THE SCOTTISH MOUNTAINEERING CLUB JOURNAL 2016

The late Mike Don on Liathach, looking south to Maol Chean-dearg. Photo: Roger Robb.

THE SCOTTISH MOUNTAINEERING CLUB JOURNAL 2016

Edited by Peter Biggar

Volume 44

No. 207

THE SCOTTISH MOUNTAINEERING CLUB

THE SCOTTISH MOUNTAINEERING CLUB JOURNAL 2016
Volume 44 No 207

Published by the Scottish Mountaineering Club 2016
www.smc.org.uk/

ISSN 0080-813X
ISBN 978-1-907233-07-4

Typeset by Noel Williams

Printed and bound by Novoprint S.A., Barcelona, Spain.

Distributed by Cordee Ltd, 11 Jacknell Road, Hinckley, LE10 3BS.

CONTENTS

Editor's Preface

It's all Robin Campbell's fault: it was his idea, I simply adopted it and did some of the donkey work. Anyway, here it is, the new hardbacked edition of the dear old SMCJ. The old lady strolls on trailing contributors, editors, photographers and artists in her wake. I do hope you will like it. After all it's largely the same much-loved Journal in a new cover: what could possibly go wrong? (Maybe we'll find out...)

In the meantime, all the poor old Editor wants to do (apart from going away on holiday) is to thank all the people who made this edition possible. Noel Williams worked selflessly as ever, burning the midnight oil, on the layout; Ian Taylor pestered his many friends to good effect for the photographs; Andy Nisbet worked with manic enthusiasm and much good humour on the New Routes; our resident poet, Graeme Morrison, hunted down the best reviewers and made them submit reviews (some of them were even on time); Mike Jacob waxed lyrical about the last 100 Years; Helen Forde painted the pictures; Simon Richardson yet again demonstrated his vast knowledge of the winter climbing scene; Dave Broadhead continued to astound with his grip of all Munro Matters (sorry Munro Society: the List is ours); Roger Robb organised the posting of Journals to our friends in the JMCS and many others besides; Novoprint printed and bound it; Cordee faithfully delivered it; and Morton Shaw might even pay the bills sometime...If I've forgotten anyone please accept heartfelt thanks anyway.

In the midst of all this activity the Editor was mainly redundant: he simply had an amusing time chatting to all our delightful contributors who also deserve a very big thank-you.

As I say, it's all Robin Campbell's fault. Blame him: that giver of gritty advice and counsel: '...it's the buggers who think they can write and can't, they're the worst...' and '...you can always threaten to resign, there isn't a queue...'

It's my great good fortune that most of my contributors don't think they can write, but they can: and how that pleases me...

Joking apart, the Journal owes a debt to Robin that we can only try to repay by doing our level best for it. He does the Index too...With a bit of luck I may not have to resign for a wee while.

Pete Biggar

A FAST WINTER CUILLIN TRAVERSE

By Finlay Wild

ON SUNDAY 14 FEBRUARY 2016 Tim Gomersall and I completed a Winter Cuillin Ridge Traverse[1] from Sgùrr nan Gillean in the north to Gars-bheinn in the south. Our route took in all 11 Munro summits, Bidein Druim nan Ràmh, and included the TD gap. We started at Sgùrr nan Gillean at 7.40 a.m. and touched the cairn on Gars-bheinn at 1.54 p.m. The summit to summit traverse took 6hrs 14mins and 17secs.

The Cuillin Ridge in prime winter condition on the morning of the traverse. Photo: Finlay Wild.

We had heard that the Cuillin traverse was in excellent winter condition and were aware of several parties who had completed traverses in the past few days. The weather looked to remain good for Sunday, if a little windy, so we arranged to drive up to Sligachan and sleep in the van. I was excited to share this adventure with 23-year-old Tim who already has many impressive mountain feats to his name including sixth place in the Glen Coe Skyline race last year, the Cuillin Greater Traverse record, and an eight hour winter round of Glen Coe to name just a few.

Setting off at 5.25 a.m. to walk in up the south east ridge of Sgùrr nan

---

[1] The Cuillin Traverse winds its way through this edition of the Journal in serpentine fashion from the electrifying speed of the young heroes through more sober accounts by older members to terminate in a sideways glance by the poet. It is a fascinating paradox that if we take speed as the criterion of excellence then the perfect traverse is impossible. Fortunately there are other criteria. (Hon. Ed.)

Gillean we were brimming with enthusiasm. The weather was clear and we could gradually make out the familiar mountain masses as the dawn developed. Popping out on the south east ridge and seeing the main Cuillin spread out before us in its winter coat lit by early morning light was breathtaking, beautiful and incredibly exciting. We have both spent a considerable amount of time in the Cuillin in summer conditions – what would it be like in winter?

Tim Gomersall traversing Sgùrr a' Ghreadaidh. Photo:Finlay Wild.

Several factors were key to our fast and light approach. The snow conditions were excellent, with both a decent base and a forgiving fresher covering on top. The weather was clear and the wind not too persistent. Several parties had been along the ridge in the past two days and so there was a trail already broken – which took a very good line for at least ninety percent of the route.

We also had the advantage of light equipment. In particular, we both wore Salomon X-Alp Carbon GTX boots – which at 500g each are essentially a stiff running shoe with an outer gaiter. These take a crampon remarkably well. We decided to take two ice axes each, to allow a maximum of soloing, and used one technical and one super light axe each for the majority of the time. For the multiple abseils we took a 38metre length of 8mm rope, and a 26metre length of 6mm cord. We took many

Tim abseiling down King's Chimney: one of the few difficult moments of the traverse as the rope proved a little too short, necessitating an unexpected down-climb. Photo: Finlay Wild

slings and lengths of abseil tat although, as we hoped, all but one of the abseils we made had already been equipped by recent teams. In addition we had a small rack of nuts and four quickdraws, for use on the In Pinn and TD Gap. We took just over a litre of water each and ate mostly gels and jelly babies.

Setting off from Sgùrr nan Gillean we were incredibly excited. Getting the timing right with days off work, weather, snow conditions and partner had all come to pass: now we could get on with the task at hand. Tim set a blistering initial pace and fell back on his alpine experience to rig the first abseil extremely quickly. From then on we developed an efficient partnership, soloing and running between the more technical short sections or abseils.

Having a broken trail which was in the right place was the key to our speed. Also the recently used abseils were visible, quick to find and safe to use – they didn't need to be dug out, re-equipped or hunted for. We moved very quickly between the abseils on Sgùrr nan Gillean, Am Basteir, Basteir Tooth, the second and then third tops of Mhadaidh. At times we were were overheating in just a single thin top layer, but as we got to Sgùrr na Banachdaich and the change of general ridge direction, it got a bit colder in the wind. Reaching a wintry In Pinn, Tim took the lead and we simul-climbed up to the summit block: 3hrs 15mins had elapsed. After a quick abseil and another gel we continued and warmed up. Abseiling *King's Chimney* we should have used both ropes, but didn't and had a short awkward down-climb.

Finlay leading the Theàrlaich–Dubh Gap: a problem wisely avoided by the soloists Moran and Richardson. Photo: Tim Gomersall.

Approaching the TD Gap I was apprehensive. Things were going well but we still had this final technical obstacle to overcome. Many winter traverses descend into Coire a' Ghrunnda from the gap, but we felt that the ideal aesthetic was to include the climb out of the gap. After a brief pitiful attempt at some lassoing of the top of the gap from abseil, we descended and I set off on an anxious lead. To my delight, I found several positive hooks which I had no idea were there, despite knowing this short section well in summer. It's pretty steep with poor feet placements and my forearms were screaming, but at least it is short and fairly soon I was up out and delighted. Tim followed up and we went on.

The sun came out now again and it was getting hot. We also picked up the pace slightly and enjoyed a brilliant romp up Sgùrr Dubh Mòr. Racing down the snowy gully towards Caisteal a' Gharbh-choire was certainly easier than ascending it in summer, although we had to make a few minor route changes in these winter conditions. From Sgùrr nan Eag we stayed close, pushing each other on, and finally, in a pretty knackered state, reached Gars-bheinn and its eagle's eyrie panorama.

The smiles say it all: the end of the traverse on Gars-bheinn. Photo Finlay Wild.

We took in the ridge and that favourite view across to a snow topped Blàbheinn, before stumbling our way down the south-west screes to the track and some water. A friendly family on holiday squeezed us into their car at Glen Brittle and dropped us back at Sligachan, for a much needed cup of tea.

WOOING APHRODITE

By Murdoch Jamieson

A PENCILLED IN WEEK free from work just happened to coincide with high pressure sitting over the UK. Guy Steven was in North Wales; we chatted and I agreed I would come down and get involved. Everyone was out on the crag. *Jub Jub Bird* was chalked, along with a few other routes that escaped my list from my time living there in 2012.

Iain Small was roaming the Highlands and at the last minute mentioned that he was around. Paul Tattersall offered me a few day's work taking some folk hill walking. Typically my love for the Highlands overpowered my North Wales plan; I stayed at home.

Aphrodite on the Central Slabs of the Shelterstone in the Cairngorms was next on my list. My apprenticeship has made a logical progression over the years: *The Pin, The Harp, The Missing Link, Thor* and *Cupid's Bow*. After *Run of the Arrow* I decided against going back. I like steep routes with holds and gear, not slabs with no holds and no gear. But time moves on. Iain said he was keen to have a look at *Aphrodite* so we agreed to pay the slabs a visit.

Three hours later I took my belay apart and started climbing rightwards towards Iain. I was ready to go home. I had just experienced one of the longest and most uncomfortable belay episodes in my climbing career. Pitch 2 of *Aphrodite* is short: its tough British 6b moves, pulling through an overlap, are protected by a peg.

Iain probed up and down the initial moves, unlocking the sequence. After clipping a quickdraw to the peg, he climbed back down to the belay. Then up again, tested the knifeblade by yanking the quickdraw, it snapped clean off! A bit of a nuisance to say the least. Our modern approach with micro wires and tiny cams was useless. There was nothing nearby to protect the moves, just a few small cams above the belay. A fall from the overlap would result in a body breaking smash on the slab below.

Iain was persistent though. He kept having a look. Up and down, up and down...up and down. Unable to commit. 'No wonder,' I thought. 'I would have given up ages ago.' I could sympathise with his frustration, but the latter soon wore off. His commitment and determination is something else. Something to admire. After a grey atmosphere came over, he admitted defeat and went off right towards the *Thor* stance.

I was pretty chilly after a lengthy hanging belay. I must admit I thought we were off home. On arrival I realised we weren't. Iain handed me the rack. From here I could traverse left (the same as *Run of the Arrow*) to get us back onto pitch 3.

Jees! A slight shock to the system, but off I went. Arranging some small wires, you commit to some smeary moves then the climbing eases but the gear is way below. I gained the junction where *Aphrodite* heads straight on and *Run of the Arrow* turns hard left. Both routes share the same cluster

Iain displaying the feeble broken peg. Photo Murdoch Jamieson.

of gear. Annoyingly it is a bit fiddly and committing to place any. Standing on the little foot ledge below, I spent a bit of time scoping the slab above. Featureless.

'Move up then right to a crack…' the guide said. Committing to this sequence, I found myself on some pretty blank rock. Seriously blank rock. I did remind myself that I was on a Cairngorm granite E7 so what was I expecting? I kept trying to move, strain to stand and hold onto nothing. I fell off. Maybe this is a bit too much for me?

Back on the footledge I decided that it was impossible. Bailing left on to *Run of The Arrow* felt quite appealing but I just couldn't. I then tried moving right from where I was and a crack appeared; a few laybacks and another little ledge was reached. I felt rather committed as my gear was out of sight. Cautiously I moved up. I still had the *Cupid's Bow* mantelshelf above. I remembered Jules Lines suggesting that it was a good idea to do *Cupid's Bow* prior to *Aphrodite* to remind oneself of the committing move. Having already ticked that route a few years ago, I couldn't be bothered redoing it. Finding myself below the mantel, maybe Jules's suggestion wasn't such a bad idea. Looking down, my ropes just lay pathetically down the slab. The gear miles below. A fall from here would be massive. Stupid in fact. I committed. Gear was reached, then the rap station.

Back at the car, we said our farewells. It was late and we were both knackered. Iain was for the Raeburn hut and I was off back to Inverness. Nothing had been agreed for the next day. I think both of us had been harbouring the same thought on the walk out, but nothing was said. Just after I started driving I sent a message to Iain suggesting we go back the next day. As I pressed send, I received a message from him asking if I was keen for a re- match! The only issue was pegs. Neither of us had our winter racks with us. Scanning my mind: who on earth at 11 p.m. on a Wednesday night would not mind digging out some pegs for me? Donnie Williamson! Having sent text messages in all directions, we settled for meeting at the car park at 8 a.m.

Funnily enough Iain had his peg hammer with him. But this was no ordinary peg hammer. It originally belonged to Alister Moses, who was on the first ascent of *Aphrodite* with Rick Campbell! This peg hammer fell into Iain's possession when he was helping his friend clean out his father's garage, and for some reason Alister's Peg hammer was there. It was just about to be sent to the skip before Iain adopted it. (For the record though, this hammer was not used to place the original pegs in the overlap).

Same drill: I did pitch one, then Iain set to work and placed two fairly decent knife blades. Up and down, up and down, Iain couldn't unlock the sequence. We swapped positions. Trying to surmount this desperate overlap was not an ideal warm up for me. After some arm circles and testing the pegs, I was back at the belay. I untied and pulled my ropes, took a minute's rest then went for it. Committing to a sequence, I latched the jug on the slab above. A sigh of relief from us both. It was in the bag! Yesterday's chalk was still there on the pitch above. It's fresh in my mind. What can go wrong now?

It started to rain. A shower, a passing shower we thought. It was sunny in the distance. It seemed quite localised. It stopped. Phew! So we both hung on the belay, chatting about the world whilst watching the slab's

Murdoch Jamieson surmounts the stiff overlap on pitch 2. Photo: Iain Small.

painful refusal to dry. I was on the sharp end again, tapping my foot with impatience. Rain. More rain. We convinced ourselves that it would stop, things would dry and everything would be fine. After a while we decided that it just wasn't happening. Rapping off, floundering around in the wet vegetation, the midges were out. Why was I not in North Wales?

The weekend came and went. The stable weather system was beginning to break down with rain in the mountains. I did some work, clipped some bolts and placed some wires at Super Crag. Wednesday came again and

Murdoch Jamieson starting up pitch 3: 'the wet streak at the top of the slabs looked insignificant despite causing havoc in my mind.'   Photo: Iain Small.

the weather looked dry. Surely the weekend's rain won't have affected the slabs too much? Iain and I teamed up again and trundled back to the Shelterstone. Walking round the toe of the Bastion, we were welcomed by a very damp looking slab. Scoping the line of *Aphrodite*, there were two main wet streaks to contend with. One just after the belay, the other over the *Cupid's Bow* mantel, at the most runout part of the route. What do you do now? We thought we might as well try it and see what happens. I had been nervous the previous week, but even more so now, knowing what lay ahead.

Each move up, I became more committed: chalking and brushing each brick edge as I went. 'This is stupid!' Somehow I justified continuing. Arriving below the mantel, I could stand fairly comfortably but felt rather alone with no belayer or gear in sight, just the ropes hanging hopelessly down the slab, disappearing under the now distant overlap. Things were damp and I retained no knowledge of the moves from the previous week. I brushed and chalked, brushed and chalked... brushed and chalked. Estimating how far I would fall if I slipped, I concluded it would be best if I didn't slip. All I had to do was get stood up on the slopey ledge at eye level. But how to do it? It can't be that hard! Finally I committed, cringing as I went, closing my eyes, but trying to relax at the same time.

Iain Small Rigs the ropes before abseiling from pitch 2. Photo:Murdoch Jamieson.

It was over. That was it. All I had to deal with now was the final dripping crack and lethal wet plantlife to gain the rap station, but at least there was gear close by. Of course this whole pantomime would not be complete without something else going wrong. The slabs can be descended by two abseils. Hanging at the *Thor* belay, we tried to pull our ropes. Stuck! Of course it was late, cold and we were both tired. Iain volunteered to prusik up to sort the issue. In retrospect, I bet he wished he hadn't after realising it was a pathetic blade of grass causing the issue 55m up. The midges welcomed us back when we arrived at our sacks.

Would I rather have spent my week off in North Wales cruising around on chalked up classics? No chance!

OSSIAN'S CAVE AND ITS VISITORS

By Robin N Campbell

Ossian's Cave viewed from below. Ossian's Ladder ascends the vegetated gully directly below the mouth of the cave. Photo: L.St.C. Bartholomew (Sept 1931) SMC Image Archive.

IT MIGHT SURPRISE TODAY'S climbers that Ossian's Cave in Glen Coe was once a popular destination, so popular that it housed Visitors Boxes or Books for many years. But it wouldn't surprise the tourist passing through the glen, who is bound to wonder about what caused that mighty gash on the face of Aonach Dubh, and what is it like inside? If they could go there to look, they would. And of course the Cave deserved a name, just as did the gaping grotto on the Isle of Staffa. Both caves were named after Celtic heroes from the Romantic poetry of James Macpherson, verses in English allegedly translated from – it has long been agreed – non-existent Dark Age Gaelic sources. According to Macpherson, Ossian was born on the banks of the Cona, so it was Ossian's Cave.[1] For those ignorant members who have yet to explore the Cave, it is reached by a two-pitch open, grassy chimney (*Ossian's Ladder*) from the Sloping Shelf below. The Cave itself is a vast echoing space resembling the nave of a cathedral, but the vegetated floor rises at a steep angle, so that it is awkward enough even to find comfortable footing there, and as a dwelling it is out of the question.

One of our own authentic heroes, Godfrey Solly – our 9th President, took an interest in the Cave. He made the earliest recorded ascent to it (discounting Ossian in the 3rd Century) at Easter 1894 along with Norman Collie and Joseph Collier. The trio spent part of Easter Week at Clachaig Inn before moving on to Fort William for their triumph on Tower Ridge of Ben Nevis. Solly had the idea of placing a tin box – he had kept his snow spectacles in it – in the Cave for the use of Visitors, and Collie's entry in the Clachaig Inn Visitors Book[2] states that 'we left a small tin box with our cards on a ledge inside the cave'. This tin box was retrieved from the Cave by the Club's then Secretary Alexander 'Sandy' Harrison on 31st August 1930, who had found it 'rusted up'.[3] Here is the list of names recovered by Harrison:

Easter 1897. W. Cecil Slingsby

18-7-1898. John H Bell; H C Boyd; W Douglas; W W Naismith; I C Napier[4]; R G Napier; G T Parker; H Raeburn

---

[1] The poems appeared in three publications in the early 1760s, with a collected edition, The Works of Ossian, in 1765. All are widely available from a variety of internet sources, including the National Library.

[2] The Clachaig Inn Visitor Book was presented to the Club by the proprietors, the Gourlays, and is item 14 of the Club's main Deposit (Acc. 11538) in the National Library.

[3] Harrison visited the Cave along with J.H.B. Bell and L. St Clair Bartholomew. He published the fact of his visit and the full list of surviving names as a Note in *SMCJ* 19/110, p. 140–1. He does not say what form these names took, whether they were business cards, or scribbled notes, etc.

[4] Probably J.S. Napier, who was one of the large Club party infesting Lochaber that week.

27-6-1902. A E Robertson; A W Russell

27-9-1902. Arthur C Brown, 2 Grosvenor Terr., Dundee; W A Brown; A C M'Laren

9-6-1905. A C M'Laren; L G Shadbolt; Osmund P Shadbolt

29-6-1905. Francis Greig; Walter Greig; Adam Smith Jnr; P C Morris; John E Davie

27-8-1905. Hugh Stewart, Trinity College, Cambridge; C R Beard; H MacRobert

31-3-1907. R W Worsdell; G T Glover

6-6-1908. L G Shadbolt; A C M'Laren

1-8-1909. David C Stuart; James Keay; E V M'Lean

17-7-1914. G Bulkeley, Helensburgh; H I Bulkeley, Royal Engineers

15-10-1916. George Paul; Lawson Paul, 82 Buccleuch St., Glasgow

4-4-1920. George Paul; Lawson Paul

23-7-1920. Wm Redpath, c/o M'Kay, 3 Hope Park Cres., Edinburgh; James H Bell, Auchtermuchty

18-8-1920. H F Godwin (F&R CC); G E Smith (F&R CC); Ilse M E Bell, Auchtermuchty

13-9-1920. B Ward-Thompson (per proxy[5]), Blackburn; A S Pigott; Morley Wood; John Wilding

21-6-1922. Wm T Elmslie (F&R CC), Christ's College, Cambridge[6]

?-?-1928. E Burt (on Quittance No. 111[7]), Cabane de Bertol

to which we must add:

31-8-1930: James H B Bell (again); L St C Bartholomew; A Harrison

Most curiously, the names of Collie, Collier and Solly were not found in the box. Of those known to have visited the Cave next, Alex Fraser and

---

[5] B. Ward-Thompson was a photographer of note. Perhaps the Pigott party used his carte-de-visite to leave their names. It is hard to think of another means of ascent 'per proxy'.

[6] William Thorburn Elmslie went on to become an important English churchman. He also compiled (and ascended) a list of 347 hills over 2,000 feet in England. See *Fell & Rock Journal* 9, p. 344ff.

[7] Probably it was the Quittance that belonged to the Cabane de Bertol, rather than Mr. Burt.

George Sang in September 1894 failed to find the tin box,[8] William Brown and William Tough in July 1895, and George Gibbs in 1896 did not mention it in their accounts,[9] but Slingsby's party found it in 1897,[10] and so did John Napier and Harold Raeburn in September that year. Raeburn commented with his customary heavy wit that 'We found the metal box, written of in the Clachaig book, guided thereunto by certain minerals placed in a peculiar and symbolic manner on one of the ledges of the cavern, the meaning whereof to the initiated being, "Cache—seek and ye shall find." Therein did we read the names of certain high-priests of Oromaniacal mysteries…'[11]

Returning to 1930, Harrison supplied a replacement bronze container containing a book, and this was carried up to the Cave by an Edinburgh JMCS party – Iain H Ogilvie, Gordon Lindsay and Alan Horne on 24 November 1931.[12]

Godfrey Solly, now a venerable member of 77 years, was provoked by these events to write for the *Journal* about the Cave and his original visit to it.[13] He began by referring amusingly to Harrison's Note as by 'Alex. Anderson', and repeated this error at the end. Getting the Club Secretary's name completely wrong is surely one of the few privileges of age. He moved on to consider how and when the Cave became known as Ossian's Cave, and observed that it was not ascribed to Ossian in 'Black's Guide to Scotland' of 1843 (3rd Edition), but was by the time of the 12th Edition in 1850. There is a reference to the Cave as Ossian's in the *Inverness Courier* for 18 July 1843 in which there is advertisement of a tour between Glasgow and Fort William via Loch Lomond 'by Steamboat and Four-Horse Coach', the coach being the 'Marquis of Breadalbane'. The coach would visit 'the Meeting of the Three Waters, the Black Hill, with Ossian's Cave, along the beautiful valley of Glencoe'.[14] So it may be that the origin of the name should be sought in Dumbarton (the home of the steamboat companies) around that date.

Solly's next question concerned ascents to the Cave prior to his own. He recounted an interview in 1894 after their climb with 'a young

---

[8] See entry in Clachaig Visitors Book.

[9] Brown's visit is recorded in his 'Climbing in Glencoe', *SMCJ* 4/19, pp. 48–51, and in the Clachaig Visitors Book. Gibbs' visit was mentioned in an unattributed letter to Wm. Douglas which appeared in abbreviated form as a Note in *SMCJ* 4/21, p. 178. The actual letters (there were two) are included in the grangerized proof copy of Volume IV put together by Wm. Douglas, which is item 41 of the Club's main Deposit (Acc. 11538) in the National Library.

[10] See entry in Clachaig Visitors Book.

[11] 'A Wet Day in Glencoe', *SMCJ* 5/25, p. 28

[12] Note, *SMCJ* 19/113, p. 361

[13] 'Ossian's Cave', *SMCJ*, 20/120, pp. 389–93

[14] More information about these elaborate tours may be found in Alan Brown's *Loch Lomond Passenger Steamers 1818–1989*. Alan T. Condie Publications, 2000.

shepherd named Neil Marquis, who lived in a cottage on the main road about opposite to Loch Triochatan, and who was reputed in the glen to have made the ascent alone by means of a tree.' Census records allow a shepherd called Nicol Marquis to be located at Achtriochtan in 1881 and 1891. However, Nicol would have been 58 in 1894 – not at all liable to have been described by Solly, age 36, as a 'young shepherd'.[15] So it is far from clear who it was that Solly's party interviewed – perhaps one of Marquis's sons, but at any rate Solly conceded that 'it seems probable that Marquis had got up, or thought he had'. Solly also knew from information given to him by an unidentified friend that someone from a shooting party at 'a lodge near King's House' – so probably Black Corries – had climbed into the Cave before 1894, but no further information about this has come to light.

At the end of his history of the Cave, Solly returned to his original ascent, noting that 'I wrote our names in pencil on a scrap of paper which I put into the box' – contrary to Collie's note in the Clachaig book. In this case, we should surely prefer Collie's version, written in the immediate aftermath of the ascent: perhaps the 'names on a scrap of paper' occurred only when Solly re-visited the Cave at Easter 1897 with 'W.C. Slingsby, J. Maclay and W.P. Haskett Smith'.[16] Godfrey Solly's set of *SMCJ* volumes is now in the hands of Chris Robinson, the Chairman of the West Highland Museum in Fort William. Solly's journals are extensively grangerized with all sorts of interesting Club material, including the correspondence he received after his article appeared from Alex Fraser, Arthur W Russell, and George Bennett Gibbs. After Solly's death, the next owner of the Journal set, apparently Mary Rose Fitzgibbon – a stalwart of the Fell & Rock CC, continued to grangerize it occasionally.

In 2001, Bill Wallace, a former Club Secretary, presented me with a large metal deed box containing a variety of Club relics which he had discovered in his garage. I inventoried the objects I could make sense of, and most of these are now safely in our NLS Deposit, but there was also a mysterious old notebook without covers, permeated with heavy black mould marks, and containing mostly illegible names and other writing. The book has 160 pages, of which many are blank, and there are a number of loose page fragments of which five have some writing on them. I added pencilled and ringed numbers to the pages, for reference, and put the five fragments in acetate sleeves. I had a closer look at this last year, and came to the idea that it might have been an Ossian's Cave Visitors Book. As I

[15] The date of Marquis's ascent in given as 1868 in the 1949 Glencoe Climbers Guide, but Solly reported no date, and I have been unable to find any source for this date of 1868.

[16] Oddly enough, although Slingsby's 1897 visit is recorded in the Clachaig Visitors Book, the party listed there does not include Solly!

deciphered names and dates, this notion received steady support. There was a conclusive loose fragment bearing the remark 'This is Ossian's Tin/ Don't pinch it' and a very suggestive poem (dots indicate indecipherable sections, slashes mark line-breaks, and square-bracket words are guesses) on pages 5 and 7.

"A damned moist, / unpleasant place!"

Carry me back to green / Glen Etive That's where I want to be Carry me back to green / Glen Etive That is the place for me	"Footholds and handholds / fail"
	I know that there's a / ridge of porph'ry Waiting for well-nailed / souls Carry me back to green / Glen Etive
I want to see the / climbers clinging Clinging with ...... /.........	Near where the ....
I want to hear the scrape / of clinkers As they.............................	
	Air 'Carry me back to green Glen Etive'
	John W ...., Ed. JMCS
O'er [Hill] and [Fell] just keep / on swinging	[Peter] Cunningham, Glasgow JMCS
.... boot-scarred? / trail Sometimes I hear the angels singing – page break here	9th Sept. 1933

Surely the poet meant that the Air should be 'Carry me back to Old Virginny', composed by James Bland, who also composed the air used for our Club Song.

The dates recorded in the book run, more or less consecutively from 1933 to 1936, and the decipherable names found are as follows:

14-4-33. J [Adam], P Macdonald

?-8-33. [Roy] Mizon, Hull

9-9 33. John W ...., Ed. JMCS; [Peter] Cunningham, Glasgow JMCS

12-9-33. [L] Rham, Lausanne, Switzerland[17]

?-9-33. George G Murray, Monkham's Lane, Woodford Green, Essex; Andrew Paton, 100 N Cathcart Road, Glasgow

---

[17] G. de Rham is listed as a Guest at an Edinburgh JMCS Meet at Kingshouse, 16–18 September 1933 (*SMCJ* 20/116, p. 156). We may infer from the report that on the 17th Marjoribanks, Ogilvie, W G P Lindsay and Rham made 'a slimy ascent to the cave, presented Ossian with a waterproof cover (once the property of Mr Woolworth) for his damp visitor's book, and left him a tip of 500 Soviet inflation roubles.' Rham's name and address is on one of the paper fragments, and although there are other names on it, they are illegible. The roubles and waterproof cover have disappeared.

17-9-33. ...... Cameron, ... Lodge, Kinloch[leven]

?-?-33. Mabel Sinclair; Robert Cairns (both Creagh Dhu M.C)[18]

9-6-34. G L Lister, Leeds

4-7-34. Margaret Simpson, ARGS; Andrew Paton[19]

22-7-34. Jack Gardner; Charles F Tomkins; Graham Young

4-8-34. J A Brown, Killearn; T D MacKinnon, Milngavie (both Glasgow JMCS)

19-8-34. Alec Dickson; D M Ryan (both Oxford University)

22-8-34. A A B. Martin; J R Myles; G A R Spence (all Grampian Club)

23-9-34. D R A Hotchkis

18-11-34. James Brown; A M Spence (both Grampian Club)

22-4-35. C G Cowen; T H Savage (both Fell & Rock CC); R H Fidler

6-5-35. Ian G Charleson; Woodhurst E Forde (both Edinburgh)

19-6-35. M C Matheson; A E Sharp; James R A White (all St Andrews University)

8-7-35. A.D.M. Cox; Elliott Viney (both Oxford University MC)

?-7-35. D. McGovern, L. CC, Glasgow

?-7-35. John B Nimlin, Ptarmigan CC; D H ...., Broughty Ferry

4-8-35. G G ....; G Arthur; C R Steven (all SMC)

6-8-35. W D. Alexander; P T Dawson (both Camp Hill Old Edwardians)

29-9-35. D F T Colbeck; R D Hugentobler; D Irvine-Robertson (all Heel Club)

1-6-36. D J Fraser

7-6-36. John B Nimlin, Ptarmigan Club; Robert A Peel, Scouts Alpine Club

27-6-36. A. Lavery; W. Wassell (both Lomond MC)

3-7-36. L A Shoubridge [Miss]; John L. Wood, Glasgow University

12-7-36. G N Sayer; R C Stewart

---

[18] This is a surprising entry, since it is common knowledge that the Creagh Dhu MC doesn't admit women to membership.

[19] An Andrew Paton wrote a piece about Ossian's Cave for the *Scots Magazine* in 1938, but I haven't managed to locate it.

9-8-36. Ivor Gess; G M Guild; William Lynch; G McG Richardson (all Lomond MC)

9-8-36. Alex. P D Thomson; Robert Thomson (both Lansdowne School of Physical Culture), Lansdowne Crescent, Glasgow

23-8-1936. James R Graham; James C Malcolm (both 20th Paisley Rover Scouts)

28-8-36. R Macdonald, Ikot Inyang, Itu, Nigeria; J A B Macdonald, 18 Learmonth Terrace, Edinburgh

13-9-36. James R Graham; A M Livingstone; James C Malcolm (all 20th Paisley Rover Scouts)

Card without date: L M & Dora Myers, 57 Parliament Hill, Hampstead NW3

Although there is no record in the *Journal* of this book being removed and replaced, the Dundee *Evening Telegraph* for 26 September 1936 carried a sensational item headed '**MOST HAZARDOUS CLIMB IN BRITAIN/ Visitors' Book Left in Ossian's Cave/ Task That Glencoe Guides Will Not Face**'. After further abuse of the cowardly guides of Glencoe, the item concluded by noting that 'A new visitors' book has just been left in the cave'. Perhaps it was the enterprising 20th Rover Scouts of Paisley who put it there, but somehow or other it made its way to our then Secretary, J. Logan Aikman.

The fate of the post-1936 Visitors Books is unknown, and so far as I know there is no longer a Visitors Book there. Peter Hodgkiss bemoaned its absence on p. 86 of his Central Highlands Guidebook (1994). He suggested that the Book was the sole attraction

An entry in the Ossian's Cave Visitors Book.

Photo: Robin Campbell.

which induced climbers to visit the Cave, and concluded his off-putting description with the observation that 'there have been several accidents to climbers descending from the Cave'. I know of only two accidents, though there have doubtless been others. The first concerned a civil engineer Kenneth Dodgson working on a road construction project nearby in 1939. Dodgson attempted an ascent late on Saturday 18 September and became cragfast. A shepherd raised the alarm locally, but rescue was not effected until the Sunday morning by a party from Glenfalloch (presumably Inverarnan, the headquarters of the Glasgow JMCS) 'including four lady climbers' who lowered a rope to him from above, which allowed him to descend safely to the Sloping Shelf (Dundee *Evening Telegraph* 20 March 1939). It would be interesting to know more about this rescue. The second accident occurred in June 1972. A party of schoolchildren from Hermitage Academy, Helensburgh were taken to the Cave by John Hendry, assistant headmaster, and Sheila MacBeth (PT instructor). On the descent one of the children fell and dragged Mr Hendry from his stance. He fell to the Shelf and later died of his injuries (Aberdeen *Press and Journal* 10 June 1972).[20]

Despite Peter Hodgkiss's negative evaluation, my own view is that the Cave is such an outstanding rock feature that it would be a poor sort of climber that would not wish to explore it. If there is no longer the inducement of a Visitors Book, then there is perhaps the allure of possible climbs from the Cave. Dougal Haston and I climbed the right-hand white wall in 1965. We had the idea of swinging left into the continuation of the dyke above the Cave, but a close look at the hideously exposed overhanging traverse pitch discouraged us. I wrote about this line in 'Once and Future Dreams' (*SMCJ* 37/192, pp. 725–6), and the self-modelled hero of Haston's novel *Calculated Risk*, John Dunlop, made a fictional solo ascent of the line. Perhaps if four lady climbers from Inverarnan had dangled a rope from above, we might have made more of an effort. But without undue difficulty the first pitch of the *Girdle Traverse* may be taken from the Cave to join *Fingal's Chimney* and continue by that route. On the east side of the Cave, originally named Abortion Wall (censored by the then Editor), escape is possible by Dave Bathgate's 1967 route *Flip-Out* (freed by Ken Johnstone in 1977). And last year a most impressive new line *The Return of Finn MacCoul* was found there by Iain Small, who has done so much to revive interest in Glen Coe's classic ground. Perhaps, too, a way might be discovered at a lower grade to traverse from the mouth of the Cave into *Shadbolt's Chimney*. So it may be that Ossian's Cave has a future as well as a past, and – who knows? – it might one day be furnished with a new metal box and Visitors Book.

---

[20] The press cutting describing this unhappy affair is included in the Solly Journal set.

AIN'T LIFE GRAND

By Grant Urquhart

ON A FEW OCCASIONS over the last four decades I have been enticed by my old schoolfriend Philip Todd to eschew my terrestrial comfort zone and venture onto some of the great desert rivers of the American North-West. Phil has appeared in these pages before in articles by Iain Smart, Malcolm Slesser and indeed myself (albeit under a not-so-thinly disguised alias). The discerning reader may also recognise him as the publisher of 'The Big Eye of Summer', the indispensable anthology of Smart's stories. Corpulent of habitus, derelict of hygiene, he is nonetheless a superb travelling companion on account of his unquenchable energy and enthusiasm. Mathematician, classical scholar, musician, author of both fiction and mathematical software, he is never short of a conversational gambit. Having in turn introduced me to climbing, skiing, and (abortively) kayaking amongst many other activities, he also initiated me into the great American pastime of 'river floating', as a result of which I and my family have enjoyed a number of splendid multi-day raft trips in the wilds of Oregon, Washington and Idaho.

Grant Urquhart battling Hance Rapid. Photo: Lisa Galbraith.

After many years of fruitless applications Phil finally hit the jackpot with a permit for the Grand Canyon of the Colorado in 2014. These permits are immutable – 8 people, 18 days, 280 miles, no excuses (I did try, pleading rafting incompetence and inexperience, dodgy shoulders and craven cowardice, but was of course ignored).

So, in late August Ian Lochhead and I made our way to Flagstaff, Arizona. Ian is another old friend who accompanied Phil and myself on many of our early somewhat deranged mountain adventures. He is also an accomplished kayaker, having co-authored with Phil the first guidebook to Scottish white water. Since those glory days he has sadly been seduced by the Nineteen Holes of Shame, though he does claim to bag the odd Munro.

Whilst awaiting the rest of the crew, and after a day spent in hideous jet-lagged bickering round supermarkets gathering our share of the (copious) provisions, we relieved the stress with an ascent of the fine Humphreys Peak (12,633ft) in the nearby San Francisco mountains. The trailhead is only 14 miles out of town; from there a good trail leads pleasantly through flower meadows before entering dense alpine forest of aspen, fir and spruce. As this thins out, the trail steepens and provides some easy scrambling between photogenic twisted bristlecone pines and other tundra scrub vegetation. Once the ridge is reached the going becomes easier and there are splendid views of the surrounding volcanic remnants and the desert beyond, leading all the way to the Canyon rim. The summit is Arizona's highest point, and there a friendly local joined me in photographing the superb panorama (Ian having mysteriously failed to appear).

The next day we met up with the US-based contingent – Phil, Hannah, Naomi and Moira Todd, Lisa Galbraith and Tom Gall, all experienced white-water rafters or kayakers. Phil, Moira and Ian planned to kayak, with the rest of us and our extensive creature comforts sharing three sizeable rafts. Lisa had descended the river twice before, by raft and kayak, which could have been very useful to us if only she'd been able to remember a damn thing about it. Flagstaff is a surprisingly cosmopolitan little town, and we made full use of its excellent brew-pubs and restaurants.

The following morning, after picking up our rafts and other paraphernalia from our outfitters, the excellent Ceiba, we made our way to the starting point at Lee's Ferry. The encyclopaedic ritual formal briefing from the Yogi Bear-style park ranger was rendered more entertaining by the fact that our glorious leader was by this time almost completely deaf, and despite nodding along sagely had in reality no idea what everyone else was talking about. I did drift away a bit myself, but do recall the warnings about avoiding scorpions – 'Anybody here been scorped? You probably won't die, but may need evacuation. Anybody been evacuated from the Canyon?' One of the other party launching that day (a bunch of lean and hungry-looking non-raft supported kayakers) admitted he had been winched by helicopter from the middle of the river when his raft had become irretrievably wrapped round a rock by the ferocious current. By now I was acutely aware of my status as team duffer.

At length we got everything rigged and onto the great river. The next two and a half weeks were a kaleidoscope of extraordinary physical and visual experiences, so many that a small sample will have to suffice – and yes, there was a bit of climbing!

The first thing we found out was that Blockhead, despite 40 years' experience of white-water kayaking, had forgotten how to roll. This

Naomi Todd climbing in Blacktail Canyon. Photo: Grant Urquhart.

allowed him to enjoy some extreme swimming, and us rafters to practise rescuing him. Moira on the other hand, despite capsizing a dozen or so times, managed to roll every time – no easy feat in the maelstroms of huge waves and raft-eating holes which characterise the bigger rapids. At the start of the Class 8 (out of 10) Hance rapid she contrived to lose her paddle, something I would have imagined to guarantee a long and turbulent swim. But no, displaying an icy composure, and with the aid of two hand rolls, she arrived at the bottom right-side up, even retrieving her own paddle. I have rarely been so impressed. Later she was to run almost the whole of the fearsome Lava Falls upside down, barring a brief roll upright in the middle (thereby spoiling her chance to become perhaps the first person to run it entirely submerged unintentionally, as opposed to as a deliberate stunt – the water runs so fast that it only takes about 30 seconds). We never found out if Phil could still roll, as he rather annoyingly refused to be upset, an achievement which I attribute to both his considerable skill and experience, and the fact he is built rather like one of those bottom-heavy wobbly dolls which always rights itself no matter how far over you push it.

Negotiating these rapids in a raft is no less of a challenge. Though much more stable, a heavily home-brew laden raft suffers from considerable inertia. Manoeuvres must be planned and started well in advance, and faulty positioning on entry is not corrected easily, if at all. At the start of Crystal rapid I was so concerned to avoid the notorious mid-river hole that I began to pull towards the bank too early and clipped a rock with the bow. This spun me round so that I entered the first big waves at an angle, with the downstream oar trapped under the raft. Losing the oar would have led to the raft flipping in the hole with all manner of potentially embarrassing consequences, whilst hanging on to it could have seen me unceremoniously ejected. Fortunately, more by luck than skill, I contrived to turn the raft with the other oar until both could be freed, then row forwards like buggery, in the end missing the edge of the abyss by a good couple of feet. There are well over a hundred named rapids in the Canyon, and though only a few offer such a major challenge, most require attention and respect. On some days the big ones come along every mile or so, resulting in a pretty adrenaline-charged few hours.

Between the rapids lay long flat sections, perfect for rowing gently while enjoying the remarkable visual effects created by the great multi-layered and variously-hued walls of limestone, sandstones and schist, red, orange, ochre and black, appearing to move in a measured three-dimensional orographic ballet, a live tutorial on the processes of geology and the reality of geologic time whose unravelling was the Canyon's unique gift to science. These periods of awe-struck contemplation were enlivened by periodic Captain Bligh-like outbursts from the Glorious Leader, enraged by some perceived breach of National Park rules or river etiquette. The generous-spirited among the galley-slaves were inclined to attribute such intemperance to frustration and isolation borne of deafness,

Grand Canyon above Nankoweap – Redwall Limestone. Photo: Lisa Galbraith.

though the majority thought he was just being a miserable old misanthrope.

Our leisurely schedule also allowed plenty of time for land-based indulgence. Camp was made each night on the pristine sandy beaches which line the river, fine dinners prepared and washed down with copious quantities of Tom's splendid home-brewed ales. Musical instruments were played with varying levels of competence, culminating in a fine if unusual Burns Supper, complete with haggis, whisky and recitals. The prize for most surreal moment, however, went to Tom for his bravura performance, dressed in makeshift kilt and sporran, of Robert Service's The Cremation of Sam McGee.

Our other terrestrial indulgence was the exploration of some beautiful side canyons. These are many and varied, some with turquoise pools and polished limestone walls, others featuring dramatic gorges cut in biscuit-layered sandstone. A light rope and a few nuts and slings allowed the livelier members to penetrate much further into these than most river-runners achieve, albeit with a few exciting moments.

Having survived 120 miles and most of the big rapids, we awarded ourselves a rest day at Blacktail Canyon. While the sybarites lounged in its shady depths, Tom, Naomi and I explored. A first giant chockstone was surmounted via some sketchy moves protected by a single nut, trainers sliding on slimy walls, the belayer chest-deep in water. Above, another blockage was passed by squirming through a narrow gap under a huge boulder. This gave access to the upper canyon, from where we were able to exit via some easy scrambling to cross the slope above, notable for an extraordinary variety of striking desert succulents, some in flower, back to the sandstone cliff overlooking our campsite. Descent appeared impossible, but by repeatedly traversing ledges we found a route pioneered by the area's famous Bighorn Sheep. These were spied more than once, leaping fearlessly between ledges on the sandstone precipices, though it was the rams' impressive cojones in the literal sense which most attracted the admiration of the young ladies.

A couple of days later in Matkatamiba Canyon we traversed narrow ledges of Tapeats sandstone a hundred feet or so above the river to reach beautiful sculpted swimming pools. In Havasu Creek, the hike was enlivened by sightings of various lizards, small mammals, birds and butterflies (luckily the rattlesnake I almost stood on was fast asleep!). We emerged into a vast amphitheatre of rock, big enough to hold a symphony orchestra and full audience, a perfect place for silent meditation. Exploration of Tuckup Canyon was a little more demanding, requiring a long unprotected lead up a moderate slab, followed by exposed traverses and another boulder squeeze.

Though much of the rock in the Canyon is not suitable for climbing, there is still a great deal which is, from bouldering close to the river, to established longer routes on the walls of the main and branch canyons, to multi-pitch epics of which Zoroaster Temple is the most celebrated. A well-organised team would have plenty time to sample some of these, or to pioneer new problems or routes almost at will.

Sixteen days passed all too quickly and we found ourselves outwith the National Park, assailed by jet-boats and waspish swarms of Vegas-based helicopters as we floated gently night and day between the great banks of filthy silt left by 25 years of drought and the consequent dramatic shrinkage of Lake Mead. Naomi's 12 hour shift rowing our 3-raft pantechnicon was probably just twenty-something showing-off, but gave us older members time to relax, while regularly watching great chunks of

Naomi Todd traversing in Tuckup Canyon. Photo: Grant Urquhart.

the silt-banks calving off like some satanic negative of a pristine glacier snout. Tedium was periodically relieved by mooning other river users, enthusiastically led by our distaff contingent, and hence generally receiving an enthusiastic reception and reciprocation. After setting up the last camp on a mud flat in 40°C heat, we found there were ice-cold beers remaining in the depths of the last cool-box, and later, that Tom had inadvertently brought a keg of 14% proof barley wine in place of the light hefeweizen he had intended, consumption of which led to a fittingly spaced-out finale to an exceptional trip. Rather surprisingly, we had survived with no raft strandings or flippages and no kayaking or scrambling injuries, only a few insect bites and some calloused hands and feet to show for our adventures (though it took months for my shoulders to recover from all that unaccustomed rowing).

Next morning the outfitters arrived bang on time to pick us up at remote Pearce Ferry, deep in the Mojave Desert, and before we knew it we were deposited in the epicentre of tackiness that is Las Vegas – never has the expression 'from the sublime to the help-ma-boab' seemed more appropriate. The dislocation was partly alleviated by a visit to the beautiful Red Rocks National Park, then it was the long journey back to quotidian life.

REPULSE AND REPRISE

By Stephen Scott

Lochnagar from Meikle Pap. Photo: Greg Strange.

BANNERS OF RAGGED STREAMING CLOUD, laced with snow, screamed from the corniced lip of the plateau. Below, in a wild calm, a climber worked, uncovering thinly iced interconnecting grooves, scraping at the powder, looking for holds and protection, steadily working upwards towards a leering harsh granite tower… and the tearing wind. His partner watched, shivering, cold, perched on an edge that dropped in a relentless grey wall of rock to the hard packed snow of the gully 100 metres below – they were alone.

It was late… too late. Confidence waned with the light until finally, there was none.

That was then. Today was different, for twenty years they had been waiting, for conditions, weather and opportunity. Undiminished by the long wait, their desire drove them here, into this window, they were ready. It was cold, very cold. Occasionally the corniced rim revealed itself through the dense cloud.

Over to their right another team chatted, easing the tension.

A succession of deep grooves covered in crusted powder brought them back below the granite tower again. The section that led here had been stubborn, yet well protected, and harder than the pitches below.

Belayed, the leader methodically racked the gear. Nuts, pegs, slings, warthogs and hooks. The notch above is the key; he knows it will be hard. Moving to the top nut, to save the belay and reduce drag, he attaches a long sling and clips in the left-hand rope. Safe now, he pauses, before making a blind strenuous swing across a rib to the right. With the weight of the exposure sucking he pulls stiffly onto a narrow foot-ledge to the spurious security of a peg at the back of a deep niche. Long sling – left-hand rope. Rest. Breathe…

Now out of sight of his second, a difficult sequence right leads into the base of another steep bottomless groove. Feet bridged, relaxed, with a nut in and a good hook, he looks up. The rock is smooth, dark and uncompromising, bare of ice and holds. Three metres above, below a slight overlap, is a rusty wire. A shallow crack on the right wall provides placements for a couple of nuts, he hammers them in. Torqueing a pick in the thin crack at the back of the groove, mono-points on bare granite, he commits. Immediately it is awkward, steep and insecure. Using the balance and guile derived during those years of stealth, he gains and clips the rusty wire.

Standing tenuously, his calves are screaming now. He has his right front point in the crack and his left scratches at the rock, holding. A wig of turf sits obligingly within reach… Reaching up he gently, so gently, swings his right pick into the turf, it's solid and holds. Holding position to avoid dislodging his feet he swings his left axe for a solid placement – the turf melts. He matches picks, and making do with the one solid placement, pulls up and locks off urgently. Scraping at the rock with a front point it grips, he transfers some weight and moves up, it grips, he doesn't fall. Above, the crack widens into a fist width pod. It takes a solid hex, the first good piece for five metres. Jamming his left hand into the crack he pulls up, hammers his right pick into the turf and rocks over. Secure now, he rests. Panting hard he realises how rank his breath has become, his mouth is arid. He looks up…

A crack on the left takes a small wire, the tip of a pick, followed by a crampon point. Another sequence on the thinly iced rock, another gentle pointinpick-chippedice leads suddenly onto a knife-edge of snow where the ridge falls vertically to the distant gully bed…

Three metres of vertical granite cleft by a wide undercut crack bar access to the final pitches – the crux in summer. But this is winter. Deep powder banks up at the foot of the crack and through a hole the steep gully ice stares up from blue below. Stand on the bridge, clip the solid in situ nut then try and find a piece of good ice or a reliable hook, foot high, just one decent placement…

It's done… not over, but he knows it's done.

No dismal, long walk down in the harassing wetness of a storm.

Quiet fulfilment, satisfaction, smiles and above all, respect.

Eagle Ridge Direct (VI, 6), Lochnagar
Rick Graham, Steve Scott – 22 Feb 2013

A NIGHT ON THE OLAN

By Fiona Murray

IT WAS SEPTEMBER 2012, I was heading to France and meeting up with Thomas, a French climber I'd got to know in 2006 when he and his family were living in Edinburgh. I felt stressed. I had recently bought a house in Aviemore and was in the middle of organising carpets and furniture and I even considered cancelling my holiday as I was to move in the day after my scheduled return. But life is for living and the carpets could wait.

Thomas met me at Lyon Airport in his newly acquired Mercedes van. The forecast was reasonable although it was plain if we were going to do anything high up then we would have to do it in the next couple of days. Thomas had some routes in mind and suggested that we head to the Écrins so we drove to the roadhead at Le Désert en Valjouffrey (1250m). I didn't know this side of the range, all my experiences had been on the bolted granite in the Ailefroide valley so I was excited to be exploring a new area. We parked up and had some food. Thomas then handed me a topo, it was of a route on the 3564m Olan called Via Devies-Gervasutti, an 1100m outing up its North-West face.

'Are you sure we have enough daylight for such a long route?' I said. After all it was mid-September. Thomas shrugged and said that most of the route was easy so we would move quickly. He is an experienced Alpinist and I trusted his judgement, so we turned in to get some sleep.

The alarm came too quickly at 3.15 a.m. I hadn't really expected to be springing into action so early in my holiday. We set off walking at 3.45 and arrived at the Refuge de Font Turbat (2169m) at 6.15. We waited for daylight to come before heading to the base of the route so we had a rest at the Refuge and changed into stiffer boots and got lightweight crampons out for the steep snow cone approach. Half an hour later we were leaving the hut in the gloom. I began to get a glimpse of the scale of the Olan and a feeling for the remoteness of this area.

At the bergschrund it took us a while to work out exactly where the route started. The gap between the snow and rock was frightening and I was already feeling that this wasn't such a good idea. Thomas managed to find a way across and he was quickly leading the first pitch while I balanced on a snowy ledge above a dark, cold chasm. 'Safe!' The pitch was tricky and awkward, the rock cold and gritty, I was moving slowly and felt stiff and clumsy – not a good start.

The initial pitches were not too hard and we were moving quickly. The angle then eased so we moved together for the next few pitches. The rock was poor; I hadn't been on such chossy rock since a trip to the Andes in 2001. I was trying to climb as fast as possible, but, with little confidence in the rock, I was placing lots of gear on my leads. As always Thomas was super-fast and efficient and I'm sure I was seconding his pitches slower than he'd led them. Nevertheless we continued to make steady

Fiona Murray on questionable rock on the Via Devies-Gervasutti on the Olan.
Photo: Thomas Lieutard.

progress until around the half-way point when we encountered some route finding difficulties.

Thomas was on the lead and was trying out various options up a chossy chimney when a huge block came flying down. Thankfully I managed to dodge it but clearly the rock quality was not improving with height. The time was just being eaten away; I got to the point where I decided not to check my watch anymore and just try and relax, after all we had head torches! Thomas got us back on route and after nearly 40 pitches and 11 hours of climbing we reached the top at 7.30 p.m. Now for the fun of getting down.

The recognised descent was the North Arête but in the impending gloom I don't think we actually found the correct starting point. I was completely in Thomas's hands. We didn't have any guidebook description, however Thomas had been up (and down) the North Arête a few years before so he was confident. It was pitch dark by now and we had the best part of 1000m of rock to descend and then a further few hundred metres to get back to the refuge, this was going to be a long night! Thomas went first on each abseil, his torch beam sliding into the void, and by the time I got down he had already got an anchor ready for the next abseil.

Arriving on a sloping ledge after the fourth abseil I found that Thomas had already put some tat around a block; I kicked the block:

'Are you sure this is solid enough?'

The author following on rather better rock on the Olan. Photo: Thomas Lieutard.

'Yes, of course.'

Thomas was just beginning to disappear over the slabby edge when there was a loud grinding noise. The block is moving! It slithers towards Thomas! Caught in my head-torch beam I was expecting that to be the last sight I would have of him before he plummeted over the edge. I shouted 'Thomas!' but he was still there. The green Black Diamond Camalot that we placed as back-up had held; the slithering block missed Thomas and he pulled himself back up to the stance. I think we were too shocked to speak much. We just concentrated on finding another abseil point and checking the ropes which had been mashed by the block; we now had more tat for setting up the abseils! A couple more and we found some pitons on an easier angled ridge.

We had clearly missed the correct descent as most of the abseiling had been down steep overhanging terrain. Thomas reckoned the angle was now easy enough for some down-climbing. This came as a bit of a relief to me as the abseiling was getting far too stressful. We down climbed for a good while, however, on checking my altimeter we were still above 3000 metres. After another 100m or so of descent the angle steepened so we were back to abseiling.

It was now 3 a.m. and we were both feeling tired. After getting the ropes stuck on consecutive abseils I suggested to Thomas that we rest for a while and wait for daylight. He took some persuading but eventually agreed to stopping on a tiny ledge. There were a few pegs so we could attach ourselves to the rock and I began to remove my boots and get my legs in my rucksack for added warmth. I was really cold and hungry and tried to get comfortable. Within a couple of minutes Thomas was snoring: I couldn't believe it. I was fearing that I'd never get off this mountain alive yet Thomas could sleep! I did eventually drop off but only very briefly before Thomas woke me:

'Fiona, we must get going.'

'Why?'

'A storm is coming.'

I swivelled my head to the west and could see flashes of lightning illuminating the distant sky. Could things get any worse? I was even more panicked now and felt doomed. Would I ever get to move into my newly acquired house and walk on those lovely new carpets? I even suggested to Thomas that we should phone Mountain Rescue. I was beaten. I couldn't take any more. He was adamant we were fine and looking back now I do feel stupid for even considering it.

Back on with the boots, repack the rucksack and yet more abseiling. We were halted again pretty quickly by further rope problems; they just seemed to be sticking all the time. Whilst abseiling I had noticed a fairly large ledge with overhanging roof so we decided to climb back up and take shelter; the storm was getting closer and we needed daylight. It was now 5.30 so not too much longer to wait. At 6.30 we began to move again and by the time we found a suitable abseil point we could see in the gloomy daylight that there were only one or two abseils left before we reached the slope below and that's when the storm hit, wet snow began falling just as we were coiling the ropes.

At least we were off the rock face but now the really scary part began. The terrain was awful, steep slabby ground with lots of loose rock and grit on top. We found a dyke of rock which provided some solidity but this was little comfort as the sleety snow was turning everything slippy. The thunder and lightning was now above us cracking and booming around the valley. We eventually found a narrow mountain path which contoured around to the east and I began to feel a bit happier as the terrain was easing. That feeling didn't last long for we were now faced with descending a steep couloir of blocks.

'I'm not going down there!' The couloir looked like a death trap especially with the covering of slushy snow. Thomas looked at me:

'You have no option, it's the only way down.'

I just wanted to cry, I felt helpless. After a few minutes of whingeing, reality kicked in and I had to move. It was the only way down and my feeble behaviour was not helping anyone. The couloir was as bad as I expected, loose blocks slithering under each footstep, I yearned for solid ground. It came eventually and we were at last on a path leading back to the Refuge.

I've never been so happy to see a Refuge, it was 12 noon and we were

safe. It had taken 16 and a half hours to descend from the summit of the
Olan. We were both soaked to the skin and freezing cold. We stripped off
and wrapped ourselves in the rough blankets in the Refuge. Lying down
I began to experience violent shivering. My entire body was convulsing
for the next half hour or so before I managed to drift off into a fitful sleep.
By four in the afternoon we were pulling on our wet clothes and boots
for the trek back to the van. We'd survived the Olan!

OUT

By Hamish Brown

Out!
All mothers ask
Where are you going?
Out.
Yes Mum.
No Mum.
Out
Out, for ever
Out
   to Ochils
   to High Alps
   the Himal
   the dreamed places
   of rationed time.
Out.
  Out.
   Out.
Till they shove me
      in.

THE BUGS I KNEW

By Gavin Anderson

Bugs McKeith, from a photograph in 'Mountain Lover' by Dennis Gray, reprinted by kind permission of the author.

I THINK IT WAS Patey who once said, there are bold climbers and there are old climbers, but there are no old, bold climbers. I belong to the second category. Nowadays, my climbing is limited to the occasional foray onto vertical plastic and the more frequent reminiscing about the good old times with a hefty dose of name dropping of the great and sadly often deceased heroes of yesterday. Let's be honest, I knew of them but didn't know them, although I once passed a scowling Haston, loping up the Mound Steps with his entourage frantically scampering after him. My American friends had never heard of any of them, Smith, Patey, Brown, Cunningham. Each side of the Atlantic has its own brand of parochialism, its own pantheon of heroes. Not even the mention of Dougal, the Leonardo of Lagangarbh could quicken the pulse. It was when I saw the eyes rolling, I realized I was becoming the classic bore. Then I happened to mention Bugs McKeith, and my friend came to life.

'You knew Bugs McKeith?' A gasp or two later he informed me, 'Bugs McKeith. He was a legend!' and gave me a brief run down on his ice escapades and how Bugs had more or less singlehandedly revolutionized North American winter climbing.

'Yes. I knew him pretty well in his early days,' I said, modestly. I knew what I was doing. The effect was gratifying and for a few delightful minutes I went up in his estimation. When he repeated, 'You knew Bugs McKeith,' he looked at me in awe and then said, 'Awesome,' which everyone did then before it was supplanted by the easier on the tongue 'Wow!' I knew Bugs had done some ice climbing in Canada, but was not aware of the extent of his pioneering or his reputation.

My friend lent me his guide to Canadian ice-climbing, which was dedicated to Bugs McKeith. Flicking through the pages I noted that many if not a majority of the climbs were first done by the same Bugs. There was a section on how he had revolutionized Canadian ice climbing techniques, stirring up the local climbing pot in general, as if he were a MacInnes, Cunningham and Chouinard all rolled into one eccentric genius. Looking him up on Google I found out some interesting facts unknown to me, for instance that he was married and had a daughter.

His daughter was born a few weeks after his death, and consequently has no memories of him, although she must have picked up the sort of information that tends to cling to one so colourful. She was interested in hearing from anyone who knew her dad. It was funny thinking about Bugs as 'Dad,' but this is more or less the letter I sent her. It doesn't pretend to be a mini-biography of his Scottish years; nor does it say much about his climbing exploits, which can be pieced together from other sources. It's a patchwork of snapshots of an influential mountaineer and rich character in his salad days in the 1960s.

Dear Arran,

I knew your Dad pretty well in his early climbing days, and I am happy to pass on any memories I have to you. Of their nature they are random and scattered. Remember all these events took place more than half a century ago.

He was different from the others in the Edinburgh climbing scene in that he went to a private school, Daniel Stewart's, lived in the Georgian New Town, and spoke with a modified pianos-and-kippers accent. From your Edinburgh contacts you will know what that means. Although unusual, it wasn't irredeemably so. In the Edinburgh climbing scene it was the thing to be aggressively working class, but there were not a few interlopers from the middle classes trying to hide the fact that they went to Heriots by lifting pints of heavy, mangling their vowels, and dropping their Ts. Some even went to the extent of wearing flat caps à la Creagh Dhu, but nobody was fooled. Karl Marx had a word for these dropouts from the bourgeoisie, which escapes me now. Some English writers have depicted Bugs's speech as a caricature of the wee Jimmy type of Scotsman with a 'hauf 'n hauf' in each hand. Their ears may not have been attuned to the upper-class accent of Edinburgh, found in the pages of Alexander McCall Smith but not in the Sunday Post. However it was more likely he was guying them, and playing the Scots character for the tourist trade. As far as I know he never wore a kilt.

I first came across him riding a kid's bike with the logo Al McKone printed on the main frame, a self-imposed nickname. This was at Blackford Hill in Edinburgh, whose potential for climbing went unexploited till your dad came along, and which despite his espousal never did become the resort de jour. He was still a schoolboy at this stage, but even then you could feel the will power in him that told you he was going to do things his way. I remember what with all the variations of spelling of his name you mention, that he spelled it Alasdair, in the Gaelic fashion.

To tell you the truth, Arran, I was not overly impressed by your dad at first sight. He seemed to me to be too sure of himself for what he was, a fifteen- sixteen-year-old; and all that Al McKone nonsense was such a deliberate way to establish himself as a character. Later I saw that the play-acting was an irremovable mask concealing the enigma that was the real Bugs. The dynamism was annoying as it pointed up my indolence and lazy acceptance of the status quo, but I got over it once I became infected by his enthusiasms.

But then Bugs was full of surprises. He made a ton of first ascents, but instead of naming them after boring topographical features like North Buttress, or ephemera such as pop songs, he would take flights of fancy into the weird, and come up with for example *Shazmakelmanov*, which sounds like cod-Russian, but imitates a climber screaming, 'Sheesh man, I'm coming off!' Other inventions included the pseudo-scientific, *Brachistochrone* in Arran, and the laconically descriptive, *Blank*, a slab route on Goatfell.

Funnily the most colourless name he gave a climb was one that may have been his most significant achievement in Europe, the first ascent of the *West Rib* of the Blaitière, for which lapse of imagination he was chastised by no less than the Editor of the Scottish Mountaineering Club Journal for the douce nomenclature when it could have been *La Voie Écossaise* to match the *Voie Britannique* of Whillans and Brown. In the same season he climbed the Bonatti Pillar. His only comment on this magnificent ascent was that his feet felt cold after taking them out of their bivouac booties in the morning. Come to think of it the bland name when one is expecting something more grandiloquent was probably a joke in reverse; the sort of twist in the tail that Bugs enjoyed.

When first infected by the climbing bug he would clamber up anything remotely scalable, old stone walls, railway sidings, medieval towers and turrets left over from the days of Bruce and Wallace – believe it or not there were plenty of them still standing – which made excellent climbing walls before there were climbing walls. He would stem his way up, palms pressed outward and feet bridging at full stretch on no discernible holds. It was levitation in its purest form. I discovered a quarry in Clermiston Woods and proudly showed him it and the lines I had sketched out on it. Before the afternoon was over he had more or less wiped out my efforts, zapping the crag with seriously sketchy routes.

More bizarre and Bugs-like, he pre-enacted (is that a word?) Monty Python's intrepid ascent of Kensington High Street laybacking horizontally up the gutter before Monty Python, but then he was Monty Python to the life. I don't think he received any royalties. In a rush of common sense, he picked a quiet street in Comely Bank to exercise his inventive instincts.

He liked to climb trees swearing that they provided an excellent surrogate for the real thing. Walking my dog along the tow path of the Union Canal one day, I wasn't entirely surprised to hear a voice calling me from above. I looked up to see Bugs sitting comfortably perched way up amongst the branches of a sycamore, so high it made me nervous. Luckily a policeman was passing by. I hoped he would order Bugs down. He looked up, shook his head and muttering something about 'silly students' resumed his patrol. Eventually, much to my relief, Bugs decided to come down. I wouldn't say he was fearless, very few of us are, but he was as near as you could get to it. Trees could be put to use in several ways. For example you could swing from branch to branch, à la Johnny Weissmuller, an excellent arm muscle developer. Of course, if there was an audience present he would do the whole high-flying circus act, swinging on one arm chimpanzee style, calling out for Jane. Sadly no leotarded lady of the jungle answered his call.

More reprehensibly he used trees to practise the new stick and pick technique in ice climbing. Maybe it was this arboreal climbing that sharpened his proficiency on ice. Who can tell? Verging on the criminal he used to hammer pitons into tree trunks to practise artificial climbing. What can I say? Remember this was in the Dark Ages as far as awareness of the environment was concerned, but there was really no excuse. We all did it but to a less intensive extent than Bugs, a pathetic cop-out you'll agree, but then every vertical surface was for him a Siren call for a climb.

He would roam far and wide from the standard climbing resorts, 'discovering' (shades of Columbus and the New World) new crags in odd little nooks and crannies of the Highlands and Lowlands. Many of these neo-Buachailles comprised more vegetation than your average haystack,

Bugs taking his ease on home soil. Notice the straps of the inevitable Tiso sack.
Photo: courtesy of the Mike Galbraith collection in the SMC Image Archive.

distance lending more enchantment than the view deserved. One such 'find' in the dreich hinterlands of Dalwhinnie was heralded as a Llanberis Pass in miniature. As far as I could see it was like the Welsh original in two respects: it was in the shape of a valley and it rained a lot. The route we tackled was basically a tree climb interspersed with rock outcroppings. Tarzan might have enjoyed it. At least it got us out of the house on a miserable day, and we saw some new ground. Probably I am being unfair. Maybe we picked a bad route on a bad day; maybe we lost the way. All are possibilities.

But then we lacked Bugs's optimistic eye of faith, which together with his drive made him the powerful and successful climber that he became. The majority of his climbs were of good if not of superb quality, witness his series of new routes on Creag Dubh at Newtonmore, not forgetting the iconic *Scots' Pillar* on the North face of the Eiger, in a class of its own, which he shared with MacEacheran and Spence.

I can give an instance of your father's determination. We were climbing on Slime Wall on Buachaille Etive Mor in Glen Coe. I was reluctant to embark on the intimidating traverse onto the route. The day and place were dark, dank and sombre. The line of the climb was ferociously exposed. I advised caution due to the dubious conditions. I said, 'It's wet. Bugs.' But that didn't stop my partner.

'No! It's bone dry!' He shouted back to me and there the die was cast. I followed gingerly, not having much fun on it. It wasn't dry; it wasn't soaking wet; mottled I should call it with every chance your feet would slip on a greasy smear of lichen. Bugs dismissed my pessimism, declaring it a 'magnificent route and a magnificent day on the hill.' There was no gainsaying him. I didn't enjoy it. It was too desperate for my comfort. To be so successful you had to be a bold climber, but then he never did become an old climber.

He was artistically talented, and would do impromptu paper sketches. Anyone sitting behind a pint in the pub might find themselves the subject of an impromptu sketch, caricatured but not cruelly. Many of these drawings found their way into dustbins, an action surely regretted by their sitters. I don't know where his paintings went, but you can get a fair idea in a self-portrait of him climbing ice in the frontispiece of the Canadian waterfall-ice climbing guide. Music and birdsong were other areas where his talents blossomed.

It was winter 1962, an enormously snowy year. I was pontificating on the importance of the novice mountaineer going through the prescribed steps in the correct order before admittance to the inner circle, plodding up thousands of feet of snow, such as the *Central Gully* of Ben Lui before tackling the single ice pitch of the *Upper Couloir* of Stob Ghabhar, all this in tricounis. Crampons were not only considered unsporting, they were an outrage against the Scottish Bens. All this was more or less straight from the pen of J. R. Marshall's magisterial article 'Modern Scottish Winter Climbing' in the *SMC Journal*. I was laying it down about chopping steps in snow, before tackling hard ice like I was handing down the Ten Commandments. Bugs was present at my oration. I asked him his thoughts. Mimicking me none too flatteringly he intoned, 'My preferences are rock, ice,' hesitation, 'stamp collecting,' then in an apologetic whisper, 'snow climbing.' He had them rollicking in the aisles. Much of his success was due to this sticking up two fingers at traditions, in this case sacrilegiously strapping on crampons and assaulting the Ben before the appointed hour.

One example of his mad zany japes will suffice. I was tramping up knee-deep snow towards the *Central Gully* of Bidean nam Bian, when I glanced over to the other side of the corrie. There was your dad chopping his way up vertical ice on Stob Coire nam Beith. He was on a new route, nothing unusual in that, except he was still in his pajamas! He looked over and grinned in that conspiratorial way he had. No, it was not sartorial amnesia. The day was grey, and this was his way of brightening it up. I hoped he was wearing something more substantial underneath, but with Bugs you could never tell.

He could pick up a guitar or a penny whistle and throw together a medley of Irish and Scots folk tunes without any hesitation or prompting. Refusing to restrict himself to the conventional instruments of the orchestra, he would burp the Hallelujah Chorus from Handel's Messiah from start to finish, and then in celebration of this virtuosity he named the most sought after new route on Traprain Law *Burp* which was a dig at those who wanted to call it something more fitting, i.e. more grandiose. When in the pub, he would sit scrunched up in a corner, as if he wanted to be unnoticed, yet with a sly grin written over his face, like a scheming leprechaun ready to pounce, and then he would announce some truly bizarre scheme, such as carrying helium in your rucksack to get up to the hut on Ben Nevis.

He is supposed to have said that he left Scotland as being too small a theatre for his talents. For my money this does not sound like the authentic Bugs, and the statement came from Haston, but then who knows? He once told me that *Cenotaph Corner* was just another pissy little route in the Pass. Make of that what you will.

I climbed a lot with him in the early sixties. We were meant to go to the Alps together, but had a falling out (I can't remember why). The truth is Bugs was streets ahead of me as a climber and that can be pretty scary. He went anyway and ended up doing sterling routes such as the North Ridge of the Peigne in his first Alpine season.

My most outstanding memory of your father was witnessing his baptism as 'Bugs.' We were in the Achray Hotel in the Trossachs, having been climbing all day on Ben A'an, beautiful in autumn colors, Pre-Raphaelite according to your father, his way of reminding us he was a bit more than a climber: he was also an artist. The pub was crowded with Glaswegians, amongst them was a very rough crowd of youngsters who kept proclaiming that they were, 'Frae Brigtoon and proud of it,' challenging anyone who wished to dispute this fact to 'step ootside and get their heids kicked in.' None of our gang was remotely interested in taking up their offer which made them more and more irate. They were desperate for a fight. Up to this moment Alasdair had been entertaining us with his musical talents, twittering like a songbird. This may have been the occasion when he did the Hallelujah Chorus. He was especially annoying to the thugs, who kept telling him to shut up in more and more unprintable forms. If it had been me I would have shut up in mid-chorus, but your father kept twittering away without heed to the physical danger. Irritated beyond belief they told 'Bugs Bunny to shut the fuck up!' He didn't, but the name stuck.

When I think of your dad what comes to mind, but what I can't describe,

Arran McKeith at the Drey in Glen Coe standing by her father's inscription.
Photo: Arran McKeith.

was his irrepressible zest for life. I am reminded of this by a photo of him with his Canadian chums. He is sporting an enormous piratical beard but it is the characteristic grin, still in place, which captures the eye and has stayed in my memory.

If he were alive today he would be verging on his seventies. It is difficult to think of him earthbound like the rest of us. It may be of small consolation to you, but your father will never grow old.[1]

---

[1] Alasdair 'Bugs' McKeith died on Mount Assiniboine as the result of a cornice collapse in 1978. (Ed.)

44

THE ALPINE TRILOGY PROJECT

By Ross Hewitt

ALL IT TOOK WAS A three-word text, Brenva is good, to motivate my Italian friend Enrico Mosetti to jump in his car and drive seven hours from the Italian-Slovenian border to Chamonix. It would be the first route of my Alpine Trilogy Project, taking advantage of the short window for skiing big steep mountain lines in late May.

The project was simple, a personal challenge to ski and photograph three of the biggest, baddest and hardest ski lines in the Alps: Switzerland's iconic Matterhorn, the Himalayan-sized West Face of Mont Blanc, and the historic Brenva Spur on the East Face of Mont Blanc. This project would be challenge enough just to ski, but to carry the extra 2.5kgs of my SLR camera and take photos of my partners on these steep faces would add another level of difficulty that had me second-guessing my likelihood of success from the start. I guessed it might take five years to ski these major lines.

THE BRENVA SPUR

A 3 a.m. alarm tore us from our dreams in the Cosmiques refuge. After forcing down as much food and water as possible, Tom Grant, Enrico and I headed out into the night to ski down the Vallée Blanche.

It was ink black and the usual summit reference points were cloaked in darkness. My powerful torch light seemed to be absorbed in the dark

Sundown at the Cosmiques Refuge. Photo: Ross Hewitt.

Tom Grant on Col de la Fourche with the Brenva Spur behind. Photo: Ross Hewitt.

rather than lighting up my path. After a quick transition we started skinning into Cirque Maudit, still in the pitch black.

At Col de la Fourche we met with dawn and bathed in the alpenglow as the sun crept over the eastern skyline. That moment of first light is one of revelation for the ski-mountaineer whose senses have been deprived in the dark, inducing fear, anxiety, doubt. Now the way ahead becomes clear, calm is restored and you feel the low point in your soul disappear. In front of us the Brenva Face revealed all its magical hidden secrets in a scale that was difficult to judge due to the sheer size of the east face.

The air was still and a blanket of cloud was drawn over the landscape below keeping Italy snug. Most people would still be curled up in bed enjoying a lazy Sunday morning, dreaming of cappuccinos and pains aux chocolats to start their day. As the sun's ray passed horizontal, every snow and ice crystal sparkled, and the temperature was so pleasant we climbed in thin mid-layers. We soon joined the curling arête of the Brenva Spur and covered the final few hundred metres to the pyramid rock tower, gatekeeper to the serac exit onto Col de Brenva.

Stamping ledges in the snow we clicked into our skis and soaked in the magnificent surroundings. The vast east face of Mont Blanc lay to our right, a labyrinth of couloirs, buttresses and tumbling seracs that held historic Alpine climbs such as *Route Major*, testament to a bygone era of adventurous times.

Boot-deep sun-kissed powder over the glacial ice waited for us on the upper section, but you are never quite sure if the ski edges will touch the ice. After the first turn revealed no surprises we skied some cautious turns allowing our sluff to run in front until we had passed a section of really

Enrico Mosetti on the crest of the Brenva Spur. Photo: Ross Hewitt.

Tom Grant on the Brenva Spur. Photo: Ross Hewitt.

shallow snow over the ice. From this point the angle eased allowing us to open it up more and a dozen turns of sensuous skiing took us to the arête. From there we dropped right onto wide open slopes holding perfect spring snow and dropped a further couple of hundred metres in five or six swooping turns back to Col Moore with big smiles on our faces.

THE WEST FACE

Three days later we were back at the Cosmiques refuge. Once again the alarm pulled me from my sleep at an ungodly hour, but my excitement levels rose as I looked out the window and was greeted by the rest of the

Ross Hewitt on the West Face of Mont Blanc. Photo: Guilhem Martin Saint Leon.

galaxy twinkling in the night sky. I made my way out into the cold pre-dawn air joined by a few of the strongest 'under the radar' skiers you could ever meet: Mikko Heimonen, Jesper Petterson and skier-journalist Guilhem Martin Saint Leon. As we skinned up Tacul the temperature continued to drop and the cold wind increased in strength making it feel pretty uncivilised. On Col Maudit the wind was driving snow and we stopped to put on all our spare clothes.

Suffering in silence we plodded on feeling the altitude and trying to keep our extremities from freezing. On the summit it was a relief to drop down the Italian side a few metres and get out of the north wind. Below us the vast West Face rolled over out of sight and filled us with nervous excitement. We had estimated 1 p.m. would be the ideal start-time, which gave us a few moments to get ready.

The top few turns were pretty scratchy and we could feel the glacial ice underneath, but after 100m we got onto good snow alongside a buttress. Below we skied a fantastic long pitch on what must be the highest spine in Europe.

We were all working hard at around 4500m: like race-pace hard when you smell the blood in your nose, trying to keep to time, knowing that that would be the only way to negotiate safe passage through the glaciers 2000m below.

A short traverse over a snowy rock rib took us into the South facing Saudan line, a 50° couloir that fell away below us for a 1000m. Now that the exposure had eased we could relax more and enjoyed good consistent

Mikko Heimonen on the West Face. Photo: Ross Hewitt.

snow that continued all the way down to the lower apron. As we crossed the bergschrund we had been skiing hard for an hour and a half and we were still above the top of the 3424m Petit Mont Blanc.

Our route from here was to skin to the shoulder above the ancient Quintino Sella bivi hut and then ski the west-facing couloir down to the Dome Glacier. Our timing was perfect and the 600m couloir skied so well on creamy spring snow that we skied the whole 45° shot together without stops in under five minutes. The Dome Glacier lay in front of us and its crossing had been a big question in our minds, but, after roping up, it only took a few minutes and the weight of uncertainty was lifted. Now on moderate terrain, a couple more hours would get us to the road where a friend would pick us up.

THE MATTERHORN
Now, in early June, only Mikko was still psyched and we headed in to ski the Matterhorn the hard way. Because the refuge was closed due to renovations, we were carrying a tent, sleeping bag, stove, and a gallon of water each on top of the usual stuff. It was difficult to know what to expect on the face, as so few people had actually skied it. A local guide had told us it wasn't very steep but it sure looked steep from below!

I went to bed early setting the alarm for 2 a.m. Sleeping intermittently, I kept thinking that the streetlamp was really bright. When I finally poked my head out the tent, there was the Matterhorn, lit up like a stadium under the full moon. Inspired, the whole day was filled with sights of amazing natural beauty.

The Matterhorn in the Moonlight. Photo: Ross Hewitt.

Mikko Heimonen on the Matterhorn. Photo: Ross Hewitt.

The tip of the Matterhorn was the first thing to be hit by the rising sun and it resembled a blade with blood-red streaks on it. We continued climbing up the face aiming for the central couloir that ended at the rocky headwall. I was conscious that the temperature was rising fast which would eventually make the face an unsafe place; speed would be our friend.

From the top of the skiable terrain the first turn would be on sustained, unforgiving 55° spring snow. Simply standing stationary and holding an edge had every fibre in the body working overtime. Mikko left the sanctuary of his ledge and, with axe and pole in one hand, committed without hesitation into a series of beautifully-linked chop turns that you'd have been proud of with fresh legs on a lift-accessed Midi North-Face run.

Now it was my turn. A heady mix of excitement and nerves. The face was really exposed looking down a uniform rock slab covered in some snow for 1000m. I had been focused on locking my body into a stable platform to shoot from and now I needed to loosen my muscles and refocus on skiing. Skiing second, I had to avoid where Mikko had skimmed the softening snow and find my own edgeable spots.

Side slipping a few metres let me get the feel of my skis underfoot and edge grip and I felt ready for that all-important first turn. Time to commit… no problem, this is going to be fine. As we dropped height and the angle eased to the 50° range, the snow softened further and the turns became softer and more rounded. Once we entered the central snowfield

Ross Hewitt on the Matterhorn. Photo: Mikko Heimonen.

the angle was around 45° and we had a lot of fun skiing fluidly and playing with the sluff down to the lower rocks.

The angle increased here and it took some time to find our bootpack to lead us through the lower slabs. Below, the lower crux traverse led through a peppered icy zone to take us to the bergschrund.

Amazingly we had pulled off the Alpine Trilogy Project in just ten days; skiing the Triple Crown of alpine steep skiing routes with a SLR and without a heli or external assistance. It hadn't really sunk in yet, but I had an enormous sense of satisfaction and happiness from the skiing, the wild situations and the performance we had put in. I knew they would be my last turns of the season and some of the best of my life.

GOING, GOING, GONE...

By Phil Gribbon

HAVE YOU EVER STOOD by the edge of a toppling cascade spilling into unseen space and watched mesmerized as a snowy hillside is sucked swiftly and silently into the gloom of Glen Coe? For years I have lived with this indelible memory imprinted in my mind. It lurks there, a bleak image with its reminder of human mortality and fraught with implications beyond my ken. Although it would have been better not happening, it was an invaluable lesson. This experience may have kept me alive for longer, and one should always give thanks for that gift.

If I had made one further little step onto the treacherous snow in the narrow runnel then my fate would have been decided. Doomed from the start, I briefly would have become a mere helpless bit of bouncing flotsam on top of a moving maelstrom of cold meringue and at the end of the ride to be swallowed in measureless mass, buried, suffocated, concreted, forever gone. These were the last moments of my companion. Time standing still, seconds without end, both above and below the churning snow, speeding ever quicker into the gully system that snaked towards the valley floor...

Did he have time to think in his downhill career? Does life go past in pictures conjured out of memory, or does the immediacy of the moment swamp everything? Was there a sensation of tossing about on a glorious frenetic helter-skelter ride, never unaware of waiting oblivion in the squeezing compression of final entombment? Who knows, but if that false step had been mine this would never have been written.

It happened this way. We had sat in comfort in St. Andrews and hatched our plans, sipping our morning coffee and proposing our first outing together. Glen Coe was always a popular choice, it was neither too far nor too taxing, and was full of challenges for a satisfying day out on interesting hills. We mooted that a traverse of the Aonach Eagach, the notched ridge along the northern flank of the main glen, would be a suitable objective; nothing definite, of course, just a possible option.

We planned to stay in Lagangarbh. Lying close to the foot of the Buachaille and at the head of Glen Coe, the hut would be our suitable base for the occasion. We wrote for the key and requested permission to stay in the revered club hut. We anticipated sampling its icebox rigours, snugly cooking close to its burning gas rings, then creeping upstairs to its mattrazenlager boards under the roof space and snuggling deep into somewhat skimpy sleeping bags. Once embedded, with more clothes added, one could lie comfortably and mentally mull over the objective for the morrow. So, the plan was to go along its length, traversing east to west, starting short side up and ending long side down..

Our visitor had little idea what was on the menu but he was game for the venture. Yes, we told him, expect a demanding day with short daylight hours to force us rapidly along the ridge so that we have sufficient light for the descent beside Clachaig Gully and towards the pleasures of a frothing quaff in the cosy cramped bar of the welcoming ancient hotel. We thought we knew it all, everything had been taken into account, and nothing could go wrong.

Way back in those bygone days the winters were always harsh and reliable, so they say. Piercingly cold north-west squalls had brought in December. Biting winds had trailed curtains of driving snow across the ridges. Up there the broken crystals had filtered into every sheltered cranny, sinking down behind every obstacle to sculpt their insubstantialness into fragile drifts that grew out over the corrie headwall.

The morning dawned fine, with blue skies and racing clouds, and a stiff boreal blast whipping spindrift plumes off the ridge. It suggested an adequate struggle ahead. There were three of us. We didn't consider an alternative objective and with carefree spirit toiled up the approach slopes picking out the most interesting route to the first summit. Once there on top of Am Bodach we paused, hunched deep in our Grenfell jackets against the chill, watching the speckled sun patterns pick out bright snow patches as they shifted along the irregular contorted gully heads and across the buttress tops above the long southern slopes. Carefully we edged down frozen ground, with no crampons for safety nor even tricouni nails on our boot edges as ice biters and scratchers. Our excuse for such barely functional footwear was that it was all the rage in those days. Who would wear crampons, if you had them, on Scottish hills?

There were no footsteps to follow, just frozen ground and sastrugied drifts, all virgin ground without trace of other scramblers. We were treading a route along our own personal mountain world. Years later I found a lone photo that showed our promise for a joyous day ahead. Two figures, axes swinging, unknowingly walking onward, sharp and clear in the sunlight with those dappled wispy clouds drifting across the sky. Sad cuttings were there too, the unwelcome news, front page stuff, and indistinct figures coming and going outside the hotel; yes, that was his wife, my heart still bleeds. However, up on the high ridge we were inspired and motivated, alive and relishing the brilliance of the day, the future unknown.

The hours slipped by unnoticed, up and down we went, nothing too demanding, full of interest, treading the singular line along the ridge. An earlier district guidebook says the Aonach Eagach is the narrowest and most difficult of the ridges on the mainland and that in addition to the charm of the rugged and picturesque pinnacles on the ridge the climber has most wonderful views of Bidean nam Bian, the Lochaber mountains and the deep valley of Loch Leven: all true, of course, but hardly written in the modern idiom. Today the Munro book states that in winter the whole traverse is a serious mountaineering expedition that may be difficult and time-consuming. That is more like it; otherwise how to explain where did all the daylight hours go?

We were at the crawl-up step-up pinnacles when a stuck-on mass of sculptured snow showed its skittery fragility. I never touched it, honest, but a cornicey cold chunk of bleached scenery churuumphed off into the steep northern corrie on its own volition. We exchanged doubting glances, aware unconsciously that this was a salutary warning from the gods. However there was little alternative but to continue carefully onwards along the ridge.

Time had become of the essence. It was growing bleakly gloomy when we reached the section of ridge sloping up towards the last summit of Sgòrr nam Fiannaidh. Clouds now had shrouded all the mountains. To go over the final highest top and try to descend towards Clachaig in the

'Deep into that darkness peering, long I stood there wondering, fearing,...'
Edgar Allan Poe. 'The Raven'. Woodcut by Helen Forde.

gathering dark was courting benightment. Leftwards we could see an escape route going downwards across a relatively gentle open slope with bare patches of open frozen ground separated by narrow strips of crossable snow. We were now well past the many treacherous gullies that were known to lure unsuspecting ridge escapees into trouble. We had stumbled on a clever circumvention down to the road, but we were about to be proved so wrong.

We began slanting down, stepping cautiously. Looking down hopefully and then up suspiciously we assessed frequently our choice of route. We had crossed a series of minor snow runnels, splitting up helpful strips of bareish ground. We reached a runnel that was wider, deeper and would need more than several quick steps to cross. I put a foot on it and sank in too far. I stopped, and looked upwards. Above was a contiguous innocuous broad snowfield that ran up to a ragged cliff that edged the misting main ridge. No, be careful, stop, step back, reconsider. A vital sixth sense was unconsciously lurking on my shoulder. It shouldn't be true, because guardian genii don't talk to unsuspecting humans, do they? I waited, silent, standing still on solid ground. Below me the second man plodded unhesitatingly onwards into the blameless morass. The third man was following behind in his footsteps and, hesitating, could only watch unbelievingly what was about to unfold.

Without sound one sensed the surface was quivering, then moving, splitting, fracturing, breaking, building, gathering speed, sucking down a seemingly endless snowfield. Of the second man there was no sight or sign. He was gone...

Somehow we got down to the road. Broke the news at the hotel. Waited until some searchers gathered. Went and shone lights at crumpled avalanche debris. Nothing there. Vanished. Gone...

Methodically at dawn we returned, swept across the surface, looking, peering, wondering, too aware of what we could find. We humans lack animal instincts but they don't. It was a wee terrier dog that stopped and snuffled into the snow. The crofter got the shovel and dug. The dog was right.

I waited a bit. Face it, man. One hesitates to acknowledge the proximity of death.

His blanched bent arm rose stiffly out of the avalanche debris. His frozen fingers were without his gloves. His axe was away and would never wave to deride the grey heavens.

Gone, and now only the memory...

TORRIDON AND KINLOCHEWE MOUNTAIN RESCUE TEAM

By Charlie Rose and Successive Team Leaders[1]

WHEN I FIRST CAME to live in Alligin at Easter in 1966, Anancaun (Field Station for the Beinn Eighe National Nature Reserve) was the designated MR Post for the area. In those days rescues were organised on an ad hoc basis by Dick Balharry[2], the then Reserve Warden, assembling local volunteers at the behest of the Police. Usually Sergeant Donnie Smith would appear to take over actual team leadership for the duration of the rescue. Rescues on the core Area Mountains were often based at Glen Cottage (at that time run as a back-packing hostel by Dave and Liz Goulder).

Following the Feith Buidhe Disaster in November, 1971, Hamish MacInnes was consulted by the Scottish Office and in liaison with affected Police authorities, proposed the setting up of additional volunteer civilian mountain rescue teams in areas palpably not yet covered. Hamish asked me if I could raise a team in this area; the incentive was that the Police Budget would cover equipping and maintaining the team and we would become a part of the overall network with all the attendant benefits (access to training courses and seminars, helicopter assistance, etc).

At about the time the team was being formed, the Scottish Youth Hostels Association built a new modern hostel in Torridon and immediately agreed it should be designated the new MR Post for the area, and that the team might use it as its headquarters. Neil Reilleay, the first warden and his wife Irene, became enthusiastic helpers providing storage and accommodation for the team equipment and rooms for meetings, etc. Whenever a call-out occurred they would stay up all night if necessary providing hot drinks, a phone link, and unflagging support. All subsequent wardens and their wives have been equally supportive and played a major role in the efficient functioning of the team. A further incalculable bonus to the team has been that we have always been able to recruit able-bodied and often experienced, helpers from the hostellers staying at the time.

Initially, the team was composed primarily of local crofters, stalkers and foresters from the surrounding sporting estates as well as the personnel of the Beinn Eighe nature reserve together with some older stalwarts who, while no longer able to go on the hill, did sterling work manning the base radio and providing a courier link between it and the

---

[1] This article by our late member Charlie Rose was in the possession of Torridon Mountain Rescue Team at the time of his death. It was decided to publish it and updates on the Team's development by subsequent Team Leaders as a tribute to Charlie and the vital work of the TMRT and indeed of all our Rescue Teams in Scotland. (Hon. Ed.)

[2] The late Dick Balharry, a distinguished naturalist, became an honorary member of the SMC in 2010. (Hon. Ed.)

nearest telephone – frequently an all-night vigil. There were relatively few team members who had previous sport-mountaineering experience but the outstanding strength most could bring to any rescue was their intimate knowledge of the local hills and their fitness; they knew the best route to take under any conditions and were undeterred by the vilest weather. In addition, the team benefited from the wholehearted co-operation of our local general practitioner. Over the years the incumbent has changed several times but all have been universally supportive, coming on the hill when the occasion permitted, running first-aid courses and always on hand to field casualties the moment they were brought off the hill.

In the early days facilities were limited. We had few radios and helicopters were scarce. I vividly recall one search situation where the Wessex we had been allocated successfully terminated the operation by flying low over widely scattered groups of searchers with the winchman sitting in the open door displaying a large piece of cardboard with GO HOME written on it!

Over time steady progress was made. Police liaison improved, courses were held at Glenmore Lodge in first aid and dog handling. Exercises were held with RAF MR Kinloss and with Helicopter Wing, Lossiemouth. Improvements in basic equipment, especially in numbers and performance of walkie-talkies and the allocation of a MR Band together with the introduction of Sea King helicopters gradually altered the entire MR scene and speeded up reaction times.

Compared with some other teams we had a very sleepy wee corner of the Highlands. For many years we averaged about four full-scale rescues a year with perhaps twice as many alarms which did not, in the end, necessitate calling the whole team out. However, in the seventeen or so years I was the team leader we encountered a dozen fatalities, many broken limbs and assorted injuries and many lost individuals, together with the usual crop of bizarre incidents – individuals or even groups of people who inexplicably 'vanished' from their companions wandering round the back of Beinn Alligin, Beinn Dearg, or Beinn Eighe because they had been busy blethering, didn't have a map, or had caught sight of Loch Maree in the distance and thought it must be Loch Torridon! I sometimes wondered whether we weren't in the business of rescuing mountains from the more zany behaviour of the human race. At the end of it all, however, the real reward comes with the elation we all feel when we have succeeded in rescuing someone who was in serious trouble and we can say, 'Yes, it WAS worthwhile.' And I wonder if anyone ever spares a thought for our wives and families who have to spend days and nights worrying about us in the most appalling weather?

TERRY DOE, TEAM LEADER 1987–1994
One evening in 1977 I knocked on the door of Charlie Rose's house in Alligin, introduced myself and said that I was interested in joining the

A Sea King involved in a tricky rescue on East Buttress, Coire Mhic Fhearchair, Beinn Eighe. Photo: TMRT Collection.

Torridon and Kinlochewe Mountain Rescue Team. He looked surprised and asked 'why would anyone want to get involved with mountain rescue?' I replied something like 'You did' and went on to explain that I was an active mountaineer and that I had spent the previous four years working as a full-time mountaineering instructor at an outdoor centre in Applecross. I was now employed as a deer-stalker/manager on a local sporting estate and that I would shortly be moving into Balgy Lodge, across the loch from his house. I was taken on and very shortly, presumably because of my background and experience, I was appointed Deputy Team Leader.

Call-outs at that time consisted mainly of searches and recoveries with the occasional need to set up anchors to lower the stretcher off steep ground. Many of the jobs were over-nighters involving many hours of stretcher-carrying only made easier by attaching the wheel when we eventually reached the path. Helicopters did not fly at night but would endeavour to pick us up soon after first light. We had no radio communication with the aircraft so resorted to using flares and hand-signals from the winchman hanging out of the side door. One day whilst involved in extricating a crag-bound walker from high up on the south side of Liathach a very large, highly polished, bright yellow RAF helicopter arrived on scene and went on to complete the job. This was our first sight of a Sea King helicopter and the first time it had ever been used in a mountain rescue situation in Scotland.

In 1987 I moved to Kinlochewe. On occasions over the previous ten years Charlie had asked me if I would step up to become Team Leader. Only now did I feel settled enough to take on the role. I was excited by the challenge because I realised that the Torridon MR Team had to modernise in order to cope with the increase in the numbers of people visiting the local hills and going out in hostile weather conditions.

I identified areas where the Team needed to make changes. A general meeting was called and officers elected. The Team Leader acted as chairman and secretary. Officers elected were: Deputy Team Leader, Treasurer, Training Officer, Medical Officer and Equipment Officer. These general meetings were to be held annually. A priority was to gain charitable status which we did.

The Scottish Youth Hostel Association gave us permission to upgrade the store and equip it with shelves and hanging racks with a separate area where we eventually installed a telephone and our base radio. The Youth hostel was an official mountain rescue post, I later gained permission to designate Anancaun Field Station in Kinlochewe an official mountain rescue post, which gave us access to all the kit required to equip it for free. An unofficial post was established at Craig, by Achnashellach, next door to Chris Mackenzie the keeper's house.

The Team equipment was out-dated and needed to be replaced. We had been issued a new base radio and a couple of hand-held sets but we required more hand-held. I approached the Howard Doris Trust who stumped-up £936 to purchase three radios which were located one at each MR post. This meant an advanced unit carrying first-aid could be on its way to the casualty before the bulk of the Team arrived. We purchased climbing ropes, pre-stretched ropes, new stretchers, casualty-bags and much more. I approached Sprayway who gave a 50% discount on their Gore-Tex Torridon mountain jacket and over trousers. We purchased fifteen sets and were able to help Sprayway with their advertising. A donation from Boots Across Scotland charity went a long way toward covering the cost of purchasing the new equipment required, plus donations received from grateful rescued and bereaved families. One lady left the Team £15,700 in her will, (ironically we had recovered her body from Moruisg, Glen Carron). In 1992 we took delivery of our first Team vehicle, a 4x4 Ford Transit donated by British Telecom. The rear of the vehicle was filled with kit and fitted with a base radio which meant we had a mobile base: a massive leap forward and a great asset.

The Team needed to train regularly. I put this statement to the Team at an AGM. I proposed the Team should meet monthly, the first Sunday in every month. Most members agreed to Team training but some were worried about training on the Sabbath. I suggested that training would not be compulsory and that each team member should look to his own conscience. Initially I took control of the monthly training, concentrating on personal MR skills required for both summer and winter conditions. Navigation, safe movement over steep ground and use of ice-axe and crampons. Later, crag rescue skills were covered and the correct use of technical kit involved in stretcher lowering and hauling. Team members were encouraged to attend external MR courses at Glenmore Lodge and Shell Seminars.

The Team was fortunate to have as our Medical Officer, Dr Andrew Brown our local GP. Andrew was also a Surgeon Commander in the Royal Navy Reserve and was well qualified to instruct us on trauma injuries. He undertook to train us during our monthly training sessions on mountain first-aid and made himself available during the de-brief of recent incidents involving injuries. For the very keen first-aiders he also ran weekly evening sessions at his home which gave us the chance to pick his brains on matters that might be worrying us. I tried to ensure that there was a first-aid component in every monthly training session, usually involving packaging the casualty and loading him on the stretcher in ever more awkward situations. During a conversation with an old friend now working as a ski patroller I asked where the ski patrol went for its medical training and could he supply me with contact details. Months later five naïve Team members headed south in the new Team vehicle to the North Staffordshire Royal Infirmary, Stoke-on-Trent, for a five day Emergency Medical Technician Course. There then followed one of the most intensive, stressful, five days of medical training any of us had ever undertaken, culminating in an easily-failable examination. We all passed and were very grateful to return to Torridon.

By the time we were due for re-validation the British Association of Ski Patrols had set up their own Emergency Medical Technician (EMT) courses. The courses were held much closer to home and were based entirely on mountain rescue situations so we attended these in the future. The EMTs became the front-line in casualty management and generally took control of the casualty on the hill, but it was still very important for the other team members to keep their first-aid skills up to date and they were encouraged to do so.

Helicopters were soon recognised as an extremely useful asset in mountain rescue. Initially the Team had no radio communication with the helicopter until the winchman was landed on scene, later if possible we would loan the crew one of our hand-held radios, even later the crew would arrive on scene with their own hand held mountain rescue radio. After a time we were able to speak to them directly when they were able to change their radio frequency to ours. RAF helicopters were not allowed to winch our mountain rescue stretcher; this meant waiting for the aircrew to lower their stretcher or to transfer the casualty from our stretcher to theirs. Medics working on a casualty were sometimes hassled to prepare the casualty for winching before he was stabilised and it took a lot of courage to tell the aircraft to go away until it was called in. Sometimes the helicopter would go straight to the scene of the incident and double strop the casualty without apparent concern for the individual's injuries. These were all matters that needed to be resolved and the Mountain Rescue Committee of Scotland (MRCofS) stepped in to convey the Team's concerns to the RAF.

The Team involved itself with the local community by providing safety cover for charitable sponsored walks including for the Highland Hospice, Lochcarron Heritage Museum and Highland Cross. We used these events as a valuable radio communication training session. We also gave the local children an annual rock climbing and abseiling day at Ardheslaig Crag which proved very popular and supplied us with a couple of future Team members.

The period between 1987 and 1992 was a very busy time for the Torridon MRT. There was so much to do to modernise the way the Team was managed and equipped, and to prepare it for the challenges of the future. I was so grateful for the support I received from Team members. The Team of the future has been built upon the solid foundations we created together.

(During the period 1977 to 1987 two years went by without a single call-out. In 1993 the Torridon MRT attended 13 incidents, four of them involving fatalities).

SEAMUS MACNALLY, TEAM LEADER 1994–2000
Terry Doe stepped down as Team Leader in February 1994 and after a brief three years as a member I was voted into this role. At that time there was still a good number of local members and support for the team was excellent. Bill Taylor was treasurer, and Cam Macleay became training officer, with Nick McNeil and Tom Forrest as deputies. Throughout the six years other office bearers included Dickie Livingstone, Chris MacKenzie, Mike Dunlop and Neil Hinchliffe.

Quite early on I decided the office bearers should meet regularly and this started the cycle the team now has of committee meetings almost on a monthly basis. This shared the burden of decision making and also kept the whole process democratic and open. Team members were always

The Team training on Beinn Eighe. Photo: Gerry MacPartlin.

welcome to attend meetings too and discuss whatever was on the agenda. Money was never plentiful and at one stage the contents of our current account was perilously close to zero, but we were not alone among teams in that situation, especially on the west coast and further north.

At this time I was also a member of the local Coastguard team and was starting to train as a search and rescue dog handler so life was never dull and being around other rescue organisations allowed a good insight into the world of rescue and the politics of the whole business.

One aspect not mentioned often enough is the support team members receive from their families, because without it the structure would soon break down. A certain amount of guilt still exists over the number of week-ends when I was at meetings or training and therefore not around for the family. In that first year as leader, the number of events attended related to mountain rescue was more than 70 (training, administration, call outs, giving talks, and SARDA).

Rescues often involved long stretcher carries with casualties, usually at night and in wintry conditions. The helicopters, both RAF and Coastguard, were good but we as a team had to work hard on numerous occasions when they were unable to offer support. There is however, no better way of bonding folk together, than long hours on the hill under arduous conditions, when all the training kicks in and the outcome is successful.

Fatalities were, and still are unfortunately, not uncommon and this brought another side to mountain rescue which is dealing with the survivors and the friends and family of the deceased. The Police are good at dealing with the necessary officialdom, whereas the team are good at handling the nearest and dearest and absorbing the sadness of the moment. After these events the leader often has to deal with correspondence from friends and family. One particular incident involved two young winter climbers who were avalanched due to a cornice collapse at the top of their route. One died at the scene and his companion was found stuck in the snow with various injuries. Both were stretchered from the back of Liathach in the dark, down to the roadside to a waiting ambulance. The mother of the young man who died wrote to the team thanking them for their assistance and asking about the circumstances of the accident. Thus began a correspondence lasting a couple of years, which only ended when the lady eventually managed to visit Torridon, and with a companion, walk in to the corrie where her son had fallen. This, thankfully, gave her some peace of mind and closure of a kind.

The team continues to thrive and adapt to changing situations, and it was a privilege to have had the title of Team Leader for a few years. After two terms in post I felt someone else should have the chance to take over, as I am not a believer in the same person taking on such a role for decades. Fresh ways are good, although having the chance to continue as a deputy with the next two leaders, hopefully meant the wheel was not reinvented too often, while allowing new ideas to come to the fore.

NEIL HINCHLIFFE, TEAM LEADER 2000–2010

When I joined the team in 1994, Seamus (MacNally) was leader. Seamus was an extremely fit and capable guy living right next door to the team base, and with his search and rescue dog, Max, fulfilled this role perfectly. However, prior to the AGM in Feb 2000, Seamus decided he would be stepping down as team leader...so then, and, following much badgering, I was pushed into the spotlight.

Other than fitness, dedication, and the ability to work as a team, it is prudent always to be aware of the strengths and weaknesses of those on a rescue with you. However, it was now crucial for me also to know absolutely everything about each individual team member. This would clearly include their skills within mountain rescue, but also other attributes e.g. who knows a particular area backwards; the order they would arrive at base; who is capable of carrying specific, large, heavy items of kit up the hill. And then there were the purely personal and perhaps even private characteristics that you had to be up-to-date on, for example, who didn't really like the thought of flying; who wasn't so happy on exposed terrain; who was dating who. All these factors, plus dozens more, were always crucial to ensure that we, the team, executed the rescue as swiftly, safely, and professionally as possible, for the benefit of the person in difficulty.

The complexity of modern rescue ropework: an example of the techniques team members have to master. Photo: Gerry McPartlin.

Since moving away from the Torridon area, I have been attached to Skye MRT, and the Hebrides SAR, (and before Torridon, Killin MRT), and whilst each team may have a totally different terrain to cover, the enthusiasm is omni-present. I can also recall many times when individual team members' lives have been literally on the line, as rescues evolved, and in hindsight, I would love to see these achievements recognised formally.

Regarding the recent announcement of a new team base being erected this year...this event hasn't come soon enough. Even in the early 2000s this proposed new base was considered essential in order to help concentrate all the professional attributes of the team into one purpose-made spot. The effects of this will inevitably help even further to ensure that anyone requiring rescuing in Torridon's mountains will receive maximum assistance.

EOGHAIN MACLEAN, TEAM LEADER 2010–2013
I joined Mountain Rescue as a very young 18 year old in 1973 when I became a member of Braemar MRT and was around MRT until retiring in 2013. My first stint of training was winter skills at the Lodge. I think this has changed a little bit in 40 years. My first meeting with Mr. Mountain Rescue, David 'Heavy' Whalley, was on a winter mountain rescue in the Braemar mountains when it was so cold that the Wessex blades were frozen and it could not leave the ground.

On coming home to Wester Ross I joined the Torridon and Kinlochewe MRT that was made up of shepherds, keepers, fishermen and a few climbers. During my time in the Team I held the positions of Deputy twice, Treasurer for 10 years and Team Leader for three years, taking over from Neil when he left for pastures new. My spell as TL was not the busiest time for mountain rescue in Wester Ross but in the six weeks before I retired we dealt with six incidents one of which was a fatality on Moruisg.

MR has changed over the years and at one time you would always have your Sunday dinner as early as possible as you knew the telephone would ring in the early evening and you would most likely not see home again till Monday morning. Some of these rescues could last for 2–3 days.

For a time Susan my wife had to put up with two sons and her husband on a mountain rescue. Our oldest son Scott and youngest son Ryan were both in the Team. Ryan is still a team member having joined when he was 16. I enjoyed my time in mountain rescue and still miss the callouts.

(Torridon Mountain Rescue Team is now led by Arjan Hendriks who was appointed in 2013.)

SIXTY YEARS ON

By Dennis Gray

WRITING THIS IN JULY 2014, I am reminded that it is now sixty years since Joe Brown and Don Whillans, made one of the most historic breakthroughs in British Alpine history, completing in record time, during July 1954 the 3rd ascent of the West Face of the Dru, and pioneering their new route on the West Face of the Blaitière. On this latter the Fissure Brown and the less vaunted Whillans Crack near the summit of the route, were both accomplished at a new level of free climbing in the Western Alps.

We are now living in a more affluent and egalitarian society, but to understand the true nature of these achievements, one must appreciate that for two working class climbers originating from the mean streets of Manchester and Salford, to have developed the skills, knowledge and ambition to undertake such feats was remarkable. Their abilities had been developed during an apprenticeship served on the British hills, with a few fledgling ascents in the Mont Blanc range.

However, these two climbs were to be no fluke and both Brown and Whillans subsequently enjoyed mountain careers almost without parallel in British climbing history. How did this come about? They were I think fortunate to develop their skills with some other highly talented and more experienced mountaineers from their own social milieu and backgrounds, some of whom were slightly older such as Nat Allen and Don Cowan who also possessed the same drive and initiative: this being crucial if you enjoyed only limited holidays, lacked finance and transport and needed to rely on rudimentary equipment. They had to seize every opportunity afforded to them whenever it presented itself.

Easter 1954 was a typical example of this when a Rock and Ice Club meet was held on Ben Nevis. I was 18 at the time, but having been an active climber for seven years, I was well attuned to the thinking and way of life of my companions. And in retrospect though we were ambitious, we were more light-hearted and jolly than most of the tight-lipped athletes that one meets on the crags these days.

We camped high in the Allt a' Mhuilinn. I shared a tent with Ray Greenall and Joe Brown, pitched on snow a foot deep when we arrived, but a sudden rise in temperature and a rapid thaw left us stranded in a quagmire. The tent was at best rudimentary and we spent the rest of our stay in wet clothes and wet sleeping bags, baling out water which oozed through our makeshift groundsheet.

By the time we had returned to Manchester our bodies had wrinkles all over them like prunes, and Joe, influenced by his recent army national service, declared after careful inspection that we had developed trench feet!

As daylight dawned on our first climbing day, Rock and Ice parties

Joe 'Morty'Smith and Joe Brown. Photo: Dennis Gray collection.

headed off for different objectives, Don Whillans and Nat Allen to essay a possible new rock route on the Càrn Dearg Buttress, Ron Moseley and Don Cowan to attempt the unclimbed *Point Five Gully*, whilst Joe decided that we three ought to inspect the also still virgin *Zero Gully*. Early in the morning we climbed straightforward slopes to the base of the climb, dodging a bombardment of falling ice from out of the gully itself. After several hundred feet, at the foot of a steep ice pitch Ray and I installed ourselves, well belayed, deep inside a cave type opening while Joe prepared to lead the pitch. He put his head out of our sheltering hovel, found nothing was falling and began cutting steps.

The rope moved stealthily out until suddenly a noise like a bren gun popping followed by screaming missiles told us, cowering deep into our fissure, that all was not quiet on the Zero front. The rope sagged, and grating tricounis gave the signal that Joe was retreating.

'Whoops!' Into our shelter he dived as a larger missile whizzed past its opening. 'The ice is in bad condition,' he informed us. 'We'll have to retreat!' An hour later we were still in the cave waiting for the ice to stop falling. As the morning progressed and the temperature began to rise it became worse, stirring Joe into activity. 'We can't stop in this hole forever,' he said. 'Coil the ropes and we'll jump for it!'

'Jump for it?' Ray and I echoed.

'Yes, jump out of here, slide down and brake with your axe before reaching those small cliffs in Observatory Gully. We'd better unrope!' So we untied and coiled the ropes, but Ray and I cowered deeper as more ice-blocks thundered by outside.

Joe climbed to the edge of the cave, looked up once more to see if anything was falling, explained, tongue in cheek, that the idea was 'to descend the same speed as the falling ice' and then nonchalantly leaped out into space. He landed several feet further down, then careered down the slope at an oblique angle in a perfect standing glissade at a speed I have only seen equalled by falling bodies, covering perhaps five hundred feet in seconds. He crowned this performance with a swift roll over, head up and face to the slope, and with a deftly executed braking movement stopped himself a short way above the barrier crags, got up and ran out of the path of falling debris. Ray and I followed his actions wide-eyed.

'You next,' I suggested.

'You're kidding! You can go'

I crept to the edge of the cave but a large ice-block screamed past and I scuttled back to the fielding bosom of Ray. Faintly we could hear Joe yelling, 'Come on you ninnies!' Out to the lip I crept once more, looked up the bulging ice of Zero, then looked down to Joe waiting impatiently below. 'Jump!' he shouted, and with rather too much impetus I sprang far out as a falling icicle burst about me. I hit the slope with a bone-shaking jar, then shot out into space once more in a complete somersault so that when I landed again I slid rapidly down the snow head first.

I had kept hold of my axe but try as I might I could not get myself the right way up. I got on my side but I was still head first and as I swooped down like a swallow. I became conscious of two things – the line of cliffs directly in my path and Joe running across to try to cut me off before I shot over them. Somehow, on easier ground but still moving at high speed I managed to right myself at last, then in a panic, lying on my axe and pressing with all my strength I stopped my flight almost dead. My shoulder and arm were almost torn out of joint, but I managed to get to my feet in time to greet a panting Brown with a grin.

After this performance, no name-calling or cajoling would persuade Ray to imitate my antics. Finally, he stepped boldly on to the slope, facing in, and slowly and methodically kicked his way down. Falling ice exploded all around him but he resolutely ignored this and when a minor particle hit him he just shrugged this off. Watching was more frightening than the action, and it was with relief that we welcomed Ray to where we safely waited, at which he proceeded to give us a short lecture: 'Always be in control!' It was a happy threesome which headed back to our wet tent: what was that against the hot brews we could make inside it?

The next day Joe teamed up with Don Whillans to investigate further the possibility of a major new route on the Càrn Dearg Buttress. After several false starts Don had made good progress the day before, and as they left our campsite he was confident that he and Brown could finish the climb off. I lay in our tent doorway watching them and by noon they had overcome the first difficult section of the climb to reach the base of the most striking feature of their route, a deep crack. This was their forte and leading through they soon had this behind them and were nearing the top of the buttress. Success by then seemed certain, when from out of the CIC hut, situated across the Glen there emerged two SMC worthies who, brandishing their ice axes like claymores, shouted across 'Ye Sassenach Bastards!' That is why the eventual new route climbed that day by Brown and Whillans came to be called *Sassenach*.

In the late afternoon I was persuaded by Don Cowan to accompany him on an ascent of *Tower Ridge*. I had never climbed with him before this event, but the speed with which we subsequently accomplished this climb, in perfect conditions, seemed miraculous to me then. Cowan, one of the silent figures of The Rock and Ice, was then the club's most accomplished and experienced mountaineer. He had introduced first Whillans and then Brown to Alpine mountains, and despite having just two weeks holiday on each occasion they had achieved some classic ascents.

Tall, with fair curly hair and a marked south Yorkshire accent, his forte was Alpine and Scottish winter climbing, and his speed, route finding, and fluency on the Tower Ridge that day made me realise yet again what a wealth of talent the group contained. We soloed the Douglas Boulder Direct, the seven-hundred-foot introductory buttress of the ridge, and moved thereafter with rope coils. Normally I don't climb like that if I can avoid it – I would sooner solo or move more slowly and belay – but with Cowan I felt safe. We overtook many parties and among them, as we set off across the Eastern Traverse which avoids the major obstacle of the ridge, the direct ascent of the Great Tower, were two ropes, two men and a woman, and two women.

We completed the traverse successfully, a wonderful airy situation to which I have returned many times, then climbed to the summit of the Great Tower. From there, we descended slightly, crossed the Tower Gap with a swift look down *Glover's Chimney* and finally, almost at a run, climbed the upper slopes of the ridge to reach the summit plateau of the Ben. The sun was shining, there was little wind, in fact the day gave us the first feeling of spring, and a view that is unsurpassed I believe anywhere in the British Isles.

Two hours after leaving our tents, *Tower Ridge* behind us, we were glissading down Number Three Gully on perfect snow, unaware that one of the parties we had overtaken was in serious difficulty.

In the rope of two which had climbed the Eastern Traverse after us, one of the women had fallen during her ascent of the Tower. Her companion had held her, but she had fallen about forty feet and had badly hit her head on the rock. The remaining four members of the party were not able to pull her back up, and all they could do was to make good her anchor and go for help.

We had just settled in for the night when the call for help reached our tents, and putting on cold wet climbing clothes on top of warm wet underclothes was an effort of will. A Creagh Dhu party was camping close by, so a Rock and Ice group set off with two of the Dhus to try to climb up the flank of the *Tower Ridge* and reach the injured climber from the Tower Gully. Whilst other Rock and Ice members climbed to the summit of the Ben and descended *Tower Ridge* to the scene of the accident. I was in the second party with Whillans, Brown, Slim Sorrell and Don Chapman. Despite everyone being tired from a hard day's climbing and the night dark, overcast with thick clouds which had drifted over at sunset, we reached the summit plateau without too much difficulty by the slopes of Càrn Dearg.

Finding the top of *Tower Ridge* was no easy task in the darkness with a wind whipping snow in our eyes, even though I myself had been there only a few hours earlier. In the end we tied our ropes together and, anchored by the rest of us, Joe found the finish of the ridge. He and Don Whillans, held from above, climbed down to the Tower Gap, then, forming a rope of two were somehow able to reach the rope on which the unfortunate woman (we found out later her name was Betty Emery) was hanging. But their combined efforts could not raise her an inch. Eventually they were joined by Bob Hope of the Creagh Dhu, Don Cowan and Ray Greenall who managed to climb up and out of the Tower Gully to join them on a ledge cut out of the snow below the summit of the Great Tower.

Even with all five men pulling they still could not move the woman back up the cliff face, so, held from above, Joe climbed down to her: but unfortunately by this time she was of course dead. Small wonder they could not move her for she was jammed into an angle in the cliff face, and Joe had a difficult task to free her body.

While this was going on, Slim, Don Chapman and I up on the Ben's summit plateau were in real danger of becoming exposure victims. This is a challenging place to be on a dark night, with a bitter wind blowing, for its very form seems to invite extreme weather conditions to develop swiftly. We had no means of communication with those below so, after cutting ice bollards and anchoring the rope to these, we crossed the plateau to the summit observatory ruins and tunnelled into these, buried but accessible under the snow. From then on the night seemed endless, we had no food and the cold bit deeper and deeper as the hours ticked slowly by until we couldn't keep still for a moment. We were cheered by the arrival, shortly before dawn, of the R.A.F Mountain Rescue; their well-provisioned and equipped team sporting flasks of coffee, primus stoves and food.

At first light we descended *Tower Ridge* and shortly after, as we reached the Tower gap the four men of the Rock and Ice and the Creagh Dhu stalwart appeared carrying the body. Events moved rapidly after that, including a brief incident as we were manoeuvring the body across the Tower Gap. An R.A.F officer appeared, took command and proceeded to give Whillans his instructions of how to do this, and when he didn't take

Don Whillans. Photo: Mike Galbraith collection.

any notice, a dressing-down. He was in charge now and would suffer no insubordination! Don soon let him know that he was not a member of H.M. Forces nor ever likely to be. But once onto easy ground we were all happy to hand over to the Rescue boys who from thereon, quickly and efficiently completed the task of getting the corpse down to the road head.

An amusing sequel to this rescue was the typically inaccurate press reportage. Nat Allen and Ron Moseley took no part in the operation for the simple reason that they did not get back from climbing till the rescue parties had set out. They spent the night in their sleeping bags and only heard the news when we returned to camp the next morning. Yet somehow Nat appeared in some of the media reports as the hero of the piece, while the ones involved were barely mentioned!

That day marked the end of the Rock and Ice meet, today's climbers may be surprised to read that we only had a four day holiday, Manchester to Fort William and back. All the club members were working, and that was a typical Easter break in 1954. Getting to the hills took a huge slice out of such a break, but somehow we felt it worth the effort. It was experiences like the night spent out on the *Tower Ridge*, that I am sure gave Don and Joe the confidence to move on to such challenges as the West Face of the Dru, then seen by other British Alpinists as being beyond their compass. At that time it was regarded as the hardest route in the whole of the European Alps.

EXPECTATIONS AND OUTCOMES – A CAUTIONARY TALE

By Dave Broadhead

I HAD LONG SINCE lost count of abseils by the time it was finally dark enough to switch on our head torches. By now the angle had eased off so we were able to continue down-climbing without the ropes. Reversing our route of ascent down the wide rocky couloir seemed interminable and the expectation of another pleasant night in the cosy Envers des Aiguilles hut looked increasingly unlikely, with the outcome of our climb more and more uncertain. Thankfully there were plenty of in situ anchors and we were spared the endless meanderings which had eaten away the precious hours of daylight on the climb up. What continued to slow us down was the inevitable fankle each time we threw down the ropes, no matter how carefully we had tried to coil them. With the gradual onset of darkness I had suggested that it might be prudent to find a suitable spot for the increasingly inevitable bivouac but Adam was keen to carry on, reminding me that we were seasoned Scottish winter climbers, well used to finding our way off the hill in the dark. As I continued to press my case, my determined companion suddenly claimed to recognised some distinctive rock features from the morning's climb, not far above the terrace where we had left our axes, crampons and, in Adam's case, boots. Once again the prospect of warm cosy blankets in the hut spurred us on. While mainly focussed on the business of getting down safely, my thoughts frequently wandered onto what had lured us into this precarious situation in the first place and what would be the outcome?

Adam Kassyk and I had started our July 2015 Alpine season gently, in the scenic Vanoise. Feeling a bit rusty, the classic WNW Ridge (400m IV) of the Pointe de l'Observatoire (3015m) had taken us almost twice the guidebook time and we were a bit late for dinner but it was an enjoyable rock climb and we felt we were off to a good start. We had then climbed the Ordinary Route (PD) of the Aiguille de Tre-la-Tête (3892m) where it became clear that snow and ice conditions were far from ideal, following a poor build-up of snow over the winter and very high temperatures early in the season. We were the first party on the climb for ten days. After wending our way up the complex glacier, the final exposed snow arête turned out to be an intimidating 150m ice rib, fortunately not very steep but requiring delicate down-climbing on front-points and dinner-plating picks, relying on a meagre selection of three ice-screws for runners and belays. Agreeing to stick to rock climbs in future, we had joined the Alpine Club meet at the campsite in Argentière as planned but soon discovered that climbing from the Chamonix valley with the help of the extensive mechanical uplift available caused its own frustrations. Despite taking the first cable-car up to the Plan de l'Aiguille and enjoying Les Lépidoptères (D. 5a oblig.) in reasonable time and style we tried to

Dave Broadhead leading the couloir on the Aiguille de la République.
Photo: Adam Kassyk.

continue up the Ordinary Route (AD) on the Aiguille du Peigne(3192m) but chose to turn around before the summit so as not to miss the last car down. Turning our backs on the fleshpots we decided to go up to the Envers hut for a few days as this seemed to offer a selection of classic rock routes in the traditional style. When we eventually reached the hut and spoke to the guardienne, the poor condition of the glaciers reduced our choice to the dramatic Aiguille de la République (3305m) (D inf.) which looked well within our capabilities.

Feeling fit and acclimatised, with a borrowed copy of the excellent Michel Piola guidebook to keep us on route we left the hut in darkness at 5 a.m. and climbed the short heavily crevassed Trelaporte glacier to gain the rocks above. Two French climbers were some way ahead of us and we soon came to a broad terrace where they had left their axes and crampons, tempting us to do likewise, with Adam leaving his mountain boots too. By the time we reached the broad rocky couloir which gives access to the final ridge, the French team were well ahead and passed us later on their way down while we continued determinedly upwards. In retrospect, we should have agreed some sort of turnaround time, but while the climb was going well that was the last thing on our minds. After climbing a couple of tricky pitches on the ridge near the summit we were happy to miss out the final bolt ladder and started our late afternoon descent with a dramatic 50m free abseil back down into the top of the ascent couloir.

As I followed Adam across a tricky couple of moves in the darkness we suddenly came across two sleeping bags stretched out on a ledge. One of the slumbering figures jumped to his feet and after a brief exchange came out with something along the lines of 'Aah Scootland benneveespointfiveadrianswol many times I climbed. You must rappel from zee bolt. Then traverser across to your gear.' Pulling on his boots but not bothering to tie them he nipped back across the tricky moves and showed us exactly what he was talking about. Naively confident in his friendly advice we thanked him and abseiled down into the maw of what turned out to be a particularly awesome chimney-couloir, past some enormous chock-stones with no sign of any lines traversing out or any possibility of climbing back up. I had started the route with ten metres of abseil tat, allowing some reassuring back up to the more dubious looking anchors.

A few rope lengths down the couloir while waiting for Adam to follow I was alarmed by a great clatter above me and immediately feared one had failed. To my enormous relief a strained voice from above assured me that apart from a sore back he was fine, having taken an unexpected swing in the darkness. To add to our discomfort the trickle of water down the back of the couloir had soaked the ropes and was starting to dampen our clothing. At the next ledge there was no dissent at my suggestion to stop and wait for daylight before we became totally wet and hypothermic. It was about 1 a.m. when we finally hunkered down, wearing every scrap of clothing and sitting on everything else. Thankfully it was a mild night and there were not many more hours of shivering darkness to endure before it was light enough to continue down until a final abseil landed me on a spacious sloping ledge at the mouth of a shallow cave. Below, a large gap separated the steep ice of the glacier from the buttress and I knew straight away that without axes and crampons there would be no further progress. Immediately I fished my phone out of the rucksack and switched on, relieved to see three bars of reception. When Adam duly arrived he agreed straight away with the decision to dial 112. There really was no other sensible alternative.

At the other end of the phone we had already been reported overdue by the hut guardienne and having established that we did not require

The second winchman joins the first and Adam on the ledge above the bergschrund.
Photo: Dave Broadhead.

immediate assistance, we were told to wait for an hour or so. Meanwhile
the mountain inflicted its final cruelty. Remarkably, on none of our many
abseils had the ropes jammed, until this very last when my relatively new
red rope stubbornly stuck. Attempting to climb up a few metres under yet
another improbable chock-stone to try and free the jam, I soon decided it
was tempting fate to push myself any further and simply reached up as
far as I could manage, cut the rope and salvaged thirty metres or so.

We heard the Gendamerie helicopter before we saw it but when that
machine came into sight, a tiny dot among the surrounding peaks and
glaciers, I felt an amazing surge of relief and happiness as it flew straight
towards us. With impressive skill in view of the enclosing walls of the
couloir, the pilot lowered two rescuers onto our ledge then backed off
while we got sorted out. With brusque efficiency we were helped to stash
all our dangly bits of slings and gear out of harm's way inside sacs before
the chopper returned to pluck us off. Adam went first, delivered to the hut
just around the corner before returning for me. As soon as my feet left the
ground we soared up and away from the cliffs, swinging precariously on
the end of the wire suspended mid-air above the mighty Mer de Glace
before being hoisted up onto the landing gear then hauled into the relative
safety of the floor of the cockpit. One can only admire the bravery of the
men who choose to do this dangerous job on a daily basis, who seemed
to want little in the way of thanks as I was carefully pushed out again
minutes later onto the grass in front of the hut.

A welcome late breakfast at the Envers hut after the rescue. Photo: Dave Broadhead.

The two guardiennes were very pleased to see us again and soon produced jugs of tea and an enormous breakfast which we wolfed down in the sunshine on the terrace in front of the hut. They had been following the progress of our rescue on their short-wave radio receiver. Adam went inside for a short sleep, during which time we watched two further helicopter rescues, which made me feel a little bit less pathetic. As a final act of kindness an old pair of plastic boots was produced for Adam, fortuitously a perfect fit for the long walk down.

Over the next few days, with Adam hors de combat there were plenty of opportunities to recount and reflect on our experience with the rest of the Meet but the thought of our gear still sitting on the mountain continued to rankle with me. By offering to pay his train fare up to Montenvers I was able to persuade Max, a strong and steady English alpinist with a spare set of crampons, to head back up with me to try and recover it a few days later. This proved to be something of a fool's errand, as the continuing thaw had melted the precarious snow bridge linking the glacier with the foot of the buttress. Good sense prevailed at this point and we turned around without pushing our luck any further, but I now felt a lot better about the lost gear, having at least tried to get it back. I also finally came to terms with the ignominy of getting into the situation in the first place. No matter how wise and experienced you might think you are, with plenty of good outcomes under your belt, do not get lulled into the smug expectation that it will never happen to you.

PLUKES, POCKMARKS, WARTS AND ALL

By Mike Dixon

WHICHEVER WAY YOU APPROACH Ben Avon there's one thing guaranteed: it will not be a short day. It's a mountain of contrasts, even contradictions. Despite being the largest area in Scotland over 900m and rising to almost 1200m, a sense of elevation is strangely absent. The mellow farmland stretching to Aberdeenshire in the east is set against the grandeur of the Garbh Choire of Beinn a' Bhuird to the west. It feels remote and wild yet your eye is caught by the patch of lushness near Braemar. Much closer to the north are the obvious land rover tracks on the opposite side of the River Avon and beyond those the ubiquitous wind turbines scything the air and occasionally our feathered friends. You're in the Cairngorms but on the fringes of things. From the north you get the best impression of what to expect, a high tableland studded with tors, the latter compared to warts in all the literature.

Leabaidh an Daimh Bhuidhe – the summit tor of Ben Avon – to the left, Clach Choutsaich to the near right. All photos (except p.80): Mike Dixon.

The trickle of walkers heading for the summit tor from the Sneck rarely stray further east. If this was the only rock intrusion on the mountain it would still make it a fairly unique hill. For many it is the mountain's raison d'etre. One very windy November day, as two friends approached the summit, they became extremely worried they might fail to scale the last obstacle and tick yet another Munro off their lists, further satisfying their obsessive-compulsive dispositions. The thought of having come so far for nothing appalled them. They grabbed a lull in the gales and scurried off, job done. With advancing years both would now decry this blinkered focus.

Another friend was not so lucky. On the three day expedition segment of his Summer Mountain Leader assessment the Glenmore Lodge instructor actually banned his group from climbing the final tor, fearing they'd be blown off like crisp packets. Poor Robin didn't seem to have much luck with Cairngorm summit tors. On an icy February ascent of Beinn Mheadhoin above Loch Avon I watched from above as he attempted the decidedly tricky step left on that summit tor. His left foot shot off the sloping rime, his body twisted back 180° to allow him to slide gracefully down the initial slab and land immaculately on both feet. He decided against a second attempt. Ben Avon itself was successfully climbed a few years later in good conditions. His even greater reward was to climb the hill from the east and experience some of its more out-of-the-way delights.

From the summit and indeed a long way off, the compact, dome-like tor of Clach Choutsaich is bound to attract your attention. To keep to the skin allusions that this hill seems to generate, it could be described as an enormous pluke. It is harder to climb than the summit tor and even more to its credit is neither a Munro Top nor figures in any such silly list. Some fine potholes adorn its pate.

Whenever I've been up on the plateau I've wandered randomly over to

Clach Choutsaich dwarfing the figures in front of it; more difficult to ascend than the summit tor.

Michael Barnard on the FA of The Lone Stone, E2 5b, on the ridge leading up to Clach Fiaraidh, Ben Avon. Photo: Alan Hill.

whichever rock formations have caught my eye. It's a bit like being the ball bearing in a slow motion, gigantic pin-ball machine. The tors are hard to resist, sometimes I've returned to the same ones in the same day. It's good to have a vague agenda in these times of targets, tick-boxes and accountability. The walking, once on the plateau, is very pleasant. High water is welcome on a hot day from burns which snake up close to the table's edges. Apart from other walkers round the main summit it will be just you and the occasional hare, dotterel and ptarmigan.

Just what is it about these tors? Monumental. Totemic. You see shapes in the formations…heads, rhino horns, elephant ears and tusks, knuckles, boxing gloves, cockscombs, piles of dinner plates, stacks of giant pancakes, gargoyles. The rock is solid, rough and reassuring. There's a strong temptation to play on them even if just a basic King of the Castle. Those with a penchant for jamming will home in on some very enticing cracks. Recently climbers have started formally recording new routes on the larger tors.

The Tomintoul approach is the bike-friendliest and one of the best ways to visit the choicest tops and tors in one circular sweep. The road by the River Avon is tarmac for a substantial distance to Inchrory. Beyond is still a good cycling surface. Tomintoul has an atmosphere of languid decline but with the new mountain bike trails in Glen Livet its fortunes might hopefully improve. It's one of those places you say you should really spend more time in but never do; in that respect it's not unlike Dundee or visiting the in-laws. The village once had a kindly benefactor who pumped an estimated £5 million into the upkeep of his favourite highland spot. At the time he was deputy head of finance for Scotland Yard, part of the Metropolitan Police. He had been given the job of supervising a secret cash account used to fund covert operations, so secret that only he knew where the money was spent. A kind of latter day Robin Hood, this prince of thieves was just that, a thief, and his crimes taught the Met the importance of accountability even for their accountants. 'Lord' Tony Williams pleaded guilty to 19 charges of fraud and embezzlement asking for a further 535 offences to be taken into account. For an accountant he sounds quite an interesting chap. His punishment was three years free board and accommodation, no council tax or utility bills and a protected pension. You cannot but warm to the man. Many of the locals still speak highly of him and are grateful for his philanthropy. The Gordon Arms Hotel is now showing signs of a resurrection, proving his investments were not all in vain. Tomintoul was in the news more recently for its medical services. Let's hope now that you don't have to postpone your heart attack or stroke till after the paramedics' tea or lunch breaks.

This way to the mountain is through an enclosed but charming slot of a valley, shadowing the river Avon. Once past the opulence of Inchrory, the NE outreaches of the hill are right in front of you. From where I abandoned my rusty steed it was only 700m of height gain to the summit. If approaching via Corndavon Lodge you pass Loch Builg and some

'Aiguilles des Cairngorms'? Clach Bun Rudhtair.

lochans just south of it, a rarity for the hill. The only other similar stretch
of water is in the corrie under the West Meall Gorm Craig: Lochan nan
Gabhar, green and beckoning. Of course the River Avon has its own
attractive sections: there being one lovely pool west of the Linn.
Compared to the more showy tors these liquid jewels are very discreet.

   Arguably the finest tor in the Cairngorms is a tri-pinnacled cluster on a
spur north of the top of Stob Bac an Fhurain. Perhaps Tom Patey wasn't
being entirely ironic when he referred to his formative mountain range as
'aiguilles'. Clach Bun Rudhtair has a 25m central 'stack' which must be
one of the hardest mainland tops in Scotland to attain. I don't know what
grade it is but at one point I used a finger lock, not something normally
associated with scrambling. You have to reverse it too. On its summit it
has the deepest pothole I've seen on a Cairngorm tor, but it is not
continuously six feet deep in its circumference. Its base is a giant bucket
with a very high back like that of a throne. In the early editions of Henry
Alexander's Cairngorm guide the Central Top was still considered
unclimbed. Richard Frere summarised the main routes up it in the 1947
SMC Journal and was the first to record/claim first ascents. Were it in the
Peak District or roadside Deeside it would figure in some climbing
guidebook and every line and boulder problem would be named and
graded. Even the two tops either side of it have their moments, offering
some interesting scrambling. A Yorkshire friend awarded it the ultimate

The Central Top of Clach Bun Rudhtair.

accolade: 'It wouldn't look out of place down in God's Own County alongside Brimham or Almscliffe.'

There is masses of rock on the spurs up to both West and East Meur Gorm Craig. Will climbers ever go up there and explore these and the other smaller tors? I would have laughed at this suggestion until what I experienced in Wales recently. In previous years I had become aware there were now more people bouldering in the Llanberis Pass than actually climbing on the surrounding cliffs. Taking a walk up to pay my respects to Cloggy, I arrived via Snowdon's long, deserted NW ridge over the summits of Moel Eilio and Moel Cynghorion. On the final rise to the Llyn D'ur Arddu was a black crash mat and two young men crimping on a the overhanging side of a 3 metre boulder. Behind, *Great Wall* and the upper section of *Great Slab* were attracting the early evening sun and turning golden. These two had been up most of the day. There'd been no one else on the cliff and they had no intention of climbing any of the classic lines either. They were content to play at moves, lie in the sun and enjoy the setting. The next day they were heading for more of the same amongst the giant rockery on top of Glyder Fach. If this attitude seeps north, eastern Ben Avon could become a very attractive destination for the game these climbers play. The potential is vast. So if you're up there on a hot day and think you're seeing giant beetles on the skyline, don't worry you're not hallucinating.

The pockmarked summit of Clach Bhan: evidence of millennia of creation by geological process is ironically contrasted with much more recent human marking on the moorland in the background.

One of the north-easterly tors, Clach Bhan, is riddled with fissures and a fabulous array of potholes, from baby bear porridge bowls and potties, right up to Jacuzzis and swingers' hot tub sized models. From here it's a quick descent north to the River Avon and bike. In an hour I was back at Tomintoul. Funny how you always rush in and out, often oblivious of the subtler charms of the valleys. The plateau has just the opposite effect and slows you down to soak up the atmosphere. You come away with a mind decluttered and rebooted. The elemental fusion of sky, space and rock can be a potent mix.

SENSE AND SENSIBILITY

By Gordon Smith

EARLY ONE WINTER MORNING, many years ago, I pounded the familiar trail from the distillery up the Allt a' Mhuilinn to the CIC Hut on Ben Nevis, wading yet again those awful, sucking bogs. I was looking that day to 'do' the winter route *Astronomy* on the Orion Face, and I bumped into Englishman Dick Renshaw who was hanging around outside the hut at that hour like common riff raff. Now, in those days Dick was one of the stars of the British mountaineering firmament. Already he and Joe Tasker had climbed the notorious *Gervasutti Route* on the East Face of the Grandes Jorasses. They had climbed the North Wall of the Eiger in winter. They even had travelled to the Himalaya in order to make a bold alpine style ascent of the mountain Dunagiri.

So it was, early that winter morning, that I met Dick Renshaw, the famous mountaineer, outside the CIC; and being a patient and a gentle soul he agreed to go climbing with an uncouth young wannabe like me. Now, it just so happened that I had been wanting to climb *Astronomy* for some time. This was because when I was a wee nyaff and a beginning winter climber I had been on the Ben climbing this and that with Post-doctoral student Steve Rasher when those Big Boys of Scottish Winter Climbing Allen Fyffe, Hamish MacInnes and Big Ian Nicholson had made the so-called second ascent of the route as stars of the BBC. For the occasion the riggers had strung cables hither and thither between camera nests across the North Face of the Ben. John Poland in his helicopter had whizzed noisily around, dipping and pirouetting like a dragonfly searching for its mate and TV cameras had pointed their long and nosy snouts from this nest and that nest searching, like gluttonous machine-guns, for some vivid little bit of excitement with which to titillate the viewers; perhaps even secretly hoping to capture death, disaster and TV Audience Ratings with all three of our heroes tumbling to their excruciatingly humiliating and public ends. Fortunately they did not.

For some unfathomable reason on the first winter ascent of Astronomy the original team had decided to do their ascent 'Big Wall' style as if, that is to say, they were human spiders bolting their way up the enormous and precipitous granite flanks of El Capitan or Half Dome in Yosemite Valley, or the vertical and ice-streaked granite spire of a Torre somewhere in the deepest south of South America, and climbing through adversity and appalling privation for days and days on end. Thus our men on Astronomy had hauled the leader's sack, and the second and third man had not even bothered to climb the cliff much at all but in large part had followed up the ropes on jumars. Something similar, indeed, had also been true of the second ascent. And what with all the fuss, movie-making, folk squabbling, hauling sacks of provisions and so forth, our TV Stars had perforce to bivouac en route; and that is a miserable thing to do on a dank and frigid

Scottish winter mountainside at night, squirming around and battling it out together as a group of three huddled on a rocky ledge full of lumps and bumps, dug out of damp powder, and big enough for two only. Oh, and don't forget the temptations afforded by the CIC, the hut stove red hot glowing; steaming brew mugs, and silver flasks reeking heavily of Old Talisker or Laphroaig or some other hideously expensive single malt, being passed freely among its rollicking occupants. It was sitting so very close, just a couple of little abseils and an easy wander down for those lonely and tormented souls stranded in their purgatory with their buttocks numb and frosted and suffering with their cold, wet feet.

What a to-do, then, for a little climb on the Ben! But thus it was that I'd seen *Astronomy* being climbed by three of the top men of the day, and I knew even then that soon it would have a stellar reputation. I wanted to climb it. And today, I felt, was to be that day. Dick was wandering around outside the CIC looking lonely and unattached and so, being an unabashed and entirely selfish git, I just hollered out to him:

'Hey you! Aren't you Dick Renshaw? I heard you might be up here. D'you want to do a climb? Come on Jimmy, let's go and do *Astronomy*!'

Without any respect for my elders and betters, nor even any pretence at democratic discussion about what he might want to climb, nor even any thought as to whether he might not want to climb with me! But being the gentle, patient sort, Dick just went along with my puerile arrogance.

That morning, therefore, saw us heaving through the drifts and blizzards, sweating it out towards the shadowy North-East Buttress of the Ben, seen darkly through the scudding clouds and swirling spindrift, and thence to the foot of *Astronomy*. Now, I never was one to take much heed of guidebooks and rarely did I carry one. They are, after all, expensive luxuries and always I felt that I had more important things to do with scarce pennies, things like buying pudding suppers from notorious Hell's Kitchen down in Caol or yummy Mars Bars from the confectionery shop and café at Inverlochy. Besides I liked to follow where my own instincts led me, even though they might be wrong, and go where I felt looked to be good climbing. Anyway, who cared! I didn't even know if *Astronomy* was in the guidebooks, but I was sure that I knew where it went.

For some reason, I know not why except that it just seemed logical to me, I always had it in my mind that *Astronomy* started directly from the foot of *Minus One Gully*. And this was in spite of the fact that I had watched our heroes starting their climb for the cameras some way up the hill from that point. But then, of course, if you do read The Guidebook, it does start from the toe of the buttress, right at the foot of *Minus One Gully*. At least the summer rock climb Astronomy does. Oh the cheaters!

'Och come now, cheps, it was just for the condeesh'ns. A wee bitty better poseesh'n, what, for the TV cemeras! And mair snaw! Mair drama! Ye've got to conseeder the audience. Efter all, ahem, we are TV Stars, ye ken. Ahem.'

Anyway, I certainly knew where *Minus One Gully* was because I'd climbed the gully before, in the winter of 1974, with that same Rasher with whom I had been wandering around on the Ben during the BBC *Astronomy* circus. And so at least Dick and I had no trouble locating the start of our climb.

The Rasher, my regular winter climbing partner, had been a Post Doc. in some or other scientific discipline, but not I fear in mathematics or physics, at the University that I briefly attended as an undergraduate in between truant trips to the Ben and other climbing stops. He owned a dark green Mini Traveller without heater which was more rust and holes than bodywork: facts very fine for ensuring that the occupants did not get uncomfortably warm while travelling to and from the mountains in winter. It had brakes that squealed like traumatized piglets more than they slowed the car down and a steering wheel that used to take a considerable amount of time and thought vacillating over whether or not to indulge the driver's intentions. But with a degree of not entirely subtle encouragement and with the judicious help of a Bleuet stove to warm up the old oil congealed in the engine pan and get things flowing, The Rasher could usually persuade the dreadful thing to go. And then, once he'd got the damned thing going, he loved to terrorize me on our winter climbing trips, especially at night, by driving around each corner we arrived at in a series of straight lines:

'Har, har, har, mathematically the shortest and most efficient way, you know, to travel around a curve, har, har, har! Has to do with chords, what!'

Or so he observed, assuming my ignorance.

I was afraid, as I sat there on the wooden crate that served as passenger seat trembling with cold and terror while The Rasher cut his corners, that the unwillingness of the steering wheel to guide the car around corners was probably the true basis for his curious claim; the ultimate if not the proximate cause hiding behind his irrational utterance. Sir Isaac Newton, in figuring out his calculus for establishing the area under a curve, may well have regarded his curve as an infinite series of straight lines but I imagine that the straight lines that Sir Isaac had in mind were probably a little shorter and more closely fitting than the straight lines that The Rasher's car used to take around corners. But never mind, I digress…

In those days my climbing relationship with The Rasher was probably founded on the fact that he had that car of sorts, and he was willing to drive to and climb anything that I was stupid enough to want to climb; and I was, by all accounts, nothing if not stupid, and, of course, entirely mercenary. But by the next winter after that The Rasher had disappeared; possibly because his Post Doc was up, or perhaps because the dreadful car had vanished, along with its owner, into one of its rusty black holes; or perhaps because car and owner had simply pranged trying to go around some particular corner which did not properly accept straight lines; or perhaps, even, because my nerves were completely shot and I refused to countenance travelling with him any more. Or because, and this has only just struck me as I write, he no longer could countenance climbing with me! Anyway, for whatever reason our ways parted, leaving me always on-the-scrounge for partners willing to climb whatever I wanted to climb and condemned, always thereafter, to travelling on my thumb, so to speak.

Thus it was that I had been looking for a partner when I bumped into Dick, the quiet English gentleman, at the CIC, and I roped up therefore with that patient fellow at the proper spot, right at the toe of the buttress next to *Minus One Gully*. And we began to climb upwards through the usual nasty Ben Nevis weather.

Being that selfish git I had assumed the lead right at the start, and being notoriously short-sighted I just followed the end of my nose. This had been bent by a boxing glove that I had failed to notice, until after the fact, when I was a pubescent and bespectacled schoolboy entirely without boxing ambitions. The result was that I tended always to the left. But, being the gentle, quiet, patient sort, Dick simply, and without a doubt foolishly, succumbed to my nonsense,

'No problem, I'll just follow you along.'

The climbing was essentially mixed; some snow and bits of rock sticking through, but not a lot of ice to begin with. We kicked off the game by trending up and right for about half a rope length on pretty easy ground before the peculiar influence of my nose started to draw us off to the left and therefore, almost immediately, up a well defined and steep little corner deep in loose snow and lumps of ice; and thence up slabs, walls and grooves, and over a tricky overhang on the left, which were all well plastered with powder snow, but not too much ice; and so on into the clouds.

Travelling thus we arrived, after several pitches that involved some difficult mixed climbing, at a very steep pillar not so far from the middle ground of *Minus One Gully*. With Dick belayed securely somewhere low on the pillar, I climbed a difficult mixed wall to reach a narrow band of snow beneath a sharp, overhanging prow. What could be seen of this prow was bounded at its bottom end by the snow upon which I was standing and at its top end, and not so very far up at that, by the bad Ben Nevis weather that had been bedeviling us all morning. That prow gave me pause. I could just make out, however, through the falling snow and my frosted spectacles, a crack clogged with ice above the undercut start, taking pretty much a direct line up the edge of the prow and disappearing off into the clouds. It looked a little tough and therefore I turned my face to the left and around the base of the prow in the direction of the vague shadows of *Minus One Gully*, looking for a diversion; and I turned my face also to the right, to where my narrow band of snow disappeared into the clouds, looking for an alternative. But it was not to be because very insistently the crack above was beckoning:

'Come on boy, come on! Be bold! Don't shilly-shally! Strike out! Strike out while the iron is hot!'

Thus obediently I dragged my way up past the undercut base of the prow and feverishly I set about hacking my way up the overhanging crack above.

That overhanging crack was not easy at all! It went, however, and it went quickly and with the rope hanging free and naked behind me. I recall, now, that when I was young my usual strategy, when the chips were down, was to batter on regardless hoping to get out of the jam before it was too late. Eventually the difficulties eased back less than vertical into snowy slabs and icy grooves that led to a significant snow patch lost somewhere in the fog. Fortunately, it just so happened that I found, sticking out of the patch, a small rock that could be cleared of its cap of snow. There I sat, hooded against the weather, a monkish figure squatting upon a rock somewhere upon the Orion Face of Ben Nevis. Trying, of course, to keep the rope secure and my partner well belayed; but as I sat I wondered where exactly I was, having wandered to this position with little or no idea where I was going. Suddenly, as if commanded by genie or by the twitch of a satanic finger, a hole appeared in the streaming blizzard, briefly allowing me a good look down to the foot of the face.

Now I knew, possibly because I had watched those Hard Winter Men climbing the route but more probably, due to the fragmented nature of my memories of that event, because I had heard about it somewhere else, that *Astronomy* was supposed to go up the obvious corner bounding the left flank of the Great Slab Rib. I wasn't absolutely sure of my information but I was absolutely sure, looking down during that brief interlude in the blizzard, that the Great Slab Rib was below us and that we had not climbed up any corner bounding it. In fact I could see little bits of our trail, starting from the mess of trampled snow at the toe of the buttress and the foot of *Minus One Gully*, moving up and right for a little way and into the foot of that short corner low down, and then intermittently coming up the slopes directly towards the pillar, hidden below me, that I had just climbed.

Now, I was not overly inclined to abseil back down and go the correct way for a proper ascent of our intended route, that is to say into the corner bounding the Great Slab Rib, just to be able to say for the record that I'd done *Astronomy*. The blizzard, you see, was building itself back up into a vile shriek and I was eager to finish whatever it was we were climbing and get on down to somewhere sensibly warm and dry. Whatever it was we were climbing it was close enough to *Astronomy* anyway, so who was to care? Just so, in those youthful days, was I lax with attention to detail, not caring much about following the exact path so long as I kept within the general ballpark of what I wanted to do; and, of course, so long as I did get in the most exciting climbing possible. We had passed, at least, on the correct side of the Great Slab Rib, that is to say on its left side, even though we had passed at some distance from it; and we were headed pretty directly towards the crest of the North-East Buttress, unseen above us in the swirling clouds, which had always been our target; and the climbing certainly was great stuff. We were doing OK!

But here we are at the overhanging prow and I have a dreadful, nay a shameful, admission to make. Dick, being the gentle, patient, methodical sort, took his time following the wall below the difficult crack; and then he was patient and deliberate also in his treatment of the undercut crack itself, the crack that had given me trouble but which I had taken at the canter, if not the gallop, in order to get up before falling off. He also had insisted upon pulling down on the climbing ropes, in a curious manner, as he climbed, possibly to ensure that I was still alive and was paying attention. Or perhaps he was just falling off and I didn't realize it. Meanwhile I was sitting up there with my legs straddling my rock, and with the howling gale blowing reams of powder snow down the neck of my cheap and porous red nylon cagoule (clearly a forerunner of today's Gore-Tex, £7 only from Nevisport – not today foolish reader but years and years ago, in the distant past, when I was young and both the universe and the money supply were significantly less inflated), hauling at the climbing ropes, and getting more and more impatient as the minutes rolled by. Dick, I must admit, didn't take forever to follow the pitch but then 'forever' tends, in such circumstances, to be a relative term. And it did seem to me long enough to warrant 'forever' in my lexicon, but then I may have been a little harsh. Whatever, my lack of patience began to take its toll; and therefore I shouted down at him:

'Come on! Come on! This is taking forever! Bloody hell! Hurry it up, will you! Pull your finger out, Jimmy.'

Now Dick can't have taken so very long, for we ended up completing the entire route in just five hours. But I was cold, sir, yes, very cold; and being that cold was making me irritable! In addition there seemed to be so little movement being transmitted through the ropes that my impatience was becoming more and more roiled up; yet slowly and methodically, though almost invisibly as it seemed to me, the ropes did creep in and in his own time Dick appeared below me out of the storm, taking my beastly manner calmly in his stride.

'That was a bit hard, wasn't it, youth?' Says he, the patient and methodical archetype of Quiet British Understatement.

I was glad that he had found it hard and I knew that he meant it, for Dick rarely spoke and, when he did, invariably he meant what he said. Now we just had to finish off the climb and get back down to the CIC before my shivering and disagreeable carping turned into something more chilling.

We climbed therefore up to the top of our snow patch and continued thence through the clag, which was once more thickening like pea soup, up lovely steep corners and grooves and slabs lathered in powder snow and lined with ice and swathed in storm. We were heading always, so we hoped, directly towards the unseen crest of the North East Buttress above us. I was concerned, as we hustled rapidly along under my baton however, that we might fall down the other side of the buttress; you have to remember, what with the storm and with me being blind as a bat, and with my spectacles opaque with frost and clogged with powder snow, I didn't know if I could stop in time! But no, suddenly the grooves dropped down to the left, depositing us on a short convex slope which I recognized as being the top of *Minus One Gully*, where it coincides with the crest of the buttress. Around us, as we stood there considering what to do next, the air was so thick with flying snow, spindrift, and spiralling cloud that it was hard to tell what was buttress, what was gully, which way led upwards, and which way down.

With blizzards raging about us we feared that my overly approximate navigational abilities might hinder us in descending from the summit plateau to the saddle between Càrn Mòr Dearg and Ben Nevis, leading us early into a classic but unwelcome slide over the Little Brenva Face and down towards a sudden and very permanent conclusion to our adventure. We decided, therefore, to turn left and concluded instead by scrambling down the crest of the buttress itself and traversing across into the snows of Coire Leis.

Once into Coire Leis we traipsed along on our crampon points around the base of the North-East Buttress and back down to the CIC; and to a last farewell for Dick was staying on. From the CIC I carried on down the Allt a' Mhuilinn alone: always to be in search of partners; always to be wanting to climb the things that I was stupid enough to want to climb; always to be travelling everywhere, rain or shine, on my thumb. And I have never seen Dick again. I can only hope, however, that he learned his lesson from this stellar experience and subsequently has taken greater pains to vet prospective climbing partners more thoroughly both for sense and for sensibility.

And was that, then, the famous climb *Astronomy*? No. The trouble with not knowing where you're going is that often you don't go where you thought you were going; and reading The Guidebook post hoc instead of a priori inevitably reveals that you certainly didn't climb where you thought you had climbed or what you had intended. So it was that I recognized recently what I had always suspected: we had not climbed *Astronomy* for that route wanders first one way, then the other, to finish three quarters of the way up the face in *Minus One Gully*. Such a climb, of course, would have been far too complicated for a simple minded fellow like me to follow, especially without a guidebook. Thus we had pursued, instead, an appropriately simple and direct line up the far left side of the Orion Face from toe to crest, taking in an impressive pillar close to *Minus One Gully*, head on. And that, therefore, was our *Wandering Star*!

Now, it should be noted that our old *Wandering Star* route may have been eclipsed by the stiff efforts of the modern 'mixed men' who in winter hang about like rabid bats under every overhanging nook, cranny and belfry vaguely touched with frosting on the Ben's northern flank, however:

> The splendours of the firmament of time
> May be eclipsed, but are extinguished not;
> Like stars to their appointed heights they climb…
> [Shelley *Adonaïs*]

(Readers may have noticed a trace of Jane Austen in the title).

THE EAGLE RIDGE

By Iain Smart

IT WAS SEVERAL YEARS since I had been on steep rock and I was trailing in confidence behind my friend the Reverend Archie Guthrie, a sprightly escapee from the pulpit. We had elected for the *Eagle Ridge*, an exacting climb, at least for two people old enough to have bus passes and more sense. It is a classic route, graded Severe and its details are given in numerous guide books where its difficulty and exposure are described in neatly moving, carefully balanced prose.

Eagle Ridge, April 2011. Photo: Richard Ball.

For the next couple of hours we needed all our resources to exert precise control over our bodies. Interesting things happen when you commit yourself to an exposed rock climb near the edge of your ability. All the physical survival mechanisms switch on: heart rate speeds up increasing the blood supply to brain and muscle; fingers read the rock like Braille and eyes transmit data about the geometry and texture of the coming holds. Your brain assesses the likelihood of the next move succeeding and, given the okay, you proceed. All this processing happens somewhere in the border territory between your conscious and subconscious. All very interesting, but why take these unnecessary risks in the first place? After all the most deeply programmed routines in our brains are to do with our survival. It thus seems counter-intuitive for intelligent people to be enjoying the exposure and unnecessary risk of playing this version of Russian roulette. Deliberately exposing yourself to danger can only mean that deeply embedded survival subroutines within the brain insist on being exercised from time to time in a real situation; otherwise they become rusty and may fail you if they are suddenly needed after a long period of disuse.

On this brilliant spring day of warm rock and gentle breeze we had everything in our favour. Once committed, my initial caution soon vanished under the functional imperative of securing my survival. We led through taking alternate leads sharing the risk. I actually enjoyed solving the geometry of the various moves. In spite of my bus pass, my passport into old age, I still had sufficient suppleness and strength of muscle to operate competently. Archie got the crux pitch and had a bit of trouble but did it well.

We topped out with a feeling of exhilaration; surviving a risk makes the world seem brighter and more colourful. If we had just walked up along the path this feeling would have been muted. I mentioned this to Archie as we unharnessed and coiled our rope.

He seemed to know all about it.

'Yes, this is survivor's joy; the afterglow of an adrenalin buzz is the reward for exposing yourself to a dangerous task. Technically what we have just done is referred to among the climbing cognoscenti as "feeding the rat." It is something within you that requires you to test yourself against danger from time to time. Some are afflicted by it more extremely than others; their rat would regard the *Eagle Ridge* as an insubstantial snack. The desire is worse – or is it better – when you are young, when you are exploring the boundaries of your ability; but some have to feed the gnawing of the rat far into old age. I don't know whether to envy them or not. Fortunately we two have only a mild case. I suppose the urge is the psychological equivalent of a "war game", serving to practice our responses to any real emergency that life may subject us to. I often talk to my Bible Class about it.'

'Your Bible Class? What on earth has feeding the rat to do with a Bible Class? '

He sensed my inability to follow the logic.

'Life is to do with survival. Feeding the rat is an example of exercising a primitive survival routine. Way back in the days of the hunter-gatherers we probably had to use these routines for real every other day.

In the modern world we have to exercise more sophisticated survival exercises – how to solve life's problems skilfully without hammering too many pitons into the social fabric. That's what I talk to the Bible Class about – ethical survival skills.

I tell them that "forty days in the wilderness" is a metaphor for real life where survival depends on route finding in difficult terrain; the wilderness of life is beset with loose rocks, holdless slabs, dodgy abseils, dangerous paths with blind ends, serpents, scorpions and all kinds of predators, the worst of them are of the same species as us.'

He noted my dismay and added, 'Of course there are many quiet waters and pastures green in the wilderness but these must be kept secret as they attract developers.'

I wasn't sure what he was rambling on about but it was fairly robust stuff; his Bible Class was certainly not for cissies.

Neither was the summit of dark Lochnagar; it was only May and a series of late winter squalls had started to sweep in from the North Sea. We left with the wind at our back, pursued by snow flurries, silver in the intermittent sunlight, down the long descent into the shelter of the Ballochbuie forest. Here we entered a different world of mighty trees, red-brown in the passing shafts of sunshine, grey and ancient when the snow storms swept through. We crossed the Dee by the little white bridge near the Garbh Allt Sheil to where we had left my car. As we drove back to Glen Muick to pick up the car we had left in the morning at the start of our traverse, I asked where we would go for a bite of supper.

'Not tonight, Josephine,' he replied. 'I'm off to a dance in Aberdeen. I'm playing second accordion for the first half of the evening, then I have to go to chair a meeting of the Kirk Session.'

Then, noting my dismay added, 'Making a transition from delicate fingering on the box to theological mantelshelfing with my Elders is just another move in the wilderness of everyday life. Both the band and my Elders are less forgiving than the *Eagle Ridge*. Today's climb was a good training session.'

SOLO CUILLIN

By Simon Richardson

I HAVE TO CONFESS that Skye has always been a bit of a mystery to me. And as my wife keeps reminding me, I do have a history of underestimating the Cuillin Ridge. I first attempted to traverse it in 1985 and cheerfully left Sligachan at 9 a.m. one sunny September morning telling my girlfriend that I'd meet her in Glen Brittle at 5 p.m. I had only reached the summit of Sgùrr Alasdair by the appointed rendezvous time, so I cut short my traverse with two Munros to go. In hindsight it was a pretty good effort for an unseen attempt, but it was absolutely the right decision to descend, as Christine and I were married soon after.

During the following three decades my climbing rarely took me in Skye's direction, and when it did, I was drawn to its wild coastline rather than the Cuillin. I finally filled the hole in my climbing CV with a south to north traverse in August 2010. I wasn't especially fit, the Ridge was a little damp and I decided not to carry a rope and bypass difficult sections like the TD Gap. All in all, I found it a rather gruelling affair, and limped back to the car that evening with my tail between my legs knowing that I'd underestimated the Ridge once again.

Like many climbers I dreamed of climbing the Ridge in full winter conditions. Roger Everett and Guy Muhlemann invited me to join them for a three-day traverse way back in February 1986, and I've kicked myself ever since for not joining them. Since then, I've never felt confident enough to predict the correct conditions, but winter climbing in the Cuillin has now been revolutionised by the Internet. The new ingredient is local mountain guide Mike Lates who posts on the spot conditions on his blog as part of a single-minded mission to promote winter climbing on Skye.

In February, Mike made it crystal clear that the Ridge was in exceptional winter shape and it had been climbed three weekends in a row. Conditions had not been as good since 1986. Finlay Wild and Sam Gomersall had set an astonishing new winter record[1] and Uisdean Hawthorn had climbed it alone in eight hours. At least a dozen other teams had completed it in perfect conditions under windless blue skies. I had visions of a mellow outing, following existing tracks and utilising the in-place abseil anchors. And surely cramponing along consolidated snow was going to be far easier than scrambling along rough and bumpy rock. In fact it was likely to be straightforward, so why not do it alone?

The weather became less stable at the beginning of March. It was staying cold, but fresh northerlies were bringing consistent snow to the North-West. It looked like the opportunity was slipping away yet again, but then the forecast changed and a weak ridge of high pressure was forecast for the weekend of 5–6 March. The Met Office insisted it was

[1] See the first article in this Journal. (Hon. Ed.)

The West Ridge of Sgùrr nan Gillean.
Photo: Roger Robb.

only going to be a transient break but indicated a dry interlude from Saturday afternoon through to Sunday morning before the next front rolled in from the west. This was my chance, but rather than having a single clear day, I was going to have to do the route over two half days with a bivouac.

Christine was away, so Roger Webb kindly agreed to be my back marker. We arranged that I would text him on Saturday night, and again when I had reached the end of the Ridge the following day, before descending to the mobile-free zone of Glen Brittle.

I woke up early on Saturday morning with an inch of snow on the car and a strong blustery wind. The cloud was low and the Ridge was covered in mist. The whole enterprise appeared hopeless, but a brief clearing over Am Basteir eventually stirred me into action. I left Sligachan at 9 a.m. and when I reached the snowline at 500m my pace slowed considerably as I broke through deep crusty snow. Surprisingly there were no tracks, and when the inevitable cloud came down my lack of Cuillin knowledge immediately began to show. It was over 30 years since I'd climbed Sgùrr nan Gillean and I was unsure of the correct route. Eventually I stumbled upon the South-East Ridge, and scrambled upwards until I reached the summit in a full on blizzard.

It was like climbing on the Ben on a bad day, so I didn't linger except to check the time. It was now 12.30 p.m. and there was no sign of the forecasted break in the weather. I may as well start along the Ridge, climb over Am Basteir and see what happens after that, I thought. Once again there were no tracks, but at least there was now a defined ridge to follow. I found the short abseil down *Tooth Chimney* easily enough and soon summited Am Basteir. Mike Lates' brief description of the winter traverse from page 298 of his guidebook became my talisman. Mike mentioned an abseil into Lota Corrie and magically I found the abseil sling buried under three feet of snow.

I wasn't sure of the location of the Basteir Notch and climbed to the top of the Tooth before I realised my mistake. I descended back to the col and slithered down the through route to enter King's Cave. Despite the weather, I was starting to enjoy myself, but in my enthusiasm I moved too fast and my heel jammed in a crack and I ended up hanging from my boot just above the flat snowy floor of the cave. The situation was amusing at first, but when I realised that my boot was well and truly stuck it didn't feel quite so funny. Thinking quickly I managed to hook an abseil sling with my axe, pull myself upright and gently step down to the snow.

After abseiling down *King's Cave Chimney*, I became disoriented on the featureless snowfield below, but eventually found the col just west of the Tooth. The only option in the poor visibility was to follow the crest over Sgùrr a' Fhionn Choire, which involved some noticeable up and down. The cloud thinned as I approached the summit of Bruach na Frìthe and looking down I could see that I could have avoided all the climbing by simply walking up a snow slope to the right.

As I descended towards An Caisteal, the clouds finally parted and I was treated to the stupendous sight of the Ridge in all its winter glory stretching out before me and curving in a great arc around Loch Coruisk. I was expecting it to look alpine with a mixture of rock, ice and snow, but everything was pure white. It was more like Alaska than the Alps, and An Caisteal looked particularly spectacular with white encrusted towers overhung by delicate cornices.

I had my second excitement of the day traversing a notch near the top of An Caisteal. The miniature col was formed by deep cut gullies either side topped by a cornice that extended over the east side by a metre or so. As I stepped down into the notch the cornice toppled over which was a good thing, but then the snow collapsed beneath my feet and I fell about a metre landing spread-eagled across the knife-edged col eyeballing the steep gullies either side. A careful long stretch with my left axe reached a good placement and I breathed again.

The traverse across the delightful intricacies of Bidein Druim nan Ràmh was Scottish mountaineering at its best. The entire Ridge was covered in a layer of soft squeaky ice and every placement was perfect. I'm sure there are cleverer ways to cover this ground, but there were no tracks, so I simply followed the crest. The exposure was exhilarating, the views stupendous and the climbing immensely enjoyable. Slowly I began to appreciate what all the fuss is about. The Cuillin Ridge in winter was fully living up to its billing as 'probably the greatest single climb to be had in Britain.'

The three towers of Sgùrr a' Mhadaidh were sensationally exposed. Somehow the uniformity and smoothness of the snow and ice exaggerated the angles and drops. It reminded me of Cerro Torre, but the climbing was easy with perfect névé instead of Patagonian bottomless rime. Two climbers finishing a route a rope length away accentuated my isolation, but it was comforting to receive a reassuring wave. The descent from the third summit was tricky. Mike described down climbing an unlikely looking twisting gully and I was singing his praises out loud when I found the abseil sling buried under fresh snow at the end of an exposed traverse at its western end.

The abseil took me into the col of An Doras, which was completely free of wind. It was 5.30 p.m. and I still had a little daylight left, so I set off up Sgùrr a' Ghreadaidh but cloud quickly came in, so I did the sensible thing and climbed back down to the sheltered bivvy site. I brewed up, cooked some pasta and sent Roger a text saying all was well. I dug a trench in the snow, lined it with my rope and a lightweight pad, snuggled deep into my sleeping bag and settled down for a comfortable night.

In the early hours the mist cleared, and although it was still overcast, I could see the outline of Loch Coruisk and the reassuring lights of Elgol below. By morning, the overhead cloud had descended a little lower but I felt good and was confident that the forecast high pressure would hold on. My hopes were soon dashed when I reached the summit of Ghreadaidh and saw a mass of cloud coming in from the sea. Sgùrr Alasdair and the In Pin had already disappeared in the gloom but helpfully it stayed clear on the long traverse across to Sgùrr Thormaid. The climbing continued to be exposed and absorbing but I started to encounter a new obstacle in the form of windslab on south-facing slopes.

I had lost my way in mist near the summit of Sgùrr na Banachdaich on my summer traverse and I was anxious not to make the same mistake again, but fortunately the cloud was thin enough for me to be confident that I was on the correct descent. The windslab had now become widespread and the only way to cross it was to dig deep with each placement to find purchase in the névé underneath. It was slow going and desperately hard work but at least I was dealing with the terrain safely.

The mist came down for real as I made the long haul up Sgùrr Dearg where the Inaccessible Pinnacle was almost invisible in the gloom. Before I set off I'd decided that my objective was to traverse the Ridge and not to climb the In Pinn, so I passed it without a backward glance. I was now concerned about finding the easy way down the snow slopes bypassing An Stac. The snow was waist deep in places, but fortunately there was no windslab and I made a lucky route finding decision traversing along a ledge that took me back to easy ground near the crest.

Earlier in the day I'd spotted a series of impressive ice streaks on the north face of Sgùrr MhicCoinnich, and these distinctive lines of white set against black gabbro guided me through the cloud to the head of Rotten Gully and the foot of the imposing north ridge. Tricky route finding low down and then a narrow crest took me to the summit. I couldn't remember the location of *King's Chimney*, but once again Mike's terse but accurate description guided the way. I breathed a sigh of relief at this point. I'd pretty much cracked the Ridge now, and just had the TD Gap to go.

At the foot of the chimney I realised I had relaxed too soon. Sgùrr Theàrlaich looked a formidable obstacle. The slabs on the east face were dangerously loaded with windslab. The snow was built up in layers up to a metre thick and all set at a dangerous angle. There appeared no possibility of going that way so I attempted a direct ascent up the crest. It was steeper than it looked and the ice thinned, and for the first time in the whole traverse my tools hit underlying rock. The way ahead looked difficult, so I carefully climbed down back to the col. As I considered my options I regretted not bringing a fuller description, as I couldn't remember the way I'd gone in summer. Eventually there was nothing for it but to venture onto the horrible east face. Once again it was a matter of excavating each placement as I gingerly traversed from one hanging slab to another not knowing whether it would link together. Finally I could see it was going to work and I pulled onto the summit a relieved man.

Where now? Mike's description spoke about the TD Gap as if its location was obvious, but when I'd made my summer traverse I'd avoided the Gap by descending into Coire a' Ghrunnda. All I could do in the mist was to climb down the crest from the summit, which became increasingly awkward and I was forced to abseil into a snow chute on the side. Carefully I followed it to its end and moved along a shelf where I found an abseil sling. Feeling happier, I set up the abseil and started down only to realise the real abseil point was hidden a couple of metres lower.

I was soon in Coire a' Ghrunnda and making my way back up to the crest. Surely I'd cracked it now? My sketch map showed a subsidiary peak before the Dubhs, but it was steeper than I remembered. My intention was to follow the true line of the Ridge at this point, and ascend Dubh na Dà Bheinn instead of the Munro summit of Dubh Mòr which lies off the main crest. When I reached the subsidiary summit, Dà Bheinn loomed out of the mist straight ahead. Climbing it was awkward; in fact it was far more difficult than anything I'd encountered elsewhere on the Ridge. Steep sections exited onto windslab-loaded terraces that had to be traversed looking for the next runnel of ice. There was no way of knowing whether it all connected up, but after a couple of blind alleys I pulled onto the summit.

The crest ahead was exposed and technical and I felt pleased with myself when I found a bypass on the left side. Once again it was slow going through dreaded windslab, but at least it was downhill. Eventually the steep ground was behind me and I set off at pace down easy slopes.

It was nearly 4.30 p.m. and I was confident that I was going to finish in daylight so I texted Roger to say that all was well and I was about to start Sgùrr nan Eag, the final straightforward Munro. As I put my mobile away a nagging feeling made me turn on the GPS to check my position. It took a while to interpret the tightly-contoured map, but eventually I realised that I wasn't on the main Ridge at all. Somehow I had strayed onto the Dubhs Ridge and was almost at Sgùrr Dubh Beag. Gradually it all began to make sense. I had mistaken the subsidiary top for the lower of the two tops of Sgùrr Dubh na Dà Bheinn and had just traversed the tricky crest of Dubh Mòr.

I suppressed a rising sense of panic. In the remaining hour of daylight I had to find my way through the cloud back to the main Ridge otherwise I'd be spending a second night out. There was nothing for it but climb back up to the summit of Dubh Mòr, reverse the difficult climbing, and then find a way across the head of An Garbh-choire to gain the col below Sgùrr nan Eag. I decided not to text Roger about my predicament – he was better off not knowing for now. Reversing the way I'd come over Dubh Mòr was awkward, but at least I knew the way. Once I broke out into the traverse leading to the col I blindly linked shelves and waded through thigh-deep snow across discontinuous gullies until I finally reached Bealach a' Gharbh-choire.

I traversed under the east side of Caisteal to reach the long slopes leading up to Sgùrr nan Eag. As if to tease me, the cloud thinned a little so I could see the Dubhs behind me and the enormity of my route finding mistake, but once on the summit I could see the way ahead to Gars-bheinn. At last I could relax, and for the first time on the traverse I saw the occasional faint footprint in the snow.

I reached the summit of Gars-bheinn 30 minutes after dark and then plunged down a helpful snow gully cutting through the screes on the south face before traversing round to reach the Coire a' Ghrunnda path. It was late when I reached Glen Brittle and I bivouacked by the beach with the reassuring sound of waves lapping the shore not far away.

Next morning there was no sign of any life so I set off walking up the glen. I was lost in thought and completely content. The Cuillin Ridge in winter had been a truly remarkable experience. The climbing was outstanding and the situations spectacular, but it was the unique Scottish mix of mist and wind, cornices and windslab that had made it so memorable. And once again I had completely underestimated the Ridge, but this time my lack of knowledge had intensified and magnified the experience. Finding my way in difficult visibility along largely unknown and untracked terrain had been one of the toughest challenges I'd ever faced in the mountains.

After three hours of walking I flagged down a vehicle just before Carbost. As I stepped into the warm car and smiled at the friendly driver, the Cuillin spell was finally broken and the adventure complete.[2]

---

[2] Both Moran and Richardson provided lists of equipment, clothing, food and drink used, and Wild provided a photo of equipment etc. If anyone would like to see lists or photo I'll be happy to oblige. (Ed.)

THE GALLOWAY CLIMBS OF GEORGE FRASER

By Stephen Reid

IN AN ARTICLE in the *Scottish Mountaineer* in February 2010, Sue Agnew wrote of her uncle George Fraser who died together with his climbing partner Mike Harris in 1959 whilst attempting the first ascent of Ama Dablam (6812m) in Nepal. In remarkably similar circumstances to Mallory and Irving, Fraser and Harris were last spotted some 300m from the summit; then cloud and snow obliterated them from sight. They were never seen again. Movingly, Sue described her trek in Nepal to retrace her uncle's footsteps and locate his memorial cairn. She also wrote about him as a climber of note, known to Hard Rock aficionados as the first ascensionist of *Dragon* on Carnmore Crag which he climbed with fellow Cambridge graduate Mike O'Hara in 1957. As the Scottish Mountaineering Club's guidebook writer for the Galloway Hills however, one short paragraph caught my eye and it was this:

> George was, from an early age, a rock climber. Born in India in 1931, he lived in Galloway when his father retired from the army. George used to take my mother up some of the lovely Galloway granite outcrops, in little more than hob-nailed boots with a rope wrapped round his waist. I have a few scribbled records of routes around Dungeon Hill and Craignelder, long before the area was explored more fully and formally recorded first ascents.

In an article entitled 'Dungeon Days' in the *SMC Journal* 2005, I had compiled what I thought at the time was a reasonably comprehensive history of climbing in the Galloway Hills, albeit rather slanted to my own involvement, and I hadn't even known of George Fraser – all at once the significance of *Central Route* on Craigdews recorded by a G. Fraser in the 1950s became apparent, and in fact I had already become intrigued by this long climb, originally graded Hard Severe, that turned out to have a 5a pitch in it. However, nobody I had spoken to among the Galloway cognoscenti at the time had any idea who G. Fraser was.

I contacted Sue via the Mountaineering Council of Scotland thinking I would soon get hold of copies of his first ascents and how interesting they would be, but it turned out things were not going to be that easy. Sue's mother Mollie (George's sister) had died in 1982 but the family still owned a house in Gatehouse of Fleet in which various photo albums, diaries and other records were stored. Sue however lived in Ullapool – her father, Captain Jock Agnew, who had been married to Mollie, now lived in Norfolk having long since retired from the Merchant Navy – and neither of them visited Galloway very often.

Several years passed before I was finally able to meet up with Jock in Gatehouse of Fleet. Numerous tin trunks and deed boxes had been extracted from the attic and half a day was spent leafing through them. I came away armed with Mollie's diaries and a few photos, but of George's

Mollie and George Fraser in 1951. Photo: Agnew family collection.

diaries and route descriptions, which Sue was sure would be there, there was frustratingly no sign. Reading through her diaries, it became apparent that Mollie was an accomplished climber in her own right, later joining the Pinnacle Club and recording routes such as Kipling Groove amongst those she had done in the '60s. There were a few tantalising entries on climbing in Galloway but no route descriptions.

It was about a month later that I finally received an e-mail from Sue with an attached scan of seven route descriptions and other notes that had been typed up by George and which she had found at her house in Ullapool. I duly set about trying to tie in the descriptions with the occasional mentions of climbing in Mollie's diaries. From George's notes it was obvious that he had wandered far and wide in the Galloway Hills and scrambled in many areas. He had visited Black Gairy on the Merrick, Yellow Tomach, the Tauchers (where he describes what are obviously the *Organ Pipes* and *The Couloir*), the Dungeon of Buchan, Craignaw, the Lamachan Hills and the Rhinns of Kells. On none of these though are climbs recorded although possibilities are mentioned.

Convinced that most if not all of these seven climbs would since have been claimed by others, I set about repeating each of them with a view to correcting the historical record in the next SMC guide. This in itself was a fun exercise but what I was not prepared for was how the standard of grades has slipped over the intervening years, especially when one

Jock Agnew scrambling on the Clints of Dromore in 1959. Photo: Agnew family collection.

considers how poor the protection available was in the 1950s compared with the racks of cams and wires we climb with nowadays. On Craigdews for instance, *Central Route* (Hard Severe and with mention of a jammed knot runner) is described along with two others, *Holly Route* (Difficult) and *Oak Route* (Moderate). As mentioned above, *Central Route* with the original finish is considered to be VS 5a these days, whilst *Holly Route* had been recorded in 2000 by Alan Murdoch and Andrew Fraser as *Vorsprung Goat Technique* and graded VS 4c, later upgraded to HVS on account of suspect rock. *Oak Route* turned out to be the only climb on the list which had not been claimed since and was rather broken but we felt worth Severe, 4b.

On Craignelder, short easy-angled slabs on Big Gairy are dismissed as not worth recording, but higher up the hill he writes that, 'The most prominent feature is a slender pinnacle some 80ft high, Craig an Eilte itself, the Rock of the Hind which gives the best climbing, including Flank Route (Very Difficult).' I was extremely surprised to find that this took the same line as my own 1992 VS *The Fleshmarket*, rather than one of

*Stephen Reid on Craig an Eilte discovering to his amazement that his 2 star climb The
Fleshmarket (VS) is the same as George Fraser's 1950s Flank Route (Very Difficult).
Photo: Bob Bennett.*

the easier climbs to either side of it. A strenuous gritstonesque jamming
problem with skin devouring properties, I was thoroughly glad of my
Galloway double rack of cams when I repeated the climb over two
decades after my 'first ascent' and it is really hard to understand how
anyone could ever have graded it V Diff.

   The place George and Mollie and their various friends visited the most,
presumably because it was so easy to get to, was the amenable south-
facing buttresses of the Clints of Dromore near Gatehouse of Fleet. On
what proved to be Central Buttress, *Two Pitch Route* (Difficult) was a
favourite – this turned out to follow Andrew Fraser's 1981 climb *Left of
Centre* (Difficult) to where it eases and then made a long traverse right to
finish via the upper half of my own 2001 route *Quoth the Raven* (HVS
but only MVS in the upper section).

   The final two routes described, also at the Clints of Dromore, are on

George Fraser on Fionn Buttress, Carnmore in 1958 a year after the first ascent.
Photo: Agnew family collection.

what George called Overlap Wall, since named Black and White Walls. Here *Corner* (Very Difficult) was apprised to be the same as my *Honeysuckle Groove* (Hard Severe) but with a left-hand finish, and *First Overlap* (Severe) was later taken by my own *Stupid Cupid* (VS), both climbs I had recorded in 2001.

On the list of climbs there is no record of when the first ascents were made or who made them though it can be assumed that George probably led all of them. From Mollie's diaries and what seems likely to have formed part of her Pinnacle Club application, we know she was in on ascents of *Central Route* on Craigdews (December 1955) and *Overlap Wall* and *Two Pitch Route* at the Clints of Dromore (April 1955). It is probable these were with George and though it is not certain that these were first ascents, no earlier ones are known. The dates the other climbs were done and the climbers involved are unknown. Other intriguing questions also remain unanswered.

The first is what was this list of routes and notes compiled for? Edward Pyatt's *Where to Climb in the British Isles* published in 1960 refers to a

Mollie Fraser at the Clints of Dromore in 1959. Photo: Agnew family collection.

'fine pinnacle on Craignelder which has been climbed'. Most of his notes on this area obviously come from Ado Waldie's article 'Rock Climbs in Galloway' in the *SMC Journal* of 1958 but this one doesn't and it seems likely that George compiled his list for this book. Following on from that, the obvious next question is were these seven routes all that was done? It seems unlikely, especially in the light of a comment such as *Flank Route* giving the best climbing on Craig an Eilte – how would they know this if they hadn't done other things there too?

One feels there is more to be discovered, George's diaries for instance, if they turn up, might give more detail, and so far, the only Galloway climbing photo that has come to light shows Jock Agnew (a self-confessed non-climber) scrambling at the Clints of Dromore, albeit with a rope visible in the background.

But to date all further enquiries have proved fruitless and attempts to trace George's diaries via Cambridge University and the SMC have drawn a blank. Nevertheless, it has been fascinating tracking down these climbs and repeating them, and it will be a nice touch, after a gap of half a century, to be able to finally assign correct first ascent details to them in the next SMC *Lowland Outcrops* guide.

Acknowledgements:
I am very grateful to Sue Agnew and her father Captain Jock Agnew (MN retired) for their invaluable help in compiling the above article and for their permission to reproduce the historical photos included. Also to Andrew Fraser, Kevin Howett and David McNicol for their sleuthing activities on my behalf and to Ian Magill, Steve Goodwin and Bob Bennett for checking the climbs with me.

NOT A SUNSET SONG[1]

By John Hay

One of Strachan's buses in a snowy Braemar. Photo reproduced from a painting by courtesy of the Ballater History Society.[2]

SUNSET BUTTRESS − BILL BROOKER'S climb with the romantic name seemed to a fourteen year old an enticing prospect on the crags that are wild and majestic of dark Lochnagar. No thought of a Scylla or Charybdis here to ensnare the unwary, just glorious Cairngorm granite sparkling in the sunlight.

31 January 1953 was an ordinary Saturday morning when, clutching an ex-W.D. axe, I set off on Strachan's bus heading for the dark mountain. During the break at Ballater I overheard the drivers discussing the 'coarse weather' and the likelihood that the road would close. Visions of that

---

[1] This reminiscence was to be called 'A Wild Day with Two in a Bed' but thinking that this would bring instant rejection by the Hon. Ed. It was changed to what is perhaps more accurate.

[2] I am grateful to Derek Pyper for sourcing the photos used in this article. (Ed.)

Kenny Winram relaxing on the beach at Glen Brittle. Photo: George Davidson.

glorious sunset were fading fast. Nor were they helped by some forcefully expressed opinions that anyone venturing onto the hill today was 'gie mad'. A bus was leaving for Aberdeen in ten minutes and, it was suggested, that was the sensible choice for this youngster.

In those days there were competing services on Deeside, but Strachan's was the preferred choice of the Aberdeen climbers with their bulky packs, axes and assorted paraphernalia, not to mention their distinctive aroma after a weekend of bothy life. Only the posh people took the blue bus. Strachan's with their well loved and well used machines tried never to let you down. One September holiday the last bus was so over-packed that not even a sharp intake of breath by all aboard would have allowed another hiker to embark. But Kenny – not the famous Grassick but his predecessor with that name (Kenny Winram) – had the solution. Out came the rope, a skilful mantelshelf onto the front wing, a good stout belay round the headlight and he was ready for the road.

This Kenneth, as far as I am aware, was never known as the Adonis of the North so this grotesque figurehead securely lashed to the bus must have spread fear and consternation to other road users as he sallied forth bound for the silver city. But I digress.

The driver, conductress and now me in the draughty old omnibus slithered our way in what was now a blinding blizzard across the muir to Dinnet. The driver's words were beginning to ring true. The weather was 'coarse, aye gie coarse' and the road was rapidly closing. The ancient pines which had withstood the blasts of centuries were coming down like ninepins. Some skilful slaloming among the fallen giants brought us once more into open country and the long straight into Aboyne. But it had disappeared. No welcoming shelter, just a tangled mass of fallen timber and broken telegraph poles. Now my twelve-and-sixpence worth of ex-W.D. gear showed its true metal. Ping, ping, ping went the wires as I carved a new route through the tangled maze of telephone lines. Raeburn would have been proud of the axemanship. But my joy was soon cut short when in the distance the fallen trees began to shudder. It was the Roads Squad bulldozing a way through with the big plough.

Eventually we reached Kincardine o' Neil late in the day and finally admitted defeat. Refuge was sought in the local hostelry – a cheerless cold place obviously not expecting guests that day – but at least I would have a bed for the night. Well not quite. I was allocated half a bed, the other half being given to the driver in his somewhat damp greatcoat.

Next morning all was quiet but what a scene greeted us. The storm had flattened whole woodlands with not a single tree left standing. Looking across the Dee to the Ballogie woods we could see where it had cut a swathe half a mile wide and nearly a mile long with every tree broken or uprooted. The Forestry Commission later estimated that ten thousand acres had been flattened with gusts reaching 120 m.p.h. As the storm had swept in from the north the devastation was much more severe than if it had come from the usual south-west.

The North-East was fortunate that day as not a single life was lost and it kept the foresters and sawmills busy for years to come. But other parts were not so fortunate. The North Sea surge which measured three metres along the Norfolk coast swept inland causing over three hundred deaths, but in the Netherlands the number was six times that. The Stranraer to Larne Ferry, the Princess Victoria, sank with the loss of 131 lives. The surge flooded a quarter of a million acres in England and double that in the Netherlands. It was reckoned to be a 1 in 250 years event.

That morning there was no chance of getting through to Aberdeen by the main road. Instead we took a devious route via Torphins and Garlogie which included a cunning diversion through the exclusive policies of Raemoir House and driving over the front lawn. I do not think his lordship ever discovered who were the villains who had driven a 36 seater bus across his lawn; we were not sent a bill.

Almost three years later when I was gillieing in the Baddoch, the woodcutters were still trying to clear the wood around Clunie Lodge. This was described as the densest wood in Deeside. With the storm sweeping unchecked up the glen it left not a single tree standing. At night it was an eerie experience. As well as great bonfires burning the brash there were loud explosions like Chinese fire-crackers. Only later did I learn that the the military had left live ammunition buried in the ground when they commandeered the Lodge during the war. The Lodge was never again the lovely place it had been before the war and the storm so it was demolished and the stone used to make the Ski-Centre's first car park.

I never did manage to get to *Sunset Buttress*. Maybe the Fates knew more about Brooker's climb than I did and decided to spare a foolhardy youngster. Later, when guidebooks became available, I learned that the crux required combined tactics. However, I did have a memorable day.

'DEATH APPEARED INEVITABLE'
An Avalanche on Stob Ghabhar

By Ian Crofton

'AVALANCHES? NAE LADDIE, NAE IN SCOTLAND', the title of John Hay's article in the 2015 issue of the *SMCJ*, prompted me to revisit this old adage in the light of an experience my father had in the 1930s.

The flakes fell in silence through the night, soft as eiderdown, blanketing the already frozen ground. Inside the tent they drifted in and out of sleep, unaware of the new snow falling. It was too cold to slumber, though they were swaddled in layers of flannel and tweed and knitted wool, and squeezed so tightly into their sleeping bags it was impossible to turn over. Along with the cold, thoughts of what the morning might bring kept all deeper sleep at bay.

It had been a long day. They'd caught the night train at Euston, barely able to find their carriage in the smoke and smog and dark of a January evening. The train rattled its way north, clattering and juddering through the long hours, their carriage decoupled and recoupled in unlit sidings amidst clanks and distant whistles. Being impoverished medical students, they could not afford a sleeper compartment, and spent the night huddled on the hard seats of a third-class carriage.

Jock Leslie on his motorbike, 1932. This was the usual means of transport for my father and his climbing friends from the south of England up to the Highlands. Jock Leslie would drive the motorbike, the second man ride pillion, while my father, a man of diminutive stature, was put in the sidecar with the rucksacks and tent piled on top of him. On the occasion of this story, he enjoyed the luxury of the train. Photo: Crofton Collection.

No one else had disembarked at Bridge of Orchy – then, as now, little more than a small station and a modest hotel. As the light spread slowly across an uncertain sky, they'd trodden the lonely old military road past Loch Tulla, and then cut more steeply up into the southern flanks of the Black Mount. Eventually they crossed the eastern shoulder of Stob Ghabhar, and made camp in Coire an Lochan, hidden amongst the maze of ridges on the north-eastern side of the mountain. By the time they'd pitched the tent and made tea the light had begun to go. Anxious to make use of what little time they had, they started to cut a line of steps up the slope of névé above them, towards their target for the morning: the remote Upper Couloir that cuts up through the summit crags of Stob Ghabhar.

Once the dusk had turned to night, the two men returned to their camp, content with their work, and made ready for the long night ahead. Below them, unseen in the dark, stretched the frozen wastes of Rannoch Moor.

In the morning – after a full sixteen hours of darkness – they woke from broken sleep to find themselves enveloped in thick mist – and the tent surrounded by two feet of soft, fresh snow.

Shortly before his death in 2009, at the age of 97, my father wrote an account of what happened next:

> Roped up, we set off obliquely upwards. We took it in turn to clear snow and cut fresh steps. Suddenly the whole field of fresh snow, balanced on the frozen snow below, began to move downwards towards what appeared to be a vertical drop into the mist. Our ropes tightened. We swam to keep on top of the snow. We quickly panicked as we approached the cliff below. Damage or death appeared inevitable.
>
> But just before the drop the slope slightly flattened out. The snow sheet slowed and stopped. We lay on our fronts, hardly daring to breathe.
>
> I was lower. With infinite caution I stood up. Just above me there was a short clear area with the underlying ice showing no covering of fresh snow. I cautiously cut new steps up towards my friend ... Gently, one at a time, we then cut steps obliquely downwards and off the ice field to our tent.
>
> Hot cocoa and happy relief!

Counting their blessings, they struck camp and struggled through the deep snow back over the shoulder, and so, eventually, to Bridge of Orchy, to catch the night train back to London, in time for ward rounds on the Monday morning.

My father explained to me that in those days the received wisdom among mountaineers and hill walkers was that 'Scottish snow never avalanches.' Quite how this wisdom came to be 'received' is puzzling, as anyone who spends any time in the Scottish hills in winter will see frequent traces of avalanches, from the small trails of natural snowballs that have gathered size as they rolled downhill, to massive cones of debris, comprising great chunks of snow, some of them weighing several tons,

From Photo by H. C. Boyd.

SUMMIT OF STOB GHABHAR, SHOWING "UPPER COULOIR" CLEAVING N.E. BUTTRESS.

The east face of Stob Ghabhar. The Upper Couloir splits the summit rocks, while the band of crags over which an avalanche nearly took my father and his friend is half way up the face. Evidence of small avalanches is everywhere to be seen in this photograph taken in 1897. (From a Photo by H.C. Boyd.)

that have broken off and smashed down the mountain, obliterating anything in their path. Indeed, I have before me a photograph in the September 1897 issue of the *Scottish Mountaineering Club Journal* of the snow-covered eastern slopes of Stob Gabhar, including the Upper Couloir, and there have clearly been numerous small snow slips right across the face.

What is more, there had been records of avalanche fatalities in Scotland, going back well over a century. One particular disaster, said to have delivered a 'rude shock to the popular imagination', occurred in a lonely part of the Cairngorms. Gaick Forest encompasses the wild uplands between the Pass of Drumochter and Glen Feshie, and this high, rolling moorland plateau, taking in the barely discernible tops of Bogha-cloiche, Meall Odhar Mòr and Mullach Coire nan Dearcag, is split by a great, steep-sided defile, at the foot of which nestles Loch an t-Seilich. On the tussocky, midge-infested flats to the south of the loch, among a tapestry of braided streams, stands Gaick Lodge. The present structure – one of the remotest and, at 450 metres, one of the highest inhabited buildings in the country – replaced an earlier bothy. Here, early in January 1800, a party of deer hunters was staying with their dogs, braving the elements for the sake of the chase.

Some days after the hunters had set out, and had failed to return, their friends and relatives became anxious. A search party was sent out. After tramping the long miles up Glen Tromie, they came to the north shore of Loch an t-Seilich, and peered southward to where the bothy should have been. The bothy was not there.

Full of foreboding they continued along the shore of the loch, anxiety spurring them on, dread holding them back. When they reached the flats beyond the loch, they found that the bothy had been entirely buried by a massive avalanche. No one, not even a dog, had survived. They managed to dig out four of the dead men, but the avalanched snow had frozen hard as stone, and it wasn't for some months, until the spring snow-melt, that they could recover the last of the bodies.

Some suspected that supernatural agency had been at work in what became known in Gaelic as Call Ghàdhaig – 'the Loss of Gaick'. The area supposedly had its own witch, who may or may not have been an avatar of the local spirit, the Leannan Sith – 'the Fairy Sweetheart'. The leader of the hunting party, Captain John MacPherson of Ballachroan, had not been popular in Badenoch, and his habit of forcibly pressing men into army service had earned him a sinister sobriquet: an t-Oifigeach Dubh, 'the Black Officer'. It was rumoured that the disaster was a direct consequence of a pact he had made with the Devil. The Loss of Gaick was commemorated in an elegy by Malcolm Macintyre (Calum Dubh nam Protaigean), a friend of the Black Officer, and by a small monument marking the spot, bearing the following words:

In memory of
Capt'n John McPherson of Balachroan
A Valiant and Patriotic Gentleman
born at Glentruim 1724
who perished on this spot
by an avalanche in Jan. 1800
along with four companions in the chase
James Grant. Donald McGillivray.
Duncan McPharlane. John McPherson.

The present lodge was built in the middle of the flat floor of the glen, as far as possible from the dangerous slopes on either side. Nevertheless, it came close to being destroyed by another avalanche in the winter of 1911.

Strangely enough, Britain's worst recorded avalanche in terms of loss of life occurred at the other end of the country, in the South Downs of Sussex – not a place that one associates with the wilder manifestations of nature's fury. Nevertheless, on 27 December 1836, eight inhabitants of the town of Lewes were killed when an avalanche overwhelmed a row of workers' cottages.

It was one of the harshest winters on record. Snow began to fall heavily

The Avalanche at Lewes, by Thomas Henwood.
Photo: courtesy of Lewes Castle and Museum.

on Christmas Eve, and went on falling steadily for several days, creating drifts up to 3 metres deep. The snowfall, combined with the gale-force winds, served to build a vast cornice on the crest of the steep western flank of Cliffe Hill. Beneath the ever-growing cornice nestled a row of flimsy habitations called Boulder Row. On the evening of Boxing Day, part of the cornice broke off and fell into an adjacent timber yard. The residents of Boulder Row were urged to leave for their own safety – but presumably they had nowhere else to go, and the weather was bitter. At a quarter past ten the following morning disaster struck. The entire cornice collapsed. The Sussex Weekly Advertiser carried a report of an eyewitness testimony:

> The mass appeared to strike the houses first at the base, heaving them upwards, and then breaking over them like a gigantic wave. There was nothing but a mound of pure white.

Local people at once launched a rescue operation, digging as fast as they could through the compacted snow. Seven people were pulled out alive; but eight others were not so lucky, dying of crush injuries, suffocation or hypothermia – or a combination of all three. They were buried at South Malling parish church, where, on an inside wall, there is a tablet commemorating the disaster. Not long afterwards an enterprising local opened a new pub where Boulder Row had once stood. He gave it a darkly humorous name: the Snowdrop Inn.

The day I took the photograph overleaf, in June 2014, miniature seracs tumbled across our approach to a 'summer' ascent of *Prore*. My cousin Nicho Mailaender (whom my father had introduced to climbing in the

One of Scotland's most notorious avalanche venues, the Great Slab of Coire an Lochain. Photo: Ian Crofton.

early 1960s) complained that he had never before 'begun a climb in a bog at the bottom of a bergschrund'.

Cornice collapses are, of course, much more common in Scotland than the South Downs. The earliest record I have come across of such an occurrence relates to James Hogg, the Border poet and novelist known as the Ettrick Shepherd (1770–1835). I found the following account while researching *Scottish History Without the Boring Bits* (Birlinn Books, 2015). It's from *The Book of Scottish Anecdote* (1888), edited by Alexander Hislop:

> James Hogg and his father were out on a hill one wintry day during a snow storm, looking after the safety of the sheep, when the old man having inadvertently gone too near the brow, the snow gave way, and he was precipitated to the bottom. The Ettrick Shepherd, alarmed for the safety of his father, looked down the side of the hill, and not only saw him standing on his feet seemingly unhurt, but heard him crying out at the top of his voice – 'Jamie, ma man, ye were aye fond o' a slide a' yer days; let me see you do that.'

So not only an early record of a cornice collapse, but also of a sitting glissade.

***

It was as well for the world that my father survived that snow slide on

Stob Gabhar in the 1930s. In the 1950s, as professor of respiratory diseases at Edinburgh University, he headed the team that pioneered the first effective treatment for tuberculosis, using a combination of different antibiotics. This 'Edinburgh Method' was eventually adopted all round the world, saving millions of lives.

John Crofton climbing the Dent Blanche, Switzerland, in the 1930s. My father remembered being extremely tired that day (it's a big mountain). He thought that might explain (if not excuse) the shocking state of the knot at his waist. Photo: John Kendal.

My father was a modest man, a soft-nosed atheist who would have hated to think there was such a thing as Providence. He would have said that if he had been swept over that cliff on Stob Gabhar by the avalanche that shouldn't have happened, someone else would have come up with the Edinburgh Method. But though he was a man of small stature and amiable nature, he had a powerful personality, a gritty determination and a great ability to inspire others, and it was those qualities that enabled him to achieve something for which the rest of the world has had cause to be thankful.

THE PARADOX OF THE QUIXOTIC MOUNTAINEER

By Alastair Reid

TO THE COMMITTED MATERIALIST, mountaineering can only ever be perceived as an absurd endeavour or politely excused as a perverse form of exercise. 'There is nothing up there, what's the point?' they cry.

The mountaineer is indeed the modern quixotic knight, armed with his delusions. Swapping the lance for the axe and tilting at ice faces, strung out in extremis between the poles of elation and despair, good weather and bad, up or down? No cosy sofa or bed can keep him home for long, regular meals are not required, no deprivation is quite bad enough. These are errant ideas to the modern man of comfort who shops…in the pathos of our age.

Out for no obvious material gain yet costing much, he continues to climb as an act of faith and in the hopeful promise of a genuine revelation but tragically attains neither. The only realism is the healthy physical feelings it induces in the mountaineer, in the delicious fight, flailing himself to exhaustion in some solitary dancing groove, encased in snow and darkness.

He curses the happy mediocrity of the harried man in the street but wishes that somehow he could simply be one and forget it all, dismiss it. Unable, instead he drinks to excess, hoping to obliterate the mundane reality of unfulfilling work, taxes and rent in a euphoric Dionysian stupor. 'Wake up you fool,' they say… 'I am awake…I was tilting at my windmills'.

A self-imposed outcast of society, misunderstood and bereft of true lasting contentment, no climb will ultimately suffice. Like a junkie, each successive hit is ever harder, ever more intoxicating and coming down from the beautiful high is painful. He spends his mad youthful days in the mountains as an unconsciously driven and iconoclastic revolutionary at whatever grade climbed, thinking elitism is a ruse, the true 'grade' is the emotion that only he felt.

He imagines the possible imprint of climbing on his soul, whose existence is vehemently denied by psychology quacks, yes, whilst the ego is king? Agreed, notions of the eternal cannot be rationally guaranteed, they are purely emotive, but he feels deeply, senses there might be something beyond his ken. It's all been said before.

His idealistic philosophy chooses to affirm the primacy of the spiritual nature of man and the existence of the soul against the ultimate fallacy of wanton acquisition and by his senseless though ritualistic quixotic actions he negates the equally illogical pronouncements of our control obsessed political age, in the hopeless quest for something called *freedom*.

Mountaineering may ultimately be fruitless folly, yet the challenges are freely chosen and private, the friendships real and the memories enduring. It is the personal enactment of a fantastical dream and the heroic mythos in an age with no dragons to slay. The fulfilment of desire, the necessary prerequisite for action but leading to the pain-creating dilemma of Buddhist thought and still, there on some lost summit stands a Madonna, waiting in serenity for the supplicant's lightning conversion.

Nobody cares and why should they? Except maybe some others who share the same felt angst of their earth-bound predicament. The high mountains of ice and rock whilst echoing naive notions of some bright airy heaven, in reality mirror the stark existential alienation of his experience, cold, vast and empty. The stars refuse to talk, it seems the nihilists have won. The quixotic mountaineer is a paradoxical being, even to himself, who pushes for the answers to questions he knows that only death will provide, whilst holding on for dear life.

A HILL

By Hamish Brown

A hill
wiping its eyes
of night's rain
and hoping
perhaps
if the sun shines
people will ant
their ways up
by myriad lines
for a summit
sunset smile.

FINAL FAREWELL TO THE BENS

(Lines excerpted from Angus Macleod's translation
of Donnchadh Ban's 'Cead Deireannach nam Beann')

I was on Ben Dobhrain yesterday,
No stranger in her bounds was I;
I looked upon the glens
and the bens that I had known so well;
this was a happy picture –
to be tramping on the hillsides
at the hour the sun was rising
and the deer would be a-bellowing.
The black-cocks and the grouse cocks –
the sweetest music ever heard
was their sound when heard at dawn of day.

Blithely would I set out
For stalking on the hill passes
Away to climb rough country,
And late would I be coming home;
the clean rain and the air
on the peaks of the high mountains,
helped me to grow and gave me
robustness and vitality.

Farewell to the deer forests –
O they are wondrous hill country
with green cress and spring water,
A noble royal and a pleasant drink;
to the moor plains which are well beloved
and the pastures that are plentiful,
as these are parts of which I've taken leave
my thousand blessings aye be theirs.

(Contributed by Iain Smart)

BONKERS AND WONDERFUL

Archie's Mountain Challenge
130 Scottish mountains over 1 km high in 16 days

By Paul Fettes and Graeme Gatherer

IN JUNE OF THIS YEAR SMC members Graeme Gatherer and John Irving were involved in a mammoth, record setting Scottish mountain relay in aid of a children's charity. The challenge was to complete a continuous human power relay over and between all the mountains in Scotland over 1000m high, with 100m drop on all sides, starting and finishing at sea level. The event started on the 30 May at the north-east end with a toe dip in the North Sea by Dingwall. It finished at the south-west end 16 days later at Rest and Be Thankful (where better?) with a toe dip in the Atlantic Ocean at Arrochar. The baton that was carried every step of the way took the form of a cuddly rabbit called Rabbie with a satellite tracker on its back. In between Dingwall and Arrochar it travelled 15,000km and completed an estimated 87,000m of cumulative ascent (roughly 10 times the height of Everest).

On the way the team faced some epic challenges. The weather was unseasonably harsh. There were full winter conditions during the first week, and fresh snow down to 600m. Team members battled through

May on the ridge between Sgùrr a' Chaorachain and Bidean an Eòin Dearg from the north over Loch Gaineamhach. Photo: Kirsty Maguire.

gales, blizzards, torrential rain, and were forced to make detours round unfordable rivers. This meant some enforced route changes and two mountains (An Socach and An Riabhachan) were only ascended at the third attempt, having had two consecutive attempts aborted due to the conditions. Every cloud has a silver lining though, and midges were not a problem!

As well as completing five legs of the event, climber and cardiologist John Irving was involved in the early stages of planning the route, and helped to coordinate runners as the event progressed. Logistics were extremely complex. Ensuring that people were available in the right place at the right time involved months of forward planning, and communication. This was particularly important because for much of the route there was precious little in the way of phone reception. The fact that there were no major injuries, and no missed handovers despite the conditions was in part due to the meticulous planning and organization of the event. The route was planned well in advance and was broken up into manageable chunks, with planned and accessible handover points. A minimum of two team members completed each mountain stage in the relay. Kit requirements were similar to those used in mountain marathon events, although for some stages ice axes and crampons were carried and used.

A satellite phone was taken in the support vehicle, but was surprisingly much less useful than the satellite tracker. The tracker proved to be a

Gatherer and Irving with Rabbie the Rabbit on the summit of Stob Coire Easain.
Photo: Graeme Gatherer.

massive hit. It enabled a huge online following of the event, and ensured that people around the world could keep tabs on the progress of the challenge on Facebook and on the challenge website page
<http://www.archiesmountainchallenge.org.uk/>
It also meant that participants could follow progress and helped ensure that they were in place for handovers.

Lack of space precludes a detailed description of the route, but in brief terms it went from Ben Wyvis to Torridon via Beinn Dearg, An Teallach, the Fannichs and the Great Wilderness. From Torridon to Strathfarrar, Mullardoch, Affric and Kintail. From Kintail to Loch Arkaig via Knoydart. From Loch Arkaig via the Laggan hills to the northern Cairngorms. Thence to the southern Cairngorms and Blair Atholl, over Ben Udlamain and across Loch Ericht to The Ben Alder group, the Grey Corries, Aonachs, the Mamores and the Ben. From Nevis to Ballachulish, Glen Coe, Starav, Etive and Cruachan, up to Bridge of Orchy and over to Glen Lyon. From Lyon over Càrn Gorm to Schiehallion, then to Loch Tay, over the Lawers group to Glen Lochay and Strathfillan. Bens Lui and Oss, Ben More, Stob Binnein, Cruach Àrdrain and down the side of Loch Lomond to Ben Ime and Arrochar.

The intention had been to go around the clock where conditions permitted, but after four days the team were a full day behind schedule. Once they reached Kintail from Affric, conditions improved markedly underfoot and the team made better progress. Knoydart saw the first kayak

Sunrise in Kintail. Approaching the Five Sisters from the East. Photo: John Irving.

leg: the baton being carried out from Barrisdale to Kinloch Hourn by sea kayak. By the time the team reached the Great Glen and the Cairngorm plateau the benign weather enabled faster progress and the Cairngorm plateau saw the most productive day with 16 mountains (including five of the six highest mountains in the UK) climbed in a 20 hour period. In a traverse from Glen Feshie to Royal Deeside the team averaged less than 90 minutes a summit all day.

The second week of the challenge saw more benevolent weather and, with clear skies, concerns about hypothermia, navigation in white outs and running through cornices were replaced (for a short period at least) by worries about sunburn and heatstroke.

The challenge raised money for the Archie Foundation which is a children's charity which operates in the north-east of Scotland and was recently launched in Tayside. The first project is to help raise the money for a new and much needed twin paediatric theatre complex. More information about the charity can be found at

<http://www.archiefoundationhome.org.uk/>

A total of 57 people participated in the challenge, and more than 100 were involved in three associated charity walks up Ben Wyvis, Lochnagar and Schiehallion. Age ranges for these walks ranged from 9–87. Some of the participants in the main event had never been up a mountain before. These people were always paired with someone who had hill craft and could navigate. The challenge could be more easily accomplished by an elite team of mountain runners, perhaps from one of the top hill-running clubs, but that was never the intention and the whole ethos of the event was to be as inclusive as possible.

There are several reasons why a list of 1000m mountains was chosen: it seemed sensible to use a metric list because the maps have now been metric for several decades; the list is attractive because it is both manageable in terms of numbers – there are 130 – and attractive because these are the highest mountains of Scotland and indeed Britain – there are only four other such peaks in the UK, all in Wales; these mountains reach more than one kilometre above sea-level, a readily appreciable measurement. We used a list of mountains which have a drop (or prominence) of at least 100m on all sides. This resembles the Munros' list, but is arguably less equivocal. It is likely that if Munro had been around today he would have used a certain measure of prominence to define his list, but the restraints of nineteenth century surveying made this impossible.

The following account by SMC member Graeme Gatherer gives an indication of the complexity and frenetic nature of the event.

A THREE COURSE SERVING OF ARCHIE'S MOUNTAIN CHALLENGE

By Graeme Gatherer

Gatherer and Joe Symonds kayaking across Loch Ericht. Photo: Katie Annan.

My initial impression was that the Archie's Mountain Challenge was nothing more than another charity walk, but thankfully I was persuaded otherwise. What followed were three fantastic outings in the Scottish mountains that will live with me for a long time to come. Once fully signed up it was wonderfully addictive to follow the online tracker, imagining what others would be experiencing at that very moment in their journey over the mountains in the north west of Scotland. The first week saw atrocious wintery weather but some fine days too so there were feelings of 'thank goodness that's not me' followed by some genuine envy!

My starter finally came at the beginning of the second week. Following a rendezvous and quick planning discussion at Fersit in Glen Spean, the baton arrived by bike from Loch Arkaig and we were off... John Irving and I made good progress over Stob a' Choire Mheadhoin (1105m) and Stob Coire Easain (1115m) in a stiff breeze with just some light snow in the wind. On our descent we met a group of runners including Jon Ascroft on a recce for a forthcoming attempt at the Ramsay Round. (He went on to smash the record and complete the run for the first time under 17hrs – an incredible solo feat).

On return to the car park a quick partner swap was made, and it was back uphill to climb Chnò Dearg (1046m) this time with Phil Lacoux. We endured bog most of the way and as temperatures slowly rose we found ourselves in a constant fine misty drizzle. Phil was glad to descend on a big snowfield, and avoid the slippery boulder field we had picked our way through on the way up. On the farm track we handed over to Tom Fardon who sped off on his cyclocross bike. It had been a 17-mile day and was rounded off with a team lunch in Dalwhinnie. Not a place you'd expect to find a good bowl of sea-food chowder but it ticked all the boxes at the time!

Well that was for starters! My main course was served up in large portions three days later. Rabbie the Rabbit had covered some vast distances in the meantime through the Cairngorms and I was desperate to get involved again. This time my partner was to be Joe Symonds. A handful of years earlier he had been a medical student in my practice and we had enjoyed a few afternoon runs and bike rides in the local hills. I remembered him as a young very enthusiastic learner with a great passion for his sport. Our 4 a.m. rendezvous at the Bridge of Tilt car park confirmed my memory – he was buzzing with enthusiasm and simply raring to go albeit now with a wee bit of facial hair.

Moments later David Henderson and Mike Donald came riding into the car park with beaming smiles and tales of punctures and a night time summiting of Beinn Dearg. No rest for the wicked though as Rabbie was handed over to Joe's sister Amy who cycled off up the A9 cycle way to Drumochter Pass where she was due to hand back over to Mike (who had scarcely enough time for a bite to eat let alone sleep).

David, Joe and I made the long journey up the dirt track from Kinloch Rannoch to Loch Ericht to await the runners coming over Beinn Udlamain from the A9. David,who had been up all night, seemed so much more organised than us. He made us cups of tea and fed us in preparation for the day ahead. Our task was to complete the Ben Alder and Laggan group – this comprised seven Archies, or eight Munros in old money. It certainly wasn't long before Mike and partner Kate Annan (of Tayside mountain rescue) appeared running swiftly down the heather slopes towards us. Soon Joe and I (with Kate and David) were kayaking almost effortlessly across a near still Loch Ericht to the foot of Beinn Bheòil. The day was cloudless with blue sky and warm temperatures forecast so we planned to travel fast and light carrying minimal kit. David and Kate took some photos and then set about towing the spare kayaks back across the loch. As we made our way up the interminable slopes our friends slowly disappeared from view and we were then a very lonely pair in a very remote part of the country. Joe is without doubt the most talented runner I know. His road marathon time is nearly world class but mountain running is his real strength. As the former British fell-running champion and the holder of records across the UK, I knew the run ahead in his company would stretch me to my limits and beyond. We made excellent

Joe Symonds running off Beinn Eibhinn with Beinn Alder in the background.
Photo: Graeme Gatherer.

progress up Bens Bheòil (1019m) and Alder (1148m) and on towards Beinn Eibhinn (1102m), but I was operating at an uncomfortable pace throughout. I could feel the 17 miles in my legs from the Sunday and that discomfort never really left me all day. It was a wonderful run however over some of Scotland's more remote mountains and a journey rarely taken in entirety. We used the lingering snowfields of the winter to make rapid progress in descent whenever we could and enjoyed views as far as the eyes could see in every direction. It was a very hot day and even the herds of deer were using the snow to cool down. We found that even with drinking from streams and consuming gels on top of every summit it remained a challenge to stay properly hydrated. From Beinn Eibhinn we passed over the summit of Aonach Beag (1116m) which doesn't quite make the Archie list (because of insufficient drop) although it is a Munro. From there it was on to Geal Chàrn (1132m) and Càrn Dearg (1034m). After a long descent into the glen from Càrn Dearg I was suffering from the heat, the pace and low energy levels. I refuelled but it took some twenty minutes to feel strong again. Beinn a' Chlachair (1087m) was followed by the seventh Archie of the day – a second, slightly lower, Geal Chàrn (1049m). From our final top we could see the finish line and ran at a good pace down the fine single-track path through Ardverikie forest and past one of the UK's best known classic rock climbs, *Ardverikie Wall*. For the second time that day Joe's sister Amy (accompanied this time by Tom Fardon) cycled off with Rabbie to the next runners. Meanwhile Joe and I congratulated each other on what had been a simply fantastic run, one of the best either of us had ever done! A cold dip in the River Spean was merited and tales of the day were enjoyed with the others.

And so to dessert. Sunday at the end of the second week had Joe and me paired up again. Fortunately for me, his efforts the previous day over a number of Archies slowed him to a more reasonable pace! Still, the long slog up Ben More (1174m) near Crianlarich was done quickly and I was glad of more typical Scottish drizzle to keep me cool. We enjoyed massive snowflakes on the top and remarked on the total contrast in weather to our previous outing. Compass bearings were the order of the day and we made fast progress over Stob Binnein (1165m) and then on to Cruach Àrdrain (1046m) the penultimate Archie of the challenge. It wasn't long before we were under the cloud again and descending the ridge down to Glen Falloch. Once again keeping things in the family, we handed Rabbie over to my kids Struan and Mairi who raced along the layby to hand Rabbie over to their mum. Lynn, joined shortly after by Des Crowe and John Hepburn, made short work of the cycle southwards via Loch Lomond, Loch Long, Arrochar and on up to Rest and be Thankful where Rabbie was handed over to make an ascent of the final Archie summit Beinn Ime.

We enjoyed a pleasant afternoon picnic and waited for Rabbie to come off the hill and make the final journey of the challenge by bike down to Loch Long where fittingly he paddled into the sea with Paul Fettes who had had the crazy idea for the challenge in the first place.

A ONE DAY WONDER

By Martin Moran

4 MARCH 2016, 4 A.M. Sligachan Hotel: I am at last going to try the Ridge in winter in a day. At 61 years of age I won't have many more chances. After a brief thaw fresh snow has fallen and moist north-westerlies have produced renewed riming. Last week's tracks will be covered and the Cuillin crests will be banked up again with barely any rock showing. These are the pristine conditions I want for a journey that's been in my dreams for half my lifetime.

Garbh-bheinn, Clach Glas and Blàbheinn at dawn from Sgùrr nan Gillean.
Photo: Finlay Wild.[1]

I plan to start grandly with a dawn ascent of *Pinnacle Ridge*, reach Gars-bheinn a couple of hours after nightfall, then order a taxi pick-up from Glen Brittle to get me back to the car. The weather forecast is for showers later and strengthening winds but for now the sky is clear and the temperature 3°C. I shoulder my pack and head into the night with a spring in my step – I really do want this!

Summit of Sgùrr nan Gillean: 3hr 20min: I took the walk-in at a modest pace and reached the top of the gully between the 1st and 2nd Pinnacles

---

[1] Neither Moran nor Richardson carried cameras as they soloed the Ridge; this illustration is reproduced by kind permission of Finlay Wild.

in 2hr 10min. Dawn came with reluctance and light fog accompanied my ascent of *Pinnacle Ridge*, leaving me cocooned in an ethereal world of dim whiteness and grey shadows. My spectacles rimed up repeatedly. The snow was firm and frozen throughout. I abseiled off the 3rd Pinnacle and sooled the rest; just 1hr 15min to the top of Gillean. I smiled to think this takes about four hours when guiding a roped party.

Bruach na Frìthe: 5hr 20min. I had written a schedule for the traverse, shaving a couple of hours off reasonable summer timings. Much depended on frozen snow and good visibility. The four metre step on the ridge to Am Basteir was thickly banked and easier than in summer. I abseiled down *King's Cave Chimney* to get off the Tooth, then hit flat light and featureless terrain on the ascent to Bruach na Frìthe. It became difficult to see the lumps and bumps on my way and I stumbled a couple of times.

Sgùrr a' Mhadaidh: 8hr 35min. Visibility deteriorated further on the long descent from Bruach na Frìthe to the An Caisteal gap. I lost my sense of orientation, and started doubting whether I was even on the correct ridge. After what seemed an age the vertical wall of An Caisteal came into view. I surmounted the wall without difficulty. Every little ledge was covered in firm snow-ice. I was glad I'd gone leashless with my Nomic axes. I could swing my picks with freedom and confidence. The cloud thinned revealing Bidean Druim nan Ràmh as an iced-caked castle. This is a thorny obstacle in summer, with slippery slabs and tiring descents, but today it was a joyous cruise. Slabby grooves had transformed into genuine ice pitches. During a stop for a smoked salmon butty at Bealach na Glaic Moire, the clouds lifted briefly to reveal the glittering waters of Coruisk and Scavaig. I found the first tracks of the day descending off the 1st top of Mhadaidh. Perhaps they belonged to recent ascensionists of the *Icicle Factory*, a modern classic on the NW Face, because they disappeared at the top. I made my own trail to Sgùrr a' Mhadaidh. So far, so good; I was 50 minutes up on my schedule.

Sgùrr na Banachdaich: 10hr 15min. The mist clamped down once more on Sgùrr a' Ghreadaidh. The continuous exposure was making me palpably tense. I could barely decipher ridge from void. The summit crest seemed never-ending. On the ramp under the teeth of Thormaid I hit deep soft snow, which sucked the sap out of my muscles. My litre water flask was still full. At the first level bit of ground after the summit of Banachdaich I stopped, mixed two Berocca tablets and took a good slug of juice, which washed down infusions of salted peanuts, jelly babies, and a melt-in-your-mouth chocolate brownie. Knowing that Banachdaich was the half-way point along the ridge I realised that the traverse would take me well into the night. The key was to get across the TD Gap by nightfall. With clear sky I could easily navigate the remaining peaks to Gars-bheinn.

Inaccessible Pinnacle: 12hr. As I crossed the head of Coire na Banachdaich the cloud lifted and the sky brightened. Spindrift and vapour trails streamed off the ridge. The weather was freshening up. A squall of hail quickly passed through. On reaching In Pinn I was concerned about soloing the East Ridge in a rising cross-wind. I briefly considered trying a quick solo up the harder short side, but the ice cover was thin and the fear of getting stranded without secure pick placements made me think again. So I tied on to my rope at the base of the long side, climbed steadily up the initial groove, then made the scary step up right on to the edge. Immediately, the wind put me off-balance. I made a six metre rope loop on my harness and teetered up a move until I could hook a thin sling over the tiny spike at the crux. A squall of graupel commenced. My ropes streamed out sideways in the gale. Near to panic, I clipped in and made the perilous step on to the spike. Once established at the half-way ledge I pulled in my rope loop to retrieve the sling only to find that nothing was attached. In my confusion I'd clipped the runner into the free-hanging loose rope. I had to arrange an abseil to get the sling. I was seriously cold by the time I touched the In Pinn's summit block.

Sgùrr Alasdair: 14hr 2min. The abseil took less than a minute and I pounded down the ramps under An Stac keen to regenerate some body heat. The clouds cleared across the corrie, revealing Sgùrr Alasdair in searing white relief. Having wasted half an hour at the In Pinn the onward obstacles grew in stature. The north ridge of Sgùrr MhicCoinnich in itself counted as a lovely little alpine route. I abseiled *King's Chimney*, and hurried round to the complex linkage of slab and gully that gains the final arête of Sgùrr Theàrlaich. Hours of tip-toeing were taking their toll. Descents were becoming especially stressful. I reckoned that since starting up *Pinnacle Ridge* 80% of the traverse had been subject to terminal exposure in event of a tumble. On reaching Alasdair's summit the light was fading fast.

Gars-bheinn: 19hr 5min! I abseiled into the clutches of the TD Gap as night fell. All day I had held a resolve to climb out by the short side and thus preserve the true ethics of the traverse. Confronted by this fiercesome wall, I tied off my rope at the bottom and made several knotted loops ready for a back-roped ascent. One pull-up and I thought again. I only had a few nuts and two runner slings. The moves looked to be technical 6. If I fell here I wouldn't be finishing the ridge whatever else the outcome.

Three minutes later I was at the bottom of the approach gully on the avoiding manoeuvre, thankful for my prudence. The last portion of the ridge, a bouldery slog in summer, no longer seemed so simple. Visibility dropped to the ten metre arc of my headtorch. There would be no moonlight. A constant stream of ice spicules further confused my orientation and the continuous fogging of the lenses forced me to remove my spectacles altogether. Effectively, I relinquished all normal anchorage to the mountain. I had no map or compass, only my fund of knowledge from 45 previous traverses in summer. Yet, under heavy snow cover nothing looked familiar. On Sgùrr Dubh Mòr I made three false starts before finding a line.

Now came the most complex bit of navigation on the whole traverse –

the zigzag traverse to the Caisteal a' Gharbh-choire and the bewildering ascent to the flat-topped crest of Sgùrr nan Eag. The torch-beam threw out a backcloth of dancing flecks of white. Many times I was fooled into thinking this was a real piece of mountain. Every drop could have either been two metres or 20 for all I could tell. For the best part of an hour I found no clear point of identification, but blundered forward on intuition. The north-east wind was my best guide. I needed to keep it blowing obliquely over my left shoulder whenever I hit the crest. The way seemed interminable. At times I felt I was going mad, but in truth I was travelling well under half my normal speed. Would Sgùrr nan Eag ever arrive?

I gained a crest and followed it with blind faith until I bumped into the little outcrop topped by the unmistakable beehive of the summit cairn. The last big col before Sgùrr a' Choire Bhig was filled with soft drift and took ten minutes to cross. Occasionally I spotted breadcrumbs of ice in the snow, the remnants of old footsteps. They kept me right for the last link to Gars-bheinn. As I clambered on to the summit, my phone rang. It was Joy.

'What's kept you? It's too late for a taxi. Can I come to get you?'

I looked at my watch – 11 p.m. I was embarrassingly late.

'To be honest I don't know what time I'll get down at this rate. Thanks, but please get your sleep. There may be folk in Glen Brittle Hut and I can sleep in there.'

As if to emphasise this truth I took 15 minutes just to undo the frozen knots in my crampon straps.

Glen Brittle Hut: 23hr 30min. I strode into the blackened glen, dreaming I would see an array of parked cars at the hut, but alas, apart from the green glow of fire safety lights, the place bore no sign of life. I was too worn mentally to really care. The entrance offered a porch to keep me out of the wind and a bench seat provided a semblance of insulation. I loosened my boots, put on my down jacket, and stretched out in triumph. I had actually done it!

Sligachan: 30hr 45min: Come dawn I creaked my chilled frame into action and explored the communications potential of the glen. As expected there was zero mobile signal, and all attempts at requisition of taxis on reverse charges from the call box were refused. I began to walk and immediately cheered up. Maybe someone would be trying to escape this valley of doom by car. The only vehicle that came was upon me before I could flag for a lift. By the time I'd reached Fairy Pools car-park I gave up hope of seeing another, and struck out on the Bealach a' Mhàim path, the direct way back to Sligachan. Another five miles wouldn't break the bank after 24 hours on the Ridge.

TIME FOR THE RIDGE

By Graeme Morrison

Chaotic magma slowly cools, and yields
Its perfect crystals in a long-drawn age;
And then the Ridge is rasped by grand icefields
Or splintered by the subtle saxifrage.

In warmer years the patient circling kite
Pores on the sun-rapt lizard, and ignores
The newly upturned hull and seaside rite
Of monks who kneel before their cross of oars.

Three-pipe problematists at last divide
Substance from shadow in their earnest quest:
Though Don and Demster, Glazier and Guide
Dare name the peaks, they venerate the crest;

Till Young Men chafing in their northern tower
Ravish it end-to-end in scarce an hour.

*The Cuillin Ridge from Garbh-bheinn, late afternoon on Sunday 13 February 2016.
Photo: Roger Robb.*

NEW ROUTES

The deadline for sending route descriptions to the New Routes Editor is 30 June each year. Descriptions of some crags and routes have not been included here, but can be found on the New Routes section of the SMC website. In general this applies mainly to short routes and remote crags.

OUTER HEBRIDES

LEWIS SEA-CLIFFS, Aird Uig Area, Boardwalk Central:
London Bridge is Falling Down   35m   E5 6b ***. Sam Williams. 25 Jun 2016.
A direct line up to and through the obvious inverted V. Start by stepping off the large white boulder on to the arete right of *The River Kwai*. Step right and climb directly (bold but easy) until it is possible to cross *A Bridge too Far* and move right into the base of a prominent groove system. Climb this with increasing difficulty until nestled beneath the inverted V. Continue direct in a spectacular position (or escape left).

NORTH HARRIS, Sròn a' Sgaoth (NB 14616 03962):
Hooded Corner   65m   H.Severe 4b *. John Mackenzie, Andrew James. 19 Apr 2016.
This climb is on the steep nose of the crag that contains the corner of *Aon*, situated just right of the shallow approach gully. A very prominent jutting block has a straight corner to its left which provides the route. Start from the toe of the buttress just right of the gully.
1. 35m Climb straight up to a steeper exit, some loose rock, to then cross a grassy terrace to below a clean slab.
2. 30m 4b Climb the slab to the base of the corner and up the corner steeply on flat holds. Continue in a good position to the top; a bit mossy but an obvious line.

Creag Beag Upper Tier (NB 220 028):
Above the lower tier which is next to the road, scramble steeply to the Upper Tier which is on perfect rough gneiss. Although the routes are short, the climbs are good and very gritstone-like. From the Lower Tier an 'Easter Island statue' is obvious up and right. This is 8m high and contains three routes.

The Maoi   E2 5c **. John Mackenzie, Andrew James. 21 Apr 2016.
The block-topped slab is climbed directly up the middle to the top block. Step right to finish; immaculate.

Maoi Grooves   VS 5a *. Andrew James, John Mackenzie. 21 Apr 2016.
Just right of the slab are curving grooves. A tricky start below the left one followed by easier climbing.

Maoi Cracks   Severe. Andrew James, John Mackenzie. 21 Apr 2016.
The wall just to the right via twin cracks with a clump of heather; pleasant if undistinguished.
Well to the left of *The Maoi* is a much taller thinner buttress with a groove on the left.

Avoiding the Issue 16m VS 4c. John Mackenzie, Andrew James. 21 Apr 2016.
An open chimney lies left of the rather dirty lower groove. Climb this and step back right and climb up to horizontal cracks. Traverse left below a smooth block delicately to arrive at a heathery bay and finish up this.

MINGULAY, Undercut Wall:

Bird is the Word 110m Douglas Russell, Ally Swinton. 17 Jun 2015.
Start in the middle of the platform at the right side of the wall.
1. 45m 5c Start up a corner until below an overlap and surmount this on the right. Continue on jugs upwards keeping right of the bird shit ledges and aiming for the big roof. Make a hard move to gain a big guano ledge.
2. 50m 5c Traverse 6m left along a break, pulling through a roof on the left-hand side. Continue up the wall until a left-rising traverse is reached. Make a hard move to gain the traverse and follow this into the cave on the lip below the big roof.
3. 15m 5c Move left round a bulge, then pull up and right to below the final hanging corner. Commit to pulling into the corner and continue up this to the top. A good exposed pitch.

ST KILDA, Stac Lee:

A route description from Mike Lates for the easiest line of ascent (V.Diff; 4a may be generous). But not a FA.
An easy angled gully runs leftward in the south wall guarded by 10m of smooth slabs above the green carpet. A good nut belay in the short overlap guarding the slabs can be used to safeguard the landing process.
1. 15m 4a Ascend directly above the anchor onto the slab (crux) then continue boldly but more easily to gain the groove. Good peg belay.
2. 35m Easy ground leads to a good spike anchor in the upper wall.
3. 8m 4a Climb directly above the belay on big holds to a broad ledge. Traverse right 4m to spike belays in the upper wall.
4. 15m Walk further right until the ledge narrows (8m) with a recess above (good peg runner). Ascending direct looks easier than it is (H.Severe?). Instead, step horizontally right 2m to gain a crack and spike before scrambling up to the jumbled block belay and abseil point.
5. 100m Rise leftward with walking and grade 1 scrambling in a superb position to reach large boulders just above the old bothy. There is rock protection if the gannet and guano hazards pose a danger.
6. 150m Continue on rock for 30m before heading up more directly through deep nests. Gain the crest of the West Ridge and follow this past one false summit to a tiny cairn on top.
Descent: Return to the jumble block anchor above pitch 4. Sixty metre ropes will reach the start but retrieval may be awkward; a 10m sling from the blocks will take the ropes beyond the lip and 50m ropes reached the start of the route.

INNER HEBRIDES AND ARRAN

RUM
Trollabhal, Harris Buttress:

Archangel Route, Architectural Finish 60m H.Severe 4b. Ewan Lyons. 22 May 2016.
From the grassy ledge below the big groove, traverse 5m right along a fault, then

up vague grooves to an easing. Continue up slabs just right of a large groove to below a convex wall. Climb the wall trending left to the top.
Note: The editor has also climbed *Archangel* and found it at least Severe, maybe more. Agreed by Ewan Lyons.

Hallival:
Colin Moody notes *Honky Tonk* and *Salad Days* are independent routes.

MULL
Calgary:
Sea Spray 12m Severe *. Colin Moody, Dot MacLean. 30 May 2016.
To the west of all the routes is a bay above an undercut sea-cliff. Scramble down into the bay to start. Follow a shelf out right to a short corner-crack. Climb the corner-crack and easier ground above.

Balmeanach, Charlotte's Cave Area (NM 443 330):
The cave is just south of a non-tidal stack. West of the cave is a short quartz wall.
Left Crack V.Diff *. Colin Moody. 24 Jan 2016.
Right Crack Severe *. Colin Moody, Dot MacLean. 12 May 2016.

Unnamed Cliff (NM 442 326):
This quartz cliff is just north of the breccia and limestone cliff (Scottish Sport p325). There are many horizontal breaks and the climbing is similar to Lake Louise. The crag dips down to the right where it is usually clear of the sea. Facing north-west, it gets the evening sun and it dries quickly. There is a huge boulder at the left-hand side. More routes will be added and a topo should appear.

Montpellier 14m 5/5+ *. Colin Moody, Dot MacLean. 8 Oct 2015.
Start about 10m left of the huge boulder at a short corner. Start up the corner, then swing right and up; continue to the base of a corner. Climb the rib on the left.

Window Pecker 15m 6a+ ***. Colin Moody, Billy Hood, Dave Wood. 13 May 2016.
Start behind the huge boulder. Climb two left-facing corners, then swing right onto *Big Sue* and make a rising traverse to the left.

Big Sue the Happy Coo 15m 6a **. Colin Moody, Dave Wood, Billy Hood. 15 May 2016.
Climb the rib behind the huge boulder and finish over the overhang.

Silver Shieling 16m 6b **. Colin Moody, Fiona Murray. 1 Jun 2016.
Start about 10m right of the boulder below the widest part of the lower overhang. Climb this, then bridge past a potentially loose block at the next bulge. Climb up joining the next route for a move at about one-third height; finish through a square slot in the top overhang.

Lachlan 16m 6a+ **. Colin Moody, Chris Cartwright. 7 Jul 2015.
The next line to the right has a bulge at about 6m and finishes up the short open corner.

Otter Job 16m 6a+ *. Colin Moody, Cynthia Grindley. 24 Jul 2015.
An easier line just right up corners, moving up left to finish up the last route (crux).

Otter Fridge 16m 6a+ **. Colin Moody, Cynthia Grindley. 19 Jul 2015.
Just right, climb up over a couple of bulges to finish up another bulge.

Theresa 16m V.Diff *. Colin Moody, Dot MacLean. 1 Oct 2015.
At the right-hand end of the crag (near sea-level) is an obvious pillar with two overhangs. Start on the left side of the pillar and climb up and step right onto the pillar above the first overhang. Climb the second overhang and continue up the pillar and then the face above.

Creach Beinn (NM 626 295) 200m West-South-West facing
8 routes on SMC website.

Kintra, Ice Wall:
Ice Burn 20m E8 6c ***. Dave MacLeod. 20 Mar 2016.
The striking crack-line cutting through the impressive leaning wall on the left side of the crag, right of *Right Wall*. F8a+ climbing with excellent protection, although very difficult to place. Scramble up ledges to gain the crack which leads with increasing difficulty to a slot before the crack fades. Lean left from the slot and make leftward moves on crimps to the top.

Grasas Saturadas 20m E6 6b **. Dave MacLeod. 21 Mar 2016.
The steep crack running up the right edge of the crag, just left of the right arete, but right of *Casa de mi Padre*. Start easily up the groove and walls above to gain the base of the crack on good holds. Climb this with difficulty, also using the right arete.

Kintra, Pigeons Cave:
Stop the Pigeon 25m E5 6b ***. Dave MacLeod, Natalie Berry. 22 Mar 2016.
In the centre of the wall is a large overhanging barrier. This route takes a line through the triple roofs on the left side of this feature. Well protected. Start up a diagonal overlap/groove for a few metres then break out left and climb the slab arete to a stance below the second roof. Arrange overhead protection, then make steep contorted moves rightwards through the roof to gain another good stance below the final roof (more good gear). Pull through this more easily and up easy ground. Take care with loose blocks on the last few metres.

Fionnphort, Dun na Torran (NM 35518 17099):
3 routes on the SMC website.

Uisken Crag (NM 38629 18257):
6 routes on the SMC website.

Knockvologan:
5 routes on the SMC website.

Rum View (NM 296 227):
2 routes on the SMC website.

ERRAID:

Rhythm and Stealth   12m   E3 6a **. Adam Russell. 16 Apr 2016.
Excellent climbing up the blunt, initially blank looking arete to the right of *Blood Orange*. Start at a down pointing spike and climb direct to the big ledge via some obvious poor holds and well camouflaged good holds. Finish up *Blood Orange*.

Unnamed Crag (NM 301 189):

2 routes on the SMC website.

SOA ISLAND:

Soa lies about 3km south of the south end of Iona and a similar distance west of Eilean nam Muc. It is really two islands, joined by a beach that can be approached by a sheltered bay on each side. It is a heavenly spot and would in fact make a great spot to camp. There are some small grassy spots that would take a tent or two. The island is ungrazed and has a beautiful array of flowers and lush vegetation. The southern half of the island is very rugged indeed, a paradise of ancient gneiss, with ponds of rainwater trapped on its surface. At its highest point it rises to 35m above the sea.

The southern coast is where all the significant climbing possibilities lie. The rock is Lewisian gneiss and reassuringly solid, having been pounded by the Atlantic. The centrepiece is Dubh Artach Cove with, from left to right as seen from the sea, a beautiful leaning wall, (Dubh Artach Wall), with a fierce right-hand face (The Banded Wall), and a great corner running the full height of the island (*Dubh Artach Diedre*), bounded on the right by a huge slab (Dubh Artach Slab). To the right again is a fine arete and then a wall, somewhat shorter with fine rock (Dubh Artach East). Further east from the Dubh Artach area is another deep cleft and this also provided a fine climb.

Dubh Artach Diedre   30m   Severe *. Chris Dickinson, Alastair Walker, Billy Hood. 16 Aug 2015.
The giant diedre at the back of the cove. Start at the bottom of the cleft and climb up the corner with occasional moves out onto the slab. At the top easy rock leads to the summit of the island.

Happy Hoody   25m   V.Diff *. Billy Hood, Chris Dickinson, Alastair Walker. 16 Aug 2015.
A few metres right of the Diedre is a broad rib. Climb this and continue up the slabs above.

Basil Brush   30m   Diff. Alastair Walker, Chris Dickinson, Billy Hood. 16 Aug 2015.
In the centre of the great slab. Climb to a short left-facing corner, surmount this and continue pleasantly up slabs to the top of the island.

Perfect Penguin   30m   Severe **. Chris Dickinson, Alastair Walker, Billy Hood. 16 Aug 2015.
The great slab is bounded on the right by a left-facing corner. Climb up into this to reach a fine flake at the top. Step left and climb the impending wall on good holds. Continue straight up the slab above, passing a big ledge before the final short wall.

Simple Simon   15m   Diff. Chris Dickinson. 16 Aug 2015.
Just right of previous route, climb up onto a slab and follow the left-facing diedre to the top.

Chunky Chimney   10m   Diff. Billy Hood. 16 Aug 2015.
Climb the stepped chimney to the large platform.

Sloping Steps   12m   Severe *. Chris Dickinson. 16 Aug 2015.
Just right of the chimney is a set of sloping steps with sparse protection. Nice friction moves characterise the wall between the first and second steps.

Ants Arete   10m   Severe *. Alastair Walker, Chris Dickinson, Billy Hood. 16 Aug 2015.
Start at foot of the prominent arete and make an awkward move up left into a groove. Reach up to better holds on the arete and climb this to the large escapable ledge. From here there is an optional finish (VS 4c) up the steep 5m wall behind the ledge by the obvious crack.

Book at Bedtime   10m   VS 4c **. Billy Hood, Chris Dickinson, Alastair Walker. 16 Aug 2015.
The obvious and classic diedre that bounds the very steep wall on the right-hand side and runs the full height of the cliff.

Gerbils Groove   10m   Diff. Chris Dickinson. 16 Aug 2015.
Climb the obvious groove to the right of the book without difficulty.

Singing Seals   20m   VS 4c ***. Chris Dickinson, Alastair Walker, Billy Hood. 17 Aug 2015.
This fine route is on the seaward face of Dubh Artach Buttress (left of the great corner). Climb up left onto the prow above the huge lower overhang. Tackle the steep prow, starting from a ledge on the left, on good holds in a very exposed position.

Mighty Minke   20m   HVS 5a ***. Billy Hood, Chris Dickinson, Alastair Walker. 17 Aug 2015.
Left of the previous route and the lower overhangs is a prominent rightward diagonal that finishes through a break in the upper overhang. Follow the diagonal throughout, steeper than it looks with increasing difficulty. The crux move is close to the top attaining a thin hanging ramp that leads through the overhang. An excellent route.

Groaner's Groove   16m   E1 5b **. Chris Dickinson, Billy Hood. 17 Aug 2015.
Left of Dubh Artach Buttress at the back of a recess is a fierce and overhanging corner-crack. Wild bridging leads to an awkward narrowing where the footholds run out before finding small holds again to gain the top. A real tussle!

Kwivering Kormorant   20m   Severe 4a *. Alastair Walker, Chris Dickinson, Billy Hood. 17 Aug 2015.
Further east from the Dubh Artach area, on the right side of a deep cleft that cuts into the cliffs, is a wall partly occupied by birds. This route follows the obvious crack that misses all the nesting ledges. The route can be reached either by a step

across the deep cleft after descending a slabby groove or by an easy sea-level traverse in from the east. The crack has an awkward start and a steep finish.

COLONSAY
Note: Iain Thow notes that on the Colonsay map (Inner Hebrides p196), the location/numbers for Sliabh Riabhach and Meall a' Chaise are transposed.

ISLAY
Sanaigmore Area, West Wall (NR 229 718):
The west side of the outer promontory holding Leac Dubh has dramatic dipping strata and the ledges are used by nesting seabirds. To the right of the dipping strata is a vertical fault.

Sea Dog Serenade   18m   Severe *. Graham Little, Peter Dewhurst, Christina Woodrow. 26 Aug 2014.
Scramble down from the west and across to a rock ledge at the base of the clean vertical fault that lies just left of the corner formed by *West Wall* and the north facing cliff line. Climb it using good holds on the smooth section high up.

DUN BHEOLAIN, Shelf Wall (NR 208 689):
Anaconda   25m   E2 5b **. Graham Little, Carl Schaschke, Ron Kenyon. 20 Jun 2015.
Follows the striking diagonal dyke that snakes across the centre of the wall. Start at the right-hand side of the big sea pool. Follow the dyke to a roof, move left below it, then climb a slot (crux) to regain the dyke and thence to the top.

Agoraphobia Groove   40m   E1 **. Ron Kenyon, Graham Little (alt), Carl Schaschke. 20 Jun 2015.
This route tackles the third groove round the corner from Shelf Wall i.e. to the left of *Avatar* and *Aldosterone Grooves*.
1. 25m 5b Climb the superstructure to reach the groove, then climb the groove to belay a short distance above.
2. 15m 5a Traverse hard right for about 9m and then climb up to make an abrupt and sensational finish, passing through a notch in overhanging flakes.
Note: Although the Inner Hebrides & Arran guidebook mentions only three steep grooves there are in fact four, with the fourth giving access to the awesome 60m wall mentioned in the Shelf Wall introduction.

The Geo, Back Bay Wall (NR 210 689):
This is the banded wall that sits above the head of The Geo. Although it has a southerly aspect, it can at times be damp due to water dripping from the turf capping. There is a good belay on a huge block well back from the top of the wall.

Tibia Test   14m   E1 5b **. Graham Little (unsec). 22 Aug 2014.
Start just right of a recess. Climb up to a good pocket, make committing moves leftwards to good holds, then climb steep rock above. At the top end of the grade with fiddly gear placements.

Fibula Fun   14m   VS 4c **. Graham Little, Christina Woodrow. 22 Aug 2014.
Start to the right of the recess below a series of small roofs high up. Climb straight up, wending between the roofs, moving out left under the top one.

Graham Little on the FA of Anaconda (E2 5b), Dun Bheolain, Islay. Photo Ron Kenyon.

Tip Toe   10m   Severe 4b. Graham Little, Christina Woodrow. 22 Aug 2014.
Climb the wall just to the left of the open groove, followed by the obvious slabby groove above (sometimes wet).

SOUTH OF PORTNAHAVEN, Hidden Geo Area (NR 174 513):

Ironheart   15m   E2 5b. Graham Little (unsec). 23 Aug 2014.
Start at the *Rust and Bone* belay at the bottom right-hand corner of the obvious rust coloured slab. Gain and climb the hanging groove above the belay (minimal protection) to gain a short ramp. Climb it and the easy slab above.

Hidden Geo, Shadow Side:

The north facing side of the geo is mostly very steep and tends to be damp.

Out Right   15m   V.Diff. Graham Little. 23 Aug 2014.
Start on a flat jammed block in the back of the geo (above tidal influence). Take an ascending line diagonally rightwards, initially by rounded flakes.

The Rift:

Just to the south and parallel to Hidden Geo is a very narrow cliff flanked rift. The north facing side of The Rift is a vertical wall, whilst the south facing side is a steep slab.

Reach for the Sky   10m   Severe 4b **. Graham Little. 23 Aug 2014.
Start below a crack in the middle of the south facing side, between two inky black pools. Climb by flakes and the crack above.

Split Wall Geo (NR 176 512):

This geo lies to the west of the Overhanging Wall Area. It has a south-east facing flank with the right side split by a vertical chimney/crack (*The Split*) and the left (seaward) side sliced by a distinctive left-slanting fault (*The Cut*). The first three routes start at high water mark so require the appropriate state of tide and calm seas. Access to the starts is either by abseil or by scrambling in from the left.

The Code   12m   Severe. Graham Little, Christina Woodrow. 11 Jun 2015.
To the left of *The Cut* lies an obvious groove (*The Groove*). Climb the rib to the left of *The Groove*, step up onto flakes, move left, then finish straight up.

The Groove   12m   V.Diff *. Graham Little, Christina Woodrow. 11 Jun 2015.
Climb the obvious groove.

The Way   12m   VS 4c. Graham Little, Christina Woodrow, 11 June 2015.
From the start of *The Groove*, move up and right then up onto a ledge. Climb the steep wall, with some fragile looking holds, moving left to finish.

The Cut   13m   Severe *. Graham Little, Christina Woodrow. 5 Apr 2015.
There is a ledge well above high tide accessible by abseil. From the ledge climb up to reach the striking left-slanting fault then follow it.

The Split   18m   VS 4b **. Graham Little. 11 Jun 2015.
Climbs the obvious chimney-crack from a poor stance just above high water mark (abseil in).

No Holds Barred 16m E2 5b **. Graham Little (unsec). 20 May 2015.
The head of the geo becomes a narrow gulch. At one point it is possible to step across onto the wall from easy-angled rock on the north side. Start at this point. A couple of long reaches gives access to right-facing flakes. Climb these to a horizontal flake. Move left to gain a hidden mineral vein (well seen from below) which is climbed followed by easier rock to the top. Protection on the first third of the route is very limited and the route is at the top end of the grade.

KILCHIARAN BAY GEO (NR 198 602):
4 routes on the SMC website.

The Fan:
Note: The route *Rust* (Inner Hebrides p212) should be E1 5b, not VS 5a.

ARRAN
A' CHIR, Coire Daingean Face:
Note: *Intruder* (Inner Hebrides p229) was climbed in 1974 not 1947. FA list is correct.

CIOCH NA H-OIGHE:
The Great Escape 95m E7 ***.
A new description from Jules Lines. The first pitch is new.
1. 25m 6a Climb a small V-groove 10m right of *Abraxus* to the roof (direct over the roof is a similar grade but on crumbly rock), traverse left under the roof and pull up right onto the belay ledge.
2. 40m 6b From the left side of the ledge, make awkward moves up and right to gain a big thread in the base of the groove. Climb the groove until it dwindles before making committing moves left to reach some hidden pockets and low cams. Climb directly up the improbable wall following the obvious groove lines to a resting ledge. Traverse right for 3m to a letterbox pocket (and thread) for protection and move back onto the ledge. Climb leftwards up the slab on friction holds until it possible to gain the base of the incredible flake-crack. Follow this in a superb position to belay on *Tidemark*.
3. 30m 6b Gain a narrow sloping shelf 3m above the belay, small wires in this and a C3 000 with a possibility of skyhooks up on the left. Make difficult and bold moves to gain the groove on the right leading to a large spike. Pull onto the slab above and veer slightly left and up this to its top. Easier climbing remains.

UPPER GLEN SANNOX, Creagh Dubh (p267):
Arran Blonde 175m H.Severe 4b **. Andrew Fraser, Ian Magill. 25 Jul 2014.
An excellent route on this most neglected of cliffs, comparable in style and quality to *Pagoda Ridge*. A future obscure classic? It climbs the left edge of the crag's main wall, which seen from the left forms a ridge. The bottom of this is undercut with two possible lines. Easy slabs and turf lead to underneath the left-hand line, an undercut left-facing corner-crack (25m 3b) Climb the steep corner-crack to the ledge above. Move round left onto the edge and continue up this to slabs below a wall. Traverse right for 3m to a corner (30m 4b) Surmount the bulge above the belay and traverse left to the edge. Climb the ridge over bulges to a heather ledge (25m 4a). Climb the crack behind the belay and continue up the ridge (35m 4a). Climb up to and over the final tower, then traverse right along a heather ledge for

15m to belay beneath a large detached flake in the headwall (35m 4a). Climb slabs to the summit (25m 4a).

15 Minute Ridge Direct 45m Severe *. Andrew Fraser, Ian Magill. 25 Jul 2014.
The original 1945 route on the crag avoids the lovely twisting cracks up the front of the ridge.

SKYE

SGÙRR NAN GILLEAN, Bhasteir Face:
Indian Buttress 80m HVS. Mike Lates, Mo Barclay. 9 Sep 2015.
Takes a central fault up the buttress left of *Deep Chimney*.
1. 25m 4c Climb a thin crack past a bulge at 5m and continue more easily to belay 3m below the next tier.
2. 30m 5a Tackle the overhung groove directly, then continue easily to a large block below the next tier.
3. 25m Easy climbing to a horizontal break.
Exit to the West Ridge by traversing above *Doctor's Chimney*.

SGÙRR NA H-UAMHA:
South-East Face 110m Mod *. Iain Thow, Margaret Carlisle. 12 Oct 2015.
About halfway along the South-East face, below the steepest buttress, is a small separate outcrop with a left-facing gully starting just left of this (the winter II in the Cuillin rock guide). Start just left of the gully and scramble awkwardly up leftwards to reach a shelf below steeper more continuous rock (a scree shoot goes down left to easy ground from here). Work left up excellent gabbro to the edge overlooking the gully further left, then climb the edge steeply to a perch where it is possible to walk leftwards across the gully. Climb a slabby rib on the far side, dodging a steep wall using the gully (one move here might just be Diff, but by a good runner). Easy scrambling continues up to the South Ridge.

East Ridge 180m Grade 2/3 *. Iain Thow (in descent). 21 Oct 2003.
Avoid the steep rock at the foot of the ridge by coming in from the left low down, then go up to a shelf (this looks easier to reach from further left). Dodge the next steep buttress by a groove on the left. Much easier scrambling continues direct to the summit. Probably done before.

AM BASTEIR, North Face:
The Breadline 70m V,5. Mike Lates, Mark Francis, Murdo Nicholson. 22 Nov 2015.
1. 40m Follow the start of pitch 2 of *The Deadline*, then continue directly up the off-width corner. Surmount the final small roof to a large ledge.
2. 30m Continue with good climbing to belay at a prominent pinnacle on the east ridge of Am Basteir.

BASTEIR TOOTH:
An Inconvenient Tooth E8 6c. Dan McManus, Ross McKerchar. 8 Jun 2016.
Climbs the front of the prow of the Bastier Tooth.
1. 20m 6c Start directly under the huge roof on the front of the Tooth. Follow a thin crack to ledges and some loose rock on the right arete. Pull up and right to a

Dan MacManus and Ross McKerchar on the FA of An Inconvenient Tooth (E8 6c) on the Basteir Tooth. Photo Malcolm Davies.

shelf with a break and many possible cam placements. A big hold above the shelf allows a reach left to the beginning of the huge roof, the start of the hard climbing, where micro cams can be placed. Wild moves lead along the lip until possible to rock over onto the face. Delicately move left to the arete and up to a ledge.

2. 20m 6a Climb easily up the arete to an even bigger ledge and continue onto the wall to the right of the arete. Tricky moves left on the lip of the roof lead to better holds and gear back on the arete. Finish straight up the left side of the arete.

SGÙRR A' BHASTEIR, North Face:

Raborigine 90m III. Mark Francis, Murdo Nicholson, David Bowdler. 28 Feb 2016.

Asnow bay lies 10m left of *Mike the Bhasteird*. This route climbs leftwards out of the bay, and finishes to the left of an obvious impending wall. Climbed in 3 pitches.

White Diamond 70m IV,4. Mark Francis, Alan Gorman, Murdo Nicholson. 13 Feb 2016.

Thirty metres right of *Mike the Bhasteird* is a thin groove leading to the top of the buttress, right of a diagonal turfy break. Climb this in two pitches, avoiding a steep wall low down on the right, trending back left into the bottom of the groove and following this to finish on easy ground.

SGÙRR A' BHASTEIR, South-West Face:

Wimplash 90m III. Mark Francis, Murdo Nicholson, Mike Lates. 13 Dec 2015.

Thirty metres left of the pinnacle of *Running on Numpty*, is a shallow groove with a short corner to start. Climb this, then go left to finish up icy ledges.

BIDEIN DRUIM NAN RÀMH, Central Peak:

The south-east face of the Central (highest) Peak has a steep crag with a prominent right-facing corner on its right-hand side. This is best reached from Bealach na Glaic Moire. Ascend the initial ridge of the West Peak then descend down rightwards past a gully/corner to reach an exposed and narrow ledge which is traversed right and around to the south-east face of the Central Peak. Descend 30m to the base of the corner. This approach reverses the upper section of the Druim nan Ràmh ridge described in *Skye Scrambles*. Due to the complex approach and descent it is best to carry sacs.

Descent from the summit of the Central Peak follows the main Cuillin Ridge. It is achieved by going over the summit for a short distance and then descending the south-west face via a basalt dyke chimney. A short downwards traverse left and then right leads to the 'Bridge Rock'. A short scramble across this soon leads down to Bealach na Glaic Moire. Follow a descending terrace rightwards to gain a scree gully leading to the floor of Coire a' Mhadaidh and eventually the 'Fairy Pools' path.

All the President's Men   60m   E1 5a/b *. Andrew Wielochowski, John Mackenzie, Mike Mavroleon. 11 May 2016.
1. 30m 5b The big obvious corner has three potential undercut starts. Climb the middle one and then move up right into a crack system. Follow this until holds allow moves left into the main corner. Climb the fine corner to an alcove stance. A very good pitch, reasonably protected.
2. 30m 5a Continue up the corner more delicately for around 15m, to reach a brown horizontal cone sheet below the corner's capping overhang. Traverse rightwards to the arete to step down at a pointed block; all this very exposed. Continue easily up the arete.
Scrambling for 50m leads to the ridge which is followed to the Central Peak.

Lower Central Buttress   50m   Severe. Andy Moles & party. 31 May 2016.
The three peaks of Bidein are divided on the Coire na Creiche side by North Gap Gully and South Gap Gully. There is a third gully in between, leading to a notch in the Central Peak. This route takes a central line up the buttress between North Gap Gully and this unnamed third gully, coming in from the left. It is not particularly recommended.

SGÙRR A' MHADAIDH, North Face, The Amphitheatre:

Spectacula   240m   VI,6. Uisdean Hawthorn, Dougie Russell, Adam Russell. 27 Feb 2016.
Climbs the wide icefall on the left side of the amphitheatre 20m down from its top. Pass an overlap at 30m by a hanging icicle and continue with interest up steep ice steps and snow.

Spirulina   240m   V,5. Uisdean Hawthorn, Lea Macleod. 28 Feb 2016.
An icefall in the top left corner of the amphitheatre. After 35m, take the wide crack to the left into a bay follow ice steps trending left until it joins *Spectacula* at its last steep step.

SGÙRR A' GHREADAIDH, Coruisk Face:

Griffin 200m III,4. Sandy Allan, Andy Nisbet. 25 Feb 2016.
An ice line on the left side of the face above the terrace, possibly close to the upper section of *Terrace West Buttress*. Start by gaining the left end of the terrace by snowy grooves (not included in length). Above and left is a huge recess not far below the main ridge leading up to Sgùrr a' Ghreadaidh. Take a zigzag line mostly on steep snow, trending left to a ramp with an ice covered right wall (60m). From the top of the ramp, climb a short steep ice pitch to a snow terrace with the huge recess at its right end (50m). Continue diagonally left up an icy fault (50m) before a short chimney led to the main ridge.

Skyefall 250m IV,5. Dave McGimpsey, Andy Nisbet, Steve Perry. 28 Feb 2016.
A more direct and much steeper ice line on the left side of the face above the terrace. Up and right of the recess mentioned above is a right-slanting gully which leads to a platform some two-thirds of the way up the main ridge to Sgùrr a' Ghreadaidh. Flowing down from this is a fine ice line. Start briefly as for *Griffin* and continue to reach the base of the ice (20m). Climb ice leftwards to reach a ledge, at the right end of which is a steep stripe of ice leading up towards the gully system (50m). Climb the ice and two short ice pitches leading left to snow (60m). Continue up snow and the gully to the ridge.

SGÙRR A' GHREADAIDH, North West Face, An Doras Buttress:

Gauche 145m IV,5 **. Steve Kennedy, Des Rubens. 28 Feb 2016.
An icefall forms down the corner of the summer route. A steep bulging section on the second pitch (turning the overhang) forms the crux. The final wall above the snow terrace was negotiated by the chimney left of the exposed arete followed by the summer route.

SGÙRR A' GHREADAIDH, Summit Buttress:

King Snakes 105m IV,4 *. Steve Kennedy, Andy MacDonald. 6 Mar 2016.
This route takes a line of ramps running up the right side of *Hamish's Chimney* (bisecting *Virgin Arete*). Start about 20m right of *Hamish's Chimney* and climb the obvious ramp up left. A long poorly protected pitch leads to a point below an overhanging wall and into the upper section of *Hamish's Chimney*. A finish was made up mixed ground on the left of the chimney.

The Healer 55m IV,5 **. Andy MacDonald, Steve Kennedy. 6 Mar 2016.
A wide steep icefall forms on the right side of the lower buttress (well right and below *Hamish's Chimney*). Situated about 50m from *North-West Ridge*. The icefall was climbed in one long pitch to easier ground. Either finish up *North-West Ridge* or descend by a shelf on the left towards *Hamish's Chimney*.

COIRE NA BANACHDAICH, Banachdaich Gully Area:

Spaced Nonety 200m IV,5. Mark Francis, David Bowdler. 15 Jan 2016.
This route is loosely based on the summer route *North Rib*. Ten metres inside *Banachdaich Gully* on the left-hand side is an obvious groove running parallel to the gully. Climb the groove to a short wall (crux), above which follow short chimneys to easier ground. Trend leftwards to finish up icy grooves.

SGÙRR THUILM:

Ridge Repellent 55m II/III. Mark Francis, Alan Gorman. 14 Feb 2016.

Well to the right of South-West Buttress is a line of broken rocks, cleaved with gullies. This route follows an obvious icefall at the right end above a large apron of scree.

Low Crag:
(NG 439 247)   Alt 400m   North-West facing
Park Lane   90m   V,4. Pat Ingram, Mike Lates. 15 Jan 2016.
Climbs the most prominent fault in the left wall of the bay.
1. 50m A direct start was avoided by the vegetated groove 5m right. Traverse delicately left to gain the main groove which gives good mixed climbing to an obvious ledge.
2. 40m Traverse left and finish up broken terrain above.

SGÙRR DEARG, North Face:
Inaccessible Icefall   250m   IV,4. Sandy Allan, Andy Nisbet. 24 Feb 2016.
An ice line which formed on the very left edge of the face, starting some 100m away from the steep Coruisg sidewall of An Stac and the Inaccessible Pinnacle. Start with easy ice, then a wide 50m icefall heading towards the sidewall, then climb ice on a rib at the left end of a steep band and quite close to the sidewall. Finish by snow trending away from the sidewall and a short groove to the crest of Sgùrr Dearg.

SGÙRR DEARG, South Buttress:
White Lightning   200m   IV,5. Guy Robertson, Uisdean Hawthorn, Adam Russell. 26 Feb 2016.
An excellent pure ice route following the obvious snaking groove / gully bounding the right side of South Buttress (left of *In Pinn Fall*). The route was climbed in three long pitches, all of which gave interest; the first with a tricky vertical step, the second with an excellent narrow runnel, and the third with thinly iced slabs. Above this easier climbing allowed a traverse away off right back to the An Stac screes.

SGÙRR MHICCOINNICH, North Face:
North-East Gully   VI,7. Guy Robertson, Uisdean Hawthorn, Adam Russell. 26 Feb 2016.
A brilliant short route with a sustained and well-protected crux pitch. Follow the summer line throughout.

Crack of Dawn   180m   VII,8. James & Doug Sutton. 14 Jan 2016.
By the summer route, the first pitch is the crux.

Note: Mike Lates notes that the initial 25m crack of *Mongoose Direct* is good. The direct continuation looked dirtier. Instead, he climbed cleaner rock 5m to the left for 15m to the foot of a good crack (pitch 3 of the normal route?). This was one 40m pitch from the start.

SGÙRR THEÀRLAICH, Stone Shoot Face:
The Bogeyman   70m   VI,7. Michael Barnard, Mike Lates. 17 Jan 2016.
The obvious steep fault-line between *Hobgoblin* and *Hi Vis*. The first 6m is the technical crux but the main pitch is very bold and insecure throughout.
1. 40m Climb the fault-line to below its short final crack. Step left to a belay.

2. 30m Move into *Gully E*, then finish up and right.

Mr Charlie 40m   VI,7 *. Michael Barnard, Mike Lates. 17 Jan 2016.
The fine vertical crack starting near the top of the Great Stone Shoot and leading directly to the summit block of Theàrlaich.

SRÒN NA CÌCHE, Western Buttress:
Coronation, Jubilee Variation 180m HVS *. Mike Lates, Chris Sutcliffe. 1 May 2012.
The 'formidable wall' contains a trap dyke mistaken for the 'fine crack' of the original route (its pitch 5).
5. 45m 5a Reach the foot of the dyke by a rising leftward traverse (10m). Climb the dyke directly to a bulge at 10m. Turn this and continue with interest to a ledge with a huge block.
6. 50m 4b Climb good rock above to the fault of *Boomerang* (10m). Cross this and continue directly by a series of short grooves & steps. Finish by a basalt groove to a good ledge.
7. 35m 4b Rise left to gain the corner formed by a very steep clean wall on the left. Follow this until the angle eases on the shoulder of *West Gully*.
8. 50m Finish up the shoulder on good rock.

COIRE A' GHRUNNDA, Sròn na Cìche, South-East Face, The Esplanade:
The name given to the crag situated below and to the right of the upper path leading to the South Face, a short distance before the Lower Buttress is reached (*Cuckoo Groove*). The crag stretches for some distance along the east side of the lower corrie and presents a very steep easterly aspect divided by a prominent cracked slab (south-east facing) forming a dog-leg. The following routes are located on the slab.

Cockatrice 35m HVS 4c **. Steve Kennedy, Cynthia Grindley. 25 Jun 2016.
The left-hand line. The upper part is sparsely protected. Start near the base of the right-facing corner bounding the left side of the slab. Climb a short way up the initial slabby corner before stepping right onto a pock marked slab which is followed to a ledge at about 12m. Continue up a large flake on the right which leads to a shallow corner. Climb the corner to a quartz studded fault. Move slightly left along the fault, then climb blind cracks in the slab above a few metres right of the corner, moving into the corner higher up. Climb the final slab right of the corner finishing with some thin moves out rightwards near the top (avoiding the grassy corner) leading to the easy upper slabs (35m). Belay well back at some blocks.

Chimera 35m   E1 5a **. Steve Kennedy, Cynthia Grindley. 25 June 2016.
The right-hand line. A fine but bold route particularly in the upper part. The lower section takes the line of the pale coloured right-facing corner/ramp leading rightwards under a roof to the right edge of the main slab. Start up the undercut corner a few metres right of *Cockatrice* and climb the ramp to the roof. Move right under the roof onto the exposed edge passing some hollow sounding blocks. A blind crack leads up and slightly left, to the end of a quartz studded ledge. Finish fairly directly up the cracked slab above taking a line a few metres right of *Cockatrice*.

South Crag:
Owl Chimney IV,5. Mike Lates, Nathan Adam, Lucy Spark. 16 Jan 2016.
Follow the summer line with continuously awkward, well protected interest.
Requires good conditions to justify.

North Crag:
Self Slabuse 80m III 4. Mark Francis, David Bowdler. 16 Jan 2016.
A direct start to Slab Buttress. The left side of the slab is bounded by a short wall.
Climb a groove leading into the corner and follow to its finish.

SGÙRR ALASDAIR, South Face:
The Sheriff's Ransom 50m V,6 *. Michael Barnard, Mike Lates. 19 Jan 2016.
A steep well protected first pitch followed by a bold and slabby second pitch
(though would be considerably easier under neve). Start below the obvious
chimney-crack between *Skye High* and *West Gully*.
1. 25m Climb the fine chimney-crack to the mid-height ledge and belay on the
left.
2. 25m The exposed ramp up and left. Either continue up easier ground or move
left to abseil as for *Skye High*.

Theàrlaich-Dubh Gap Walls:
Tre Difficile 25m V,6. Michael Barnard (unsec). 16 Jan 2016.
An alternate pitch up the long side of the TD Gap. Start just left of the *Original
Route*, below two parallel grooves of which the left one is undercut. Move up the
right groove (crux), then step left and follow the left one to below the obvious
chimney-slot. Move left into another groove and finish up this.

SGÙRR NAN EAG, West Flank:
Age Concern 320m IV,4 *. Steve Kennedy, Des Rubens. 27 Feb 2016.
The West Flank was in unusually good condition with extensive areas of ice and
neve which provided an excellent mountaineering route up ground left of *Western
Buttress*. The difficulties are confined to the upper section. Start at the right end
of the cliff band which stretches across right from the mouth of the upper corrie,
about opposite and level with the right side of South Crag. Climb easy mixed
ground up rightwards into a snow bay below *Western Buttress*. An obvious snow
gully leads back diagonally left, terminating below the upper steeper face. A fairly
direct line was followed in the upper section, initially into a snow bay, followed
by an icefall turning a large undercut block on the left. Ice-covered slabs and short
grooves lead to a steep final buttress. A line of iced up grooves in the centre of
the buttress provides an excellent finish.

SGÙRR NAN EAG, Coire nan Laogh:
The Scorcher 215m HVS 5b **. John Mackenzie, Noel Williams. 9 May 2016.
A good route, to the right of *Golden Calf* (SMCJ 2014), which weaves a way
through the lower slabs and overlaps, then climbs a basalt dyke cutting through
the central Barrier wall at its highest point. Start by a short pillar.
1. 40m 4a Climb its right corner and pull over an overlap above to belay. Walk
left for 15m.
2. 20m Climb the slabs past a flake to belay under a large tongue of rock that lies
below the Barrier.

3. 25m 4c Traverse horizontally right under the Barrier to reach a lower ledge just right of the trap dyke.
4. 45m 5b Move left to some holds left of the trap dyke and climb steeply up and right and then follow the dyke up the wall to reach the upper slabs. Continue up then right to a large flake and niche.
5. 55m 4c Move left to the trap dyke and follow to where it swings left and becomes a trench. Step right onto an immaculate slab and climb straight up this on perfect rock keeping left of a smaller dyke.
6. 30m Simple slabs and scrambling lead to the top.

MARSCO, North Face, Coire nan Laogh:
S Gully   150m   III *. John Jackson, Martin Holland, Lorn Smith, Linda Gentlemen, Gareth Robinson, Joanne McCandless. 28 Feb 2016.
The central S-shaped gully of the corrie. The main pitch is the final bend of the S from a shelf at half -height on the left-hand crags. Above this a variety of finishes are possible to the summit ridge. Ice screws and warthogs useful for runners and belays.
Note: Previously climbed by Mike Lates.

MARSCO, South-West Buttress:
The following routes climb left of the amphitheatre on which *Odell's Route* is based. There is a lower left buttress with the first route while up and right, across an easy ramp, is an upper right buttress with the second route. There is also an older route (1995) on both sections but the line has yet to be rechecked. Diagram and photos provided.

Araminta's Buttress   100m   V.Diff *. Jim Cooper, Peter Walkington. May 2012.
The left side of this buttress is formed by the gully to the left of the crag which is *Fiacaill Geal*. The right half of the base of the buttress is barred by a line of overhangs. Twenty metres left of these is a short grassy gully line. This worthwhile route climbs the broad rib immediately left of this.
1. 35m Climb the broad rib directly up to a grassy ledge at 25m. Climb the wall above.
2. 35m Climb the wall behind, then easy angled rock up to a line of overlaps at 20m. Avoid the overlaps by stepping round to the right and climb more steeply up to a large ledge.
3. 30m Take the attractive ramp on the left, then go up and right to the easy angled ramp.

Araminta's Wall   130m   Severe **. Jim Cooper, Peter Walkington. May 2012.
This starts from the easy angled ramp, towards the centre of the upper right buttress and 70m right of the finish of *Araminta's Buttress*. Start at a dark brown 5m wall with a line of square-cut holds leading diagonally up right to left. At the top of this is a short deep groove leading up left to right. A fine climb with an air of seriousness.
1. 35m Climb the dark brown wall from bottom right to top left and into the groove above. Follow this up and right for 4m and step right onto a wall. Climb straight up to the middle of three large shelving ledges.
2. 35m Climb the wall above by a series of short corners and grooves to a horizontal ledge that traverses much of the crag.
3. 15m Traverse left easily.

4. 45m Up and left are many short grooves and walls. Pick a way diagonally up left to the top of the crag. About halfway up this pitch, the 1995 route crosses and may provide a better finish up right.
To descend, take an indistinct deer track that leads horizontally left across the top section of the gully.

CAMASTINAVAIG, Far Cliff:
Gogglebox 10m VS 4b. Mark Hudson, Nicola Bassnett, Roger Brown. 20 Aug 2015.
Left of *Obligation* the cliff turns a corner to a scrappy bay. This route gains and climbs the slim wall 3m left of the grassy corner. Climb past overlaps to gain a pedestal to the left of the face. Step back right onto the face and climb direct.

Obligation 10m HVS 5b. Nicola Bassnett, Mark Hudson, Roger Brown. 20 Aug 2015.
Take a direct line up the overhanging crack immediately left of *Vox*.

Vox 10m V.Diff. Mark Hudson, Roger Brown, Nicola Bassnett. 20 Aug 2015.
Takes the chimney of jutting steps on left-hand side of the *Haiku* roof.

OLD MAN OF STORR AREA:
Desperate Remedies 25m E1 5a. Richard Ive, Chris Underwood. 5 Jul 2015.
Limited protection and unnerving rock make this a serious, but memorable undertaking. The climbing requires a confident approach. Start as for *The Old Boy*. From a belay at the back of the pinnacle, traverse diagonally rightwards towards the Old Man for about 5m. Climb boldly for the grassy ridge opposite the Old Man. Finish steeply by continuing to the turfy top. Descent was made by down climbing *The Old Boy*.

RUBHA HUNISH, Meall Deas (Right-Hand Section):
Passing Out 48m E5 6a ***. Nicola Bassnett (unsec). 10 Sep 2015.
A splendid climb situated between a large (unclimbed) west-facing corner on the left and *Whispering Crack* on the right. A plumbline crack system joins the latter route in its upper reaches. The lower section includes a shallow right-facing corner with three spaced overlaps, which present the cruxes.
    Start atop a steep grassy slope and follow a shallow cracked groove for 8m until a step left brings the corner into line. Above the second overlap make moves to gain the main wall on the left, before stepping back right to reach the final tricky moves and the sustained soaring crack line. Finish up the final section of *Whispering Crack*.

Copperhead Road 70m E2. Ian Parnell, Sandy Ogilvie. 13 Aug 2015.
Start right of the flying buttress right of *Whispering Crack*, just before the end of the wall at an area of more amenable grooves, and before the Gothic Walls begin. The route is identifiable by the crack-line of pitch 2, which is just right of a steeper smooth shield of rock. Worthwhile with occasional vegetation not affecting the climbing on pitch 1.
1. 35m 5a Climb cracks and grooves trending slightly rightwards to a small stance below an overlap guarding a shallow right-facing groove split by a hand crack.
2. 35m 5c Climb the crack to reach a big left-trending ramp. Follow this past a steep short crack before finishing up a short steep wall.

The Headland, Seal Buttress:
Rosie 20m VS 5a *. John Lynch, Mike Lynch, Bethan Davis. 1 May 2016.
The route follows an obvious shallow groove on the left-hand end of the buttress. Starting off a flat boulder immediately above the sea, trend slightly left then follow the obvious right-facing groove line to a tricky and slightly steeper exit direct through an overlap.

NA HURANAN:
Earth, Wind & Rock 40m Diff. Daniel Heaton, Andrew Heaton. 19 Aug 2015.
This route starts at the right-hand end of a low black wall some 100m west of Gauger's Pinnacle. The cliffs at this point form two distinct tiers separated by a wide heathery band.

Step on to the rock ramp at the right-hand end of the wall but then go straight up onto the thickly vegetated deep ledge. Cross the undergrowth diagonally leftwards to an obvious wide exit cleft marked by a large boulder leaning against the back wall. Once at the boulder, climb up it and follow through the cleft at the top. Belay placements are well back from the lip (use a 60m rope).

NEIST, Upper Cliffs, Seagulls Sector:
Button Up 35m E2 5b *. Nicola Bassnett, Roger Brown. 24 Aug 2014.
The big face immediately right of *Route with a View* has some vertical weaknesses in its lower blank section. This route traverses the cliff at mid-height. On its right-hand side, where the wall gently angles back towards the gully, a leaning flake rests against the bottom of the face with stepped blocks beneath it. Start 3m left down from the gully and gain the flake. A curving finger crack offers plenty of gear before the crux moves on positive rugosities that follow the shallow groove. The holds improve and the climbing eases as welcome protection arrives on the right below the overhang. Traverse left on good holds in a spectacular position to reach a good perch. The following groove using laybacks, bridging, and jamming is surprisingly unrelenting.

Financial Sector:
The Price is Right 30m E1 5b **. Nicola Bassnett, Roger Brown. 28 May 2014.
This takes a vertical line to finish up the final crack of *Insider Dealing*. This and two other routes share a start, which takes the corner of the alcove. Start at a disjointed crack to the immediate right of this and continue straight up, as it veers left. Step right into the U scoop of *Inside Out* and quickly meet the mid-height ledge. The prominent steep crack above is climbed using help from various nubbins on the right wall. This leads to the right side of the *Insider Dealing* overhang and its crack above.

Note: Andy Moles notes an obvious direct start to *All the Small Things*, avoiding the bold lower ramp of the original, making the route E4 6b * (29 May 2016). He thought the original was ** rather than ***, the traverse right at the top feeling like a major cop-out. The direct finish is very safe but he couldn't do it.

Gritstone Reminiscence Area:
Note: *Seven Days* and *Braveheart* (SMCJ 2014) follow the same line.

South of the Steps, Sonamara Area:
Forbo 20m H.Severe 4b. Nicola Bassnett, Roger Brown. 23 Jul 2014.

A knobbly crack immediately right of *Fizzy Pop* is very often wet. When dry it offers pleasant climbing on good handholds, despite a dubious sounding well inbedded block. A short wall with quirky holds gives fun climbing before the shared easy top.

ELGOL, Schoolhouse Buttress:
Honeystick 12m E4 5c. Andy Moles. 5 Jun 2016.
The neat arete of *Bee Keeper's Bother*, climbed on its steep right side all the way. Good climbing but eliminate. Protection is tricky to find and place (small cams). Stepping around at the last big hold on the arete to place a side runner in *Bee Keeper's* would make the route E3, and might be sensible.
Note: *Bee Keeper's Bother* was thought HVS 5a.

ELGOL, Suidhe Biorach, Prince Charlie's Cave Area:
Arch Buttress 35m E1 5a *. Mike Lates, Lucy Spark. 15 Oct 2015.
Tackles the obvious seaward face of the buttress containing the arch immediately east of Prince Charlie's Cave. Start by the central groove which steepens sharply at 15m. Make a leftward diagonal traverse to a subsidiary groove and good wires. Climb directly to the top but step left to finish avoiding the vertical peat.

RAASAY, Beinn na h-Iolaire, Southern Buttress:
Six by Six 20m E3 6a ***. Nicola Bassnett, Roger Brown. 30 May 2014.
This excellent route takes the striking central line of weakness in the wall to the left of *Stollen*. The deceptively steep lower wall allows small and difficult to place protection but gives way to more relaxing climbing above.

Calum's Crag:
30's the New 20 10m V.Diff. Rosie Lynch, Rich Armour. 6 May 2016.
The obvious crack to the left of *Calum MacLeod*. From the block follow the well protected crack for a few metres before working into the groove and onwards to the top.

Ocean-Going Cliff:
Note: *Raucous Summer* (SMCJ 2015) is the same as *Schapps Route* (SMCJ 2014).

RONA:
This low lying tranquil island, sitting between Skye and Applecross, holds a surprising range of quality climbing across the grades with plenty of room for more. Once on the island it makes a leisurely base thanks to a well equipped bunkhouse, good access tracks and a supportive warden. There is scant previous climbing history and the following list charts climbs made in Aug 2010, June 2011, and Aug 2015, with only the cliffs nearest to the central settlements looked at so far.
    The Rona landscape is similar to Raasay north of Brochel but with heavier tree cover in places including some ancient forest, deep cut inlets and plenty of wildlife. Its barren undulating ground rises to 125m on Meall Acairseid, and is covered in glacial hummocks and blanketed in knee-deep scrub and bogs. Once off the two tracks northward (to the lighthouse) and southward (to the ruined chapel of An Teampull), it is difficult to get around.
    The island is seemingly all composed of gneiss, but with a huge variety of types

ranging from sharp red sheets through gritty grey bulges to gnarlier knobbled walls. Almost all are compact and trustworthy, in beautiful and remote positions. The taller crags often have undercut starts with gentler faces and slabs above, giving climbing similar in style to north Raasay. Venues have been laid out in three areas as approached along the tracks from Big Harbour.

Access is from Portree or north Raasay by charter. There are three holiday cottages and a well equipped bothy on the island. Contact Bill Cowie, Island Manager, on ronalodge@isleofrona.com or visit <www.isleofrona.com> to look at options.

Acairseid Mhòr, Summerhouse Slab:
(NG 61474 57142)   West facing
This is the first of a couple of venues which lie within easy reach of the pier and bunkhouse. It is a continuous steep slab, 12–15m high with a gentler tier of curvier clean slabs above, only a few minutes north of the bunkhouse, visible in profile on the horizon above the trees and level with the Rona Lodge summerhouse.

Escapee   15m   Diff. Mark Hudson. 27 Jun 2011.
Climb the central cracks with a cleaner wall to the left.

Beware Block:
(NG 61809 57241)   North-West facing
This fierce 12m overhanging block lies just off the track across marshy ground just east of the turbine, and holds some characterful routes either side of a dark central cleft. Leave the track at the Rona Lodge gate and cross the marsh following the fence for 50-60m to the cliff.

Beware of the Bill   12m   E3 5c **. Nicola Bassnett, Mark Hudson. 24 Aug 2015.
The main overhanging wall is taken by a powerful and direct line of cracks 2m left of the dark corner-cleft and finishing up a V-groove.

Fairies Versus Giants   12m   H.Severe 4a. Mark Hudson, Roger Brown. 24 Aug 2015.
The huge steps just right of the central cleft, finishing directly up a thin crack.

An Teampull Path Areas (Southwards):
A handful of pleasant venues clustered around the initial sections of the An Teampull path and best accessed with reference to that track.

Saturday Cliff:
(NG 61774 56818)   South-West facing
This 15m vertical sea-level wall is highly conspicuous during the boat approach to Acairseid Mhor, lying 100m south of the pier across an inlet. Access is tricky, either by leaving the track 200m past the turbine, cutting back down to the inlet and boulder-hopping 400m along the south side and round the point. Or, longer but easier, by following the An Teampull track for 600m as far as the 'Hamburger Cliff' and then dropping westwards down the valley to the shore. The cliff is steep and compact, split into two aspects by a central overlapping groove, with climbing characterised by small sharp holds. Two worthwhile lines climb the right-hand aspect either side of a mid-height bulge.

Spindrift 15m E1 5b *. Nicola Bassnett, Roger Brown, Mark Hudson. 22 Aug 2015.
Gain and follow slanting cracks past the left-hand end of the overlap, finishing direct.

Henningsvaer 15m HVS 5b *. Nicola Bassnett, Mark Hudson, Roger Brown. 22 Aug 2015.
Make a sharp pull onto the wall further up the slope and move urgently past the right end of the overlap, finishing up the wall to the highest point of the cliff.

The Bulge:
(NG 61768 56625) South-West facing
This beautiful rounded 12m bulge of gritty rock gives short and easy routes. It lies only 50m north-west of the An Teampuill track, accessible from the same point as The Shoulder, visible as a dome to the right of the track, in line with the pier in the bay below.

Rocky Bag 10m Diff. Mark Hudson. 28 Jun 2011.
The groove on the left and the arete above.

Heavy Shoe 10m V.Diff. Mark Hudson. 28 Jun 2011.
The central cleft via a steep start followed by higher slabs.

The Shoulder:
(NG 61832 56515) North & West facing
This prominent 15m feature, visible from the bunkhouse, presides over a bend in the track. It is a patchwork of slabs, ribs and walls of differing rock types split into many sections by diagonal fault-lines and grassy breaks. The northern aspect holds pleasantly angled slabs, while the west facing facets offer steeper fare in a series of bulging walls that extends for 100m. The leftmost of the westerly facing buttresses is composed of orangy rock, which has an overhanging start with an easier-angled slab above.

Eagles Dare 18m VS 4b. Roger Brown, Nicola Bassnett (alt), Amy Fuller. 25 Aug 2015.
Climb the orange roof at its widest point on adequate holds, then the clean slab above. A higher pitch can be added by scrambling down left to the base of a 4m vertical crack in a grey wall.

Wooden Wall:
(NG 61601 56515) North-West facing
This rounded 12m crozzly wall is split into two aspects by a blocky gully, giving characterful climbing on amazing knobbly folded 'wood bark' holds. Visible from the bunkhouse to the south-west, it holds a commanding position over the Big Harbour. Make a 200m bushwhack westwards from the An Teampuill track from a point just beyond The Shoulder.

Should Be 8m Diff. Mark Hudson. 28 Jun 2011.
Climb the left end of left-hand wall on huge holds.

Sticks and Stones   12m   V.Diff.   Roger Brown, Mark Hudson. 28 Jun 2011.
Take knobbly steps up the middle of the left-hand wall and the centre of the wedge above.

Would Be   12m   Severe. Mark Hudson, Roger Brown. 28 Jun 2011.
Climb up to and follow the obvious diagonal crack in the left-hand wall, then the right edge of the wedge above.

Splinter   12m   V.Diff. Mark Hudson. 28 Jun 2011.
Climb cracks, a flake and then gentler upper slabs 5m in from right end of the right-hand wall.

Lighthouse Path Areas (Northwards):
These three areas are accessed using the tracks leading northward out of Big Harbour. More remote but giving some of Rona's best rock and situations.

Meall Acairseid:
(NG 62100 57598)   NW facing
This 40m broken cliff lies on the north-west shoulder of Rona's highest hill. A clean slim face higher up gives good almost mountainous positions above a scrappier lower section. The shoulder is part-visible from the track by the Beware Block. Access by dropping down for 100m north-west from the Meall Acairseid summit, or (shorter) follow old the Acairseid Thioram track from the turbine past the Beware Block and across 3 or 4 small valleys until the face appears on the right.

Prospect of Skye   40m   Severe. Mark Hudson, Roger Brown. 27 Jun 2011.
A good exposed route once up onto the main face. Scramble to the centre of the heather ledge at 10m. Make a steep start through a light green lichenous break, moving directly up to a dark wedge slot and over two overlaps above (step right then back left). Move leftwards across the smoother upper face following a prominent break. Finish by stepping off a flake to take the final wall direct.

Open Book   12m   Diff. Mark Hudson. 15 Aug 2010.
A short shallow open-book corner at the right end of the cliff.

Extra Slab:
(NG 62511 58643)   West facing
A beautiful and secluded gritty 15m slab with a clean sweep of rock that is not too steep and highly protectable. Take the signposted footpath from 'Escape' cottage towards the lighthouse through the old Acairseid Thioram settlement. Once past the ruined community, turn northwards off the main lighthouse path onto a subsidiary path, where the cliff is soon seen nestled in trees 100m to the east of the path.

Extra Time   15m   Severe *. Mark Hudson. 29 Jun 2011.
A lovely direct climb taking the thin central cracks and overlaps.

Extra Slice   15m   V.Diff. Mark Hudson. 29 Jun 2011.
Follow cracks and overlaps 1m in from the right edge.

Satellite Cliff:

(NG 62864 59147)   West facing
A striking and remote 30m cliff with strong natural features holding some of
Rona's longest and most sustained climbs to date. Follow the signposted
lighthouse track from 'Escape' for 15–20mins beyond the old settlement and past
the Extra Slab turn-off. Once over a low wooded shoulder, the cliff is easily seen
in a prominent position on the east side of the open valley ahead and 100m east
of the track. Both routes breach the sharply-undercut base via stiff bouldery starts,
giving access to a central scoop and onto divergent natural lines that find ways
through the near-vertical walls above.

Secret Weapon   30m   E2 5c *. Nicola Bassnett, Mark Hudson. 23 Aug 2015.
A sharp pull over the shallowest point of the undercut base gains the central scoop.
Step left to climb the increasingly strenuous left-rising diagonal crack. Finish up
a clean vertical crack on the higher tier.

Satellite   30m   HVS 5b ***. Mark Hudson, Nicola Bassnett. 23 Aug 2015.
An intriguing boulder-problem start 3m right of the shallowest point allows moves
back left into the scoop. Follow the line of right-rising ramps, and then the soaring
vertical crack that runs right to the top of the cliff, with lovely VS climbing all
the way.

NORTHERN HIGHLANDS NORTH

BEINN DEARG, West Buttress:

Double Salchow   350m   IV,4. Dave McGimpsey, Andy Nisbet. 3 Mar 2016.
A continuous line of ice (and snow) which forms just right of the crest right of
Silken Ladder and left of *Peace Process*. The lower half forms in a shallow gully
with the steepest section (crux) just below a terrace. Continue slightly left and
back right on lower angled ice, finishing by a line leading left below a steep tower.

BEINN DEARG, Coire Ghranda:

Ice Bomb Direct, The Mind Bomb Finish   VIII,7. Guy Robertson, Andy Inglis,
Nick Bullock. 7 Mar 2016.
As per the original line, but on the final pitch climb the overhanging chimney-
groove direct all the way. Superb, outrageously steep and well-protected (ice
screws on the first ascent).

KLIBRECK, Creag an Lochain:

Skinny Dip   120m   V,4. Sandy Allan, Andy Nisbet. 9 Mar 2016.
An icefall which formed some 50m left of *Little Tower Gully*. Steep snow led to
a 60m pitch of ice, at times thin and serious. A large cornice was 50m away and
only passed by traversing right until beyond *The Breck* where it ended (not
included in length).

Veterans   200m   V,6. Sandy Allan, Andy Nisbet. 9 Mar 2016.
The next fault to the left of the Y-gully on the north facing cliff is blocked low
down by overhangs with a fringe of icicles. The first pitch is serious despite the
grade and the turf needs to be well frozen. Start to the right of the icicles and climb

very steep turf before traversing left across the ice line to the left edge of the fault. Climb up to cracks in the sidewall (50m). Continue up easier grooves (50m), then easing ground to the top.

KEANCHULISH INLAND CRAGS, Morning Wall:
The Deer Shoveller   15m   E5 6a. Ian Taylor, Tess Fryer. 22 Jul 2015.
A line up the left edge of the main buttress, just left of *Steel Spider*. Some poor rock in the lower section. Gain then pull over a roof to a small broken flake (Rock 1 in horizontal crack on the right). Make a long reach to better holds and continue more easily.

BEINN MÒR COIGACH, Garbh Choireachan:
West Ridge Direct   100m   III,5. John Higham, Iain Young. 27 Feb 2016.
Climb the ridge as described in the Northern Highlands North Scrambles in two and a half pitches to the main ridge. Generally straightforward ground under powder snow with a couple of technical but well protected steps.

STAC POLLAIDH, West Buttress:
Western Buttress Edge Route   120m   VI,7. John Higham, Iain Young. 26 Feb 2016.
Start at the toe of the buttress and climb via turfy grooves on the right of Baird's Pinnacle to belay in the notch between the pinnacle and the mountain. Traverse right then move up and right via short walls and corners until a traverse left can be made via a very awkward step around a nose to belay on the crest. Move up and left on easier ground to belay on slabs above the terrace. Move up and right as per the summer route until a hard move gains a belay below the fine corner described in summer (just left of the crest of the buttress). Climb this with the help of crucial turf blobs at the top, crux, then move right to the wide crack and awkward move to belay on the summit ridge. Climbed under exceptionally snowy conditions with frozen turf, though would be easier with more ice.

The Evolution of Wings   30m   E5 6a **. Ian Taylor, Tess Fryer. 27 May 2016.
A counter diagonal to the first pitch of *Walking on Air*, starting at a block just to its left. Layback up the crack above to good holds. Make a hard move up and left, then a bold section leads to good holds and gear where *Walking on Air* comes in from the right. Move right and go up to a niche, then over a final bulge to the belay. For a second pitch follow *Mid-Flight Crisis* or *Walking on Air*. Grade and stars confirmed by a second ascent.

CUL MÒR, Creag nan Calman:
Buffalo Ballet   130m   VII,7. Helen Rennard, Simon Richardson. 20 Jan 2016.
As for the summer route except the left diversion up the narrow rib on the third pitch was climbed direct over an icy overhang with a point of aid.

Coire Gorm:
The Wrecking Light   160m   VIII,7 ***. Nick Bullock, Andy Inglis, Guy Robertson. 6 Mar 2016.
An outstanding icy direct line up the imposing steep wall between *The Cul* and the massive roof section of the crag. The line is an ice streak running directly up the steep slabby wall left of the great roof, right of a big black corner-groove, and

Ian Taylor on the FA of The Evolution of Wings (E5 6a), 27 May 2016. Photo: Andy Tibbs.

left of a smaller groove immediately left of the great roof. The route may prove easier with thicker ice.

1. 40m Start up a steep turfy wall and climb up for 5m on improving ice to the base of a slim icy groove. Climb the sparsely protected groove past a number of technical and tenuous moves to a ledge.

2. 40m Step right and climb the ice streak directly to an easing in angle at 15m. Continue up easier ground for another 20m to belay on the left.

3. 50m Climb snow slopes and short tricky steps to arrive below a final steep wall with a steep ice groove leading to an icicle-ridden roof (obvious from below, and just right of a steep nose of rock).

4. 30m Climb the icy groove, then the surprisingly accommodating roof in a marvellous position, leading to easier ground and the top.

STAC POLLAIDH, The Keep:

The Monkey Puzzle 35m E2 5c. Andy Tibbs, Davy Moy. 19 Aug 2010.
Start below a steep corner between *Angus the Arsonist* and the gully.

1. 20m 5c Climb the steep corner and cracks above to a good ledge on the left.
2. 15m 5a Climb onto the large block behind the belay, then the crack above to a ledge. Finish up and rightwards passing a jutting beak of rock.

Singe 20m VS 4c. Andy Tibbs, Davy Moy. 19 Aug 2010.
The furthest right line on The Keep. Start in the gully above the ledge running underneath The Keep. Climb a slim, open slabby corner feature and steep crack to finish by easier ground on the right.

REIFF, Spaced Out Rockers Cliff:
Sgeoldair 30m E5/6 6b **. Ian Taylor, Tess Fryer. 25 Jul 2015.
Start as for *Spaced Out Rockers* and follow this left for 5m, then go up the left side of a black streak to gain a small hanging corner and a good break. Move left then run it out up the crimpy wall to another good break. Go left up through a break in the overhangs (often wet but on good holds) to a ledge and an easier finish.

Rockers – The Prequel 25m E4 5c *. Ian Taylor, Tess Fryer. 26 May 2016.
An alternative first pitch to *Spaced Out Rockers*. From the same start, follow *Aqua Rambling* up the left edge of the cave to a break, then follow this left to join *Spaced Out Rockers* at its belay.

Amphitheatre Bay:
Forty Plus 25m E4 6a *. Tess Fryer, Ian Taylor. 6 Jul 2015.
Follow *Roaring Forties* for 12m and after the moves left onto the steep arete, go up to a good break under the roof on the right. Make a footless swing right to a rest below a steep groove, then finish the groove and its left arete.

Meall an Fheadain (NB 997 110):
Just under the summit is a crag that forms a band of slabby west facing walls of lovely featured sandstone some 8m high making for easy climbing in a delightful setting. Four routes on Mod to Diff were climbed by Martin Holland on 15 Sep 2015.

ASSYNT, Creag Rodha Mòr (Super Crag):
Champagne Rhubarb, Variation Finish E2 5c **. Michael Barnard (unsec). 11 Oct 2015.
From the ledge above the flake-crack, move up to traverse the headwall on pockets, finishing as for the normal route.

Le Trip 20m E4 6a **. Tess Fryer, Ian Taylor. 7 Aug 2015.
Start as for *Ruddy Glow Corner* and where it heads left into the corner, continue up the right side of a grey block to a small ledge. Make committing moves right along a thin break to gain a vertical crack and follow this steeply to good holds and an easier finish with hairy lichen.

Carcassonne Wall (NC 0758 2412):
Approach as for Ardroe Slab past Loch Dubh crags, but don't cross the deer fence.

Carcassonne Crack 15m H.Severe 4b. Rich Abell, Tom Adams. 26 Mar 2016.
Start at a flake-like rock projecting upwards to the base of the prominent right-trending crack-line (at the right-hand side of the prominent deep bay). Climb the flake and into the crag to a good ledge, then up and slightly left over a bulge to finish up slabs and cracks.

Avignon Wall 15m VS 4c *. Rich Abell, Tom Adams. 26 Mar 2016.
Start at the closest boulders to the wall to the left of the deep bay. Climb the wall, steeply at first, to reach small ledges. Go up the crack on the right, then move slightly left to another crack. Finish directly.

Langres Ledge   15m   HVS 5b *. Rich Abell, Tom Adams. 26 Mar 2016.
The obvious right-trending ledge line to the right of a slab bounding the left edge
of the highest section of crag. Climb the ledge to a bulge at its end (maybe wet).
Go up and slightly right with a couple of tricky moves to reach easier ground.

Clean Cut (Achmelvich):
Michael Barnard notes that a huge block has come off the cliff. The block formed
the side walls and arete between *Snappy Carrot* and *Calypso*, so these routes may
not be climbable now (or at least will be very different, both climbing and
probably grade-wise). No other routes are affected, though *Flawless* no longer
climbs 'the second arete from the left'.

QUINAG, Bucket Buttress:
MacFearsome Sisters   40m   VI,6. Pete MacPherson, John Lyall. 20 Jan 2016.
An eliminate but good route, with the hard climbing being new. Climb the crux
wall of *Bounty Hunter*, then the smooth corner on the right wall to join *Pick'n'Mix*.
Follow this to easier ground, then go up through the final wall on the right of a
roof.
Note: *Bounty Hunter* was thought much harder than the given III,5. More like
IV/V,5/6.

The Frontline   Severe. Michael Barnard. 29 May 2016.
As for winter, but finishing as for the next route.

Hell in a Bucket   45m   VS 4c *. Michael Barnard. 29 May 2016.
Climbs the wall between *The Frontline* and *Brendan Voyage*. From the ledge
above it, step right to take the continuation crack of *Kane Mutiny*, then step right
again to finish up a short arete.

Brendan Voyage   H.Severe 4b *. Michael Barnard. 29 May 2016.
As for winter, up cracks in the wall. From the base of the chimney, step left to
instead climb the arete to the ledge. Finish as for the above.

Kane Mutiny   V.Diff. Michael Barnard. 29 May 2016.
As for winter, starting up the groove on the right.

Skull Buttress:
This is the square-cut crag overhanging the gully on the left side of the next
buttress right of Barrel Buttress. When viewed from the top of Barrel Buttress
(recommended on first acquaintance) the cliff resembles a huge human skull. On
all the routes a shorter, easier introductory pitch leads to broken ledges below a
long and sustained second pitch up the headwall. The climbing on the headwall
is strikingly different to any of the other big sandstone cliffs in the North-West,
with no rounded features, no jamming, but lots of thin hairline cracks, crimps,
slots and flatties. The rock is generally excellent, with all routes cleaned
extensively prior to their first ascents. It would be possible to approach from the
north (shorter but boggy) but arguably better just to go over the top (about 1hr
45mins on a good path). The cliff faces north so a good spell of warm dry weather
is needed.

Jurassic Spark 60m E6/7. Guy Robertson, Jason Currie. Jul 2015.
The inaugural route provides a superb sustained outing more or less directly up the centre of the cliff. Take lots of micro wires and micro cams, but still expect to be running it out high up. Start at the col below the lower buttress.
1. 25m 5c Climb up for a few metres until an obvious line of big footholds leading out left can be gained. Follow these hard left to gain the left-slanting crack on the left edge of the cliff and follow this with interest over a bulge until a tricky move gains a good ledge. Turn the nose on the right directly and on up to a commodious block seat.
2. 35m 6b Move directly up to the base of the headwall, then left to stand on a large protruding hold. Climb directly for a couple of metres then step right onto the black wall and climb straight up again (bold) to gain the first break. Follow this right to a thin crack, just left of the obvious groove. Climb the crack up to where a perplexing move left gains better holds and a good flake which leads up to the next break. Climb the dwindling crack with increasing difficulty to a good hold from where a long stretch up right leads to improving holds and the final break. Take a deep breath, then forge directly up the thin white flake feature above to a final hard move rightwards just below the top.

Primal Dream 60m E5. Guy Robertson, Pete Herd. 6 Jun 2016.
The easiest line on the wall is also the slowest to dry, but arguably the best! Takes the obvious staggered cracks just right of centre on the headwall.
1. 25m 6a As for *Land of the Lost and Found*, pitch 1, but belay directly below the obvious black crack.
2. 35m 6a Follow the crack to a rest at the first break. Climb the right rib of the groove, then swing right to gain another thin crack which leads up right to the next break below the final soaring crack. Follow this (crux) into a short corner and so to the top.

Land of the Lost and Found 60m E7. Guy Robertson, Adam Russell. Sep 2015.
Another stunning route, taking the immaculate smooth wall left of the right arete. Start as for the previous route.
1. 25m 6a Climb directly up, then trend left to below the obvious stepped black groove which is climbed with some difficulty. Continue up over ledges to belay below a tiny corner at the base of the headwall, a few metres right of a black crack.
2. 35m 6b/c Stand on the block below the corner and stretch right to place a good small wire in the crack up and right. Climb boldly right past this to good holds and protection on the arete, then step back left and follow a faint groove more or less directly to a huge rough hold at the first break. Make a tricky move up right to gain another faint groove (RPs out right) which is followed to big flat holds which lead strenuously to the next break. Go left a short way to gain a rattling flake; stand on this and follow thin cracks to niche and block. Make hard moves past this (crux) to the upper break then pull out right to ledges. Easier cracks on the right lead up and then back left to the top.

SCOURIE CRAGS, Telegraph Crag:
The following routes lie at the right end of the main crag.

Private Investigations 15m VS 4c. Michael Barnard. 15 Aug 2015.
A shallow right-facing corner, finishing up the corner above.

Calling Elvis   15m   VS 4c. Michael Barnard. 15 Aug 2015.
The crack just to the right. The upper crack is loose and best avoided via a traverse into *Private Investigations*.

Note: *Telegraph Road* should read 'the crack 5m further right' (not 10m). Also the traverse for the descent is nowhere near 100m and just saying 'at the right end of the crag' would probably suffice.

FAR NORTH-WEST CRAGS, Creag nam Phreasain Challtuinne, Hazel Crag (SMCJ 2013):

Grasshopper   12m   VS 4c *. Jonathan & Diana Preston. 30 Sep 2015.
The slanting crack-line left of *Old Wrinkly* (cleaned).

Note: *Old Wrinkly* is also 12m and other routes are shorter than recorded, also thought to be about a grade easier than recorded in SMCJ 2013 pp500–01.

SHEIGRA, Second Geo:

Rhapsody in Blue   35m   E3 5c **. Robert Durran, Jerry Handren. 27 Jul 2015.
Abseil to the lower tidal ledge below the start of *Above the Blue*. Hand-traverse a small ramp leftwards onto the steep wall. Go up at its end, then traverse hard left to gain an obvious blunt spike. Climb steeply up the left side of the wall passing a ledge on the left to finish more easily up *Right-Hand Buttress*.

FOINAVEN, Lord Reay's Seat:

Note: Erick Baillot & Dave Kerr climbed *Fishmonger* on 16 Jan 2016, following close to the summer route instead of the more direct original line. They named it the *Misplaiced Variation*.

BEN HOPE:

Viking Ridge   600m   II. Andy Nisbet, Steve Perry. 18 Jan 2016.
The next ridge right of *Tower Ridge*. The line of least resistance was taken, while trying to stay as near the crest as was sensible. Climbed under deep snow. There was one move on the crest at about two-thirds height which was more suited to a route of Grade III.

Valhalla   600m   III,4. Andy Nisbet, Steve Perry. 19 Jan 2016.
Two main ridges right again (ignoring a minor one immediately right of *Tower Ridge*). This ridge has a triangular lower section with two legs which join below a steep slab high up. Start over a short, steep turfy wall to easy ground which leads to below the steep face between the two legs. Move out right to the right leg and climb just right of its crest to gain the crest higher up. Follow this to a lower angled section below the steep slab. Pass this on the left, close to the gully on the left, before returning right as soon as possible to an upper section of ridge, which formed a prominent skyline from the north end of Dubh-loch na Beinne. This was climbed by a snow grooves and a ramp leading right to finish just right of the crest.

Valkyrie   600m   IV,3. Sandy Allan, Andy Nisbet, Steve Perry. 21 Jan 2016.
A ridge three to the right of *Valhalla* has an apparent tower at half-height, although there is no col behind it, only a level section. This route follows a well defined gully to its left, and the steeper left branch where it splits. The gully provided

three water ice pitches low down followed by snow leading to the branch. The left branch contained a 30m snow-ice pitch up a slabby wall (no protection due to conditions) followed by several smaller pitches separated by steep snow and leading to the top.

South Tower Ridge   400m   III. Andy Nisbet, Steve Perry. 13 Feb 2016.
The ridge with the apparent tower, which actually angles back to a col and is well seen as a steep wall when approaching from the south. The initial slopes were easy by a zigzag line and not included in the length. The tower was climbed by a line near its left side followed by a diagonal line rightwards still on the steep face. An upper ridge was climbed fairly direct.

Freya   300m   III. Andy Nisbet. 11 Mar 2016.
After two more ridges which join high up, is this substantial gully. The first pitch was a waterfall but easily avoided by traversing in from the left on a deer track. Another wet pitch was passed by heather on the left, after which the gully was joined; the length starts from here. Snow and small ice pitches led to a big ice pitch, started on the left. Snow led to a fork; the left branch was taken. More snow gained another significant ice pitch, followed by icy runnels direct to the top.

Harpie   500m   III,4. Andy Nisbet, Steve Perry. 15 Feb 2016.
After the gully above and a ridge with a large steep triangular base, is this less steep but continuous ridge. There were two short tricky steps but the ridge was largely Grade II and perhaps should be graded that.

Valentine's Ridge   500m   IV,5. Andy Nisbet, Steve Perry. 14 Feb 2016.
The last ridge on the face, although still with steep ground on its right. Start close to the gully on its left and climb a big corner before exiting right along a ledge. After easy ground, climb a turfy groove some 25m right of the gully. Go up to a steep triangular buttress which abuts the main upper section of ridge and climb its left edge. Move left along the first ledge on the wide upper section and climb a tricky short wall and easier grooves (50m). Climb a steep groove and easier walls to a terrace (50m). Continue up steep but easier ground to move right on a terrace below a large, steep upper slab (60m). Climb this by a line of weakness near its right end before moving left to and finishing up the crest (60m).

PORT VASGO:
This is a site of the Scottish Primrose and while climbers may not do any harm, try not to disturb the ground at the cliff-top. The comment in the guide, 'Most of the crag does not warrant climbing' turns out not to be true. The existing routes *Faith Pays Dividends* (E1 5a) and *Revelation* (E1 5b) were thought to be E2 5b and E2 (or E3) 5c, but worth their stars. Some 100m east of these routes is an amazing prow. The rock is slightly soft but solid where weathered by the sea. The routes are described from the existing routes eastwards, although it may be easier to find the prow first.

The east side of the arete of *Faith Pays Dividends* is an overhanging wall bounded by a big gully. The following four routes are on a wall which lies east of the gully. The wall is topped by stacked flakes which are more solid than they look but still require care. Approach by abseil to ledges near the sea.

Primrose Edge   35m   VS 4b. Andy Nisbet, Steve Perry. 7 Aug 2015.
The right arete of the wall, adjacent to the big gully, is climbed fairly directly.

Kong   35m   E1 5a. Andy Nisbet, Steve Perry. 7 Aug 2015.
A shallow crack-line in the centre of the wall; further left is overhanging. Start up
a red slab, then more broken ground to reach the crack-line. Moves are made on
the left low down and on the right high up for an exciting finish.

Stac Beag Slab   45m   VS. Ian Butterworth, Gerald O'Neil. 6 Aug 1970.
A serious second pitch which is not technically difficult but needs treating with
care. Start below the right-hand side of an obvious flat-topped pillar.
1. 20m Ascend the groove on the right of the pillar to the large ledge at the top.
2. 25m Traverse left to the centre of the slab, then make an ascending traverse
back right to finish up the loose gangway. Loose and unprotected.

Stac Beag Direct   35m   VS 4c. Nick & Diane Burton, Ian Butterworth. 1976.
A better finish. As for *Stac Beag Slab* to the flat-topped pillar (20m). Climb the
steep shallow groove above (15m).

The following routes are reached by a 30m abseil down the corner on the west
side of the prow. For the first two, traverse west at high tide level round an arete
to below an alcove.

Brooklyn Bridge   50m   E1 5b. Steve & Katie Perry. 15 Jul 2015.
Climb up into the alcove. Move out right to traverse along the lip of a cave before
going up the top of the flat-topped pillar (35m 5b). Finish up the shallow groove
as for *Stac Beag Direct* (15m 4c).

Rockyfeller   35m   E1 5b. Andy Nisbet, Katie & Steve Perry. 16 Jul 2015.
Climb up into the alcove and start out right as for *Brooklyn Bridge* until below a
flake-line leading to a roof. Gain the flake-line (crux) and follow it to the roof.
Pass the roof on the right and go up to a ledge. Finish direct up the railed wall
above, no protection but 4b.

Central Perk   30m   VS 4b. Andy Nisbet, Katie & Steve Perry. 16 Jul 2015.
A line right of the corner which forms the right edge of the prow. Start just to its
right and climb up slanting rightwards to reach the rib left of a groove. Climb the
rib leftwards to finish up the next break right of the corner.

*California Gurl*s   30m   VS 4c. Katie Perry, Steve Perry, Andy Nisbet. 15 Jul
2015.
The corner itself is helpful, mostly well protected and not as hard as it looks.
Climb fairly directly to and up the corner.

Eleutheria   35m   E6 6a ****. Jules Lines. 19 Jul 2015.
A mind blowing climb up the full height of the main arete. Careful rope
management required. E5 climbing with E7 intimidation. Start on a ledge above
sea-level and below the fin. Climb up easily into the corner and traverse along
the lip of the blade (large cams) to a stopping place in the base of the arete (good
medium cams). Launch up the wildly overhanging arete on good holds to a good
rest on the arete. Climb the arete on the right past some cam placements in

horizontal slots, to another rest. Continue up the very crest, finishing on the right side.

Burn Brooklyn Burn 30m E5 6a **. Jules Lines, Steve & Katie Perry. 16 Jul 2015.
A relentless climb up the centre of the wall.
1. 15m 4a Climb up easily into the corner (*California Gurls*) and belay on a ledge near the base of the corner.
2. 15m 5c Step up and move diagonally left to gain a pocket come pod (large cam). Move up and right and back left to more protection (small cams). Move steeply up the wall to a good hold beneath a bulge and central crack above. Climb the crack (rock 3) to the deep break and exit up and left into a notch. Another arm pumping climb with no hard moves, although the best holds will take time to find on first acquaintance.

The Statue of Liberty 35m E4 5c ***. Jules Lines, Steve Perry. 15 Jul 2015.
The most amenable climb to take on the challenge of the blade.
1. 15m 4a Climb easily up into the corner to belay on a ledge.
2. 20m 5c Climb the corner for 3m to gain an obvious handrail/ traverse line that cuts across the wall (medium cams). Near the end of the traverse, go slightly down on a set of small finger rails to a rest on the arete (gear in the rail on the right). Climb the arete direct and move up to another rest (small cam on the left). Climb a vague groove in the left side of the arete to finish.

Libertas 35m H.Severe 4a. Andy Nisbet, Katie & Steve Perry. 15 Jul 2015.
A line up slabbier ground left of the prow, but with little protection. Start at the base of the abseil, below the right side of the roof which forms the base of the prow. Slant up leftwards until at the left end of the roof. Continue leftwards up a ramp and finish straight up.

Immediately east of the wall with the prow is a buttress semi-detached from the mainland. Looking from near the top of the prow is a face with a big roof near its top. Approach the buttress by a long step across the gap with the mainland. The first route was reached by scrambling down and across big slabby ramps on the north side before traversing round on to the west face (Diff). The next two routes were reached by a direct abseil.

Skull Island 20m VS 4c. Andy Nisbet, Steve Perry. 7 Aug 2015.
The left side of the face. Start from a ledge about 6m above high tide level. Climb up to the traverse ledge and continue up a crack-line which passes through small roofs between bigger roofs, also right of a prominent protruding block (a useful feature if a direct abseil approach is chosen).

Satari 25m E1 5b. Andy Nisbet, Steve Perry. 7 Aug 2015.
A parallel line to the right takes a crack-line through two roofs and passes some 2m left of the big roof. Start from a ledge just above high tide level and below another big roof well below the high one. Climb a wall to pass left of the lower big roof and climb the crack-line.

High Line 25m H.Severe 4a. Andy Nisbet, Steve Perry. 7 Aug 2015.
A spectacular line for the grade passing just right of the big upper roof. Start from

a ledge about 5m above high tide level. Move left into an open corner which starts at the right end of the lower big roof. Climb this and trend left to gain a shallow slot which leads past the upper roof to an easier finish.

Bronxie   20m   E1 5b. Andy Nisbet, Katie & Steve Perry. 15 Jul 2015.
A right-leaning corner line seen looking about 100m east from the top of the prow. This is beyond the above buttress and a deep geo with poor rock. The corner is towards the right end of a wall but an obvious ramp leading towards its base doesn't reach and an abseil approach down the line is required.

Harbour Wall:
(NC 586 650)   West facing   Non-tidal
A west facing wall some 200m east of the road end. Its top is visible from the parking spot but not obvious. Follow a signed path to approach the wall from above. The rock is a little soft.

Grid Iron   15m   HVS 4c. Andy Nisbet, Steve Perry. 10 Sep 2015.
A flake-line near the left edge of the wall, just before it turns into a north-facing wall. Climb a small right-facing flake to easier ground.

Saga Lout   15m   VS 4c. Andy Nisbet, Steve Perry. 10 Sep 2015.
Start in the centre of the wall. Gain a flaky ledge, move left, then up to finish more easily.

Mindfields   10m   VS 4b. Andy Nisbet, Steve Perry. 10 Sep 2015.
Climb a vague crack-line 3m left of the wall end.

Spectre   10m   4a. Andy Nisbet, Steve Perry. 10 Sep 2015.
The right edge of the wall. Unprotected.

Brown Slab:
(NC 584 651)   South-East facing   Non-tidal
At the landward end of the first big inlet west of the parking place is a slabby wall of brown rock, steeper at the base.

Stooky Bill   25m   Severe 4a. Andy Nisbet, Steve Perry. 10 Sep 2015.
Low down on the left side of the wall is a prominent left-slanting flake-line. Gain and climb this (easier than it looks) to the upper slabs. Finish just left of a roof.

Eat, Sleep, Climb, Repeat   25m   VS 4b. Andy Nisbet, Steve Perry. 10 Sep 2015.
Gain and follow the short, right to left rising ramp to its end before moving back right onto the main slab. Climb straight up and finish on the right of the smaller roof.

LATHERONWHEEL, Peninsula Wall:
Arch Villain   15m   VS 5a. Eleonora Di Cuffa, Andy Nisbet, Steve Perry. 17 Apr 2016.
Based on the arete left of *Positive Mental Attitude*. Start left of the arete inside the first arch and climb a wall to near a roof. Step round the right side of the arete and climb steeply to and past the roof to a short arete to finish.

The Old Man of Hoy, Spring Bank Holiday, 2016. Andrew Wielochowski leads the main pitch of the Original Route (E1 5b). Photo: Noel Williams.

Sedimentary Ambitions   12m   VS 4b *. Steve Perry, Sarah Sigley. 13 Jun 2016.
On the south side of *Reach for the Sky* is a corner leading to a triangular roof with
a soaring arete above. Climb the corner and pull over the roof on jugs. Follow the
arete and move left at the top to belay. Well protected but easy to escape.

Bedrock Area:
Dino Saurus   12m   V.Diff *. Sarah Sigley, Steve Perry. 13 Jun 2016.
Three metres left of the Bedrock area descent is a slabby scoop. Climb onto a
small ledge low down and follow a faint crack-line leading to a steep headwall
which finishes right of the highest block.

ORKNEY, Old Man of Hoy:
Space Station Finish   25m   E1 5b ***. Dan Moore, Shauna Clarke. 17 Aug 2015.
From the belay at the bottom of the final corner pitch of the *Original Route*; climb
up onto the left wall of the corner and gain an obvious left-trending flake line.
Follow this, then move left and up to a wide crack in the bulging wall above. Gain
a thin crack on the right and make tricky moves up the wall to gain a good foot
ledge below two parallel hand cracks. Climb these, then move right to a wide
crack and continue more easily to the top. Very well protected.

Rora Head, Sandy Bay:
Happy Idiots   80m   HVS. Ian Parnell, Gary Panes. 20 Sep 2015.
Midway between Mucklehouse Wall and the southern tip of Rora Head lies a bay
with a square-cut promontory defining its western side. This route climbs the
easiest line up the southern face of that promontory. Good rock, gear and a nice
adventurous feel make this route a good second route for those who've travelled
to tick the Old Man. Two old pieces of gear were found indicating that the top
two pitches may have been climbed before. The grassy rake under the promontory
accessed by abseil leads to the boulder beach. Start around on the west (seaward)
side where a short wall of good rock extends from the foot of the main cliff.
1. 25m 4b Climb an obvious right-facing groove starting just to its left to gain
the big ledge. Follow a series of steps to the base of a yellow corner with several
cracks in its left wall.
2. 15m 5a Climb a combination of the cracks to a steepening. Traverse right to
gain another big ledge and belay 5m back at a small pillar with an old in-situ
thread.
3. 15m 4c Climb a layback flake and a shallow cracked groove and belay at the
right-hand end of the ledge (signs of old tat).
4. 25m 4c Climb the crack in the eastern wall of the promontory.

Yesnaby, The Black Dyke:
Damp Wa   20m   E4 5c *. Tim Rankin, Scott Johnston. 4 Aug 2015.
A serious route climbing the centre of the wall. Abseil to the right end of the long
black ledge and belay from the rope. Move up right below a roof to a good break,
then boldly climb the right-facing groove above to a precarious step up to the
large roof. Step left and cross the roof to gain and climb the steep slanting corner-
line to finish. Inspected on abseil.

NORTHERN HIGHLANDS CENTRAL

BEINN A' MHUINIDH, Bonaid Dhonn:

North by Northwest, alternative start 40m E7 6b ***. Dave MacLeod. 7 Jun 2016.
A logical single pitch version of the route with an exciting start along the lip of the roof guarding entry to the main wall above. Start up the slab and break left up a short wall to the right edge of the roof. Swing along this on a big break and move steeply up on good holds to gain the parent route at the spike at the base of the crack.

Bonebag 120m Severe 4a **. Ewan Lyons. 11 Feb 2015.
Beyond the large bay to the left of *Route I* is a steep wall with a prominent right-facing corner containing a holly tree. Start below the large corner but trend left then back right to gain the left arete, aiming for a much smaller hanging corner. Climb this and a short slab to a heather ledge above the large corner. Pull up to a hidden groove, exit this and climb shattered cracks to easier ground. Cross *Route II* and follow a rib below a large corner with a smooth wall on the left containing an obvious overhang on the right side. Climb pink rock on the right side of the wall passing the overhang on the right to a corner. Climb this, step left to the continuation groove which leads to a smooth rib leading right to a heather ledge, and finish by the blocky arete on the left. Be careful of some loose rock here and there.

Murdoch Jamieson on the second ascent of North by North West on the Bonaid Dhonn with the eastern peaks of Beinn Eighe in the background. Photo: Iain Small.

THE GREAT DUNDONNELL SLAB:

Sandstone Tango 100m HVS 5a **. John Mackenzie, Andrew James. 27 May 2016.

A fine route on excellent clean rock that climbs the discontinuous flakes and cracks near the right-hand side of the lower and upper tiers. Start below a short corner-crack well right of the start of *Longer, Steeper, Better* and below a small overhang bottoming a prominent boss of rock.

1. 30m 4c Move up to the overhang and climb the flake-crack on the right of the boss to a small ledge. Move up the slab to gain the next crack on the right of a smaller boss to its crest. Traverse right to a stance at the base of a deep crack.
2. 20m 4c Climb the deep crack to its short capping wall which was wet on this occasion and graded as such, probably 4b if dry. Belay on the tree above.
3. 50m 5a Move 7m right to below a fine slab right of the cracks and pillar taken by *Longer, Steeper, Better*. Climb up to a ledge and a blind crack. Step right to another and continue up and left to ledges. Step up right onto the excellent upper slab and friction up this aiming for a straight crack which is to the right of the slanting crack taken by the top pitch of *Longer, Steeper, Better*. The slab steepens below the crack which once reached leads to a heather cornice and the fixed abseil point above. A fine if bold pitch on clean rock.

   Either descend from the Terrace or continue up the top two pitches of *Longer, Steeper, Better*.

STONE VALLEY CRAGS AREA, Meall an Triubhais Dhuibh, Lily Lochan Crag:

Crack n'Slab Variation 22m H.Severe 4b. Andrew James, John Mackenzie. 2 Apr 2016.

Instead of climbing the crack in the second tier, take the clean wall to its left at the same grade and reach the base of the upper slab directly.

Arete and Crack 22m HVS 5b *. John Mackenzie, Andrew James. 2 Apr 2016.

To the right of the start of *Crack n' Slab* is a corner. Climb its right-hand edge to the base of a thin curving crack just left of a wider wet crack. Climb the thin crack with interest, well protected, to the right side of the easy slab above, up which the climb finishes.

RUBHA REIDH:

A small inlet at the north end of the lighthouse car park has some non-tidal buttresses. The first small buttress on the right after the descent gives:

Chicken Run 14m E1 5c. Nicky Bassnett, Roger Brown. 26 Oct 1999.

The finger crack left of centre provides well protected but sustained climbing.

GRUINARD BAY CRAGS, Riverside Slabs:

Winking Crack 15m Severe. Davy Moy, Kenny Summers. 14 May 2016.

Take the same start as *Blues Before Sunrise* but go straight up the large dirty crack, heading for a large orange spike. Go to the left of this and up the wall above.

Creag Càrn an Lochan Duibh:

White Stripe 45m VS 4c **. Tom Adams, Colin Abernethy. 28 Mar 2016.

Start up the glacis as for *Pink Streak* but diverge left up a vague rib between the heather ledge and the pink streak. After steepening ground, climb a crack topped

by a small heather clump and continue direct past the left side of small overlaps to reach the diagonal crack of *Pink Streak* near its top. Finish by this route.
Note: *Pink Streak* was considered worth two stars (agreed, Ed).

GOAT CRAG:
Sun Rays 7a **. Ian Taylor. Oct 2015.
Follow *Between the Monsoons* to bolt 4, then take the right-hand line of bolts to a high finish up the rough slab.

GLEN CANNICH, Creag a' Chaorainn (NH 168 338):
Don't Forget the Joker 200m IV,4. Mick James, Graham Stein. 1 Jan 2016.
Viewed from the outflow of Loch Tuill Bhearnach, there is a prominent snow bay towards the left of the crag. This route takes the first shallow turfy corner that breaks out from the far right side of the bay. Climb the corner on mainly moderate ground, passing two short steep steps (130m). Climb easier ground above by the line of least resistance to the top (70m).

STRATHCONON, Creag Achadh an Eas:
A remarkable chasm of icefalls lies on the north-western slopes of Creag Achadh an Eas at the head of Strathconon (NH 212 503), alt 400m.
   Approach from the end of Strathconon car park, walk past Scardroy and cross the River Meig at Corriefeol. The amphitheatre is found in the Allt Coire Dhughaill gorge. The lower burn is chaotic and level and blocked by obstacles. On this occasion an exposed traverse was made along the true right bank to a point where it was possible to descend to the main burn. This was crossed to a subsidiary one and a spur climbed up and over to the main burn where only then can the amphitheatre be seen. It is split into two by a narrow fin of rock and this ascent took the straight right branch which has a vertical right-retaining wall festooned with icicles along its entire length. An icefall forms close to the right wall giving the route below. A good period of frost is needed to bring into acceptable condition. A possibly easier alternative lies to its left but is rocky and probably rarely gets iced.

Dougal's Chasm 140m IV,4 **. John Mackenzie, Andrew James. 20 Jan 2016.
1. 30m Easy ice or turf to a cave pitch.
2. 45m Steep ice over and up steep steps to the top where a left traverse was made to a small fallen birch tree.
3. 35m Easily up the gully to a seeming exit on turf or ice.
4. 30m On this ascent the right wall was climbed to the top.
A tortuous descent was made down the cut-up slopes of Creag Coire na Feola, avoiding further minor ravines. A better exit would be to climb the true right bank to a much more straightforward and quicker descent.

Creag Ruadh, 740m Top, North-East Face (NH 272 544):
Creag Ruadh Buttress 105m II/III. Andrew James, John Mackenzie. 9 Jan 2016.
A smaller buttress lies near the right end of the crag ribs, identified by a tapering groove on the right side and a pointed block up and right just beyond. Hard initially, then easier; the first and last pitches are good.
1. 25m Climb the groove which steepens and narrows near the top to a nut belay above.

2. 50m Climb easily and directly above to a rib which is taken on turfy ground to below a steeper headwall.
3. Move up to the headwall and climb this centrally via steps to the top.

MOY ROCK:
Little Squeezer 6c+. Andy Tibbs (bolted Ian Taylor). 12 Jun 2016.
Between *Little Teaser* and *Pulling on Pebbles*.

STRUIE HILL CRAG:
Davy Moy & Dave Allan did 10 new climbs in Aug and Sep 2015, and thought the crag was much better than the guidebook says. The following is a new write-up.

This unusually good conglomerate crag is visible above the B9176 'Struie' road between Alness and Ardgay. Travelling from the south, park in a large pull-in on the left just past the crag where the road bends to the right. Walk 130m further up the road, then take a path up to the crag passing to the left of the pine trees, 20mins.

Grey Slab Gully 25m Diff.
Climb the gully on the left of the first clean face.

RP Slab 20m HVS 5a **.
Climb the smooth wall about 1m right of the gully, then trend right to finish up the left-facing corner-crack. About 5 micronuts or RPs are needed to protect the first half of this climb.

Austerity Wall 20m HVS 5a *.
Start 2m right of the last climb and go up to the left side of the block. Cross the bulge about 2m left of the block and finish up the right-hand crack.

Alcove Slab 20m VS 4c.
Right of the prow climb a shallow corner and a V-shaped overhang, then a slab and a steep corner.

Pink Slab 20m V.Diff *.
Climb the fine pink slab to the right of the last climb, surmount the overlap and continue up the slab.

Jungle Jim 25m Diff.
This climbs the big left-facing corner at the right side of the slabs or the slabs to its left. Start up a sometimes wet chimney.

Achilles Chiel 20m VS 4c **.
Climb a left-slanting rib then a short arete to a slab. Trend rightwards to finish by a miniature right-facing corner.

Archimedes Flakes 25m Severe **.
The obvious two flakes and wide crack to finish.

Socrates Chimney 25m VS 4c *.
The chimney-corner left of the big overhangs.

Hairy Eyrie   20m   E1 5b *.
This climb takes the high corner right of the big overhangs. Start on a block
beneath a blunt arete and follow cracks over an overlap, then move left and up
the corner.

Grey Slab   20m   VS 4c.
Further right and left of a wet streak (Struie Icefall), climb the grey wall to a
pocket. Move right then back left. At the chimney step left to easier ground.

Struie Icefall   25m   III,4.
Some winters this short steep ice pitch forms and is visible from the road. Climb
it and the heathery corner above.

About 20m further right is an area of fairly clean orange rock with three corners.

Pensioners' Partypiece   25m   HVS 5a *.
Climb a few metres up the first corner to beneath a sloping overhang. Move right
2m, ascend 3m, then step back left round a bulge. Ascend more easily to a slab
beneath a steep wall. Traverse left and climb a short chimney to easier ground.

Copernicus Corner   25m   Severe **.
Just right of the last climb, go up easily to the start of the fine open corner/groove.
Climb the corner to the notch, then step right onto the arete and climb blocks to
easier ground.

137 Not Out   25m   Severe.
The next and last steep corner to the right, the short corner above, then the corner
system above that.

NORTHERN HIGHLANDS SOUTH

LADHAR BHEINN, Spider Buttress:
Tir na h-aoise   400m   VI,6. Simon Richardson, Roger Webb. 25 Feb 2016.
A natural line of weakness zigzagging up the centre of the buttress between *Tir
na Og* and *Face Route*. The highlight is the barrel-shaped wall at mid-height on
the face.
1. 60m Gain the central snowfield from the left as for the alternative start to *Face
Route*.
2. and 3. 100m Continue directly up the snowfield to its top and climb the tapering
right-slanting gully, which begins just right of the icefall of *Tir na Og*, to where
it narrows.
4. 60m Break out right of the gully onto the barrel-shaped wall and climb steep
slabs via isolated blobs of turf and some ice before trending back left to the top
of the tapering gully. Follow this to the hidden left-slanting gully that cuts through
the upper half of the barrel-shaped wall. A serious pitch.
5. 50m Climb the slanting gully to the diagonal fault-line that crosses the upper
face.
6. 60m Follow the fault to belay just before the exit gully of *Face Route*.
7. and 8. 70m Climb mixed ground and snow slopes trending left away from *Face
Route*, to finish at the top of the buttress.

A' CHRALAIG, Lochan na Cralaig:

Poseidon   120m   III,5. Andy Nisbet, Steve Perry, Jonathan Preston. 10 Feb 2016.
The ridge right of the descent gully has a spectacular prow and right of this is a hanging ramp. Start up a lower ridge until below the prow (unfortunately escapable easily into the gully here). Make a cramped traverse right under the steep wall below the ramp and return back left into its base. Climb the ramp and a short wall on the left to finish.

The Creel   120m   III. Andy Nisbet, Steve Perry. 10 Feb 2016.
At the right end of the cliff is a right-curving snow gully (Grade I). This route follows the gully until an exposed ramp leads out left between two steep iced slabs.

Shielfish   120m   III. Jonathan Preston. 10 Feb 2016.
Start up the snow gully but take a steeper and more direct line on the right. Cross the gully and finish up turfy walls high on the left.

BEINN FHADA, Coire an Sgairne:

Cailleach   160m   V,5. Andy Nisbet, Masa Sakano. 7 Mar 2016.
The first gully right of the diagonal fault right of the big steep wall (*Banshee* starts up this fault but leaves it lower down). Start right of the fault and follow the gully to near its top (50m). A short steep ice pitch leads into the fault (50m). Finish up it (60m).

Countryman   120m   IV,4. Andy Nisbet, Masa Sakano. 7 Mar 2016.
An ice line which forms fairly regularly on the right side of the leftmost buttress (with *World's End*). Start just right of the toe of the buttress and follow ice left of a chimney, then above it to the left end of a terrace (40m). Climb the continuation iced groove for about 10m, then exit right up a slab. Move up on turfy ground, then return left to a ramp which leads rightwards up the steep sidewall of the buttress. Follow this to a ledge (50m). Continue up the ramp to a ledge, follow this rightwards and finish on to the slope above the crag (30m).

Edge of Beyond   50m   VS 4c *. Steve Perry, Andy Nisbet. 3 Nov 2015.
The arete right of *World's End*, gained by abseil from the top. It gave a sustained but serious climb with fine positions. The top of the arete is best reached by a grass rake trending up rightwards from the base of *World's End*. From a grass ledge, gain and climb the arete on its left side for 25m before crossing over to the right, then immediately back left and upwards to a small awkward roof with a wide flared crack beneath it. Climb the roof to a ledge and step left to finish past a horizontal flake in the final headwall.

MORUISG, The Great Grey Slab:

Tapering Slab   70m   V.Diff *. John Lyall. 13 Aug 2015.
The inset tapering slab on the left wall of the main slabs is followed to its end, then the edge on the left is gained and a narrow ridge leads to the top.

Tapestry   70m   Severe *. John Lyall. 13 Aug 2015.
On the first big slab left of the main slabs. Start where a tongue of rock sticks out from the lower wall, and use this to gain the slab above, then follow the edge to

a point where it takes a turn right. Go straight up the clean slab, between two thin cracks, and finish by the left ridge.

Scaled Slab 70m VS 4b *. John Lyall. 13 Aug 2015.
The second slab left of the big slabs, starting a couple of moves up the corner on the right. Follow the rib for a short way, then move left and up a shallow right-facing corner, then straight up the clean slab and final crest. Good after a loose start.
Note: This may be on the same slab as *A Right Guddle*, but keeping left of it most of the way.

Mangled Rib 70m Severe. Michael Barnard. 5 Jun 2016.
Left of *A Right Guddle* are two other main arete lines. This route takes the rib to their right.

Great Grey Shrike 75m VS 4b. John Lyall. 13 Aug 2015.
The third slab left of the main slabs. Start on the left of the lower wall. Traverse delicately right above this to gain the edge, which is followed to finish by a jamming crack.

Living Wreck 70m VS 4c. Michael Barnard. 5 Jun 2016.
The left-hand arete, taking in a couple of good sections of climbing. Climb directly up the blank slab near the base and continue more easily to below an obvious mucky corner. The clean edge immediately to its left provides the other interesting section.

Throw-Away Slab 50m Diff. Michael Barnard. 5 Jun 2016.
The shorter wide slab up and left of the other routes.

BEINN BHAN, Coire na Poite:
Wall of the Early Morning Light, Direct Start 170m V,5. Dave McGimpsey, Andy Nisbet, Steve Perry. 5 Mar 2016.
A direct but right-slanting succession of grooves runs the whole height of the cliff. The upper half is *WOEML* and a complete ascent makes a 360m natural line. Start up ice right of *The Cooler* to below the first main groove (55m). Climb the groove (60m). The next groove forks and the right branch (a steep iced corner) was climbed, returning slightly left to the main line and joining *WOEML* (55m). A wide groove (60m) followed by right traverse gains a huge groove. Climb this part way (60m), then to its top (30m), from where snow leads to the top (40m).

Coire an Fhamhair:
Nam Famhairean 410m VII,7. Malcolm Bass, Neil Silver, Simon Yearsley. 13 Feb 2016.
A big route. Takes a rising line into the centre of the face between *Der Riesenwand* and *Gully of the Gods*, before moving right from *Der Riesenwand* and accepting the challenge of the upper wall.
1. 40m Walk left along the ledge from left of *Gully of the Gods*. Belay before the ledge narrows.
2. 50m Continue left along the ledge passing a bulge and belay on cracked blocks.
3. 60m Climb up 5m to join a gradually rising leftwards line that leads to the big snow terrace on *Der Riesenwand*.

4. 50m Follow the leftwards rising traverse of *Der Riesenwand* to belay where a gangway leads off right.
5. 50m Follow the gangwaypast a hard sequence of moves round a rock barrier.
6. 60m Continue for 5m to the end of the terrace. Climb up a 5m icy groove, cross a small snow bay, then climb the fine crack and continue steeply in the same line to belay at the top of a terrace.
7. 60m Move up and right into a broad depression and climb this through a wide flaky crack and continue up fine ground till the angle eases.
8. 40m Climb easy ground to the top.

BEN SHIELDAIG, Loch Dughaill Crags (NG 833 515):
7 routes on the SMC website.

SHIELDAIG CRAGS, Creag Ob Mheallaidh (NG 8384 5385):
A slightly smaller crag just to the north-east and over a crest from the original crag (SMCJ 2011).

Fickle Flake   15m HVS 5a. Susan Jensen, Martin Moran, Andy Nisbet. 23 Apr 2016.
The crag is largely a steep wall bounded on the right by a flake system topped by a large flake. The wall is also cut by a diagonal crack running right to left from the flake system. Start up a wet patch but with sufficient dry positive holds to reach the diagonal crack. Climb the crack to its top, then finish out left.

Fickle Fingers   15m VS 4c. Susan Jensen, Martin Moran, Andy Nisbet. 23 Apr 2016.
Start as for *Fickle Flake* but continue up the flake system. At its top, step left and back right to finish more direct.

BEINN DAMH:
A Good Outcome   420m IV,4. James Edwards, Neil Wilson. 28 Feb 2016.
A line to the left of *Traveller's Tale* (no description received).

TORRIDON CRAGS, Seana Mheallan:
Note: *Reject* was climbed direct up the rib at VS 4c by John Lyall, Jonathan Preston & Jimmy Whyte on 10 May 2016.

Seana Mheallan West, Pink Walls:
John had Pasta for Breakfast   15m E1 5a. Michael Barnard, John MacLeod. 4 Oct 2015.
Climbs the bold line of weakness up the wall between *Skye and Kyle…* and … *Fish and Chips*, moving left or right as necessary.

King Solomon's Marbles   15m E1 5b *. Michael Barnard, John MacLeod. 4 Oct 2015.
The obvious thin crack between *Hadrian's Wall* and *Heather Said Sunshine* is gained directly (bold). Start on a large block and move up and left to gain the crack.
Note: The upper part of this is shown in the guide as a variation to *Heather Said Sunshine*, but this is really a separate route, probably harder than graded here.

Golden Generation 15m VS 5a. Allen Fyffe, Alan Hunt, John Lyall. 15 Aug 2012.
The slabby wall right of *Better than a Slap in the Face*. Start up a short right-facing corner, through a bulge, up a left-slanting crack, then right to break through the centre of the overlap, finishing by a blunt rib.

Seana Mheallan West, Quartz Slab:
Queen of Hearts 15m H.Severe 4b. Andy Nisbet, Jonathan Preston. 10 May 2016.
A direct line up the slab left of *Off with her Head*, passing through quartz to finish up flakes just left of the corner of *Off with her Head* (which was thought to be Severe 4a).

The Whirlwind 12m VS 4b. John Lyall, Jimmy Whyte. 10 May 2016.
The right end of the slab. Trend right to finish 3m right of a right-facing corner with loose blocks.

Celtic Boulders:
Super Pittance 10m E6 6b *. Ian Taylor, Gaz Marshall. 28 Feb 2016.
First find the Pittance boulder problem, detailed in the Torridon Bouldering Guide. Climb the wide diagonal crack, left of the problem, to a ledge. Step right and go up the wall past a good Rock 4, before a hard move gains a good hold. Place small cams (Black Diamond C3 00 and 000), then gain the edge on the right and follow this leftwards to the top.

DIABAIG, The Pillar:
Dire Straits, Diabolic Finish 10m E3 6a **. Martin Moran, Robin Thomas. 12 May 2015.
At the top of thin cracks in the upper wall, move left and make a hard rock-over move to surmount the bulge above. Move left and teeter to the top.

Little Big Wall:
An Armful 18m E4 5c *. Martin Moran, Robin Thomas. 12 May 2015.
Climbs the vague groove in the arete 8m right of *An Eyeful*. Climb the first groove with fingery moves and tricky protection, then swing boldly up right and gain a ledge. Climb cracks in the wall above to a hard finish.

Main Cliff:
Perfect Days 55m E2 **. Gary & Karen Latter. 15 Mar 2016.
1. 15m 4b Pitch 1 of *Route Three*.
2. 40m 5c Start at large pink patch a few metres left of *Route Three*. Follow twin cracks up the slab, then move out rightwards and direct by cracks aiming for thin, twin tramline cracks. Follow these which lead to the leftmost of the twin off-width cracks in the headwall. Finish up this past a small but useful rattly chokestone. Nut & maillon in situ for abseil just above.

Northern Sky 57m HVS 5a **. Gary & Karen Latter. 15 Mar 2016.
Start up *Route Two* to an obvious left-slanting, diagonal hand crack. Take this to a small heather clump, then move up to follow an obvious left-trending diagonal fault. At its end, move up to the cracks above the right edge of the large heather

bay. Follow the fine cracks to the top. Nut & maillon in situ for abseil up and right.

The Condome:
Fisherman's Dream   30m   E6 6b **. Gary Latter. 31 Mar 2016.
A direct line up the wall between *Instant Muscle* and *Rough Justice*. Start up *Rough Justice* for 5m, then move left and follow twin cracks. Where they peter out, continue direct past a peg runner to pull direct into the final crack of Condome and finish up this.

Uncaught Silver   20m   VS 4c *. Karen & Gary Latter. 31 Mar 2016.
A left-trending line starting from just below the awkward step in the gully. Follow cracks, passing through a short grassy section, sharing a short section common to Shunned.

Stars so Close   20m   HVS 5a *. Karen & Gary Latter. 31 Mar 2016.
Start just above the awkward step in the gully, beneath a small arching overlap. Follow the twin broken cracks to finish just right of a short left-facing corner at the top.

COIRE DUBH CRAGS:
These sandstone crags lie on the lower flanks of Liathath and Beinn Eighe, and are approached via the footpath from the Coire Dubh car park in Glen Torridon (NG 958 568). While the approaches generally exceed an hour, this is well worth the effort as the climbing is of good quality and the situation splendid.

Mad Man's Crag:
(NG 943 588)   Alt 400m   North-North-West facing
This is the first low lying tier of sandstone seen up on the left after crossing the stepping stones on the Coire Dubh footpath, 45mins overall. The only climbs recorded so far are on the far right end of the crag, which lies some distance left of a small burn trickling down from the prominent gully above (*Chi Squared*). A corner-crack on this section of the crag is clearly seen from the path about 5mins after crossing the stepping stones – this is taken by the following route.

The Trundler   15m   HVS 5a ***. Michael Barnard. 2 Jun 2009.
Excellent climbing up the crack splitting the crag at its highest point.

Sliced by Scree   8m   HVS 5a *. Michael Barnard . 2 Jun 2009.
The shorter stepped crack just left of the above.

Creag Dubh Beag:
(NG 936 587)   Alt 520m   North-North-East facing
This steep outcrop is passed by on its left on the ascent into Coire Dubh Beag and is well seen from the main footpath. A very fine wall with two prominent crack-lines and some potential for harder routes, 1hr 10mins.

Truly Torrential   12m   E3 5c ***. Michael Barnard, John MacLeod. 22 Apr 2011.
The left-hand crack. A bold lower section with adequate holds leading to a hard well protected finish.

Torrid Time   12m   E3 5c ***. Michael Barnard, John MacLeod. 22 Apr 2011.
The right-hand crack, gained from the ledge on the right. Sustained and superb.

To the right of the main wall the crag becomes more broken; this is the best line
of descent. Further right are some short walls and corners.

Wee Corner   6m   HVS 5b *. Michael Barnard. 2 Jun 2009.
The first corner on the right gives a nice wee problem.

The following two routes lie on the upper crag (about 5mins walk up the hill from
the top of the main wall).

Into the Red   15m   VS 5a *. Michael Barnard. 29 May 2009.
Takes the obvious two-stepped crack-line on the right side of the crag. The steep
initial crack leads to easier climbing up the corner above.

Out of the Blue   15m   V.Diff. Michael Barnard. 29 May 2009.
Pleasant climbing up the easy angled groove further right.

Hill Man's Crag:
(NG 939 586)   Alt 530m   North-North-West facing
This crag lies just across left from Creag Dubh Beag and features a very different
style of climbing; very gritstone-esque. The rock is immaculate.

Te Tahi   15m   Severe *. Alan Hill, Michael Barnard. 11 Sep 2015.
Easy but delicate climbing up the fine blunt arete at the right end of the crag.

Taniwha   12m   VS 5a *. Alan Hill, Michael Barnard. 11 Sep 2015.
Left of *Te Tahi* are two short corners. Climb the blunt arete immediately left again.

Ermine   10m   VS 4c. Michael Barnard, Alan Hill. 11 Sep 2015.
In the centre of the crag is a prominent V-groove. Bridge up this, then climb the
crack on its right wall.

In the Groove   10m   V.Diff *. Alan Hill, Michael Barnard.11 Sep 2015.
The prominent V-groove.

Fingers and Toes   10m   E1 5a *. Michael Barnard, Alan Hill. 11 Sep 2015.
Climbs the steep crack left of the V-groove before continuing up the arete above.

Block Appreciation Society   12m   E3 5b *. Michael Barnard, Alan Hill. 11 Sep
2015.
The innocuous left-slanting ramp. A cam on the right low down may be the only
gear you get! Finish right up the easier scoop above.

Keep Calm and Carry On   12m   E2 5b *. Michael Barnard, Alan Hill. 11 Sep
2015.
Start in a short corner the other side of the arete from the above and move up to
a ledge on the arete. Climb up, then right to gain holds on BAS. Finish up the
groove on the left. Basically a solo; the break is distinctly disappointing!

Big Mac's Crag:

(NG 934 588) Alt 500m   North facing
From the Coire Dubh footpath this crag can be seen to the right of, and slightly
down from, Creag Dubh Beag, 1hr 10mins.

Noo Noo 10m   Severe *. John MacLeod, Michael Barnard. 22 Apr 2011.
This route is found on the more broken left section of the crag. It climbs a three-
stepped crack-line, unfortunately escapable. The first step is avoided by taking
the ramp on the left and moving back in across a slab.

The rest of the routes lie on the steeper right section of the crag:

Ach Aye the Noo 10m   VS 4c *. John MacLeod, Michael Barnard. 22 Apr 2011.
The first main line reached here, a vertical two-stepped crack-line, the upper half
up a corner.

Raspberry Cheesecake 10m   E1 5b *. Michael Barnard, John MacLeod. 22 Apr
2011.
A steep left-facing groove, gained with difficulty and climbed with further
difficulty! Micro-cams essential.

Big Mac 10m   E1 5b *. Michael Barnard, John MacLeod. 22 Apr 2011.
The obvious steep crack has a hard middle section.

Right of this is an imposing blank section of wall. Further right the angle starts to
lessen, but the base is undercut.

Echo Falls 12m   VS 4c *. Michael Barnard, John MacLeod. 22 Apr 2011.
Start near the right end of the undercut section. Pull over the lap (crux,
unprotected), then move up and left to gain and climb the obvious crack.

No the Noo 15m   V.Diff. John MacLeod, Michael Barnard. 22 Apr 2011.
Right of the above, move up right then back left and up the slabby central groove
in the wall.

Mac-a-noo 12m   V.Diff *. John MacLeod, Michael Barnard. 22 Apr 2011.
Climbs a left-trending crack up the slabby wall at the far right end of the crag.

Proud Crag:

(NG 931 590) Alt 500m   North-East to North-West facing
The most westerly of the Liathath crags is also the most extensive. Much of it has
the feel of a miniature gritstone edge featuring micro-routes and bouldery starts,
though it does have some more substantial offerings. The outlook is superb, with
views straight up into Coire na Caime. It is clearly seen on the skyline during the
approach, and can be reached by contouring round the hillside from Big Mac's
Crag. To reach the crag directly, follow the footpath until just past where it splits
for Coire Mhic Fhearchair; from here the crag is visible lying on the crest of a
slight ridge, 1hr 20mins.

Just left of where the crag changes direction from north-east to north-west, two obvious corners are located (*Insomniac* and *The Good Soldier*); the climbs are described rightwards from this point. Three short routes have been done immediately left of the two corners.

Earth   6m   Severe 4b. Michael Barnard. 29 Apr 2011.
The short cracked nose left of *Insomniac*.

Wind   5m   V.Diff. Michael Barnard. 29 Apr 2011.
Left of the above, this route ascends a crack up the shortest part of the crag. Can be used in descent (with care).

Water   6m   Severe 4b. Michael Barnard. 29 Apr 2011.
The two-stepped crack-line left again.

Insomniac   8m   Severe *. Alan Hill, Michael Barnard 10 Sep 2015.
The left-hand corner.

Singing Winds   8m   HVS 4c. Michael Barnard. 29 Apr 2011.
The blunt arete between the two corners, finishing on the right-hand side.

The Good Soldier   8m   V.Diff. Alan Hill, Michael Barnard. 10 Sep 2015.
The right-hand corner.

Crying Beasts   10m   HVS 4c. Michael Barnard. 29 Apr 2011.
Right of the corners is a shallow hanging groove. Climb the blunt arete to its left.

Out of the Frying Pan   10m   VS 4b *. Michael Barnard. 29 Apr 2011.
The shallow hanging groove-line is also unprotected.

The Gunger   10m   VS 5a *. Michael Barnard, Alan Hill. 10 Sep 2015.
A vertical cracked corner-line with a steep start.

Into the Fire   10m   HVS 5c *. Michael Barnard, Alan Hill. 10 Sep 2015.
The fine thin two-stepped crack in the centre of the wall right of *The Gunger*.

To Squirm or Not to Squirm?   15m   VS 4b *. Michael Barnard. 29 Apr 2011.
The wide crack has a simple solution but little protection (without a large cam).

Gunk Rock   15m   VS 5a *. Michael Barnard, Alan Hill. 10 Sep 2015.
A few metres right of the wide crack is a fine vertical crack. Climb this and continue up to the top break, then step left to finish.

The Secret's in the Squidge   15m   HVS 5b *. Alan Hill, Michael Barnard. 10 Sep 2015.
A thin vertical crack just left of a corner. Climb this directly.

Golden Brown   15m   VS 5b. Alan Hill, Michael Barnard. 10 Sep 2015.
A bouldery start up the arete right of *...the Squidge*, followed by easier climbing up the wall above.

May Day Corner 15m VS 5a *. John MacLeod, Michael Barnard. 1 May 2011.
The next feature right is a left-facing corner-crack, often wet. Climb this and continue up the fault-line above, finishing up the top corner.

Blind, Crippled and Crazy 15m HVS 5a **. Michael Barnard, John MacLeod. 1 May 2011.
Climbs the steep shallow groove in the wall right of *May Day Corner*. Start 3m right of that route. Move up and left then step back right at the break and climb the groove to a ledge. Continue up the steep corner above (crux).

Right of this is the most continuously steep section of the crag, breached in its centre by a striking flake-crack.

Calling Card 12m E3 6a **. Michael Barnard, Alan Hill. 10 Sep 2015.
Start 2m right of *Blind, Crippled and Crazy*, below a short V-groove. Sustained moves lead up this, then up and right to the break (Friend 3.5). Gain the flake above, then finish up and right.

The Daddy Line 12m HVS 5b ***. Michael Barnard, John MacLeod. 1 May 2011.
The excellent flake-crack.

One for the Worm 12m E3 6a *. Michael Barnard, Alan Hill. 8 Jun 2016.
Near the right end of the steep section of wall is a thin right-trending crack. Climb this to the ledge on the right, then step back left to tackle the upper flake-crack.

White Rabbits 15m VS 4c **. John MacLeod, Michael Barnard. 1 May 2011.
Right of the steep section of wall are two thin parallel cracks leading to an obvious stepped corner. Climb boldly up these into the corner then continue straight up the wall above, moving left to finish.

Fire on the Mountain 15m Severe **. Michael Barnard. 29 Apr 2011.
Start 2m right of the above. Climb a short corner, then continue up the wall above to gain the stepped corner. Finish up this.

Liathath's Burning 15m VS 4c *. Michael Barnard. 29 Apr 2011.
Start 2m right again and go up a corner to gain the obvious left-right diagonal crack splitting the wall above. Climb this (crux).

Creag Coire Dubh:
(NG 947 595) Alt 550m South facing
The only crag here lying on the Beinn Eighe side, this lies just right of the prominent steep narrow gully which descends from the right side of Coinneach Mhòr. It has a fine outlook and being south facing, is quicker to dry than some of the Liathath crags. It has well defined left and right sections with a scramble descent in-between, though abseiling is more pleasant and the gear can be collected after the last route of the day. While the highest part of the crag is 30m, 45m of rope is needed there to reach suitable anchors back from the edge, 1hr.

Solaris   30m   V.Diff. Alan Hill, Michael Barnard. 8 Sep 2015.
Climbs cracks up the crest of the first buttress reached at the far left end of the crag.

Burning Serengeti   30m   HVS 5a *. Michael Barnard, Alan Hill. 8 Sep 2015.
The next buttress has an obvious vertical groove just left of the crest. This route climbs the fine wall left of this via thin cracks. Continue more easily to the top.

The Power of the Sun   30m   HVS 5a *. Michael Barnard, Alan Hill. 8 Sep 2015.
The vertical groove, gained via the arete below. A nasty bold move on the arete makes the route rather unbalanced.

The Sizzler   30m   HVS 5a **. Michael Barnard, Alan Hill. 7 Sep 2015.
A quality flake-crack. Continue directly up grooves above.

Note: On a later ascent, John Lyall stepped right at the top of the crack, then climbed a bulge and shallow crack.

Next is the showpiece of the crag, a fine high wall with a large flake-crack (*Coire Dubh Crack*). Marking the left end of this wall is an obvious V-groove and upper corner.

Baker Street   30m   HVS 5a **. Michael Barnard, Alan Hill. 8 Sep 2015.
Start below and just right of the V-groove. Climb a flake-crack, then step left to tackle the V-groove. Finish up the steep corner above, a long sustained pitch.

Mr Sandman   30m   E2 5b **. Michael Barnard, Alan Hill. 8 Sep 2015.
Climbs the prominent left-slanting crack in the wall right of the *Baker Street* groove, gained via its initial flake-crack. Move left to the base of *Baker Street's* top corner, before stepping back right to finish up the top wall.

Coire Dubh Crack   30m   E1 5b **. Michael Barnard, Alan Hill. 7 Sep 2015.
The big flake crack in the main wall. Climb past the lower wide crack (bold), then take the flake-crack through the bulge to the upper overlap. Step right and finish up the bold groove above.

Sandcastle   30m   E1 5b *. Michael Barnard, Alan Hill. 7 Sep 2015.
A direct line up the crest of the buttress. The main feature is a short thin flake-crack just right of *Coire Dubh Crack*. Start up a large block/pillar then climb via the arete and groove above to the base of the flake-crack. Climb the wall until possible to gain a foot ledge on the left. Move up, then hand-traverse back right to pull into a short groove below the upper overlap. Continue directly to the top.

Note: John Lyall avoided the right traverse, went straight over the bulge, through the overlap just right of *Coire Dubh Crack* and up a right-slanting crack to the top.

Nutters' Crack   30m   H.Severe 4b *.
An obvious forked crack in the next wall to the right had been climbed before (nut in-situ).

Dark and Stormy Night   30m   H.Severe 4b. Alan Hill, Michael Barnard. 8 Sep 2015.
Aims for a miniature S-shaped crack high in the next wall to the right. Some loose blocks require care.

The next three routes lie on the final wall before the descent area.

A Route of Two Halves   20m   HVS 5a *. Michael Barnard, Alan Hill. 7 Sep 2015.
The lower part of the wall is slabby and slightly undercut at the base. Step left onto this and climb to the break (crux). Continue more easily then move up just left of the central crack, before stepping left to finish up the fine top wall.

Round Heads and Cavaliers   25m   VS 4b. Alan Hill, Michael Barnard. 7 Sep 2015.
Follows cracks in the right side of the wall.

Get Your Wimple On, Madge   20m   VS 4c. Alan Hill, Michael Barnard. 7 Sep 2015.
The right-facing corner-crack just left of the descent.

The right-hand section of the crag also has a good higher bit of wall. The main feature of this is two parallel cracks, the right-hand one being set in corners.

Brexit Vote!   20m   H.Severe. John Lowther, John Lyall. 23 Jun 2016.
Follow twin cracks up a left slanting line left of 'Invaders', up a slight rib, then move right to cracks up cleaner wall, right of a dirty groove.

Invaders   20m   E2 5c **. Michael Barnard, Alan Hill. 8 Sep 2015.
The fine steep left-hand crack.

Fresh Evidence   20m   VS 4c *. Michael Barnard, Alan Hill. 7 Sep 2015.
The right-hand crack up corners.

Sands of Time   20m   E2 5b *. Michael Barnard, Alan Hill. 8 Sep 2015.
Climbs a thin vertical crack in the wall right of the arete. From above the crack. step right and move up to join the upper corner of *Fresh Evidence*.

Second Helpings   20m   VS 4c. Michael Barnard, Alan Hill. 8 Sep 2015.
The next corner/groove right.

LIATHACH, Coire na Caime, Upper Corrie:
Lost Ridge   150m   II. Andy Nisbet. 13 Mar 2016.
A ridge at the left end of the buttress left of *Gully IK*, overlooking the highest and rightmost Grade I gully on this section of face (has been used for descent, but often corniced). Start just right of the steep base of the ridge. Climb a short ice pitch and curve up left to a snow arete above the steep base. Follow the crest to a steep band of rock, passed just on the left. Finish up the crest and a short wall.

Sgòrr a' Chadail:
The Path and the Way   45m   E1 5b. Michael Barnard, Alan Hill. 9 Sep 2015.
Climbs thin vertical cracks in the wall right of *Trench Foot*. Start at the base of

that route and make an awkward move to gain the ledge at the base of the fine lower crack. Climb this, then move up rightwards to tackle the upper crack. Continue up the cracks and grooves above.

Rocking Horse   45m   E2 5b. Michael Barnard, Alan Hill. 9 Sep 2015.
Climbs what appears to be the least resistance line in the wall right of *Reflections on My Mind*. However, the lower half proves to be deceptively hard and serious. Start below a roofed section and climb up and left towards an obvious ledge. Place a cam under the roof on the right, then attempt to get established on the ledge without pulling on the large block which occupies it. If successful, continue up the groove above then move out right to go up a short left-facing corner. Traverse back left to finish up a fine crack on the left wall of the upper corner.

Ragged Glory   45m   E1 5c **. Michael Barnard, Alan Hill. 9th Sep 2015.
Excellent climbing. Start just right of *Rocking Horse*, below a vertical groove/corner. Move up this, then up and left to reach for a good flake on the edge. Step left along the ledge then up a right-slanting flake-crack to below the left-facing corner of *Rocking Horse* (finishing up this would give a good HVS 5a). Instead tackle the flying crack on the right (crux), before finishing up the cracked corners above.

Billy Goats Gruff   45m   E1 5b. Michael Barnard, Alan Hill. 18 Jun 2016.
About halfway between the crag's change in aspect and the Pale Wall (or 15m right of *Ragged Glory*) is a prominent roof 8m up, with a smooth left-facing groove below. Start below a crack a few metres right of the groove. Climb the crack until it peters out, then make a delicate traverse left to gain the crack above the roof (crux). Move up the crack, then step left to continue more easily up the cracks and grooves above.

Chevrolet   55m   E2 *. Michael Barnard, Alan Hill. 18 Jun 2016.
Aims for the right-hand crack high on the right side of the main wall (*Chadailac* takes the left-hand one). Go up the easy corner to belay at the base of the wall (as for *Chadailac*).
1. 30m 5b Step right and ascend the wall to a crack in a shallow right-facing groove. Move up this to a break, step left and continue up cracks to the top crack, then up this to the ledge.
2. 25m 4c As for *Chadailac*.

Karmacanic   55m   E2. Michael Barnard, Alan Hill. 18 Jun 2016.
Start 2m right of *Chevrolet*.
1. 30m 5b Go up the wall to a crack in a shallow left-facing groove; climb this then step left and continue up cracks to below a couple of large blocks. Step right and move up to take the obvious V-groove to the ledge.
2. 25m 4c Continue up the groove above, then up a large flake-crack to the top.

Note: *Chadailac* was thought E1 5b ** (E2 at most), not E3 5c ***.

BEINN EIGHE, Far East Wall:
Daughter of the Dawn, Direct Finish   30m   E4 6a. Graham Tydesley, Liam Malone. 4 Jun 2016.
From the belay ledge, move back right into the main line heading up towards the

right end of the roof above. Pinch up a protruding seam to gain the base of a left-facing corner. Pull across this onto the wall and then move more easily up and right to the roof and through it. Move back left into a cleft splitting the steep ground above.

Chinese Burn   50m   E2 6a *. Michael Barnard, Alan Hill. 7 Jun 2016.
A few metres right of *Epilogue/Divine Ambition* is a crack leading to a left-facing corner. Climb these to a ledge, then take the thin crack up the bulging wall above (crux) and its continuation to a ledge. Continue to the top.

Hong Kong Phooey   50m   E1. Michael Barnard, Alan Hill. 8 Jun 2016.
Right of *Chinese Burn* and left of the big corner is an obvious left-slanting crack in the wall.
1. 20m 5a Move up to climb the crack to a large ledge.
2. 30m 5b Right of the thin crack of *Chinese Burn* are two parallel cracks in the wall. Climb the left crack then continue more easily to the top.

Note: *Divine Ambition* was thought E1 5c (not 6a). *Karaoke Wall* is worth a star for its excellent widening flake-crack.

Central Buttress:
Note: Rob Adams & Fiona Murray climbed direct from the end of the diagonal line through the sandstone, moving left round the crest and up to join the normal route higher up the first quartzite band. Still VI,7 but the crux overall.

CAIRNGORMS

COIRE AN T-SNEACHDA, Fiacaill Buttress:
Smokestack Lightnin' Direct Start   VII,8. Dave Almond, Simon Frost. 17 Dec 2015.
Climb about halfway up the ramp of *Jailbreak* before breaking out right and following a corner (like a mini *Stirling Bomber*) for some 20m to join the normal route which traverses in from the right. Instead of following this, step left and climb a crack-line and subsequent groove on the left to join the normal route at its crux. The overhanging variation to pitch 3 was then freed.

MAM SUIM, Creag na h-Iolaire:
Central Buttress Direct   80m   IV,4. Simon Richardson, Michael Rinn, Ryosuke Ohbu. 30 Jan 2016.
A direct version of *Central Buttress* following the crest throughout.

Picasso   70m   III,4. Jeremy Windsor, Pablo Artigue. 30 Jan 2016.
The next rib right of *Central Ridge*.

Loose Rib   60m   II/III. Gwilym Lynn, Goran Kelecic. 30 Jan 2016.
The rib right of *Picasso* to the left of a wide gully.

Anglo-Danish Route   70m   I. Mikkel Schelde, Paul Headland. 30 Jan 2016.
The furthest right rib in the corrie. Start from the large weathered tree at the base

of the rib and climb a rocky groove past another small tree. Continue up the ridge over two further short rock steps.

CREAGAN COIRE A' CHA-NO:

Cha-cha-cha 30m V,4 or II. Michael Barnard, Simon Richardson. 1 Jan 2016.
The leftmost buttress on the cliff is cut by a prominent right-facing groove. Climb this on thin turf over a bulge to the top. Later in the season the groove will bank out and will become significantly easier.

Whaleback Ridge 40m III,4. Simon Richardson, Michael Barnard. 1 Jan 2016.
The rounded ridge about 50m left of *International Rib*. Climb up a turfy groove on its right side to a vertical right-facing corner. Climb this on huge holds and finish up the rounded crest above.

Flood Warning 50m III,4. Simon Richardson, Michael Barnard. 1 Jan 2016.
The prominent wide gully to the right of *Captain Fairweather* has a couple of steep steps in its lower half. Possibly climbed before.

Ziggy Groove 60m II. Matt Smith, Vicky Smith. 9 Jan 2016.
On Tower Buttress. The route takes the right flank of *Short Ridge*, joining it at the top. Start in a bay 5m tight of the toe of the buttress. Move up the right side of the ridge to a broad groove. Follow this taking the easiest line over steps to join the crest of the ridge after 45m. Traverse left of the crest to finish.

Anvil Chorus 50m IV,7. Roger Webb, Simon Richardson. 13 Dec 2015.
The steep crack system on the left flank of *Anvil Gully*. Technical and well protected.
1. 25m Climb the left branch of *Anvil Gully* (often climbed as an alternative to *Anvil Gully* itself) and belay below bulging twin cracks on the left wall.
2. 15m Climb the cracks over a bulge and pull over the chockstone above to gain the wide platform of *Flaked Out*.
3. 10m Take the right-hand of the offwidth cracks finishing over a small roof with a chockstone.

Grandee Grooves 60m III,5. Simon Richardson, Michael Barnard. 1 Jan 2016.
The gully line between *Duke's Rib* and *Jenga Buttress*. Start as for *Jenga Buttress* and continue up mixed ground to its left to gain a steep chimney-corner on the right. Climb this to easier ground, them move up and left to finish. Probably Grade II if the chimney-corner is avoided on the left and possibly climbed before.

LURCHER'S CRAG:

Nirvana Fallacy 200m III. Andy Nisbet. 2 Mar 2016.
A mixed line up the right side of the buttress left of *North Gully*. Start by following a ramp which curves round the right end of the buttress. This leads into a short steep groove and then a terrace below a steep wall which slants up left. Head left, then straight up until under the top end of the wall. Finish up a broken ridge which is the continuation of the wall.

Ultramontane 250m IV,5. Sandy Allan, Andy Nisbet, Steve & Katie Perry. 27 Dec 2015.
Start at the base of the buttress some 20m right of *North Gully* at a short but well

defined groove. This is well left of where the buttress base is overhanging. Climb the groove and traverse right, continue upwards, then move back left to a groove, climbed to below an awkward step (50m). Climb the step and a corner, stepping left out of it to a narrow ledge and the base of a short shallow chimney. Climb this and step right beneath a steep rocky section (30m). Climb the rocky section to easier ground and move up to block belays on left (40m). Continue up easier ground to the base of a ridge which is formed on the right bank of the right branch of *North Gully* (50m). Climb the ridge to its finish on broken ground.

Akita 250m VI,6. Steve Perry, Andy Nisbet. 22 Feb 2016.
Start some 10m right of *Ultramontane*, just before the buttress base starts to rise up right. Climb slabby icy ground up to a steepening (25m). Climb a groove to a small roof and pull over this rightwards to another groove. Step left from the top of this and climb further grooves to easier ground (30m). Climb a short chimney and more broken ground (50m). Continue up the left side of a ridge above, then its crest and joining *Ultramontane* high up.

Dotterel Direct 140m VII,7. Steve Perry, Andy Nisbet. 8 Feb 2016.
A direct line up the crest of the *Dotterel* buttress. Start just right of the crest, which is close to *Central Gully*. Make hard moves up into a right-facing corner and climb this (serious, being near the ground) to gain the arete on the left. Climb cracks and flakes just left of the crest to join *Electric Brae* (25m). Follow this up a chimney to the small col. Continue up the crest of *Dotterel* to the top.

Electric Brae 140m VI,7. Steve Perry, Andy Nisbet, Jonathan Preston. 14 Dec 2015.
A line just right of the crest of the ridge of *Dotterel* (left of that route). Start in the centre of an undercut section where a patch of turf can just be reached. Pull though the overhang and make thin moves up to an overhanging groove topped by a thin wedged block. Climb the groove and the continuation line which bends left and regains the crest. Climb a groove just left of the crest and which leads to an easier section which leads to a small col (45m). The route now joins *Dotterel* and follow that route up two long easier but good pitches to easy ground.

Snowbird 160m VI,7. Andy Nisbet, Steve & Katie Perry. 8 Jan 2016.
A line of grooves right of *Dotterel*. Right of *Dotterel* is an easier, wide turfy groove which leads to overhangs. Climb the groove and move right below the overhangs. Make a rising traverse right into a left-rising slabby corner (not the first line with a large wedged block). Go up this into a groove, climbed to a recess (30m). Climb a capped groove above the recess, then another wall to a pedestal. Climb the steep wall on the left to easier ground and follow this up through a narrow chimney slot (45m). Move left to join the upper crest of *Dotterel* and follow this for 2 pitches to the top (85m).

Strictly Come Swimming 150m V,6. Andy Nisbet, Steve Perry. 22 Nov 2015.
A line of grooves just right of the ridge of *Dotterel* and at the left side of the depression between it and *Reindeer Ridge* (*Beagle has Landed* takes grooves on the right side of the depression). Climbed under deep snow. Start down right from the crest of the ridge and just left of smooth slabs.
1. 50m Climb over a flake and move right to a steep groove above the slabs. Climb the groove and move up to a short overhanging wall. Traverse right below

this to enter and climb a turfy groove, then a well defined subsequent groove. Move right on an inset slab, then back left more easily.

2. 50m Trend right on slabby ground to enter and climb a big central groove. Continue up more easily to below a steep upper tier.

3. 50m Climb up towards a through route below a big block and pass this on the right. Continue up on blocky ground, then move right and climb more blocky ground to finish at the end of the ridge of *Dotterel*.

Have an Ice Day   140m   V,5. Steve Perry, Sandy Allan, Andy Nisbet. 12 Dec 2015.
A big groove tucked into the left side of *St. Bernard's Ridge*. Start under the right side of *St. Bernard's Ridge* and traverse a fault leftwards through a lower tier before going up to the base of the groove. Climb the groove mostly on ice (40m). Finish the groove out right to easy ground in an upper bowl (20m). Move right and finish up *St. Bernard's Ridge*.

The Force Awakens   140m   VI,6. Andy Nisbet, Sandy Allan, Steve Perry. 12 Dec 2015.
A ramp line set into the left side of *St. Bernard's Ridge* and overlooking the previous route. Go up *Have an Ice Day* for 5m until ice leads up to an overhang. Step left round this and climb a steep groove to the base of the ramp. Climb the ramp to its top (40m). Climb a groove leading up to the crest of *St. Bernard's Ridge* (20m) and finish up this.

Doorway Ridge, Far Left Start   60m   III,4. Simon Richardson, Michael Rinn. 31 Jan 2016.
Start by climbing 20m up the *Left Start to Doorway Ridge*. Break on to the mixed ground on the left and climb it directly to the triangular wall at its top (50m). Move left and up through the triangular wall on large blocks to join the original route on the easier upper crest.

American Werewolves   200m   III. Bill McConachie, Andy Nisbet, Steve Towne. 31 Jan 2016.
A ridge which forms the right edge of the buttress with *Deerhound Ridge* forming its left edge. This gives a long route with interesting moves, but escapable. A line of least resistance, but keeping as near the crest as possible, was taken to a terrace. A section of shallow ridge led to a steep wall blocking access to an upper ridge. This was passed by a rising line right leading into a narrow V-groove which lead back left to the crest. This was approximately followed to the top, finishing close to *Deerhound Ridge*.

Lupus   60m   III,5. Andy Nisbet, Steve Perry. 8 Feb 2016.
A parallel ridge to the two Canis ridges further right. Rather scrappy and escapable. Start on its right and climb a crack-line to the crest. Continue to the next tower and climb this on its left wall. A third tower was climbed more direct and a final tower was climbed by a steep groove just on its left.

Sirius   40m   IV,6. Andy Nisbet, Steve Perry. 18 Feb 2016.
A steep tower lies at the far south end of the cliff. This route takes the second groove up left from its base (*Canis Minor* takes the first groove). Climb the groove until it reaches an arete (left of *Canis Minor*). Climb the arete to easy ground.

COIRE GARBHLACH, Upper Corrie, Pinnacle Buttress:

Rake's Progress   120m   II. Sophie Grace Chappel, Andy Nisbet. 30 Nov 2015.
A shallow rake just right of the central crest (and the existing routes). Start just
up the ramp which bounds the right side of the buttress. Climb a groove to a fork
and take the left branch, nearer the crest. Follow this to an upper tower on the
crest and pass this on the left to finish.

BRAERIACH, Garbh Choire Dhaidh:

The Outback   140m   VS ***. Sarah Atkinson, John Lyall, Jonathan Preston. 29
Sep 2015.
A superb route between *The Culvert* and *The Great Rift*. Start by scrambling for
20m to a belay 5m left of *The Great Rift*, left of a smooth red groove.
1. 50m 4c Climb up to a prominent left-facing flake, to the left of and parallel
with the red groove. Follow this and continue up to a left-slanting corner. Make
a couple of moves up this, then pull out right by a steep crack, then follow a V-
groove and fault up left to beneath a left-leaning corner (this is above a left-leaning
roofed corner).
2. 35m 5a Climb the left-leaning corner, then go up right by a fault and over a
short steep wall past a peg (from *The Culvert*, which goes out left from here) to a
ledge.
3. 35m 4a Follow the stepped corners and easier ground to finish.

Aboriginal Root   150m   H.Severe *. Sarah Atkinson, John Lyall, Jonathan
Preston. 29 Sep 2015.
Scramble up easy rocks for 25m to the base of the clean, curving groove, between
Kangaroo and *Boomerang*.
1. 45m 4b Follow the groove to its end, then make a thin traverse left to gain and
follow another groove to a rock ledge.
2. 35m Continue to a grass ledge, then take cracks up a rib and easy ground to
the upper slab.
3. 45m Climb the slab between the corners of *Kangaroo* and *Boomerang*, starting
by cracks just right of the offset roofs, to finish left of the upper roof.

Re-connected   150m   V.Diff. John Lyall. 10 Sep 2015.
Ribs and edges close to *Wichity Way*, with a nice finish. Follow the first pitch of
Wichity Way, then the rib between its easy gully and prominent corner, moving
right above the big left-pointing roof. Work up left and climb the right edge of
the final corner on superb holds.

COIRE SPUTAN DEARG:

Hot Tin Roof   150m   VS. Sarah Atkinson, John Lyall, Jonathan Preston. 1 Oct
2015.
A line up the buttress just right of *Aurora*.
1. 45m 4b From the toe of the buttress, gain a thin curving flake line (next line
right of *Aurora*), and follow it up and right. Continue up until possible to cross a
slab rightwards to gain a left-facing corner, which is followed to a platform on
the right edge.
2. 35m 5a From the top of the platform, follow a layback crack, then pockets up
to the edge. Move up the edge, then go leftwards by the cleanest line to easier
ground.
Scramble to the top.

Sarah Atkinson on FA of The Outback (VS), Braeriach, 29 Sept 2015. Photo: John Lyall.

Indian Summer   140m   H.Severe. Sarah Atkinson, John Lyall, Jonathan Preston. 1 Oct 2015.
A short way up *Anchor Gully* is a fault cutting up the left wall; this route starts on the slab below this fault, then crosses it on the second pitch.
1. 35m 4a Follow a diagonal crack up the slab to gain a belay on the rib, where a ledge cuts into the fault.
2. 45m 4a Cross the fault and climb a crack and the cleanest rock on the right side of the buttress to a terrace (poorly protected).
Easy to the top.

CÀRN ETCHACHAN, Lochside Crag:
Air Strikes   150m   IV,4. John Lyall. 3 Dec 2015.
Starts approximately 30m left of *Lochside Chimney*, at the toe of the buttress. Start up a shallow right-facing corner just right of the toe, and continue by a faint fault to reach a left-slanting shelf, which leads into the gully on the left. Instead of following this into the gully, make a move right to gain the foot of a left-slanting ramp (the left of two faults), and follow this to a steep V-corner, then move right on a ledge and up a diagonal fault to a ledge. Go left up a ramp, then right and up to the left edge of a snow terrace. Skirt round the left side of the upper wall by the prominent fault.

Friendly Fire   150m   IV,6. John Lyall, Scott Frazer, Mick Twomey. 8 Feb 2016.
The next fault left of *Balaam's Donkey*.
1. 45m Slant slightly left through a short chimney slot, then up a ramp until possible to move right on ice to a parallel ramp, which leads to a belay beneath a short icy groove (the fault right of the *Air Strikes* ramp).
2. 25m Go up the awkward icy groove, then pass an overhang on the left by a delicate slab. Two tricky cracks lead to a ledge.
3. 40m Move right over a slab, then slant up left and straight up to a belay.
4. 40m A left-slanting fault gains the snow terrace, then a ledge is gained on the left and followed right to a groove up the crest of the upper wall.

Note: *Balaam's Donkey* has had a recent rockfall from low down on the right wall, and which is now a good identifying feature for the route.

BEN AVON, Creag na h-Iolaire:
The Scraggle Ladder   15m   E2 5c. Rory Brown, Peter Herd. 6 Jun 2014.
A nice climb up the unusually featured arete to the right of *The Beach*, worth a star or two. Listed as number 5 in Cairngorms p297.

Clach Bhan (NO 162 054):
The Badger's Tadger   10m   E1 5b *. Michael Barnard, Alan Hill. 19 Sep 2015.
At the south-east end of the tor is a fine east-facing slab with a small pool down on the left. Climb the slab, finishing directly over the top bulge.

Wallower   V0
Right of *The Grindstone*, move up to gain the big hollow.

A couple of good solos are possible here. To descend, downclimb and jump down between *The Grindstone* and *Wallower*.

The Shrine   8m   E1 5a. Michael Barnard. 19 Sep 2015.
The left end of *The Grindstone* slab, starting down and just left of the large block.

Dark Hollow   8m   HVS 5a. Michael Barnard. 19 Sep 2015.
On the wall left of the above, climb a right-slanting line of flakes.

Easter Island Boulder:
An impressive large boulder lies on the way up to the ridge from Clach Fiaraidh (NO 157 048).

The Lone Stone   8m   E2 5b ***. Michael Barnard, Alan Hill. 19 Sep 2015.
The superb right arete of the slabby east face. A bold route, and the easiest way up the boulder! To descend, lower or abseil down the other side using the belayer at the base as an anchor.

East Meur Gorm Craig:
That's the Badger   25m   VS 5a *. Alan Hill, Michael Barnard. 19 Sep 2015.
Climbs the buttress between *Fox Crack* and *Backslash*, which has a forking crack system. Start up the initial flake-crack, then take the steep left fork.

Fox Glove   15m   HVS 5b *. Michael Barnard, Alan Hill. 19 Sep 2015.
Just right and slightly up the gully from *Backslash* is a buttress with two prominent crack-lines; this route takes the left one. Start up the flakes on the left, then make a tricky move right to gain the crack.

Wafer   25m   HVS 4c. Michael Barnard, Alan Hill. 19 Sep 2015.
Lies on the left side of the buttress containing *99*. Start from a high grassy ledge and make an awkward move right to gain and go up a flake-crack. Continue up a left-trending crack for a couple of metres then leave it to climb rightwards up flakes (bold). Traverse left along a ledge to finish up a short crack.

Jam Raiders   10m   HVS 5a *. Alan Hill, Michael Barnard. 19 Sep 2015.
Up and right from *The Aberdonian* is a buttress with two parallel cracks in its front face and a wide crack further left. This route climbs the fine left-hand parallel crack.

Clach Bun Rudthair:
Fantasy Castle   15m   Severe 4b. Michael Barnard, Liam Malone, Graham Tyldesley. 26 Sep 2015.
Start at the far left end of the west face of the north tor (i.e. left of *Tidy Package*). Climb cracks up the crest of the buttress.

The Tax Man   10m   E3 5c. Graham Tyldesley, Michael Barnard, Liam Malone. 26 Sep 2015.
The cracks in the arete right of *Tidy Package*. A steep start followed by some delicate climbing above. RPs protect.

The House of Udge   15m   E2 5b. Michael Barnard, Alan Hill. 20 Sep 2015.
Left of *Obscure Cleft* is an obvious flared offwidth crack cleaving the centre of the tor. Start up a crack on the right, then make a tricky move left to gain the offwidth. Sustained udging follows.

Biscuitarian 20m E1 5a. Michael Barnard, Alan Hill. 20 Sep 2015.
Around the arete left of *South Crack* is a wide left-slanting crack. Climb this, then traverse left to gain the upper part of a right-slanting fault-line. Finish up the *Cream Bun Finish* (does not affect the grade).

Cream Bun Finish to South Crack 5m. Neil McGeachy, Donna Ryan. 31 Jul 2013.
Climb *South Crack* to its top. From the back of the subsidiary pinnacle, hand-traverse a ledge leftwards to make a gymnastic move and finish up large dishes and flakes.

Triple Crack Route E3 5c. Graham Tyldesley, Liam Malone. 26 Sep 2015.
1. 8m 5b *South Crack*.
2. 8m 5b Step down and right to ascend the crack to the next pinnacle.
3. 8m 5c Across the gap is crack 3. Hands, then fists, then a squirm.

T for Traverse 30m E1. Michael Barnard, Liam Malone, Graham Tyldesley. 26 Sep 2015.
A devious and entertaining route up the 'T' buttress.
1. 15m 4c Start as for *Time for T* but continue left along the break and around the corner. Go up an awkward deep groove.
2. 15m 5b Move up onto a large block in the gully then swing round right to hand traverse the break below the roof. Finish onto the top slab as for *Time for T*.

LOCHNAGAR, Southern Sector, Sunset Buttress:
Full Moon Arete 100m III,4. Simon Richardson, Sophie Grace Chappell. 23 Dec 2015.
The well-defined arete on the left side of the shallow buttress taken by *Aramis*.
1. 50m Start just 10m left of the gully of *Ham Butty* and follow a ramp rightwards to join *Ham Butty*. Continue up this to the foot of the arete.
2. 30m Gain the arete from the left and climb on to the crest and move up to a good flake. Move right around the bulge above, pull back left onto the arete and continue to a good ledge below the final steepening.
3. 20m Climb up a short groove, then step left onto the arete and continue on to a tower that defines the end of the arete. Step down into the col (the exit of the gully of *Aramis*) and finish easily to the top.

The Cathedral:
Judas Priest Untrue Finish 80m V,5. Kevin Murphy, Forrest Templeton. 31 Jan 2016.
Climb the first pitch of *Judas Priest*, but instead of breaking right when it reaches easy ground, continue directly up an obvious steepish groove parallel to the top of the second pitch of *Spellbound* onto the terrace below the bottom left of a wide, slabby chimney-corner (50m). Climb up rightwards into a hanging groove on the rib with a technical start. Follow grooves and bulges to a narrow square-cut exit at the top of a steep 15m chimney-groove (30m). A sustained and direct route of good quality.

An t-Sron, The Stuic, North-West Face:

Angel's Share 70m V,7. Simon Richardson, Michael Rinn. 28 Jan 2016.
A direct line cutting through *Solid Air*. Start midway between *Shepherd's Warning* and *Solid Air*.
1. 35m Climb a wall to below an overhanging flared chimney. Climb this with difficulty (crux) and continue up a short corner to the bay and traverse line of *Solid Air*.
2. 20m Continue up the chimney of *Solid Air* for 8m and then climb the vertical wall on the right (second crux) to where the angle eases.
3. 15m Easier climbing leads to the crest of The Stuic.

Cnapan Nathraichan:

White Mamba 150m V,4. Simon Richardson, Roger Webb. 18 Feb 2016.
A striking line based on *Green Mamba*. Climb directly up thinly iced slabs to right of the summer start to gain the main left-facing corner. Follow this to its top and exit up and right past the 'moustache' before trending left to gain easier ground and the top. Climbed in three pitches on thin ice and semi-consolidated snow.

CREAG AN DUBH LOCH, Central Gully Wall:

Note: The pegs on *Bombadillo* have gone and the route is E6 in its current state.

COIRE KANDER:

Note: *Kander Surprise* (SMCJ 2015) seems the same as *Nordwanderer* (SMCJ 2013).

Prudence 200m II. George Allan. 21 Feb 2015.
An alternative to *The Bastion*. Climb the snowfield rightwards below the initial ramp of the parent route until beyond a steep wall. Traverse back left across this via a ledge. Follow a line to the right of the parent route until near the right edge, then climb up slightly leftwards to finish via a small snow field.

Pear Buttress:

This is a name for the buttress to the right of *Twisting Gully*. It contains the route *Tora Bora* (SMCJ 2010). The following three routes are on this buttress which forms the right wall of *Twisting Gully*. Topos of the corrie provided.

Unnamed 200m III. Graham Penny, Calum Horne. 2015.
Fifty metres up *Twisting Gully* on the right wall there is an obvious icefall below an ice ramp leading to the upper slopes.

The Pear 200m IV,4. Geoff Cohen, Raymond Simpson. 11 Feb 2015.
There is a stepped fault going straight up the centre of the buttress from the lowest point to meet an icy groove leading left to the upper slopes. These lead in 100m to the top.

Spiral Staircase 200m III. Des Rubens, Raymond Simpson. 17 Feb 2015.
On the left flank of the buttress an open fault spirals up to a short ice pitch below the upper slopes.

GLEN CLOVA, Corrie Wirral:
Heather Boulevard 115m II. George Allan, John Thomas. 13 Dec 2015.
A wandering line of no particular merit on the left-hand buttress (see SMCJ 2008). Climb a ramp rightwards out of the right corner of a bay in the centre of the buttress, then continue until stopped by a very steep wall girdling the cliff. Traverse left across the buttress to finish up a shallow gully with an awkward exit.

GLEN CLOVA, Craig Mellon:
Der Anfang 200m II. Adam & Tom Harris. 22 Nov 2015.
A rib on the south side of Craig Mellon, starting at NO 265 764 and continuing in steps with many route options available. An interesting climb sticking to the hardest line, although often escapable. The rib peters out near the summit. Photo provided.

GLEN CLOVA, The Scorrie:
The Scorrie Romp 160m II/III. Brian Duthie, Forrest Templeton. 5 Mar 2016.
Start in the centre of the upper Scorrie Buttress. Follow an easy angled left-trending ramp for 45m, belaying at the foot of a steeper turfy groove with an obvious rocky pinnacle to its left. Climb this for 40m to a tree at the top. Continue for a pitch and a half up easier ground left of a small buttress to finish almost at the cairn. Descend to the left, facing back down the Scorrie.

GLEN CLOVA, Craig Broadlands:
King Herod 60m VI,7. Simon Richardson, Sophie Grace Chappell. 23 Dec 2015.
The rambling east face of Craig Broadlands contains a pinnacle that sports an impressive 60m-high front face.
1. 30m Start below the left-hand of the two right-facing grooves on the front face. Gain the grove by climbing a short wide crack on the left and traversing back right. Steep climbing over a couple of bulges leads to a left exit on to the mid-way ledge. Continue up to the prominent offwidth crack on the right.
2. 30m Climb the steep cracked wall right of the offwidth to a ledge and continue up the offwidth corner above to a second ledge. Move right along this, step down and climb a steep inset corner to a turf platform. The short bulging corner above leads to a ledge just below the summit blocks. Descent was by simultaneous abseil to avoid leaving an anchor. It may also be possible to climb down the 5m-high landward side. A short ridge of tumbled blocks leads to the hillside above.

Corrie of Bonhard:
Bamboozle Buttress 80m V,6. Simon Richardson, Adrian Crofton. 17 Jan 2016.
High on the left (north) wall of the corrie are twin buttresses. The right buttress is climbed by *Mystery Ramp* and *Cryptic Wall*. This route this takes the centre of the left buttress.
1. 45m Start at the toe of the buttresses. Climb turfy walls into the obvious corner, then steeply to a terrace.
2. 35m Climb a short chokestone chimney and wall immediately above, step left into corner up to large block on right, turn this and exit up a short ramp. Easy ground for 10m leads to the top.

Corrie Farchal:

The Seven Ages of Man 150m V,5. Simon Richardson, Henning Wackerhage. 7 Feb 2016.
The buttress between the gullies of *Age Before Beauty* and *The Art of Growing Old Gracefully*.
1. 50m Start in the centre of the buttress and zigzag up to undercut twin cracks. Pull through these (first crux) and climb slabs and turfy ledges to belay below an improbable undercut prow.
2. 50m Climb a steep groove on the right side of the prow, then traverse delicately across its front face to its left side (second crux) and continue up easier ground trending right then left.
3. 50m Finish up straightforward snow slopes to the top.

Coffin Dodger 140m IV,4. Simon Richardson, Sophie Grace Chappell. 10 Mar 2016.
The rounded icy buttress between the gully lines of *Brains Before Brawn* and *Over the Hill*.
1. 40m Start 10m left of *Over the Hill* just left of a small rock buttress and climb an easy angled icefall to below the barrier wall.
2. 30m Move left up an icy ramp cutting across the wall and continue up steeper ice to easier ground. Move up snow to belay on the left side of the diamond-shaped buttress.
3. 40m Continue up snow on the left side of the 'diamond' to gain the upper barrier wall. Breach this via short steep groove to the right of the corner taken by *Over the Hill*.
4. 30m Easy ground leads to the top.

The Last Hurrah 140m IV,4. Henning Wackerhage, Simon Richardson. 11 Feb 2016.
The discontinuous gully line between *Elder Crack Buttress* and *Farchal Gully*.
1. 40m Start 10m up and right of *Elder Crack Buttress* and climb a thin icefall up the initial wall (harder than it looks) and continue up the snow gully to below a short steep wall.
2. 50m Climb a groove through the wall and continue up snow to the next barrier wall, climbed by a steep icy groove on the left.
3. 50m Move left and finish up the final snow slopes of *Elder Crack Buttress*.

Too Young to Die 70m IV,6. Simon Richardson, Sophie Grace Chappell. 10 Mar 2016.
The steep rectangular buttress with its overhanging front face above *Farchal Ramp* is one of the finest features in the corrie. This route takes the blunt left arete of the buttress.
1. 30m Start from 40m up *Farchal Ramp* and take a diagonal icy line leading left to a snow bay on the left side of the buttress.
2. 20m Climb through the awkward overhung niche above to gain a broad overhung snow bay. Continue up turfy ground on the left side of the wall above and belay by a huge jutting perched block.
3. 20m Finish up a flared, overhanging offwidth crack to reach easier snow slopes and the top.

Too Old to Rock and Roll   60m   V,7. Simon Richardson, Sophie Grace Chappell.
2 Mar 2016.
A serious route based on the hanging icicle that sometimes forms down the
overhanging corner at the back of the overhung snow bay.
1. 30m Start 50m up *Farchal Ramp* and zigzag up the front face of the icy wall
above to gain the overhung snow bay.
2. 10m Move up to the icicle and climb it (bold and delicate) to a good ledge.
3. 20m Finish easily up the gully and snow slopes above.

The Age of Enlightenment   140m   VI,7. Henning Wackerhage, Simon Richardson.
11 Feb 2016.
An excellent route that fully meets the challenge of the overhanging front face.
1. and 2. 80m Climb easy ground to the right of *Farchal Ramp* to a slanting
chimney-slot 5m right of the initial chimney of *Age is Only a Number*.
3. 25m Climb the chimney-slot, step over the chimney of *Age is Only a Number*
and continued up the ramp above to a narrow ledge with the headwall bulging
above.
4. 15m Continue up the left-slanting crack through the headwall and swing left
to a good ledge.
5. 20m Move left and climb a short vertical icefall to the left of a prominent
jutting fin to finish.

Bassies:
Flotsam   150m   III,4. Simon Richardson. 23 Feb 2016.
The centre of the lower tier of the most easterly buttress on the North-East Face
of Bassies is cut by twin chimney-grooves. Climb the left-hand chimney to the
terrace, then continue up a left-slanting ramp through the second tier. Move 10m
right and climb a narrow right-trending corner through the third tier. Continue up
easier ground up and left to gain the shoulder of the east ridge and the top of the
buttress.

Jetsam   150m   III,4. Simon Richardson. 23 Feb 2016.
Start up the right-hand twin chimney-groove and continue up broad right-tending
ramp through the second tier. The third tier is breached by a narrow right-slanting
ramp 5m right of *Flotsam*. Continue straight up to the crest and finish up easier
ground to the top of the buttress.

Bassies Beachcombing   150m   II. George Allan. 13 Jan 2016.
Start just left of the bay with two chimney-grooves taken by *Flotsam* and *Jetsam*
and climb a zigzag line with two awkward steps, to reach the first terrace.
Continue up the left-slanting ramp of *Flotsam*, then traverse right below the third
tier to beyond the narrow right-slanting ramp of *Jetsam*, where the wall begins to
ease. Easy ground leads to the shoulder.

GLEN ESK, Corriedoune Crag (NO 434 764):
A low level cliff in a beautiful setting. From the right, the first buttress is tree
covered. To its left is a shallow gully with a short steep exit; Woodcutter's Buttress
is left of this gully.

Woodcutter's Buttress 180m II. George Allan. 28 Feb 2016.
Start just up from the foot of the gully and climb easily to the base of the headwall.
Climb away up left by a narrow ramp system.

The Discovery Channel 150m IV,3. George Allan, John Thomas. 7 Mar 2016.
The gully left of *Woodcutter's Buttress*. Climb easily to where the gully cuts into
the left wall forming an ice pitch which veers out of sight. Climb this (55m). Finish
up right or, better, climb mixed ground above (40m).

Craig Maskeldie North Face:
Note: Peter Coleman & George Allan climbed *Dochty Gully* (SMCJ 2009) on
21 Mar 1994 and assumed that they weren't the first.

NORTH-EAST OUTCROPS

SICKLE ROW TO BLOWUP NOSE:
Access to this section of the coast south of Aberdeen has become more challenging
of late. Major quarry works makes locating and assessing the Sickle Row parking
more difficult. There has also been one recorded conflict with the landowner here.
The normal Clashrodny approach is no longer possible as Scottish Rail have
closed the pedestrian railway crossing. It is now illegal to cross the railway here
and there are signs to this effect. Access must now be made from Sickle Row
under the railway or to the south as for Blowup Nose. Parking is generally limited
to one or two cars at most so car share; cars can be parked in Findon village or
better left in Portlethen.

Blowup Nose, Red Roof:
Non-tidal South-West facing
On the south side of the Blowup Nose headland is a small but impressive undercut
wall of sound red granite. It has several fine lines but closer inspection reveals
the roof undercutting the wall is considerable and provides most of the difficulties.
The wall gets the sun into the evening in summer and dries quickly, however
seepage can be a problem after prolonged wet periods. The left end of the wall
supports an impressive colony of kittiwakes but only routes left of *New Horizons*
are affected.
   Approach: As for Blowup Nose to the headland or better and slightly shorter
by parking sensibly on the road just south of North Mains of Findon farm. Pass
the farm on the south and head east through three fields down the side of the
quarry to reach the headland. The centre of the headland is split by a long narrow
inlet which cuts back inland. From the south side of this inlet descend easy rocks
south to a non tidal platform below the routes. For routes left of *Kuiper Belt* it is
wise to prefix a rope and abseil to gain the base as the rope is needed for a belay
especially on *Bird's Nest Soup*. Locate a strainer post at the head of a pile of scree
on the south edge of the headland. Abseil from here down the south edge of the
scree to the cliff-top (40m) then down the corner of *Kuiper Belt* to the cliff base
(15m).

Bird's Nest Soup   18m   E2 5c *. Tim Rankin, Daniel Laing (on-sight). 20 Aug 2015.
The steep crack at the left end of the wall. Climb the initial wall with care via its right arete, then climb the crack until the angle eases. Finish up the continuation groove.

Dark Matter   20m   E4 6a *. Tim Rankin, Russ Birkett. 30 Aug 2015.
Climb *Bird's Nest Soup* until the angle eases, then step left onto a hanging slab below another groove. Place crucial protection in the groove, then swing wildly right to climb the arete and groove to the top.

Interstellar   18m   E4 6a **. Tim Rankin, Daniel Laing. 22 Aug 2015.
The overhanging tight groove. Climb the initial arete to the ledge then a hanging corner to gain the groove. Finish straight up the fine wall above.

New Horizons   18m   E7 6c *** (F7c). Tim Rankin, Gordon Lennox (both redpointed). 5 Jul 2015.
The 6m horizontal prow and thin crack left of *Kuiper Belt* provides an impressive line with stunning climbing. Climb an easy groove to below the roof, gain the lip right of the roof crack and heel hook left to the arete. Slap up this to gain the thin crack which leads to the much easier upper wall. Incredibly well protected if you can stop to place any of it and well worth climbing as a sport route with protection preplaced. Climbed ground up with rests, then redpointed with protection in-situ.

Kuiper Belt   15m   E4 6b **. Tim Rankin. 5 Jul 2015.
The central undercut corner-line is the most obvious feature of the crag. Very well protected and there is a good belay which can also be used for routes to the left or to abb in. Inspected on abseil.

Supernova   15m   E7 6c **. Tim Rankin (head pointed). 29 Aug 2015.
The hanging ramp and small corner right of *Kuiper Belt* provides another compelling line. Climb the lower wall to the ledge below a crack right of *Kuiper Belt*, arrange protection in the roof above (small Friend in slot and micro wire in corner on right). Launch out right from the crack along the lip to gain the hanging ramp and excellent protection. Climb the ramp with a hard move at the lip to gain a good flat hold in the corner above. Continue up the corner, pull out right onto a ledge and finish up a short wall.

Perfect Vacuum   15m   E8/9 6c **. Tim Rankin (head pointed). 29 Aug 2015.
The hanging arete above the ramp gives excellent powerful climbing but is potentially serious. Climb *Supernova* to the protection on the hanging ramp, them make hard moves directly up the overhanging wall to gain holds at the lip beneath the arete (crucial rock 1). Now climb the arete to get established on the wall above. Finish up the easy groove. All protection placed on lead but left in place after a failed attempt and deteriorating conditions.

Voyager   15m   E5 6b *. Tim Rankin. 23 Aug 2015.
A wild little route climbing the steep right-hand hanging groove at the right end of the roof. Climb an easy groove to a ledge, move up to a block, then move left and up again using a rattly granite shield to below the groove. A hard move up this leads to an easier finishing groove. Inspected on abseil.

Outer Space   15m   E4 6a **. Tim Rankin, Russ Birkett. 30 Aug 2015.
Even better, climb *Voyager* until below the steep groove, then make a sensational traverse left to the base of the slabby groove. Climb this and step right to a technical finish. Inspected on abseil.

Approach Walls:
10 routes on the SMC website.

BLOWUP NOSE, South Side:
5 routes on the SMC website.

FINDON CLIFFS, The Shark Fin:
Non-tidal   South facing
A short but very steep sport climbing venue named after the huge fin of rock which protrudes out of the hillside like an umbrella above the routes. The rock is a very compact grey micro schist which is very different in style to its near neighbour, Orchestra Cave. Although not affected by rain it can be very damp and sweaty due to its sheltered location and steepness. The steeper roof routes receive little sun especially in summer but the right-hand routes and base of the crag bask in sun much of the day; a real novelty for the North-East coast! For this reason the crag really comes into its own from autumn through to spring when you can enjoy good cool conditions but be sun bathing at the belay. There can be seepage above the right-hand routes but it is only really a problem on the true finish to *Dorado*. For worthwhile conditions good air movement is needed as well as a bit of morning sun. Birds are not a problem on the current routes.
   Approach: The routes are on the north wall of the deep inlet immediately south of the Red Band Cliff. Follow the approach as for the Red Band Cliff. Once in the field, follow the south edge overlooking the deep inlet. Cross the fence and head out to the south-east end of the headland and carefully descend the grass ridge to gain easy angled rock slabs. A 20m abseil from 2 bolts leads to the huge non-tidal platforms below the cliff. Egress is via ascent of a fixed rope (jumar). Alternatively at low tide, scramble round from just south of the Rock Band cliff, jumping a small inlet (Diff).

The Cave:
At the left end of the crag the routes are short but very steep. A skilled belayer is required here as is some thought when clipping.

Closed Project
A left-hand start to *Mbenga* starting up the corner.

Mbenga   10m   8a+ **. Tim Rankin. 4 Mar 2015.
Excellent moves up the 60 degree wall and arete on the left side of the cave.

Arapiama   10m   7b+ *. Tim Rankin. May 2014.
The central line out the hanging corner in the roof and wall above. Special care needs to be taken clipping the bolts due to the large boulders beneath the line. *Warm up Start* (5m 6c) pulls on from the boulders missing out the crux roof section.

Hammerhead   15m   7c+ *. Tim Rankin. 16 May 2015.
A link up; climb *Arapiama* to the lip and take this right and up to the lower off on
Great White. A physical affair!

Great White   8m   8b ***. Tim Rankin. 5 Apr 2015.
Whacky moves through the right-hand roof. You're only cheating yourself with a
tight rope on the crux!

Main Fin:
Closed Project
Left-hand line out of *Megalodon*.

Megalodon   16m   8a+ ****. Tim Rankin. 25 Nov 2015.
The central line (directly above the maillon on 5th bolt) out the huge upper fin
has moves as spectacular as the line! Finish at the juggy break beneath the
waterfall. Reverse aid the top 5 bolts then lower off.

Right Wall:
The following routes are much steeper than they look. They are all very good but
the lip can seep badly however the finishing holds on both *Stingray* and *Barracuda*
are usually dry.

Stingray   14m   7b ***. Tim Rankin. 18 Apr 2015.
Gain the crack in the arete, climb the arete and continue up the hanging groove.
Climb the top arete direct making hard moves to a side-pull up left. Reach right
to clip the lower-off.

Dorado   16m   7b+ **. Tim Rankin. 24 Apr 2015.
Using the first bolt on Stingray, climb the corner until forced onto the arete of
Stingray. Step back right above the roof to gain the hanging ramp. Continue
straight up via a pocket of gold to the ledge and climb the slanting quartz crack
(lower off on left if top is wet - 7b) to a final hard move to the cliff-top lower-off
as for the next route.
Permadry Variation 7b+ is a logical variation which is always dry. With hands on
the ledge, move up left to finish up *Stingray*, no lying on the ledge to rest at this
grade.

Mahi-Mahi   16m   7c *. Tim Rankin. 26 May 2015.
A 'Rankin style' eliminate taking in the hardest climbing on the wall. Climb
Dorado to the ledge, then move right to climb the top wall direct left of *Barracuda*
and studiously avoiding its rest and holds in the groove.

Barracuda   16m   7a+ **. Tim Rankin. 24 Apr 2015.
Climb the roof-capped corner and swing right (best to unclip the first bolt to avoid
sharp roof edge). Climb the shallow groove to the ledge, then up left to the quartz
crack. Move back right and climb the steep upper wall using a small corner on
the right.

There is also some worthwhile bouldering beneath the routes and on the boulders
themselves. The best problems are:

Wilson Moir on Stingray (7b), The Shark Fin, Findon Cliffs. Photo: Niall Ritchie.

Fin Cave Traverse F7b. A left to right low-level traverse of the crag, starting from the red wall and traverse right with difficulty dropping down and across sloping shelves, good breaks lead to more hard moves at the overhanging arete. It is easier now to finish at the end of the wall just past the fin or link into the next problem.
Hammy Warm-Up F6a+. SDS just left of *Stingray*. Drop down right to a block on the lip and traverse the lip right to pull up into the block of *Barracuda* to finish.
Low Cave F6b. SDS in back of cave below *Arapiama*. Go up breaks, then right to the start of *Great White*, or continue along *Fin Cave Traverse* for a F7a tick.
White Snake F6b+. SDS F6c. The overhanging white calcite arete right again, finishing below the roof. Even better started from below *Great White* F7a.
On the largest boulder there are several good problems the best being the central ramp, SDS from a good edge F6b, or better SDS at the left arete and climb the ramp direct F7a.

Orchestra Cave Right Wall:
The right granite wall overhangs at 50 degrees, has no seepage and makes an excellent winter venue, receiving sun for longer than any other part of the cave. The following two routes lower off to the raised ledge avoiding big seas and are easy to strip. So no excuses really! In big seas the experienced can abseil in from the north side of the cave (spike block and large nuts in break) down an easy corner to large sloping shelves at the south end of this. Belay and abseil to an easy traverse left to the raised ledge.

La Forza del Destino 10m 8a **. Tim Rankin. 7 Feb 2015.
The grossly overhanging groove on the right side of the granite wall is much harder than it looks. Very powerful, sustained climbing.

Con Fuoco 10m 7c+ **. Tim Rankin. 21 Feb 2015.
Start up *Bittersweet Symphony*. At the 2nd bolt, step right and take the wall direct. Short but superb climbing.

CRANHILL CRAG:
The Short Hope Route 30m VS 4c. Rory Brown, Andrew Appleby. 14 Aug 2013.
The obvious curving crack-line at the south end of the cliff. Abseil to the ledge 4m above the base. Beware of some loose rock.

NEWTONHILL, Harbour Wall:
Mission Improbable 15m HVS 5a. Tim Whitaker, Jon Ashdown. 8 Aug 2015.
At the inland end of Harbour Wall. Start 2m left of the arete of *The Snirgler* below a short hanging corner. Climb the wall left of this directly to a band of more friable rock. Trend up and right to a large ledge and belay (or continue), then right to finish up *The Snirgler*. Belay stakes above Back Door wall some 30m back.

NEWTONHILL, Lower Boltsheugh:
3 routes on the SMC website.

NEWTONHILL, Green Slough:
12 routes on the SMC website.

Brown Crag:

Lobster Thermadore 15m E4 5c **. Tim Rankin, Amanda Lyons. 12 Apr 2015.
A super direct version of *Rock Lobster*. Start as for *Rock Lobster* and climb the
thin crack, but instead of reaching right to good holds make a move up left to a
good crimp and 0 cam. Continue straight up to better holds and junction with
Pinch of Salt. Finish up the fine head wall of this. Excellent sustained wall
climbing.

Brown Band Crag:

Coalition E3 6a *. Tim Rankin, Amanda Lyons. 12 Apr 2015.
Start below *The Fire Inside* and take the wall up and left to below the roof and
junction with *Devo Max*. Rock over the roof to the right to gain hidden jugs at the
lip on the next roof (crux). Cross the roof and finish direct over the upper bulge.

On the right side of the cliff is a distinctive alcove.

Found 15m E1 5b. Tim Rankin, Amanda Lyons. 12 Apr 2015.
Gain the alcove and exit it on the left, move up to and around the roof on the right.
Rock up left onto the slab and climb the centre of the steep headwall above.

NORTH OF ABERDEEN, Red Wall Quarry:

Hades (aka Demons) 22m 8b+ ***. Tim Rankin. 30 May 2015.
Climb Lucifer to the undercut break, then move right to climb the blunt upper
arete via exquisite powerful moves.

COVESEA, Boulders Bay Area:

Khmer Rouge 10m E7 6c *. Jules Lines. 5 Oct 2015.
An unprotected eliminate line up the centre of the wall between *Sandinista* and
Zugzwang. Start below a flake in the centre of the wall. Make hard moves directly
up the wall to gain the flake. Use the flake to gain a line of improving crimps and
ledge holds to gain the top.

Banana Republic, Corbyn Variation E2 5c *. Callum Johnson, Steve Carter. 12
Jun 2016.
Climb *Banana Republic* through the roof to stand on the ledge. Traverse hard left
for 4m into the middle of the wall to a faint crack. Climb this and move left again
at the top to finish.

Escher's Steps 15m E6 6b ***. Graham Tyldesley (headpointed). 21 Jul 2015.
Start up *Fascist Octopus*. Make the long reach, then move left into a capped
corner. Step left to the arete and finish up cracks and roofs to the top.

Honey Barrel 15m E3 5c **. Jules Lines. 5 Oct 2015.
The hanging arete to the left of *Roof Crack*. Pull through the guarding roof and
climb the wall into the corner. Traverse along the lip on chicken-heads to gain the
arete. Climb the arete, mainly on the left in a great position.

LOGIE HEAD:

Seahorse 10m H.Severe. Steve Perry, Eleonora Di Cuffa. 12 Apr 2016.
Directly opposite *Sea Pink* and right of *Sea Snake* is a rising flake. Layback this
to a ledge at 6m, then step left and follow a crack-line in the headwall.

North Star   10m   F7a * S1 (E5 6b). Jules Lines. 13 Aug 2015.
This route takes the arete to the right of *Dark Star*'s finish. Climb the arete on the left side via some off-balance moves to gain jugs at half-height. Continue up the arete above, making the most of the holdless pod-crack. A spotter would be handy for DWS.

Snow Crab   12m   E7 6b **. Jules Lines, Steve Perry. 12 Apr 2016.
The topless crack and intermittent seam to the right of *Sea Pink* is excellent, fingery and run out.

CULLEN AREA, Crathie Point (NJ 548 673):
1 route on the SMC website.

PORTSOY, The Needle (NJ 587 663).
4 routes on the SMC website.

ROSEHEARTY:
Note: Michael Barnard thought HVS 5a for *Lipp Service*. This would be better described as finishing directly, rather than up the right side of the overhang (a bit eliminate). *Shapeshifter* is E3 5c (not E4 6a).

PASS OF BALLATER:
Hybrid Lines   10m   E7 6c **. Jules Lines. 5 May 2016.
Climb *Smith's Arete* to the first good hold, crucifix left to the flat hold in the sidewall and continue up to the break. Finish up the crack in the vague seam in the headwall (*Peel's Wall RH finish*).

Local Anaesthetic   12m   E4 6a **. Jules Lines. 25 May 2015.
Climb *General Anaesthetic* to the hand jug 3m below the top and climb diagonally right on quartz holds to reach the top right corner of the wall.

CRAIG CORN ARN (North East Outcrops p414):
Jamming Over There   10m   VS 4c *. Steve Perry, Sarah Sigley. 4 May 2016.
Heading right from *Crackline* (which was thought **), the crag changes aspect and rises uphill. There are two crack-lines that converge into a jamming crack.

HIGHLAND OUTCROPS

DUNKELD AREA, BLACK CRAG:
Swither Wa'   10m   E5 6a ***. Alastair Robertson, Adrian Crofton. 29 May 2016.
Climbs the centre of the 'impressive overhanging wall' left of *Ugsome Fearlies*. Make some fingery committing moves to better holds and protection. Step right and climb over the overlap (crux, exciting), then move right on better holds to a junction with *Ugsome Fearlies* and good gear. Climb straight up then leftwards on good holds to finish with a grapple over the top.

LOCH NAN UAMH, European Union Crag (NM 713 843):
6 routes on the SMC website.

GLEN NEVIS, Polldubh Upper Tier, Tiara Buttress (NN 1520 6897):
4 routes on the SMC website.

Whale Rock Gorge Area:
2 DWS routes on the SMC website.

BINNEIN SHUAS:
Ardversary 190m H.Severe. Graeme Ettle, John Lyall. 2 Oct 2015.
Start at some cracked ribs just left of the vegetated groove just left of the start to *Ardverikie Wall*. The last 2 pitches are similar to *Summer Wine*.
1. 50m 4b Climb easy rock ribs for around 15m to a short vegetated step right onto a smooth dark slab. A tricky step up leads to easier clean slabs following a direct line to a shared belay with *Ardverikie Wall*.
2. 40m 4a Climb the excellent wall above on great holds; this is left of the *Ardverikie Wall* crack.
3. 30m 4a Follow twin cracks right, to cross *Ardverikie Wall* at a thread. Straight up leads to a small niche.
4. 30m 4a Step left and climb to the large grass terrace and a large block up right.
5. 40m Follow the quartz slab just to the left.

CREAG DUBH, Great Wall:
SMB 33m E1 5b *. Gary & Karen Latter. 25 Mar 2016.
A fine companion to *LMF*. Start right of that route, behind the fallen birch. Climb a broken crack and direct over a bulge to better holds. Continue direct, pulling over the bulge just right of *LMF* to a ledge on *The Brute*. Cross the roof (as for *Fou rire*) and continue to the 5 bolt ledge.

Fou rire 60m E4 **. Gary Latter, Craig Lamb, Scott Grosdanoff. 10 Mar 2016; Gary Latter, Dave McKinney (pitch 2). 25 Jun 2016.
1. 35m 6a Start midway between the fallen birch tree and *Outspan*, just right of a shelf at the base. Make bouldery moves past a good incut hold to the second break. Move left along this, then up past a left-curving flake to a large quartz recess (as for *Organ Grinder*?). Pull out rightwards and climb direct up the wall trending left to beneath the roof. Cross this at a prominent V-slot (jugs on lip), and continue easily up right edge of wall to gain the right end of the 5 bolt ledge.
2. 25m 6a Climb directly up the wall to the roof and good cams in a slot. Reach over to a good small edge on the lip, then span left to jugs. Pull over to a good small break, then go more easily up the wall above rightwards, then trending left to a sling and maillon on a tree. 60m abseil.

Mein Kampf 32m E7 6b *. Calum Muskett, Ross Creber. 30 May 2016.
Start 4m right of the *The Fuhrer*. Boulder up the wall to the right end of *The Fuhrer* gear ledge and place a good wire – your last for quite a distance! Traverse 2m to the right and make big moves on good holds to a rest beneath a small overlap. Make a tricky unprotected press up into the overlap and up again to some good crimps. Make a final bold move up to the right and finally some good gear as for *Harder than your Husband*. Finish as for *The Fuhrer* to the tree belay.

KINGUSSIE:
Note: Scott Grosdanoff in Apr 2016 climbed a line just right of *Finale*, also a left-hand finish to *Leftover*. Both E2 but peg runners used and taken out.

BEN NEVIS, AONACHS, CREAG MEAGAIDH

Tower Ridge, East Flank:
Night Fury   IX,9. Dave MacLeod, Helen Rennard. 6 Mar 2016.
Steep grooves 4m left of *The Urchin*. Start up a tricky left-facing corner to enter a larger right-facing corner. Climb this with bold moves above poor gear to thank-god runners at its top. Continue to a good belay below an overhanging barrier. Arrange poor gear in this and make committing moves over the bulge to gain easier ground and *Tower Ridge*.

Number Two Gully:
Logger's Wall   80m   V,4. Michael Barnard, Ron Dempster. 21 Nov 2015.
Lies on the right wall of *Number Two Gully*. Start about halfway up the gully beneath an obvious left-trending fault leading to a chimney higher up.
1. 30m Go up the fault for 10m to where it steepens, then traverse left before moving up (bold) to the chimney. Climb the chimney to a spike on the left.
2. 20m Climb up to an obvious system of ledges. Follow these out right and up to a large block.
3. 30m Finish more easily up the groove above.

Number Three Gully Buttress:
Gothic Edge   120m   VII,7. John Crook, Peter Graham. 31 Dec 2015.
Although only the pitch up the arete left of the *Gargoyle Cracks* is new, this combination of existing routes provides a good direct route up the buttress. Start up the Direct Start to *Gargoyle Wall* (which without ice provides a good VI,7 pitch), then follow *Gargoyle Wall* to the corner below the *Gargoyle Cracks*. Climb the arete (15m, crux) left of the *Gargoyle Cracks* and finish up the *Rok Finish to Hobgoblin*.

South Trident Buttress:
Tangerine Dream   35m   VII,8. Ramon Marin, Douglas Russell. 31 Jan 2016.
A prominent chimney-flake crack on the lower tier and to the left of *The Rattler*, finishing on the large terrace leading into *Number Four Gully*.

Càrn Dearg Buttress:
Capricorn   90m   VIII,7. Nick Bullock, Tim Neill. 10 Mar 2016.
Follow *Gemini* to a good block belay at the end of the diagonal ramp after the famous ice smear section. This is just left of the foot of the *Gemini* twin grooves.
1. 30m Pull left over a small roof to gain an ice flow and pillar in an obvious left-facing groove. There is a stance on an exposed ledge at its top left.
2. 60m Follow the icy corner until possible to gain a hanging smear out left. This leads into a more mixed groove and to a snowy ledge. Possible and good belay. Follow the technical groove straight above (quite well protected) to gain easing ground and so *Ledge Route*.

Cousins Buttress:
Note: *Cousinade* (SMCJ 2015) should have been graded VII,8.

Castle Ridge, North Face:
Note: Michael Barnard notes that the line of the *Superdirect Finish to Nordwand*

Direct (supplied by his partner) was shown incorrectly on the topo in SMCJ 2015. He has supplied an amended topo.

STOB BAN, North Buttress:
Deceptive Grooves   110m   III,4 *. Steve Kennedy, Andy MacDonald. 10 Jan 2016.
The south-east flank of the *East Ridge* is split by two gullies. This route takes the buttress between the gullies characterised by a steep triangular shaped wall in the lower section. Climb grooves running up the right side of the wall before moving diagonally left to reach the buttress crest. A thin slabby wall leads to easier ground (55m). Easy mixed ground leads onto the *East Ridge* (55m).

North-East Flank:
En Guarde   170m   III *. Steve Kennedy, Andy MacDonald. 14 Feb 2016.
To the right of the start of *Bodice Ripper* is a small pointed buttress and thereafter two gully lines. This routes starts up the left gully (via a short ridge on the left) which ends at a steep rock wall. Climb the gully, then move right below the wall to reach the base of a left-facing corner (55m). An icefall forms in the corner which is followed to a wide leftward-leaning shelf. Follow the shelf leftwards below some headwalls to reach the edge of the buttress (55m). Continue up the edge to a wide snow shelf, then up left to join the upper part of *Bodice Ripper* in two pitches.

AONACH MÒR, West Face:
Living Dead   135m   III *. Steve Kennedy, Andy MacDonald. 31 Jan 2016.
A more direct and continuous line than the original route described in SMCJ 2015 and which is superseded by the following description. Climb *Downhill Gully* to a point just below an icefall which usually forms at the first narrow section. Climb the well-defined groove on the right wall of the gully leading diagonally left until a short wall is reached on the second pitch (the original route moved out right from just below this point). Turn the wall on the left to reach a prominent left-facing corner. Climb the corner which finishes at the narrow section of the upper part of *Golden Oldy*. Finish up *Golden Oldy*.

BINNEIN SHUAS, North-West Buttresses:
Note: A correction. *Bogle Eyed* (SMCJ 2015) is roughly level with and about 100m left (east) of *Laggan Fantasy*.

Location, Location, Location via *Cave Man Start*   55m   III,5. Andy Clark, Rob Wright, Martin Holland. 6 Mar 2016.
Climb easily to a boulder ledge in the cave, arrange chockstone protection and struggle up through the hole above. Belay blocks available where the original route is rejoined.

Off Yer Knees   30m   III. Andy Clark, Rob Wright, Martin Holland. 6 Mar 2016.
Directly north of the summit is a short buttress. Towards the right-hand end of the buttress is a heathery ledge at two-thirds height. From an undercut start, climb turf and rock to near the right end of the ledge. Traverse left along the ledge to easier ground and the top 20m north of the summit.

CREAG MEAGAIDH, Meall Coire Choille-rais:

Serpentine 150m II. Simon Richardson. 23 Feb 2013.
The S-shaped line of snow and frozen turf on the south-east flank of the East Ridge. Low in the grade.

Coire Choille-rais:

The following routes lie on the triangular buttress known as Aisre-Chaim on the west side of Coire Choille-rais.

Birthday Route 160m IV,4. Simon Richardson, Henning Wackerhage. 6 Jan 2016.
A natural left to right line cutting diagonally across the buttress. Start just left of the steep lower tier where a turfy break leads up and right.
1. 50m Follow it over several short walls to gain a ledge system that leads up and right to a prominent right-leaning slot at half-height on the buttress.
2. 50m Climb a steep crack on the right wall of the slot and exit onto a ledge. Continue up walls and turfy steps to where the angle eases on the crest of the buttress.
3. 60m Easy snow and short steps lead to the plateau.

Cat Burglar 160m V,5. Simon Richardson, Pat Ingram. 12 Jan 2016.
A good route following grooves and corners on the left flank of the buttress. Start as for *Birthday Route*.
1. 40m Traverse right along a shelf to a prominent square-cut corner. Climb this to the diagonal line of *Birthday Route*.
2. 30m Continue straight up to a smooth slabby corner. Make an awkward traverse left across the left wall (crux) to a ledge. Step up, then crawl right to a good stance below the upper corner.
3. 30m Climb the corner to its top, and surmount the short steep wall above to reach the top of the steep section of the buttress.
4. 60m Continue up the easy-angled crest to the top as for *Birthday Route*.

The Day After Tomorrow 190m VII,8. Simon Richardson, Roger Everett. 9 Jan 2016.
A bold and difficult route meeting the challenge of the 'impregnable wall' on the steep front face of the buttress.
1. 25m Start just right of the buttress toe and climb blobs of turf up a vertical wall to reach a steep right-facing corner that leads to a roof. Traverse left below a hanging ramp (crux) to reach the sanctuary of a blob of turf on the arete. Pull through the overhanging offwidth above to a ledge.
2. 25m Climb the flake-crack above to a terrace. Move up the wall above and traverse 10m left along a second terrace to below a smooth right-facing corner. The only belay is a flake 5m before the corner.
3. 30m Make a hard move up the left wall of the corner (bold, second crux) to reach a ledge. Continue up the chimney-corner above to gain the slanting line of *Birthday Route*. Follow this to the stance below the prominent right-leaning slot.
4. and 5. 110m Continue up *Birthday Route* to the top.

DIRC MHÒR, West Flank:

Dalwhinnie Primary Gully 110m III,4. John Lyall. 12 Feb 2016.

On the right side, a short way before reaching Sentinel Rock, is a prominent left-slanting fault. The main steep sections are passed on the right wall.

Meltwater Channel   45m   III. John Lyall. 12 Feb 2016.
The thinly iced groove tucked in to the left side of *White Tower* and the icy slab to finish.

Ship Rock:
Icebreaker   60m   IV,4. John Lyall, Ian Thomson. 28 Feb 2016.
Climb the icy corner on the left flank of Ship Rock, then smash your way through the icicle festooned right-slanting fault to the top of the block. Ice and heather to the top.

Beyond the descent gully and behind *Carry on up the Khyber*, look out for the first metal post on top of a projecting buttress. A second fence line stops atop a further buttress.

Breathing Space   45m   IV/V,5. John Lyall, Ian Thomson. 28 Feb 2016.
Climb very helpful vertical ice to gain an icy ramp behind the projecting buttress, which is followed to the top.

GEAL-CHÀRN (DRUMOCHTER):
Gentlemen's Excuse Me   55m   IV,5 *. Gregor Ewing, Linda Gentleman, Martin Holland. 21 Jan 2016.
On the crag north-east of the one with *Flight of the Navigator* (so two crags NE of the main Creag Dhubh). The obvious ice line at the right end of the crag. GPS map reference for the start of the route NN 59950 80212 (altitude 492m). Climb steep ice or a steep ice/turf ramp on the left and then ice to a bay and good tree belay where the angle eases (25m). Climb easier angled ice and turf in the gully above (30m). A 50m abseil descent is possible from trees just below the top.

CÀRN DEARG (Monadhliath), Summit Buttress:
Of Ice and Men   100m   IV,5. Michael Barnard, John MacLeod. 6 Mar 2016.
Climbs the Monadh Lisa gully.
1. 40m Start as for *Monadh Lisa* to below the impasse.
2. 60m A short pillar of water ice gains the upper gully. Continue easily to the top.

GLEN COE

BUACHAILLE ETIVE MÒR, Creag a' Bhancair:
Note: Malcolm Rowe & Davy Moy climbed the *Original Finish to Carnivore* free on 28 Jun 1968, before the date in the guidebook or on UKC. Picture supplied.

LOST VALLEY BUTTRESS:
Moonshine   120m   V,7. Simon Tietjen, Mark Chadwick. 9 Jan 2016.
1. 35m Start as for *Moonlighting* but where *Moonlighting* steps left, *Moonshine* carries straight up the initially overhanging chimney-corner to the same belay as *Moonlighting*.

2. 35m Follow the same chimney-corner line directly above the belay. Surmount the final chockstone and follow the off-angle corner to reach the belay of *Moonlighting*.
3. 50m Move left into the *Pterodactyl* gully and follow this to the top.

STOB COIRE NAN LOCHAIN:
Shadhavar VIII,9. Uisdean Hawthorn, Iain Small. 14 Dec 2015.
Pitch 1 of *Unicorn*. Climb the second pitch of *Unicorn* for 5m until just above a small roof. Traverse right on thin hooks into a thin crack in the middle of the wall. Follow this with sustained interest and good gear to a small ledge. Trend back left to the top of the wall. Finish up *Unicorn* pitch 3 or step down and right to abb off in 60m.

CHURCH DOOR BUTTRESS:
Hoargasm 40m VII,8. Greg Boswell, Uisdean Hawthorn. 10 Feb 2016.
Start at the very toe of the buttress. Follow a right-trending crack for 10m, then pull left over a bulge to follow a very positive crack-line to a ledge. Finish up *West Chimney*.

Gates of Paradise 60m VIII,8. Iain Small, Murdoch Jamieson. 10 Feb 2016.
A set of hanging icicles further right up the crag than the summer routes. Start directly below the main icicle.
1. 20m Two short steep walls which lead to easy ledges. Trend left towards a blocky pinnacle. Climb this and belay on the right.
2. 40m Climb the steep wall and step left on the arete. On the first ascent, ice formed down the left side of the arete. This was climbed till it was possible to step right into the crack-line. Follow this into a groove which leads to a roof. Arrange protection; then make powerful moves up right to gain the ice. Follow this to the top. Gaining the ice could be easier if ice was to form further down the wall above the roof.

ETIVE SLABS:
Hammer Direct Start 35m HVS 5a ***. Gary & Karen Latter. 24 May 2016.
Climbs direct from the base of the corner. Scramble leftwards up grass from the top of the first pitch to belay at the base of the corner. Climb the main corner throughout, joining the original route above the scoop and continue to belay on the good ledge halfway up the corner.
Note: The final pitch is 70m to reach the descent path (not 35m as described in the current guide) – probably best split at the small trees after about 40m or so.

BEN STARAV, Coire an Fhir Leith:
The squat buttress that finishes at an altitude of 900m on the east flank of the north ridge of Ben Starav is cut by a couple of lines in the shape of an offset V.

The Starav Enigma 40m V,6. Simon Richardson, Roger Everett. 14 Feb 2016.
Climb straight up a line of steep shallow chimneys (the left leg of the V) cutting through the centre of the buttress. Good sustained climbing with a bold start.

The Borrowdale Conundrum 50m III,4. Simon Richardson, Roger Everett. 14 Feb 2016.
1. 35m Start at the foot of *The Starav Enigma* and climb a right-slanting ramp (the right leg of the V) to a bay.

2. 15m Step left, climb a short corner to a ledge, and move left to the arete. Follow this more easily to the top.

CREISE, Stob a' Ghlais Choire:
Central Buttress 100m VI,6. Simon Richardson, Roger Everett, 15 Feb 2016.
The south-east face of Stob a' Ghlais Choire is home to a fine narrow buttress that runs directly up to the summit.
1. 30m Start below the right toe of the buttress and climb a steep right-facing corner (bold) to enter a niche and continue up a left-slanting gully (delicate) to reach a large platform.
2. 30m Continue up the centre of the two walls above and belay below a steep left-facing corner.
3. 25m Climb the corner and belay below the final tier.
4. 15m Finish up the left-facing corner to the top.

CLACH LEATHAD, Summit Cliff:
Stone Roses 120m II. Dave McGimpsey, Andy Nisbet. 31 Mar 2016.
Based on a rib forming the right end of the face. Start up the right-hand and bigger ramp at the bottom right corner of the cliff. Climb this and another ramp on the left, set below a steep wall. Continue up snowy grooves just right of the crest to a final steeper buttress, climbed up short steps.

SGÙRR DHOMHNUILL (Ardgour), North Face:
Note: Jamie Hageman climbed the long gully at 250m Grade I on 16 Jan 2016.

BEINN MHIC CEDICH (Moidart), North-East Corrie:
Perfumed Garden 105m IV,4 *. Steve Kennedy, Andy MacDonald. 17 Jan 2016.
The most prominent and central buttress is roughly triangular in shape. This route takes the fault on its right side, starting from almost the lowest point of the buttress. A steep lower step is turned on the left wall. From the top of the fault, move up leftwards, then follow grooves to the summit ridge.

SOUTHERN HIGHLANDS

BEINN UDLAIDH:
Wind Up 60m IV,4. David Goldie, Robert Kincaid. 25 Feb 2016.
A short route between *Sunshine Gully* and *Central Gully*. Start at the left of the steep buttress that is adjacent to *Central Gully*. Climb direct up steep iced slabs then up a right-trending snow ramp to below an overhang (30m). At the right of the overhang is a steep iced corner; climb direct to the top (30m). Topo provided.

BEINN IME, Fan Buttress:
Forked Gully Buttress 60m II/III. Gerhard Mors, Stephan Mors. 22 Nov 2015.
The buttress between the forks of *Forked Gully*, via a right-slanting snowy ramp and continuing up an open groove.

BEINN EUNAICH:
Note: Ken Crocket notes that *Beaver Buttress* (120m III) was first climbed by J.R. Corbett, C.W. Parry, A.P.A. Robertson & J.H.B. Bell on 31 Dec 1927. There is a description of the FA in the SMCJ (18/105, April 1928, pp.184–5).

BEINN HEASGARNICH, Coire Heasgarnich:

Simba 140m III. Simon Richardson, Sophie Grace Chappell. 26 Apr 2016.
Start 20m right of *The Rambler*.
1. 50m Climb a parallel depression into a bay and move up to a smooth corner (the second corner left from the right edge of the buttress).
2. 30m Ascend the corner to a terrace.
3. 35m Move left onto the hanging turfy ramp and climb it past an overlap to a bay.
4. 25m Exit steeply right and continue up easier ground to the top.

BEINN CHALLUIM:

North Face Route 300m II. Simon Richardson. 30 Apr 2016.
An exposed face route finishing at the summit. Start 50m left of *North Gully* and climb a shallow left-slanting open gully to gain a couloir leading to the central 'spider' snowfield. At it top, exit via a steep wide couloir that leads to the final snow slopes and an exit by the summit cairn.

MEALL NAN TARMACHAN, Creag na Caillich:

Spooks 160m VI,6. Simon Richardson, Simon Yearsley. 14 Jan 2016.
Takes a curving line up the steep buttress to the right of *Momento Mori*. Start at a groove, 5m right of the large corner of *Momento Mori*.
1. 55m Climb the groove, passing right of a grey pillar to below steeper turfy ground. Climb steep walls, then move left to belay on the edge of a groove.
2. 50m Go up the groove, then swing right onto a turfy ramp system. Follow the ramp in a fine position to easier ground.
3. 60m Continue up easy ground to finish.

Càrn Chòis, East Face. Photo: Willie Jeffrey.

**CÀRN CHÒIS
East Face**

1. Nippy Sweetie II
2. Famous for a Reason II

Coire Riadhait:

Digital Painter 100m II. Simon Richardson. 29 Apr 2016.
The line of grooves up the centre of the rectangular buttress near the head of Coire Riadhait, starting from a small snow bay.

GLEN TURRET, Càrn Chòis, East Face (NN 798 276):

This face overlooks the Loch Turret Reservoir. Park below the dam and approach by a track on the west side of the loch.

Nippy Sweetie 120m II. Willie Jeffrey, Noel Williams. 24 Feb 2016.
Follow the obvious central gully.

Famous for a Reason 110m II. Willie Jeffrey, Raymond Simpson, Noel Williams. 6 Mar 2016.
This leftward leaning gully starts at a slightly higher level than the previous route on the right-hand side of the crag.

LOWLAND OUTCROPS

AYRSHIRE, Loudoun Hill:

Sheep Thrills 10m VS 4c. Andrew Fraser, Ian Magill, Alasdair Fraser. 26 May 2015.
A useful addition which climbs the steep wall immediately right of *Conclusion*.
Note: The present guide refers to mossy routes between Mod and V.Diff to the right of *Conclusion*, but on looking at the 1986 guide, these lie further right.

GALLOWAY HILLS, The Merrick, Black Gairy:

Overdraft Dodger 150m IV,4 *. Stephen Reid, Colin Wells, James Kinnaird. 5 Feb 2015.
A useful alternative for those chickening out of *Interstellar Overdraft* or a good route in its own right.
1. 50m As for *Interstellar Overdraft*.
2. 40m From the block belay, traverse 2m rightwards and climb the left-leaning turfy corner, stepping left to a fine view of *Interstellar's* top section, before finishing up a rib. Twenty metres of easier climbing leads to a belay on a huge block on the left. A further 60m of easy ground gains the plateau.

Kirshinnoch Ramp 140m IV,4 *. Colin Wells, Stephen Reid. 6 Feb 2015.
The huge vegetated ramp slanting rightwards from below the crux pitch of *Kirshinnoch Corner* is an obvious feature and is good when iced.
1. and 2. The first two pitches of *Kirshinnoch Corner* to the block belay in the scoop.
3. 20m Climb the vegetated groove and/or ramp on the right to a a ledge on the left.
4. 30m Continue up the ramp to an interesting exit – thread belays in boulders just above. Easy ground for 100m leads to the plateau.

Craigencallie, Low Slabs:

These are the lowest slabs in the slabby area under Main Wall and the first rock passed on the approach.

Stephen Reid on FA of Overdraft Dodger (IV,4), Black Gairy, The Merrick, 5 Feb 2015. Photo: Colin Wells.

The Lowland Clearances   40m   VS 4b *. Stephen Reid, James Kinnaird. 8 Oct 2015.
Slightly bold but on excellent rock. Start directly below a slightly blocky line up the centre of the lowest slab. Climb a short slab to the left end of a big ledge. Move up the wall and rightwards to stand on a flake (micro wires above), then stride leftwards and pull onto the upper slab. Go straight up and slightly rightwards following the clean rock to a finishing ridge.

The Farrier   30m   Severe 4b. James Kinnaird, Stephen Reid. 8 Oct 2015.
The larger looking slab just up to the right has a pinnacle on its right side. Launch off the pinnacle to gain a slim ramp leading up rightwards. Follow the left edge of the rock above with much more ease.

Right Side:
To the right of Main Wall the crag becomes more broken.

Flying a Kite   75m   H.Severe 4b. Andrew Fraser, Ian Magill. 21 Apr 2015.
Worthwhile. As viewed from the car park, this is the right arete of the main area of crags, starting at a pile of boulders in the grass slope to the right.
1. 30m 4b Climb a rounded ridge and continue up slabby walls to beneath a steeper buttress.
2. 45m 4b Climb the corner to the prominent roof, turn this on the right and continue to easier ground. Above is an easy slabby rib which leads to a belay beneath a steep wall at the top of the crag. Scramble off to the right of this.

Far Right Side:
The following routes are on short clean walls 250m to the right, separated from the main cliffs by a wide grassy slope. They dry quickly and are cleaner and less foreboding than the main crags. Descent is to the left.

The Sorcerer's Apprentice   25m   V.Diff. Ian Magill, Andrew Fraser. 20 May 2015.
The easier left-hand slab is climbed directly from its lowest point.

Fantasia   25m   HVS 4c *. Ian Magill, Andrew Fraser. 18 Jun 2015.
Lovely but serious. Up and right of *The Sorcerer's Apprentice*, and reached by a rising traverse from its foot, is a steep prow. This is climbed on its left side.

The next two routes are on the longer right-hand slab.

The Sorcerer   40m   H.Severe 4b *. Andrew Fraser, Ian Magill. 20 May 2015.
A good route. Start at the bottom of the main slab and climb cracks until it is possible to move right into a shallow niche in the middle of the slab. Continue directly to a ledge, up cracks to another ledge, then climb the wall above by its left side. Continue up walls above with an airy step left to finish.

Kite Runner   35m   HVS 5a *. Ian Magill, Andrew Fraser. 21 Apr 2015.
Varied climbing on clean rock. Start as for *The Sorcerer* but immediately move right up the right-trending ramp to good holds. Climb boldly up the thin slab above to a ledge and move right to finish up a steep and difficult corner. Avoiding the final moves of this on the right reduces the standard to VS and removes the star.

Craigdews, The Quarry:
Clearly visible on the approach is a smooth 6m wall in a small quarry which has
so far yielded one highball boulder problem.
Apprentice Wall   V5 (5c, F6c) ***. S.Fletcher. 18 Jan 2015.
Follow the thin seam up the centre of the face.

CRAIGNELDER, Big Gairy:
(NX 492 701)   Alt 325m   West facing
Big Gairy and its smaller neighbour Wee Gairy comprise the large and vegetated
cliff forming the lower Craignelder escarpment. Some excellent clean slab pitches
lurk hereabouts despite the vegetation and the approach is quick, if steep. There
are three areas of climbing. From the left these are Wee Gairy, the leftmost area
of clean slab directly above the start of the access, Paleface Area, situated to the
left of a gully which divides the crag and Main Face, the larger more rambling
area to the right of the gully.
    Approach: Follow the A712 to a parking place in the woods 0.5km west of the
Grey Mare's Tail/Murray's Monument car park. Take the forestry road opposite
(south – signed Talnotry 50m with an arrow pointing back across the road to the
car park) and follow this across the Palnure Burn, keeping right shortly after and
continuing a short distance to a small layby on the right. Two hundred metres
beyond this layby, a large cracked boulder with a huge drill hole in it will be found
in the ditch on the left (NX 48901 70742) and the slabby buttress of Wee Gairy
will be seen up and slightly left. Go straight up towards the crag heading for the
right end of a large collection of boulders situated down and right of it. Just below
these a wall is crossed above which the path becomes better defined. From here
go straight uphill to Wee Gairy (30mins from the track, 45mins from the car park)
or traverse up and right to the other buttresses (allow an extra 15mins).

CRAIGNELDER, Wee Gairy (NX 49156 70757):
A nice clean slab with all the routes being worthwhile. Due to the slabby nature
of the crag numerous variations and link ups are possible; only the main lines are
described. Micro wires and micro cams are particularly useful. There is an
excellent belay above the cleanest part of the slab and it is easiest to abseil from
this if several routes are to be done before making a final descent to the right.

Lower Tier:
The short lower slab has a couple of nice warm up routes.

The Mirror Cracked   22m   H.Severe 4b. Ian Magill, Andrew Fraser. 17 Aug
2014.
Follow the slab from right to left to a tricky finish up the fine crack at the top left
side of the crag.

Poultry in Motion   15m   V.Diff. Andrew Fraser, Stephen Reid. 14 Sep 2014.
Follow *Route 1* onto the slab and slightly left, then step up and move back right
to exit.

Main Crag:
The best part of the crag is gained by scrambling up to a large heather ledge above
the Lower Tier.
Union Jock   25m   HVS 5a *. Stephen Reid, Andrew Fraser. 14 Sep 2014.

A harder way but a safer proposition than *Independence Aye* (particularly if you take some micro wires and micro cams). Start just right of a large flake, at the left side of the main slab under a small square niche at 4m. Climb up leftwards onto a rib and follow it to a steep wall just left of the niche. Pull directly up onto the slab above and follow a thin crack (the left-hand of three thin cracks) up the wall above on its right side to a break. Step left and move up to a vague groove (the left-hand of two vague grooves). Climb the groove to a slab and finish direct.

Union Jock Socialist Version 25m VS 4c *. Stephen Reid, John Biggar. 17 Sep 2014.
Taking a series of variations to the left gives an easier but less satisfying route. As for *Union Jock* to the thin crack but climb a scoop to the left of the crack. Follow *Union Jock* up the vague groove above to the slab, then traverse left and pad easily to the top.

On Reflection 25m VS 4c *. Ian Magill, Andrew Fraser. 12 Sep 2014.
Pleasant climbing with a delicate crux at the start. Start, just right of a large flake, at the left side of the main slab under a small square niche at 4m. Climb up to an overhung niche at 4m, which is exited on its right side. Easier climbing leads up and left to a slabby ledge. Climb the steeper wall above on good holds, leftwards then rightwards, then moving left to a short corner which leads to a rising traverse up the top slab.

Independence Aye 25m HVS 4c *. Stephen Reid, Andrew Fraser. 14 Sep 2014.
A tempting option but with potentially serious consequences if you mess it up. Start at a thin vertical seam 1m right of *Union Jock* and *Route 2*. Climb the seam which soon peters out but carry on directly up to the left end of a square overlap. Step up and out leftwards to the right-hand of three thin cracks and climb it on its right to a horizontal break. Pull up to the right-hand of two vague grooves and climb it to a slab. Traverse right along an obvious sloping footledge to gain a crack on the right (and some gear) and finish up this.

Calling Card 28m VS 4c **. Andrew Fraser, Ian Magill. 12 Sep 2012.
Finish as described by John Biggar, Stephen Reid. 17 Sep 2014.
A cracking route, easy for the grade except for a few moves getting off the ground. Start under the large overlap at 6m at the highest point of the grass. Teeter up the slab slightly leftwards, then more easily up to the large overlap. Turn this on its right side, move back left, then climb the front of the flake-crack to a horizontal break. Move up the slab to climb the groove and cracks above to just below the heather, then traverse right and finish up a crack 2m to the right (or extend the traverse even further right and go up a wide crack).

Calling Card Direct 28m HVS 5a *. Stephen Reid, John Biggar. 17 Sep 2014.
As for *Route 3* to the overlap which is overcome direct at its widest point to gain the flake. Follow *Route 3* to where it moves right near the top and finish direct up the crack as for *Independence Aye*.

Whipping Post 28m HVS 5a *. Andrew Fraser, Stephen Reid. 13 Oct 2015.
Previously climbed via the Right-Hand Start by the same team. 14 Sep 2014.
A good pitch with three distinct cruxes. Start at the right-hand end of the highest point of the grass. Make a bold and tenuous traverse rightwards across the slab to

Stephen Reid on FA of Independence Aye (HVS 4c), Wee Gairy, Craignelder, 14 Sep 2014.
Photo: Andrew Fraser.

gain a rib and groove. Move up and overcome a bulge with difficulty. Step left and the next bulge succumbs more easily. Above is a blocky crack. Climb the slab to its left and gain a fine shallow flaky groove. Climb this with difficulty to a pull out right onto easier upper slabs which are followed to the top.

Right-Hand Start The entry slab can be avoided by starting up the initial groove of *Angels' Left-Hand* and stepping left.

The remaining routes start from below the step up to the heather ledge under the Main Crag.

The Angels' Share 35m HVS 5a *. Stephen Reid, Andrew Fraser. 13 Oct 2015.
Not an obvious line but good climbing throughout with a bold start. Start at a short slab just left of a boulder at the right edge of the crag. Foot-traverse the slab to a groove on its left side. Climb boldly up this until it gets rather dirty, then traverse left to a foothold in a parallel groove. Puzzle your way up the groove, then more easily to a steeper wall. Pull up into a shallow niche on the right then traverse back left and through a gap in the heather to a narrow ledge. A short crack proves more troublesome than it looks, then take a left-slanting ramp to gain the final slab and climb this directly to the top.

Variation: *Angels' Left-Hand* 28m VS 4c *. Stephen Reid, Andrew Fraser. 14 Sep 2014.
Quite tough for the grade. Start at the highest heathery triangle under the more vegetated right-hand part of the slabs and climb a short corner exiting leftwards, then trend back rightwards to join the climb above the crux groove.

Traitor's Goat 65m H.Severe *. Andrew Fraser, Ian Magill. 11 Jul 2014.
Nicer climbing than appearances suggest up the right edge of the slabs. Start at a short slab just left of a boulder at the right edge of the crag.
1. 35m 4b Climb the slab just left of a black streak and move over a bulge at 4m (all rather bold), then slightly right, before following a slab leftwards below a cracked bulge. Continue up slabs to the right end of a narrow heather ledge. Climb the bulge above and continue to a grass ledge on the right below a cracked wall (possible belay). Move up left and follow the final slab to a wide heather ledge. Scramble up this to a huge flake at an outcrop on the right.
2. 30m 4a Plough through more heather up leftwards to the steep top wall and climb its central prow, reached from the left by sloping ledges, then continue up slabs to the fine summit of Wee Gairy.

The Low Road 45m VS 4c *. Andrew Fraser, Stephen Reid. 13 Oct 2015.
A girdle traverse featuring a particularly enjoyable hand-traverse. Start as for Route 4.
Foot-traverse the slab to under a groove on its left side and go up a slab beyond to a grassy niche. Climb the short groove, exiting leftwards and overcome a difficult bulge up left. Traverse left to gain the flake on *Route 3* and go up this to the overlap. Hand-traverse this leftwards in a fine position to finish up the final section of *Route 2*.

The High Road 45m VS 4b. *Stephen Reid, Andrew Fraser. 13 Oct 2015.
Another girdle traverse, this time making a bold foot-traverse of the hand-traverse of *The Low Road*. Start as for *Route 4*.
Follow *Route 4* to the end of its initial traverse left. Step down and across heather

to a wall on the left. Climb this via a left-slanting ramp, then up through a gap in the heather to below a wide crack. Traverse left to a blocky crack and keep traversing left with feet on the lip of the slab, until slightly more tricky moves can be made into *Route 2* up which the climb finishes.

Paleface Area:

The routes lie just left of the obvious gully splitting the face.
Descent: Immediately above the routes (even before the belay), a narrow grass ledge leads right across the gully, then a steep heather face is descended diagonally rightwards (worth keeping on the rope).

Art of Darkness 80m VS *. Ian Magill, Andrew Fraser. 4 Jun 2010.
Nice slab climbing up the sweep of brown slabs 30m left of the gully. Start at the right edge of the brown slabs.
1. 40m 4c Climb for 8m to a steeper wall which is started immediately above a small spike, then slightly go left. Continue to a heather ledge, then starting at the right toe of the next slab, climb delicately up and leftward to belay on the left.
2. 40m 3b Continue up the wall above, then up a sweep of brown slabs, moving rightwards at times to maximise good rock.

Paleface Direct 80m HVS *. Ian Magill, Andrew Fraser. 4 Jun 2010.
An interesting route takes the pale sweep of slabs 5m left of the gully.
1. 40m 4c/5a Climb the centre of the lower slab direct to a heather ledge, very bold at the top. A short wall leads to the next slab (junction with *Paleface*) which is climbed delicately leftwards to a scoop. Finish up a break in between the steep wall on the right and an overhang on the left and belay immediately at a shallow groove (alternatively climb the groove left of the overhang and traverse right across the final slab to the same point).
2. 40m 4a Climb the slab above leftwards, traverse 2m left, then continue up three further pale slabs, following the cleanest line, difficulty and protection decreasing as you go.

Main Face:

The buttress to the right of the gully is larger but very broken. A grassy ramp leads up rightwards from the foot of the gully under the face. Near the right end of the ramp is a large flat rectangular stone, with an overhang immediately above it at 3m. This helps locate the following routes. A long descent lies to the right but carrying rucksacks and taking a longer way down is a better option.

Midnight Cowboy 155m HVS. Andrew Fraser, Ian Magill. 7 Jun 2013.
Superb padding on the final pitch fails to compensate for hard technical vegetation on the first two pitches. Start 10m left of the rectangular flat stone.
1. 25m 5a Climb 7m to a bulge which is overcome at its left end where heather can be grasped. Two short vegetated steps lead to another bulge. Gain this from its right end and climb it centrally to a niche.
2. 45m 5a Move out left onto the slabs and climb these boldly. Continue up further mossy slabs to the right end of a long and large curving overlap (identifiable by the odd deciduous tree).
3. 40m 4a Climb the overlap at its right end, then continue via rock (or heather according to taste) to belay 3m to the right of a corner in the final clean sweep of slabs.

4. 45m 4c Move up and right to cross a bulge with difficulty, then 15m of brilliant padding up slabs.

Eating an Elephant 155m VS. Andrew Fraser, Ian Magill. 7 Jun 2009.
A jumbo outing with some nice touches and making the most of the available rock.
1. 50m 4c Start 2m right of the large flat boulder on the right side of the overhang and climb over a bulge to a second slab. Climb this with difficulty (crux), then continue up the right side of a nose to gain steep heather. Go up this to a innocuous but hard wee wall, then up slabs to belay just short of a heather terrace.
2. 40m 3b Above and right is a corner. Take the crack on the front face, 3m right of the corner, and continue up slabs above, moving left across a steeper slab to belay up left.
3. and 4. 65m 3b Above and left is a large sweep of slabs. Take the easy slab on the right side of these slabs to go over a bulge. Continue across a heather terrace to a final 10m wall climbed on large holds.

BUCHAN HILL, Black Gairy (NX 424 813):
Viewed from Bruce's Stone, this is the largest compact buttress on the SW face of Buchan Hill, situated 400m up and right from Buchan West Crag. The easiest descent is to the right (east) although it is possible and quicker to scramble down to the left (west).

Buchan Bronco 40m VS 4c. Ian Magill, Andrew Fraser. 30 May 2015.
This climbs the three slabs on the left side of the buttress and is worthwhile and varied. The first slab is climbed centrally, the second starts by standing on the spike on the right of the slab, then traverses to its left edge and up. The third climbs its right edge then goes up left to a heather ledge below the upper buttress. This is climbed at the left, starting at a groove, then gradually moving right.

Igor, Release the Bats 40m Severe 4a. Andrew Fraser, Ian Magill. 16 Sep 2015.
Pleasant climbing up the thin ribs 2m left of *The Buchanites*, with a deviation into the groove on the right at the start of the second rib.

The Buchanites 40m VS 4b *. Andrew Fraser, Ian Magill. 10 Jun 2015
Classic climbing and easy for the grade. Start at the toe of the buttress, just left of the tree. Climb the rib, then move right to pass the overhang on its left side. Continue up the main crack-line above. The upper buttress is climbed easily just to the left of its prow.

Clothed with Sun 40m HVS 5a *. Ian Magill, Andrew Fraser. 10 Jun 2015.
Sustained and technical. On the right side of the crag is a blocky crack. Start 2m left of this and climb the wall until it is necessary to join the crack for its last few moves. The upper buttress is climbed easily just to the right of its prow.

Craig an Eilte:
Note: *The Flesh Market* (HVS 1992) was previously climbed by George Fraser and party, pre 1959, and named *Flank Route* (and graded V.Diff!)

The Freezer Section:
Some 500m down and right of *The Flesh Market*, at the lowest point of the

escarpment, is an obvious short gully guarded by chockstones, *Spindrift Gully*. An area of more continuous rock guarded by a band of overhangs lies 20-30m left of this. Descent is by a long diagonal descending traverse to the right.

Fleet Street   45m   VS *. Stephen Reid, Robert Bennett. 9 Apr 2015.
Two good pitches at the upper end of the grade. Start just right of the overhangs at a short chimney where a block abuts the main wall.
1. 20m 4c Gain the top of the block and climb up into a groove on the left. Follow the groove and/or its right arete to exit leftwards at its top.
2. 25m 4c The slab on the left leads to a cracked wall just right of an overhang. Climb the cracks to exit at a block, surmount the block and continue more easily up a stepped rib.

The Veg Market:
Marshall Law   120m   HVS *. Stephen Reid, Chris King (alt). 21 Apr 2015.
A spectacular second pitch makes this climb well worthwhile. A large horizontal flake lies on the ground 6m right of the large flake at the start of *Galloway Gallivant*. Start just left of this.
1. 30m 4c Follow a left-slanting seam boldly up the initial slab to heather. Climb the easier slab above on the right and belay at cracks on the left side of the steep wall.
2. 20m 5a Climb the crack on the right side of the steep wall until under the left end of a long roof. Traverse to its right end and climb steeply up the headwall to a slab and crack just beyond.
3. 20m 4a Step down left onto a jammed block, then climb short slabs, overlaps and bilberry to belay under a left-slanting, wide quartz crack at the right end of the clean wall.
4. 50m 5a Traverse right and climb the innocuous looking, short mossy arete with difficulty and then continue up slabs and overlaps to a block on a grass terrace.

Mental Block   120m   E1 *. Chris King, Stephen Reid (alt). 9 Jul 2015.
Low in the grade and another enjoyable route on excellent rock. A large horizontal flake lies on the ground 6m right of the large flake at the start of *Galloway Gallivant*. Start 4m right of this.
1. 30m 4c Climb a thin flake in the steep wall to a horizontal break. Hand-traverse boldly leftwards to a step up onto a ledge and heather ramp. From the heather terrace above, climb onto a block and up to more heather. Go up a bit, then traverse left to a belay at the left-hand side of the steep wall.
2. 20m 5b Climb the crack on the right side of the steep wall until under the left end of a long roof. Step into the groove on the left and climb it with bravado, passing the wedged hanging block of the name.
3. 20m 4b Traverse rightwards on grass until under the left end of a triangular slab. Climb a crack until it is possible to traverse right along a shelf in the slab and go straight up the centre to its top. Traverse horizontally leftwards on heather, passing under a chimney, to a corner with a left-sloping quartzy crack.
4. 50m 4c Climb the corner-crack just right of the left-leaning quartz crack, then pad up slabs and overlaps to the top.

South East Corrie of Milldown:
The Great Cleugh of Auchniebut (reported as a winter route, SMCJ 2013) has been found to have a traditional name of *Garrinner Strand* and also to have been

Stephen Reid on FA of Mental Block (E1 5b), Black Gairy, Buchan Hill, 9 Jul 2015.
Photo: Chris King.

climbed in summer by C.M. Allan, J. Dow, R.L. Beveridge & AN Other, as long ago as 10 Oct 1937. At a guess it would be Diff in dry conditions.

THE BORDERS, Bitch Craig (NT 199 266):

Bitch Craig is an extensive but largely broken whinstone crag flanking Bitch Cleuch on the east side of the upper Manor Valley, near Peebles. Access on foot to the start of the routes, from the end of the Manor Valley tarmac road, takes about 40mins. Most of the routes are footed by very steep grassy slopes so care is required when gearing up and when walking around in rock boots! Raptors and Corvids nest on the crag so it should be avoided during spring and early summer. There are a number of other short routes but the following are the longest and the best.

The north facing flank of the crag is a bit broken but does hold a couple of distinctive grooves. The best access to these, avoiding most of the scree, is to take a rising diagonal line from the mouth of the Cleuch.

Bitchhiker's Guide to the Fallacy 25m Severe *. Graham Little, Ryan Little. 28 Aug 2015.
This route takes the first groove on the north flank of the crag, 7m left of the large rowan tree and about 15m above the very foot of the crag. Gain and climb the interesting groove (avoiding contact with the big wedged tablet of rock near the start) to reach a grass terrace. Climb the fine little pillar above to a pinnacle belay. Scramble up and then descend to the left.

Bitchfinder Groove 17m E1 5c *. Graham Little, Ryan Little. 6 Sep 2015.
Tackles the obvious roofed groove on the north flank of the crag (very large nest to the left of the groove). Ascend bulging rock (above the mossy slab) directly to the base of the groove. Climb the groove, passing through the slot in the roof, to finish by a rowan tree. Descend to the left.

A vague path runs up the Cleuch at the foot of the scree slope. The easiest approach to the following routes is to follow this path until beyond the scree slope and then to take an left-rising line, past a little pinnacle, to reach the foot of the walls. The relatively clean, pale streaked wall in the centre of the crag is the most distinctive feature and holds three routes and a variation. The descent is down a steep grassy ramp to the left (north), not visible from below.

Three Pocket Groove 13m V.Diff. Graham Little, Ryan Little. 12 Sep 2014.
Start at the base of a slim groove, with three distinctive pockets, 8m left of the right edge of the wall. Climb it, finishing just left of the big poised block.

Zebra Crack 14m Severe 4b *. Graham Little. 22 Sep 2014.
Start 6m left of the right edge of the wall. Climb the obvious diagonal crack and the short continuation crack above the ledge, finishing to the right of the big poised block.

A Bitch in Time 18m HVS 5a **. Graham Little. 9 Sep 2014.
Start 3m left of the right edge of the wall. Climb up a scoop for a few metres, then move right and up to a big hold near the right edge of the wall. Move up and left (crux) to a ledge, then climb the centre of the short wall above.

A Bitch in Time Direct 15m E1 5b *. Graham Little (unsec). 22 Sep 2014.
Avoids the moves right and back left by climbing the groove directly above the
initial scoop.

4 further routes are on the SMC website.

GALLOWAY SEA-CLIFFS, Meikle Ross:
Greywackattack 15m VS 4c. Alex Riley, Anna Riley. 7 Jun 2015.
Climb the layback flake to the right of *Fats Waller* until an obvious left-slanting
crack is gained and followed to the top. Well protected although care needed on
the top section.

Meikle Ross, Little Zawn Area:
Bloody Arete 15m E4 5c. Alex Riley, Peter Wilkes, Lex Pearce. 23 Apr 2016.
Start just left of *Bloody Crack*. Climb the steep groove on the big block, then
move right from the small breaks to gain the middle of the face. Thin moves lead
to a big break below an overhang. Traverse to the arete and climb direct on
sidepulls, following the arete to the top. A high quality route, but serious and
sustained.

GALLOWAY SEA-CLIFFS, Portobello, March Bay:
4 routes on the SMC website.

Money Head, Cioch Area:
Sheet Lightning 25m VS 4c *. Andrew Fraser, Ian Magill. 3 Aug 2013.
Start as for *Martin's Bank* but traverse the slab up and left to the left end of the
main overlap. A short left-facing corner lies 1m up left. Climb this (crux) and
continue more easily to the top.

Pot of Gold Variation. Having surmounted the overlap, climb directly up the slabs
above at the same grade.

Banker's Bonus 15m Severe. Ian Magill, Andrew Fraser. 3 Aug 2013.
At the top right of the slabs, 3m right of *Martin's Bank*, is an overhanging prow,
split by a crack. Climb this on huge holds, then continue up the delicate wall
above.

FIFE, Limekilns:
Blackout 13m E4 6b *. Adam Russell (headpoint). 5 May 2016.
Essentially a difficult direct start to *Edge of Fear*. Start just right of the arete and
climb direct through the blackened roof with difficulty. Continue straight up to
the half-height break where *Edge of Fear* traverses round the arete (first gear).
Finish more easily up this.

MISCELLANEOUS NOTES

THE W.H. MURRAY LITERARY PRIZE

As a tribute to the late Bill Murray, whose mountain and environment writings have been an inspiration to many a budding mountaineer, the SMC have set up a modest writing prize, to be run through the pages of the Journal. The basic rules are set out below, and will be reprinted each year. The prize is run with a deadline of midnight on the last day of April each year..

The Rules:

1. There shall be a competition for the best entry on Scottish Mountaineering published in the *Scottish Mountaineering Club Journal*. The competition shall be called the 'W.H. Murray Literary Prize', hereafter called the 'Prize'.
2. The judging panel shall consist of, in the first instance, the following: The current Editor of the *SMC Journal*; The current President of the SMC; and two or three lay members, who may be drawn from the membership of the SMC. The lay members of the panel will sit for three years after which they will be replaced.
3. If, in the view of the panel, there is in any year no entry suitable for the Prize, then there shall be no award that year.
4. Entries shall be writing on the general theme of 'Scottish Mountaineering', and may be prose articles of up to approximately 3000 words in length, or shorter verse. Entries may be fictional.
5. Panel members may not enter for the competition during the period of their membership.
6. Entries must be of original, previously unpublished material. Entries should be submitted to the Editor of the *SMC Journal* by the end of April for consideration that year. Electronic contributions are preferred and should be submitted via e-mail, although double-spaced typewritten hard copies will also be accepted by post. (See Office Bearers page at end of this Journal for address etc.) Any contributor to the *SMC Journal* is entitled to exclude their material from consideration for the Prize and should so notify the Editor of this wish in advance.
7. The Prize will be a cheque for the amount £250.
8. Contributors may make different submissions in different years.
9. The decision of the panel is final.
10. Any winning entry will be announced in the *SMC Journal*, and will be published in the *SMC Journal* and on the SMC Website. Thereafter, authors retain copyright.

THE WH MURRAY LITERARY PRIZE 2016

THERE WAS A CERTAIN AMOUNT of soul-searching amongst the Judges this year before Phil Gribbon emerged as the clear winner. His article *Going Going Gone...* was felt by one judge to be 'full of flashes of light and colour'; another thought it 'blackly humorous', while a third thought it 'deeply impressive...a confession' and 'an attempt to come to terms with tragedy'. Perhaps only a very good piece of writing could evoke such strong and seemingly contradictory opinions?

Two other pieces received solid support: former winner Gordon Smith's wonderful Ben Nevis romp *Sense and Sensibility* was thought 'almost Victorian in its prolixity' – in marked contrast with Gribbon – but it flowed nicely and painted an ironically effective portrait of Smith's laconic companion Dick Renshaw: in amongst all the word-play Renshaw speaks once. It was also felt that Smith's article was good humoured and lacked egoism or posposity.

The Ben was also the setting for Dennis Gray's historical piece *Sixty Years On* which effectively combined comedy and tragedy: no easy task. This struck the judges as 'written from the heart...very engaging and of some historical value'. Perhaps, said one judge, 'it never quite sparkles though it glows pleasurably'. Other judges noted Gray's sincerity and understatement. The piece contains cameo portraits of Brown and Whillans which seem very apt.

Other work which attracted favourable comment included Mike Dixon's evocative essay on the Beinn Avon plateau, Gavin Anderson's insight into the early career of Bugs McKeith, Stephen Reid's work on *The Galloway Climbs of George Fraser*: a fascinating piece of research; and Stephen Scott's well-digested account of a winter day on Eagle Ridge. One judge thought that this might have been improved by 'something going wrong': let's be glad that it didn't! There was even a discursive essay on the nature of mountaineering itself by Alastair Reid; this was 'caviar to the general' perhaps but intrigued the philosophical among us.

The Winter Traverse of the Cuillin Ridge took a real bashing this year. Apart from Finlay Wild's wonderfully youthful account (which arrived too late to be considered), Martin Moran and Simon Richardson wrote contrasting pieces: Moran's almost as spare as himself and Richardson's with more introspection and background. Both writers shared an unexpected but most engaging fallibility.

Last year's winner Ian Crofton went into the history of Scottish avalanches. The judges couldn't decide if the link he made with his family history was more than 'tenuous', but all agreed it was interesting anyway. Lastly, John Hay's trip down '50s Deeside had a fine 'sense of place', and some fascinating information about the storm of 1953.

Some articles of Scottish interest have not been considered: this is because they came in too late. In order to be considered for the prize, work MUST be received by midnight (but preferably not at midnight) on the last day of April.

SCOTTISH WINTER NOTES 2015–16

The 2016 winter is unlikely to go down as one of the great Scottish climbing seasons. Snow came late to the mountains, and even through December, winter climbing was a start-stop affair with frequent thaws. The Highlands were then hit by an almost unprecedented series of storms over the Christmas–New Year period, which made climbing almost impossible, and the trend continued through January and February with ferocious winds. As the weather cooled down in February, the gales transported and redistributed the snow causing dangerous avalanche conditions and making mountain travel difficult. Despite the challenges, there was a high level of activity, mainly centred on calmer periods in the middle of January and February and a glorious weekend at the end of February. A major thaw in early March brought most climbing activity to an abrupt halt, although cool weather later in April brought the classic ice routes on Ben Nevis back into condition.

Second Ascent of Anubis

The most significant event was the first repeat of *Anubis* on Ben Nevis by Swiss climber Dani Arnold. The first winter ascent of this overhanging summer E8 on The Comb was made by Dave MacLeod in February 2010. It is widely regarded as the most difficult winter route on Ben Nevis, and along with *Banana Wall* in the Northern Corries, it is the only route in Scotland that merits a Grade XII rating. Arnold is perhaps best known for setting speed records on the north faces of the Eiger and the Matterhorn, but he also made an early repeat of *The Hurting* in the Northern Corries in 2012 so is no stranger to top end Scottish mixed. He succeeded on *Anubis* on his second visit – conditions were too warm in January, but the cliff was well frozen and well rimed up in March. Continental climbers have visited Ben Nevis in winter for many years, however most have focused on

Iain Small on Gates of Paradise (VIII,8), Church Door Buttress, Bidean nam Bian.
Photo: Murdoch Jamieson.

the classic snow and ice routes. Dani Arnold's repeat of *Anubis* is undoubtedly the most difficult Scottish ascent ever achieved by an overseas visitor.

Gates of Paradise

The finest new route of the season took place in February when Iain Small and Murdoch Jamieson climbed *Gates of Paradise* (VIII,8) on Church Door Buttress in Glen Coe. This spectacular route starts further right than the existing summer routes and climbs overhanging mixed ground to gain a hanging icicle. Small had noticed the icicle start to form when he made the second ascent of *Crusade* (VII,8) with Uisdean Hawthorn earlier in the season. 'The line had formed up into some ice-coated lower walls and slabs from the dripping icicle fringe, then a steep mixed section to roofs and through them to gain the icicles,' Iain explained. 'The main pitch started up a rather run-out icy arête leading to a strenuous roof with a knee-bar rest on an icy tufa-like feature. A hard pull then gained the ice and some short screws after which it was all over. With it being short, but intense, we thought VIII,8 might cover it.' The grade should be treated with caution, as Small is reluctant to give relatively short routes a Grade IX rating.

Earlier in the season in Glen Coe, Small and Uisdean Hawthorn made the first winter ascent of *Shadhava* (VIII,9) a summer E3 on the right wall of *Unicorn* in Stob Coire nan Lochan, and Mark Chadwick and Simon Tietjen added *Moonshine* (V,7) to Lost Valley Buttress. Further south, Dave MacLeod had a good day with Helen Rennard making the first winter ascent of *Southern Freeze* (IX,9), an E2 on The Cobbler's South Peak.

*Steve Perry on
Have an Ice Day (V,5)
Lurcher's Crag.*

Photo:Andy Nisbet.

The Cairngorms

The wild weather and difficult snow conditions limited exploratory activity in the Cairngorms, although Andy Nisbet used the west-facing aspect of Lurcher's Crag to his advantage and added nine new routes. The finest additions of *Have an Ice Day* (V,5), *The Force Awakens* (VI,6) and *Snowbird* (VI,7) were climbed with Steve Perry and took advantage of early season ice. Glen Clova proved to be a sheltered venue away from the westerly gales and saw activity from Henning Wackerhage, Adrian Crofton, Sophie Grace Chappell and Simon Richardson. The finest routes were *The Age of Enlightenment* (VI,7) in Corrie Farchal, *Bamboozle Buttress* (V,6) in Corrie Bonhard and *King Herod* (VI,7), an unusual pinnacle-like feature, on Cairn Broadlands.

Early in the season, the Northern Corries saw third ascents of *Pfugga-lule* (VIII,9) – Andy Inglis and Neil Adams, *Swallowtail Pillar* (VII,8) – Dave Almond and Ian Parnell, and *Babes in the Wood* (VIII,8) – Almond and Helen Rennard. Uisdean Hawthorn and Tom Livingstone also made the second ascent of *The Vapouriser* (VIII,8) on Creag an Dubh Loch. Big news in the Cairngorms however, were two ascents of *The Needle* (VIII,8) on the Shelter Stone the same weekend by Inglis and Adams, and Parnell and Kenton Cool. Although *The Needle* was first climbed in winter as long ago as February 1985 by Andy Nisbet and Colin MacLean, it is still regarded as one of Scotland's big Grade VIIIs, so ascents on consecutive days was something of a landmark event.

Central Highlands

New route activity on Ben Nevis was unusually quiet although a couple of good pitches were added in January. John Crook and Pete Graham climbed the bold *Gothic Edge* (VII,7) up the arête left of the *Gargoyle Cracks* on Number Three Gully Buttress, and Ramon Marin and Douglas Russell found *Tangerine Dream* (VII,8) the prominent chimney-crack to the left of *The Rattler* on South Trident Buttress. Later in the season Nick Bullock and Tim Neill tip-toed up *Capricorn* (VIII,7), the ice smear that often forms to the left of the twin grooves of *Gemini* on Càrn Dearg Buttress, and Dave MacLeod added a serious mixed route on the East Face of Tower Ridge. The two-pitch *Night Fury* (IX,9) had seen a couple of prior attempts and lies just left of *The Urchin*.

On Creag Meagaidh, Simon Richardson teamed up with Henning Wackerhage, Pat Ingram and Roger Everett to explore an attractive unclimbed mixed buttress in Coire Choille-rais. *Birthday Route* (IV,4) and *Cat Burglar* (V,5) took the obvious lines of weakness on the left side of the cliff, and the full challenge of the buttress was met with *The Day After Tomorrow* (VII,8) that climbs the front face.

Northern Highlands

The cold weather in January resulted in a number of significant repeats in the Northern Highlands. On Beinn Eighe, the spectacular *Shoot the Breeze* (IX,8) saw its second ascent courtesy of Andy Inglis, Iain Small and Murdoch Jamieson, and Jamieson also repeated *Bruised Violet* (VIII,8) with Guy Steven and *Immortal Memory* (IX,8) with Ian Parnell and Uisdean Hawthorn. Other notable second ascents include *Reach for the Sky* (VII,6) on Mainreachan Buttress by Inglis and Small, and *Fishmonger* (VI,6) on Foinaven by Erick Baillot and Dave Kerr.

Opposite
Andy Inglis works his way up Shoot the Breeze (IX,8), Beinn Eighe. Photos: Iain Small.

Andy Inglis on Ice Bomb Direct, The Mind Bomb Finish (VIII,7), in Coire Ghranda, Beinn Dearg. Photo:Guy Robertson.

The most significant addition to the Northern Highlands took place in mid February on Beinn Bhan when Malcolm Bass, Neil Silver and Simon Yearsley climbed the eight-pitch *Nam Famhairean* (VII,7) in Coire nam Fhamair. This major expedition takes a mirror image line to *Der Riesenwand* on the Giant's Wall and shares a pitch at half-height. Later in the month, Beinn Bhan proved a popular location as its proximity to the sea meant it avoided most of the heavy snowfall inland, and multiple ascents were made of *The Godfather*, *Gully of the Gods* and *Great Overhanging Gully*. Also on Beinn Bhan, Andy Nisbet, Dave McGimpsey and Steve Perry climbed an excellent three pitch *Direct Start* (V,5) to *Wall of the Early Morning Light* resulting in one of the longest ice routes in the country. Further south in Knoydart, Roger Webb and Simon Richardson added the long and serious *Tir na h-aoise* (VI,6) to the 400m-high Spider Buttress on Ladhar Beinn.

Cul Mòr in Coigach saw a couple of good thin ice additions with the first winter ascent of *Buffalo Ballet* (VII,7) on the south face by Rennard and Richardson and the first ascent of *The Wrecking Light* (VIII,7) in Coire Gorm by Nick Bullock, Andy Inglis and Guy Robertson. The latter team also made the long-awaited second ascent of Mick Fowler and Dave Wilkinson's *Ice Bomb* in Beinn Dearg's Coire Ghranda adding a spectacular *Direct Finish* in the process.

Skye

The Cuillin on Skye provided several of the season's finest exploratory routes spearheaded by local guide and guidebook author, Mike Lates. The Skye Winter Festival in mid January saw some excellent additions, notably the first winter ascent of *Crack of Dawn* (VIII,8) on Sgùrr MhicCoinnich by James and Doug Sutton. Mark Francis and Dave Bowdler climbed the excellent *North Rib* (IV,5) of Banachdaich Gully, and Lates made the first winter ascent of *Owl Chimney* (IV,5), but it was Michael Barnard who proved most prolific with several difficult new routes including *The Bogeyman* (VI,7) and *Mr Charlie* (VI,7) on the Stone Shoot face of Sgùrr Theàrlaich.

Spurred on by Mike Lates's informative reports, several parties made traverses of the Cuillin Ridge in February. Conditions were excellent which led to a six-hour record time by Finlay Wild and Sam Gomersall, and an eight-hour solo traverse by Uisdean Hawthorn. Attention then swung to the ice routes when Lates made the second ascent of *White Wedding* (IV,4) with Mark Francis. This route was first climbed by Mick Fowler, Victor Saunders and Chris Watts almost exactly 30 years ago. News of their ascent focused attention on the other great Fowler-Saunders route, *Icicle Factory* (VI,6) on Sgùrr a' Mhadaidh. James Sutton, Ben Wear and John Smith just beat Uisdean Hawthorn, Adam Russell and Dougie Russell to the coveted second ascent, who instead, added *Spectacula* (VI,6), the prominent line of ice to the left, before abseiling down to make the third ascent of *Icicle Factory*. The following day Hawthorn and Lea MacLeod made the first ascent of *Spirulina* (V,5), the line of ice between these two routes.

Across on the Coruisg side of the Cuillin, Andy Nisbet, Steve Perry, Dave McGimpsey and Sandy Allan had a good run of new ice routes including *The Inaccessible Icefall* (IV,4), *Griffin* (III,4) and *Skyefall* (IV,5). In a winter of difficult and testing conditions it was ironic that the most fickle venue of all, namely the Cuillin on Skye, should provide some of the finest routes of the season.[1]

---

[1] The first SMC Skye Meet specifically aimed at winter climbing took place at Glenbrittle in February 2016. Des Rubens and Steve Kennedy added new lines on Sgùrr nan Eag and Sgùrr a' Ghreadaidh: see meet report and New Climbs section. (Hon.Ed.)

Simon Richardson on Central Buttress, Stob a' Ghlais Choire, Creise.
Photo: Roger Everett.

Late Season

The March thaw was followed by a glorious period of warm settled weather that
provided superb ski touring conditions but was not cold enough for winter
climbing. The weather cooled again in April and a series of strong Northerlies
transformed the snow pack and provided some excellent ice climbing conditions
high on Ben Nevis. The late season classics such as *Point Five Gully* and
Hadrian's Wall Direct saw many ascents, together with rarely climbed objectives
such as *Orion Directissima*[2] and *Match Point*. And fortuitously, the SMC CIC
Meet at the end of April was superbly timed to take advantage of the late season
ice just before it all melted away when temperatures rocketed at the beginning of
May.

Simon Richardson

[2] Is this a deliberate misspelling of Direttissima?

100 YEARS AGO: THE CLUB IN 1916

(*Italics* indicates quotation from the *SMC Journal* or other named source.)

IT WOULD BE VERY inward-looking to go back a century and completely ignore the unprecedented challenges which faced Britain in 1916, to which the Journal only made the occasional oblique reference. This was due to the Club's apolitical nature and also to censorship imposed by the Defence of the Realm Act upon all publications, which made discussing military matters in public a serious offence. By January 1915 over one million men, including many SMC members, had enlisted in the armed forces as volunteers. Then, in March 1916 the unpopular Military Service Act imposed conscription on all single men aged between 18 and 41, which was soon extended to include married men. In May, Daylight Saving Time was introduced to maximise working hours, particularly in agriculture. The early optimism that the war would not last long had faded and in July the Battle of the Somme started. Some 60,000 British men were killed or seriously wounded on the first day alone. This campaign, one of the bloodiest military operations in history, dragged on until November, and claimed the lives of several SMC members.

Meanwhile, the Easter Rebellion in Ireland and its harsh repression, had stimulated support for an Irish republic, another morale-sapping and distracting issue which, when added to anti-war demonstrations in 'Red Clydeside' and elsewhere, rent strikes, industrial action in essential industries, food shortages and increasing women's emancipation, presented the coalition government with the task of rallying the country to the war effort.

Also in July, it was announced that a specified area, the whole of the mainland roughly north of the Caledonian Canal and including Inverness, was to become a Special Military Area to which access was only permitted to non-residents by obtaining a permit from the Commandant (Cameron of Lochiel). The Scotsman reported that *in view of the agitation in some quarters for the closer supervision of aliens and naturalised foreigners, the military authorities are confident that in taking this step they will have the support of the public. That the new regulations will cause some inconvenience will be at once apparent. Something like a Continental frontier station is to be established at Inverness, where, unless the official permit is in order, anyone will be liable to be turned back.* Travel in much of the Highlands was thus severely restricted. This was the background to a war-affected society in a state of uneasy flux, with civil liberties severely curtailed.

The 27th AGM and Dinner of the Club was held at the St. Enoch Station Hotel, Glasgow on Friday 3 December 1915, with the President, Dr. W. Inglis Clark, in the chair.

Walter Nelson, the acting treasurer, reported increased costs for publication of the Journal owing to *a temporary discontinuance of advertisements*, also that reserves had been depleted by a large donation to the Scottish Red Cross Society. The Hon. Secretary, George Sang, reported that the Club membership stood at 197. It was agreed that a special committee should be appointed to expedite the publication of the first volume of the Guide Book. Other 'house-keeping' discussions took place and Sang read the special minutes compiled for the three members who had so far been killed in action, copies of which were to be sent to relatives. Following the precedent of the previous year, the afternoon reception was abandoned as an observance of the suffering caused by the Great War.

The Dinner was an informal affair, attended by just twenty-four members only, who heard the President talk about the enduring nature of friendships nurtured in the mountains and gave an outline of military operations in the Tyrol. He also made reference to the energies of the Club in combating the enemy both at home (presumably he was referring to the spy hunt in the Galloway hills the previous year) and abroad.

Club Meets

The New Year Meet was held at Lochearnhead from 30 December to 4 January with 19 members and 7 guests attending. The weather was *wet and forbidding* but this did not deter parties from ascending the usual selection of nearby hills. Strathyre became heavily flooded; Raeburn who arrived on motor cycle, reported that *there was no Falls of Leny, but simply one rushing torrent of water, and that at one part the road was flooded to a depth of two feet or thereabout.* One party managed to make a navigational error in the mist on Ben Vorlich and descended into Glenartney and then Comrie instead of Glen Ample, assuming that fences lead in the direction that one wants to go. It's happened to me, too, and is a salutary lesson on the necessity to constantly check the compass.

The Easter Meet, which had been scheduled for Kinlochleven and the Kingshouse, Glencoe, was instead held in Fort William from the 20th to 27 April with 16 members and 4 guests in attendance although Rev. Ronald Burn did not arrive until most of the others had departed. *Many familiar faces were absent, some serving abroad, others at home on military work or other national service. Saturday was the red-letter day on the Mamore hills ... the glare of the snow and the appearance of the hills was quite Swiss ...* but bad weather ruined the remaining days' activities.

The Journal

There were three slim issues (Nos. 79, 80 & 81 of Volume 14) of the Journal at a retail price of 1shilling (5pence). None of the issues contained more than four general articles each, the rest of the space being taken up by obituaries, proceedings of the Club, notes, letters, photographs, members' war experiences, and so on but this makes them no less interesting. Unlike our present Journal, there were no book reviews or New Routes section, for fairly obvious reasons.

The February issue started with an illustrated item titled 'Sassenachs in Skye' by John Hirst which describes a fortnight in Glen Brittle in July, 1915, during which Raeburn's *North-west Corner* route on the Inacessible Pinnacle was repeated, amongst other climbs. The article is spoilt by the irritating use of multiple anonyms. There is a more lyrical piece about 'Cruachan, Glen Etive and Glencoe' by James M'Coss, which includes a boat journey on Loch Etive from Bonawe to disembark at the wooden jetty below Ben Trilleachan. Perhaps the most interesting essay is the 'Nomenclature of the Cuillin' by Colin Phillip. Unlike other Highland areas which were rich in well-authenticated names, the Cuillin mountains were *rather meagre* in place-names since they were not the haunts of sporting, pastoral or agricultural interests, leading to many points on the Ridge being named, of necessity, by mountaineers. Liathach, in contrast, was well-endowed with names for all its *rocks, ravines, small corries, etc.,* the author being given nearly one hundred of such by an old goatherd. The origin of the word Cuillin itself is discussed before an examination is made into the particularised names of peaks, corries, bealachs, etc. The anglicised interpretations of local names were mostly undisputed but there were some exceptions. For example,

Sgùrr nan Gillean, usually translated as 'peak of the young men', is given the alternative mixed Norse/Gaelic meaning of 'peak of the ghylls or gullies'. It was a universal and common complaint that the Ordnance Survey created problems by defective interpretation and spelling of place-names and that, once printed on a map, the errors became 'fact'. Appropriately, Alfred Harker continued his series 'On Some Old Maps'; the topography of the land may have been crudely represented at times but the engraver livened things up with illustrations … *a sportsman pursuing with bow and arrow some strange horned beast … and a party of gentlemen in cocked hats dissecting a whale on the shore* on a map of 1761 which is reproduced in the Journal. The difficulty of accurately representing primitive roads, bridle-paths and drovers' tracks was overcome by drawing a straight line between, for example, Fort William and Finlarig (Loch Tay), to indicate merely that *it was practicable to travel from one place to another*.

Tribute is paid to the first members to die in battle. Alexander White, a young Edinburgh lawyer, died of wounds received in Gallipoli and was buried at Warriston Cemetery in his home city. Harry Walker, a much-loved favourite of the Club, died in France and was buried in an orchard in Pont de Hem. He was born in Fife, his ancestors having been landowners near Cupar since the early 17th Century. 'Cousins Buttress' on Ben Nevis got its name from its ascent by the two Walker cousins, Harry and Charles, in 1904. Harry was also involved in a scary incident on Blaven when the leader, W. Inglis Clark, climbed to the bottom of a sloping scree ledge and discovered loose stones barely in equilibrium supporting a huge block of rock. As he touched them they started to slide inexorably downwards and he was forced to push up against them, gravity gradually overcoming his strength … *and with a frantic effort I threw myself on to it [the boulder] dragging myself over it as the murderous avalanche descended.* Walker was in the line-of-fire having refused to untie and abandon his friend. He was hit by some of the smaller rocks, which also severed the rope in two places … *this was characteristic of the man – fearless, calm and unselfish.*

There is a letter from A.E. Maylard regarding a trip to Ben Nevis the previous October and the disgraceful state of the summit … *here were strewn about in chaotic confusion old pots and pans, broken beams and planks, wood and iron of every description, bent, broken and distorted into all sorts of shapes, smashed windows … the whole appearance being one of rack and ruin.* The mess was all that remained of the meteorological Observatory with additional discarded waste from the Summit Hotel. G. Sang, in reply, said that *climbers will agree that it [the rubbish] is better there than silting up the gully bottoms or perching sea-bird-like upon the ledges. To bury it would be a herculean task demanding a continuous outlay of expensive labour and to cart it down again to the sea is out of the question.*

Of all the Journal entries perhaps the most poignant is the account by A. Robertson Wilson of his experiences at Gallipoli and how his physical recovery started *among the good old brown hills of Deeside where, amidst their peace and quiet, it is hard to realise that Europe is in a blaze.* Fortunately, the 2016 furore about Britain's relationship within Europe hasn't involved any of us in actual warfare, as far as I know.

The June issue included an appreciation of Charles Air, a Captain in the Black Watch and the third Club member to forfeit his life. He was a native of Dundee and died in the same operation as his friend Harry Walker on 25 September 1915, … *his striking personality and charm of character made him the centre of a large circle of intimate friends.* A.E. Maylard contributed an article about 'Mountains and Mists' and Gilbert Thomson wrote about 'The Winter's Weather' for those who like Monthly Records of Rainfall as bedtime reading. A. Harker continued his treatise with part 4 'On Some Old Maps', this time concentrating on the history of mountain names and the accuracy of their locations. *The same political considerations which inspired the first opening up of the Highlands by highways led subsequently to the making of a Military Survey* of the Scottish mainland, which was completed by 1755. Aaron Arrowsmith's map of 1807 was the first to include named mountains arranged in something like their true positions but place-names were a constant problem, Harker stating that *the Ordnance Survey rightly expects those who use maps of the Highlands to acquire some slight knowledge of Gaelic spelling and pronunciation.*

In similar vein, in the October issue, the topic of mapping inaccuracies was pursued by E.M. Corner who sent a series of notes about *two poorly explored districts – Wester Ross and the southern end of the Western Cairngorms. He warns that the Allt Linneach ... that drains the hollow between Braeriach and Sgor an Lochan Uaine ... becomes impassable when the snow on these huge hills is melting.* Walter Smith contributes a reflective account about 'Some Hill Roads in Scotland', mentioning *those bonny Forfarshire glens of Isla and Clova.* James A. Parker chooses 'Craig Maskeldie' (near the head of Glen Esk) and that fine area of hills for his essay ... *there is evidently a lot of climbing to be done on the north face of the craig but we had no time left for further investigations* [they had set out from Ballater and now faced a 14 mile return walk with 3,600ft of ascent] ... *they had a good hard day on the hills!*

J.H. Bell describes in detail a fortnight's holiday amongst 'Some Western Hills' with W. Ling, starting in Ardgour and finishing in the Grey Corries area, praising the delights of the upper Cour water which drains the large corrie east of Aonach Beag. The article was illustrated with some photos taken by A.E. Robertson in 1906, one of which is reproduced here.

It was announced that *Harold Raeburn is engaged (full time) in a factory doing Government work.* According to the obituary written by W. Ling, Raeburn had *always been theoretically interested in aviation, and tried hard to join the RAF*

Rum from Moidart in 1906. Photo: A.E.Robertson.

[Ling is wrong here; the RAF did not come into existence until 1918 and he meant the Royal Flying Corps] *but his age was against him* [he was 51] *and he found an outlet for his patriotism in an aeroplane factory, where he worked fifteen or sixteen hours a day. With the exception of an occasional two or three days in the Lakes or the Highlands, the mountains had to be left alone till the war was over.* The location of the aeroplane factory and the precise nature of Raeburn's employment are open to speculation but at that time he resided at an address in Partick and the nearest aeroplane manufacturer was William Beardmore & Co., next to John Brown's Clydebank shipyard on the 'Dalmuir Bend' where today the Golden Jubilee Hospital stands.

Finally, the deaths of five more SMC members were acknowledged. Just to read the tribute to Captain Ronald MacDonald of the Cameron Highlanders, for example, is enough to sum up the waste, the pain, the tragedy, the uselessness of it all, this bloody War to end all wars. Born at Glenhenisdale, Skye in 1866 he was one of those *cultured* Celts who embraced education ... *a Highlander of the best type, a man of high character and gentlemanly manner, a brave soldier and a friend unostentatiously generous.* The others were Major William Grierson MacAlister, Lieut. James Ranald Beckett, Captain William R. McJannet and Captain Thomas H.B. Rorie. Their names may not be as familiar as some other SMC members from that period and I regret that there isn't enough space to reprint more details from their obituaries for they all sound like interesting, unassuming, accomplished men.

Members' excursions

I imagine that everyone took to the hills when they had the opportunity but there is little information available other than in personal diaries. Fortunately, W. Ling kept a full record of his numerous outings and Diary 12 catalogues around thirty such entries for 1916, both in Scotland (including official Club Meets) and the Lake District. I have selected a couple of the more interesting entries:

April 21. Carn Mor Dearg. Ben Nevis.
A dull morning. R. Corry, R.G. Elwell, G. Solly, A.E. Maylard, A.D. Smith, G. Lawson & self left Alexandra Hotel at 8.15 and walked along past the distillery, then across the moor and up the ridge of Carn Mor Dearg. The snow was in good condition and as we went the mists rose and on the top 12.40 we had magnificent views. It was rather cold on the ridge but quite warm on the top where we lunched. The arête to the Ben was in good order and after lunch we went on to the top of the Ben 2.20. The Observatory and hotel were completely covered. The cornices were very fine, that at the top of the Tower Ridge looked impossible. On our way down we met 6 Lovat Scouts ascending. The Red Burn was soft and we only got a short sitting glissade. We were back at Fort William at 5 p.m. [This took place during the Easter Meet]

Sept. 10. Birkness Chimney attempt.
Fine morning. Raeburn, Field, Miss Field, Wilson, Backhouse and self rowed up the lake to below the Coombe. Then I went on and gathered Bicknell and Graham. We all went leisurely up the Coombe. Miss Field stood out. The rest roped up. Raeburn leading, self, Wilson, Bicknell, Field, Backhouse, Graham. The first pitch is up a steep wall into the chimney. Then up a steep bit, a long stride into a narrow crack, true left. Then some easier climbing to the principal pitch. This is very difficult, overhanging, a large slab which requires a strong armpull and a long

reach. Raeburn first tried it in boots, but it would not go. He then came down and took off his boots while Bicknell came up second to give a shoulder. It looked very sensational and the hold was beyond his reach. We persuaded him to come down, though he would probably have done it, if we had encouraged him. We then all went down, doubling the rope over a hitch and sliding down to save time. Raeburn and Bicknell then went on and did the gully which was wet and difficult. The rest went down to lunch, Wills and Miss Wills having come up to join us. Backhouse and Graham went to do a climb on the face. The rest went down to Lower Gatesgarth to tea.

[Birkness Chimney & Birkness Gully, Eagle Crag; both routes were climbed by Sheldon and Oppenheimer in 1903 and graded Hard Severe and Severe respectively in the 1992 FRCC guide to Buttermere & Eastern Crags. The Gully is described as a strenuous climb on good but often greasy rock whilst the Chimney is similar ... with a decidedly harder crux.]

Mike Jacob

Postscript: there is an interesting wartime connection with one Scottish hill. The German navy had discovered orders from Winston Churchill aboard a captured ship, the SS *Ben Cruachan*, which instructed captains of merchant vessels to treat the crews of U-boats as felons rather than as prisoners of war and survivors from U-boats might be shot if this was more convenient than taking them captive. So, when Charles Fryatt, captain of the SS *Brussels*, attempted to ram a U-boat in 1915 he became the target for German vengeance. In 1916, he was captured at sea and later executed, although he was a civilian non-combatant, an act which caused international condemnation.

200 YEARS AGO: 'The Year Without A Summer'

We are apt to complain about our weather, but on 7 September 1816 the Caledonian Mercury reported a failed harvest and persistent snow on the hills. Earlier, the Scots Magazine for 1 August reported a series of violent storms. But this was nothing to what was endured elsewhere in Europe early in the year: storms and floods abounded in June and July. The Cambridge Chronicle for 19 July summarized various catastrophes, such as the hurricane at Vibbel near Frankfurt on 28 June, in which 'roofs ... were torn from houses, some buildings entirely destroyed, and 400 fruit-trees torn up by the roots. The hail lay two feet deep in the streets and fields.' So bad was the weather in Germany that horses were killed for lack of fodder for them, and Karl Drais was driven to invent the first bicycle. 'It's an ill wind...' some might say.

The cause of these disasters was the eruption in April 1815 of Mount Tambora in Sumbawa, which previously lorded it over the Indonesian Seas from a height of 4,300 metres. The explosion – the greatest in recorded history at VEI 7 – ejected 163 km^3 of material which made its way to the Northern Hemisphere by the summer of 1816, bringing about The Year Without a Summer.

Unsurprisingly, little activity of a mountaineering nature was recorded that year. In the Alps, Mary Wollstonecraft, Shelley and Byron, confined to the Villa Diodati by the tempests, were reduced to writing ghost stories, of which Wollstonecraft's Frankenstein was the eventual gruesome outcome, although Byron also produced a fragment which John Polidori developed into The Vampyre. 'It's an ill wind...'

some might say. In Scotland, we know (see Ian Mitchell's *Scotland's Mountains Before the Mountaineers*) that William MacGillivray – a truly remarkable man and a formidable pedestrian who thought nothing of walking between Harris and Aberdeen University several times a year – and Major Colby were afoot on the heights, but not where or when, thanks to the fire which destroyed MacGillivray's Journals in Australia, and the bombs which fell on Colby's archive in November 1940 during the Southampton blitz. In these cases, the winds that fanned the blaze blew no good whatsoever.

Robin N. Campbell

THE GIRVAN SISTERS OF INVERARNAN INN

In the 1981 Journal, Bill Murray wrote a short obituary for Nancy Girvan, the older of the two sisters who kept the Inn at Inverarnan, which according to Bill, was in the 1930s 'the most favoured haunt of the J.M.C.S. Glasgow', and later became 'the winter headquarters of the Western S.M.C'.

Nancy and Hannah Girvan on Killin Golf Course in 1954. Photo:Tom Weir.

Recently I received a donation to the Archives from John Mallinson, a fine photograph of the Girvan sisters, Hannah and Nancy, taken by Tom Weir in 1954 during a break from ski-ing the Killin Golf Course. I had the idea of getting some more information about these Muses of the Glasgow JMCS, but my primitive inquiries soon ran into a brick wall in the form of inadequate data – or inadequate searching – at the Scotland's People online database. Bob Aitken offered to put the problem to his friend Duncan Macniven, a former Register-General, and thanks to Mr Macniven's generous efforts, we can now put together a few basic biographical facts. These hardly constitute an obituary for Hannah, by way of a complement to Bill's note about Nancy, but they provide a starting point for further research on the lives of these much-loved innkeepers.

The sisters were among the children of William Murdoch Girvan, a farmer, and Hannah Lindsay Wilson, both of Sorn in Ayrshire. Agnes McClure Girvan (a.k.a. Nancy) was born on 20 April 1901 and Hannah Lindsay Girvan on 20 April 1910. 'Nancy' was born at Auchenwrath Farm, Kirkmahoe, just north of Dumfries. Sometime after 1907 the family moved to Rowan Cottage, Tradespark, Nairn, and Hannah was born there.

At some point after giving up Inverarnan, the sisters moved to Invergarry, living in a house called Tighmony. That was their usual residence when Agnes ('Nancy') died at Raigmore on 19 February 1981, aged 79. Hannah survived until 1 February 1990, when she died at Meallmore Nursing Home, Daviot, also aged 79. Her usual residence had been 107 Balmacaan Road, Drumnadrochit and her death was registered by her nephew who lived at Corrimony, Drumnadrochit.

Robin N. Campbell

SCOTTISH MOUNTAINEERING TRUST – 2015

Scottish Charity Number SCO 09117

The Trustees met on 17 April and 16 October 2015. During the course of these meetings, support was given to:
Renovations to the Glen Brittle Memorial Hut; Mountaineering Council of Scotland – Access; Mountaineering Council of Scotland – Smart Student Weekend; Jonathan Conville Memorial Trust – Winter Courses 2015/2016; R Crawford – Dundee Mountain Film Festival; Glasgow University – Tanzania Expedition; People's Project – Criffel Footpath; Edinburgh University Mountaineering Club – Renovations to Glen Licht House; Dundonnell Mountain Rescue Team – Construction of Rescue Base; G&J Surveys – Measurement of Heights of Hills; Dr Emmanuelle Tulle – Research on Women Mountaineers; John Muir Trust – Sligachan to Coruisk and Beinn Dearg Mheadhonach Footpaths.

For the year to the Club AGM in December 2015 the Trustees were JRG MacKenzie (Chairman) (Ex officio immediate past President of the SMC), ER Allen, R Anderson (ex officio Convener of the Publications Sub-Committee), PJ Biggar, AM James, CM Jones, CR Ravey and DN Williams (ex officio President of the SMC). With effect from the Club AGM in December 2015 there were the following changes namely PJ Biggar retired by rotation but remained as Trustee in his capacity as ex officio Editor of the Journal. CM Jones and CR Ravey retired from the Trust by rotation. The Trustees wish to record their gratitude and appreciation for their valuable input over a number of years. GR Ross, SD Pearson and JAP Hutchinson were appointed as new Trustees at the Club AGM in December 2015 and in addition CR Ravey was re-appointed for a further term.

The present Directors of the Publications Company are CR Ravey (Chairman/Secretary since October 2014), K Crocket, BM Whitworth, SL Jensen and RT Prentice (Publications Manager). CR Ravey (who is both a Director of the Publications Company and a Trustee) provides valuable liaison between the Publications Company and the Trust.

The following grants/loans have been committed by the Trustees during 2015:

Renovations to Glen Brittle Memorial Hut (further loan)	£10,000
Mountaineering Council of Scotland – Access	£5,000
Mountaineering Council of Scotland – Smart Student Weekend	£3,000
Jonathan Conville Memorial Trust – Winter Courses 2015/2016	£1,000
R Crawford – Dundee Mountain Film Festival	£750
Glasgow University – Tanzania Expedition	£500
People's Project – Criffel Footpath	£2,000
Dundonnell Mountain Rescue Team – Construction of Rescue Base	£5,000
G&J Surveys – Measurement of Heights of Hills	£2,000
Dr Emmanuelle Tulle – Research on Woman Mountaineers	£200
John Muir Trust – Sligachan to Coruisk and Beinn Dearg Mheadhonach Footpaths (£6,250 per annum for 2 years)	£12,500
Edinburgh Univ. M.C. Renovation of Glenlicht House	£2,000

James Hotchkis (Hon. Sec SMT)

MUNRO MATTERS 2015

by Dave Broadhead (Clerk of the List)

This report covers 1 January to 31 December 2015. The five columns below give number, name and year of Compleation of Munros, Tops and Furths as appropriate. *SMC member, **LSCC member.

5684	Andrew R. Bonwick	2014 2014		
5685	John A. Laing	2014		
5686	Steven Gillies	2012		
5687	John McGugan	1995		
5688	Ian Purdie	1995		
5689	David J. Wood	2014		
5690	Allan McCulloch	2013		
5691	Keith Rodber	2015		
5692	Janet Rodber	2015		
5693	Campbell Matthews	2015		
5694	Lynsey Fitzpatrick	2014		
5695	Philip Tipping	2014		
5696	**Joanne Webster	2014		
5697	Chris Dean	2015		
5698	Graeme Sidwell	2013		
5699	Steve Illingworth	2007		
5700	Elaine Beattie	2013		
5701	Marie Clare Lunny	2014		
5702	Kevin Murray	2012		
5703	Claudia Zeiske	2015		
5704	Nicholas May	2015		
5705	Philip Aikman	2015		
5706	Shelagh M. Shoulder	2015		
5707	Norman Harrison	2015		
5708	Jim Hughes	2015		
5709	Graham Eccles	2015		
5710	Ian Combe	2015		
5711	Andrew Stevens	2015 2014		
5712	John Toms	2015		
5713	Peter Watson	2015		
5714	David J. Stott	2015		
5715	Hugh Willison	2015		
5716	Brian W. Ringland	2004 2004		
5717	Carl Gilham	2015		
5718	Michael Mulligan	2015		
5719	Colin Richards	2015		
5720	Geoff Binns	2015		
5721	Paul J. Worsnop	2015		
5722	Lesley Scott	2015		
5723	Andy Scott	2015		
5724	Roderick M. Kingman	2015		
5725	David White	2015		
5726	Paul Findlow	2015		
5727	Peter Duggan	2015 2015		
5728	Nick Chapman	2015		
5729	Leisha Fullick	2015		
5730	Michael Gotz	2015		
5731	Grant Maclean	2015		
5732	Steven Wright	2015		
5733	Rhoda Forrest	2015		
5734	Calum Anton	2015		
5735	David Sothern	2015		
5736	Valerie Phillips	2015		
5737	David Hall	2015		
5738	Richard Anderson	2015		
5739	Keith Small	2015		
5740	Andy Cox	2015		
5741	Steve Hawken	2015		
5742	Andrew Murphy	2015		
5743	Brenda J. Dunnett	2014 2014		
5744	Bruce Dunnett	2014 2014		
5745	Jenny Beveridge	2015		
5746	Stephen W. Kendal	2015		
5747	Roger J. Duncalf	2015		
5748	Seana Carroll	2015		
5749	John Mahon	2015		
5750	David Lees	2011		
5751	Dave Turner	2011		
5752	Ian Hodgson	2015		
5753	Dylan Ryan	2013		2014
5754	Martin Stevenson	2015		
5755	James H. Roberts	2015		
5756	Michael McGregor	2015		
5757	Phil Hadland	2015		
5758	Andrea Stanbridge	2015		
5759	Mark A. Willingham	2015		
5760	John Perkins	2015		
5761	John S. Casson	2015		
5762	Iain Macdonald	2015		
5763	John Perry	2015		
5764	Sarah J. Douglas	2015		
5765	Stephen Jardine	2009		
5766	Kathleen Lawless	2008		
5767	Christopher Reid	2015		
5768	Kenneth M. Murray	2015		
5769	Stephen Gibb	2015		
5770	Nigel Hill	2015		
5771	Arran Ellis	2015		
5772	Geoff Dobson	2015		
5773	David W. Main	2015		
5774	Mhairi A. Martin	2015		
5775	Alison D. Steele	2015		
5776	Valerie Maclean	2015		
5777	Roderick Maclean	2015		
5778	Martin Hunt	2015		
5779	Gerald T. Smith	2015		
5780	Stephen Mayne	2015		
5781	Karen Powell	2015		
5782	Keith Roberts	2015		
5783	Sandy Presly	2015		

5784	Rachel Higgins	2015
5785	Martin Joyce	2015
5786	Peter Botterill	2011
5787	John D. Howard	2015
5788	Roy Robinson	2015
5789	Jack P. Harland	2015
5790	Stephen Cottrell	2015
5791	Colin Fridge	2015
5792	Kevin Woods	2013
5793	Margaret Spalding	2015
5794	Gavin Mullen	2015
5795	Liz Walkington	2015
5796	Douglas Robertson	2015
5797	Kevin J. Whyte	2015
5798	Stuart Robb	2015
5799	John Reay	2015
5800	Helen Beatham	2015
5801	Neil Beatham	2015
5802	Anne Devey	2015
5803	David Devey	2015
5804	Ian P. Bell	2015
5805	Paul Hodges	2015
5806	Anne Foley	2015
5807	Michael Foley	2015
5808	Bob Gil	2015
5809	John Neary	2005
5810	George Devereux	2015 2015
5811	Isobel Burnett	2015
5812	Linda Thompson	2015
5813	Andrew Reid	2015
5814	Stuart Whittaker	2015
5815	Eric Rossiter	2015
5816	Margaret Kay	2015
5817	Dennis Mawhinney	2015
5818	Tony O'Kane	2015
5819	David Dunn	2015
5820	Anne Patterson	2015
5821	Tony Patterson	2015
5822	David T. Sutherland	2015
5823	Jennifer May Cardno	2015
5824	Archie Macsporran	2015
5825	Robin Wrench	2015
5826	Christopher Langthorne	2015
5827	Andy Giddy	2015
5828	Lyndon Brown	2015
5829	Dean Souter	2015
5830	Peter McIntosh	2015
5831	Grahame Connor	2015
5832	Alan Ledger	2012
5833	David Duffin	2015
5834	Steven Allen	2015
5835	Norman Wilson	2015
5836	*Gordon Ross	2015
5837	Gregor Gibson	2015
5838	Gordon Battersby	2015
5839	John Stokes	2015
5840	Ron Rawlinson	2015
5841	Jackie Wilkins	2015
5842	Derek Williams	2015
5843	Catherine L. Warwick	2015
5844	Jim Williamson	2015
5845	Andrew Liddle	2015
5846	Leo G. McClymont	2015
5847	Anthony Jackson	2015
5848	Mary H. Coventry	2015
5849	Shelagh Goodwin	2015
5850	Shona McDaid Robertson	2015
5851	David Evans	2015
5852	Rosie Crawford	2015
5853	Maureen Sillence	2015
5854	Adrian Sillence	2015
5855	Irene McCombe	2000
5856	David Meckin	2015
5857	Malcolm J. Otter	2015
5858	Andrew Chippindale	2015
5859	William Ross	2015
5860	George Dunlop	2015
5861	Bill Dickson	2015
5862	Andy Rees	2015
5863	George Watson	2015
5864	Kevin Moore	2015
5865	Philip Birch	2015
5866	David Brown	2015
5867	Keith S. Thomson	2015
5868	Alison McLeod	2015
5869	Malcolm M. Brown	2015
5870	Gerard M. Bramwell	2015
5871	Alastair D. Bruce	2015
5872	Christopher Watson	2015
5873	Monica Shaw	2015
5874	O. Fraser Clark	2015
5875	Frances Watkins	2015
5876	John C. Jamieson	2015
5877	Philip McLean	2015
5878	Sandy Scott	2015
5879	Peter Berwick	2015
5880	David Cochrane	2015
5881	Charles Evans	2015
5882	Jack Campbell	2015
5883	Christopher Abrams	2015
5884	Gill McMillan	2015
5885	Chris Lord	2015
5886	Bengt Karlsson	2015
5887	Calum G. Skinner	2015
5888	David Galsworthy	2015
5889	Steve Smith	2015
5890	Janice Chapman	2015
5891	Keith Cocks	2015
5892	Darran Moss	2015 2015
5893	John Tochel (Snr)	2015
5894	John Tochel	2015
5895	George Weir	2015
5896	*Iain Thow	1984 2004 1994
5897	Colin Priestley	2015
5898	Nicola Tod	2015
5899	Jonathan Tod	2015
5900	David Leeming	2015

Comparing this year's data with last year (in brackets): New Munroists 217 (250); males 80% (76%); resident in Scotland 64% (55%); couples 12% (16%); average age 55 (54); size of Compleation summit party 10 (10); average Compleation time 24 (23) years; Golden Munroists 8 (10). I have started every report with this summary for the past 9 years, so it is interesting now to look back on any variation or trends.

| | | | % | | | | |
YEAR	MUNROISTS	MALE	SCOTS	COUPLES	AGE	PARTY	TIME
2007–08	257	81	64	18	54	16	23
2008–09	227	79	55	12	54	14	21
2009–10	239	81	63	12	52	14	22
2010	217	78	59	15	53	15	22
2011	242	78	54	16	55	11	24
2012	248	79	63	18	52	11	25
2013	233	81	60	11	54	12	25
2014	250	76	55	16	54	10	23
2015	217	80	64	12	55	10	24
AVERAGE	**237**	**79**	**60**	**14**	**54**	**13**	**23**

Without doing any further number crunching it looks to me like things have stayed pretty steady over the years! I wonder if the low Munroist total for 2015 was a direct result of the poor summer weather? As ever there were plenty of interesting letters and I thought it would be worth looking this year at the length of time taken to Compleat a first Munro Round as the focus for my report. Five categories were chosen, with the size of the group shown as a percentage of the 2015 total.

<5 YEARS = Superfast = 6%
To climb all the Munros in such a short time takes a lot of focus, organization and determination. Lynsey Fitzpatrick (5694) 'took the great challenge of completing the Munros to raise money and awareness for the soldier's charity Help for Heroes' along with her black Labrador Rabbie. As the wife of an injured veteran with a full-time job, their Round of less than 3 years was particularly impressive. She noted that 'the Cuillin in Skye was definitely not at all dog friendly. With the help of a mountain guide, a dog climbing harness and boots made especially for him, we managed to find routes up to the summits.'

Steven Allen (5834) would probably be surprised to be described as speedy. He explained 'before I started I read about the pioneers of the 1890s and was interested to find out how they travelled to the mountains. I was struck by the fact that they would sometimes use a bicycle to reach the starting point and being a keen cyclist myself and not owning a car I decided to adopt this approach to my hill walking. If no train was available for my bike I would take the bus.'

6–23 YEARS = Nae hangin' aboot = 43%
This is the largest group, taking a less than average time. This would include my own Round of 18 years, achievable by most regular hill-goers. Steven Gillies (5686) neatly summarized the incentive for many in registering their Round. 'On completing his first Munro I told my youngest son Thomas (aged 9) about "The List" and had to admit a little shamefaced that my name wasn't on it. He was very insistent that I should rectify this as he would want to show his children and grandchildren what his Dad had achieved.'

Brian W. Ringland (5716) a rare Irish Compleater from Co. Monaghan, reported a remarkably coordinated Contiguous Compleation on 2 June 2004 with Munro Beinn Sgritheal along with its NW Top, Corbett Beinn na h' Eaglaise and Graham Beinn a' Chapuill. Martin Stevenson (5754) started his Munros with his father Roger Stevenson (3566) but has since moved to New Zealand and fitted in his Compleation on Ben Lomond on a visit home. He is now working through the 'Great Walks of New Zealand'. Bengt Karlsson (5886) is the only overseas Compleater this year, from Jackson, New Hampshire, USA. He explained his introduction to Munros 'while working in the US writing software I met Ron Bell who worked for IBM and discovered we were both avid hikers.' In due course Ron completed the 48 mountains over 4000 feet in New Hampshire and the Lakeland Wainwrights and persuaded Bengt to join him on the Munros. He has spent about 180 walking days on the task and only has 2 more Munro Tops left.

Apart from climbing all the Munros, Roy Robinson (5788) admitted that 'his other ambition in life was to play professional rugby, which I achieved in 1993.' Kevin Woods (5792) reported two Munro Rounds, finishing the second only 2 years after the first and was featured on a BBC Alba programme called 'Dha-Ochd-Dha' literally 'Two-Eight-Two'. He admitted to a cumulative count but promised 'I'm wiping the slate clean for the third Round!' John Tochel (Snr) (5893) and John Tochel (5894) father and son 'completed every hill together' and 'enjoyed a great family Compleation day on Meall nan Tarmachan, with four first time Munroists including my wife, daughter, mother and sister.'

Correspondents often omit interesting pieces of information but Iain Thow (5896) is the first not to mention his name! Having met Iain a few times I soon worked it out from his long letter which started 'Now that I'm an SMC member I suppose I'd better confess my bagging sins.' As well as reporting 'Full House' in the course roughly 7000 hill days he has finished various UK lists too numerous to mention and has an impressive tally of overseas summits. He comments 'incidentally, my vote for the naturally roughest ground goes to the Ceathramh Garbh north of Loch Laxford.' (Thankfully still a Munro free area.) Gulvain saw the Co-ordinated Compleation of Kevin Moore (5864), Philip Birch (5865) and David Brown (5866) whose Rounds of 18, 27 and 25 years respectively cross my rather artificial categories!

24–45 YEARS = Whit's yer hurry? = 35%

Munroists taking longer than average have often had an interruption to their hill-going career and seem to write the most interesting letters. Andy Cox (5740) had a particularly harrowing Compleation. After enjoying many years of ice climbing and skiing in Scotland and with only 4 Munros left he developed a neurological problem and 'now find climbing stairs difficult'. With a great deal of grit and determination he managed Beinn Dearg 'having climbed Emerald Gully and Penguin Gully previously but never summited I was able to cling to the old stone wall down the long ridge reducing the number of times I fell.' His final challenge was Conival and Ben More Assynt, overcome with the help of a friend Max, short roped and wearing a helmet!

Frances Watkins (5875) lost her husband Tim in a car crash in 2005 but 'carried on Munro bagging with much help from my friends.' Paul J. Worsnop (5721) sent a very interesting 'Munro Highlights' in which he admitted to being a Methodist minister, observing 'all in all a wonderful experience which has given me huge pleasure and many real spiritual moments – I often find God closer in the mountains than in church' though he also admitted spending 32 nights in bothies. Stephen Cottrell (5790) belongs to the small group of Munroists who do not drive, explaining 'while I was grateful for lifts to about 11% of the hills, the majority (about 75%) were climbed as a day out from accommodation, often using a bike or public transport. The remainder involved wild camping in the hills.' By the same method he is 2/3 through his Corbetts and 'hoping to climb the Irish Furths as part of an extended cycle tour.' Graham Eccles (5709) finished his letter by observing 'I suspect Sir Hugh Munro had no idea what he started many years ago. It must have brought millions of pounds of income to many areas of Scotland that would otherwise have never seen any visitors. Of course a big thanks must go to the SMC for issuing and updating the Tables.'

Kenneth M. Murray (5768) celebrated his Compleation with a toast to the late James S. Anderson (19) 'a family friend and eminent Chartered Accountant in Dundee who sparked my initial interests, both in becoming a C.A. and in climbing Munros.' Stuart Robb (5798) introduced himself as the son of 'a certain R. Robb you may know'. Roger Robb (262) is of course a fellow Dingwall resident, enthusiastic Munroist and SMC member. Stuart then went on to describe a series of incidents enlivening his Compleation on Sgùrr Dhearg (Beinn a' Bheithir). 'My brother-in-law forgot his boots and had to borrow trainers, the soles fell off both my sister's boots and had to be bound on with tape. Half an hour after starting, my father realized he had left his camera behind and had to go back to retrieve it. Then there was the new path, not marked on my old map. Despite these setbacks we all reached the summit, where it proceeded to rain.' I blame the parents!

John Reay (5799) became another second generation Munroist on Meall nan Tarmachan and reported 'sadly my father John R. Reay (3338) who had taken me up Ben Wyvis in 1973 was unable to join us due to arthritic knees. He was at Ben Lawers car park to see us off and partook in the celebrations that evening.' Some Munroists feel they have to justify having taken so long. Andrew Reid (5813) explained 'the long time to Compleat was due to a career at sea which has involved more time on the ocean than on land.' Michael Gotz (5730) commented wistfully 'I have handed over the book of Munros to my youngest daughter Martha on her 18th birthday. May she carry on from here. What will I do next? I will never do the Drumochter hills again or Schiehallion or Mount Keen. I am going to do a lot of ridge scrambling; I'll spend much time on Skye and whenever I can I'll take my sea kayak, launch from Elgol, paddle across to Loch Coruisk, pitch my tent and do the Dubh slabs in sunshine next day. Back in the tent I will look at whales and otters, write bad poetry, read good books, talk to great friends and drink very small amounts of extremely good Speyside whisky.' Malcolm J. Otter (5857) finished his letter with a short but rather beautiful poem composed 'after a bivvy beneath Mullach Coire Mhic Fhearchair.' 'Often, only the swish of the wind in the crags, the curruck of the raven or the beating of your own heart break the profound silence of the mountains.'

>45 YEARS = Nae hurry at a' = 5%

This category have extended the pleasures of climbing new Munros over almost their entire hill-going career and include nine Golden Munroists who are David Hall (5737) (59 years); Ian Hodgson (5752) (52 years); Sandy Presly (5783) (56 years); Stuart Whittaker (5814)(55 years); Gordon (better known as Curly) Ross (5836)(54 years); Catherine L. Warwick (5843)(53 years); Alastair D. Bruce (5871)(51 years) and Charles Evans (5881)(58 years). Calum Anton (5734) reported a Contiguous Compleation on 3 June 2015 finishing his Munros on Mayar followed by his Corbetts on Ben Tirram 5 hours 30 minutes later. Having climbed his first Munro in 1947 he managed to spread his Round over an impressive 68 years, nearly matching the record of 69 years set by Robert Waterson (3210). Ben More (Mull) is the most popular final Munro, but Archie Macsporran was brought up on the island and started his Round by climbing it at the age of six.

NO TIME GIVEN = Nae tellin' = 11%

Members of this category seem to have little of interest to tell me, but Shelagh M. Shoulder (5706) Compleated with the inevitable poet Roger Barr (3696). His ode 'Climb Every Mountain' ran to 15 verses opening 'It started back in the 70s/Sometime in mid-July/When Shelagh climbed her first Munro/And reached up to the sky.'

AMENDMENTS

The eight columns give number, name and year of Compleation of Munros, Tops, Furths, Corbetts, Grahams and Donalds. *SMC member. **LSCC member.

Num	Name	M	T	F	C	G	D
1746	James King	1997		2014	2003	2014	2014
1110	Christopher G. Butler	1992	2001	1995			
		2001	2009				
		2004					
		2015					
1239	Roger C. Henshaw	1993	2001	2002	2008		
5285	Allan McConnochie	2013					2014
3596	John M. Tweddle	2006	2006	2008	2015		
5415	Frank Schyvens	2013					2015
2090	John A. Owen	1999		1998	2009	2014	2015
2493	Andrew Lawson	2005			2011		2014
3463	Bill Taylor	2005	2005		2015		
573	Tommy Hepburn	1988	1988	2015			
		2014	2014				
389	Jane O'Donovan	1985			2014		
4033	Donald F. Irvine	2002	2002	2008	2015		
5716	Brian W. Ringland	2004	2004		2004	2004	
4519	Mark McKain	2010			2015		
727	Kenneth Critchley	1990			2006	2014	
3934	Alastair H. Govan	2007	2010	2014	2015		
262	*Roger J. C. Robb	1981	2002		2004		
		2000					
		2015					
1836	Wendy Dodds	1997		2000	2015		
4688	Helen Thomas	2010			2012	2015	2015
4689	Michael Thomas	2010			2012	2015	2015
4483	*William A. Forbes	1986	1995	2002	2002	2006	2014
		2009			2015		
5288	Jamie Dobson	2013	2015	2014			
4054	Kenneth C. Ballantyne	2008	2007	2005	2015		
3438	Hazel Strachan	2005					2011
		2008					2012

Num	Name	M	T	F	C	G	D
		2010					2012
		2012					
		2013					
		2014					
		2015					
4890	Peter H. Grayson	2011	2011	2015			
2533	Roger Jamieson	2001			2015		
5186	Tim Searles	2012		2015			
5044	Chris S. Peachey	2012	2015	2012			
4572	John Spiers	2010	2015	2011			
2412	Dave Windle	2000	2010	2004	2015		
		2015					
1911	Martin J. Almond	1997	1997	2014	2012	2015	2013
		2006					
2003	Bob Macdonald	1998	2006	2006	2006	2015	2014
3493	Andrew Lawson	2005		2015	2011		2014
3468	John Henderson	2005			2010	2014	2015
2308	Simon Waddicor	1997			2007	2015	
2114	Thomas Bailey	1999			2015		
		2015					
1891	Dave Marshall	1993	2015		2014		
		2010					
		2014					
4151	Norman Wares	2008	2010	2011	2014		2015
1170	Elaine S. Fenton	1993	2014	1994	2010	2015	2015
1169	Garth B. Fenton	1993	2014	1994	2010	2015	2013
5360	Alan S. Hardie	2013	2015				
182	William Steele	1978					
		1986					
		1991					
		1997					
		2000					
		2005					
		2010					
		2014					
4625	Jim Bull	2010				2015	2013
2612	Rick Ansell	2001	1999	2015	2014		1997
4611	Tom Pattison	2010			2015		
1664	Ian H. Hill	1996			2005		
290	Kenneth J. Maciver	1982		2002			
		2000					
		2009					
		2015					
1345	Brian Norman	1994		2015			
2091	Roger Holme	1999			2015		
1533	Graeme Morrison	1995			2009		
		2009					
		2014					
		2015					
983	John Inglis	1988			2001		

Num	Name	M	T	F	C	G	D
		2015					
4396	Mark Gibson	2009	2013		2015		
3018	Matthew Linning	2003			2015		
4320	Andy Barnett	2009			2015		
4460	Christopher J. Smythe	2009	2012	2012	2015		
375	Robert H. Macdonald	1984	2008	1989			
		1987					
		1990					
		1992					
		1995					
		2002					
		2007					
		2011					
		2015					
1853	Anne J. Fletcher	1997		2000	2015	2015	2002
5057	Robert Philips	2012			2013	2014	2015
107	*Andrew Nisbet	1972	1991	1991	2000		
		1984					
		1996					
		2009					
		2015					
4006	Chris Pine	2007		2015	2012	2013	2014
3461	Patricia A. Chapman	2005			2012	2015	
3462	Adrian W. Chapman	2005			2012	2015	
5458	Trevor Willis	2014	2015				
5855	Irene McCombe	2000			2015		
2272	John E. McPherson	1999			2015		
3885	David Batty	1994	2011	2013	2014	2015	2014
		2011					
4037	Sue Lyth	2008	2011	2011			
		2015					
3305	Janet Pitt-Lewis	2004			2015		
2940	Neil Fullwood	2003			2015		
2355	George D. Smith	1995	2000				
		2015					
332	Stephen Bateson	1983	1994	1983	1996		
		1995					
		2015					
5506	Alistair Deering	2014	2015		2015		
2125	James Henderson	1999			2008	2014	2015
		2011					
5361	Fiona Clark	2013		2015			
5362	Stuart Clark	2013		2015			
3112	Bert Barnett	2001	2002	2002	1998	2000	2012
		2001	2009	2007	2007	2009	2013
		2009	2015	2015	2013		
		2012					
2433	Alan Rowan	2000		2011	2009		
		2011					
		2015					

Num	Name	M	T	F	C	G	D
1797	Elaine Stewart	1997		2003	2015		
5896	*Iain Thow	1984	2004	1994	2004	2007	2004
		2008					
4787	Brent Browning	2011					
		2015					
4122	Kennedy Hamilton	2008					
		2015					
364	J. Brian Dick	1984	2015	2006			
		1992					
		2000					
		2015					
3465	Colin F. Morsley	2005	2009	2010	2015		
2871	Peter Hamilton	1992		2002	1997		
		2002					
		2008					
		2015					
5505	Allison Robertson	2014			2015		

The dreaded heighters were at it again in 2015. Turning their attention away from the 282 Munros, with the assistance of some members of this Club and The Munro Society, Messrs Barnard, Jackson and Philips lugged their GPS equipment up some Munro Tops instead, resulting in some minor alterations. Creag na Caillich on the Tarmachan ridge was re-heighted as 914.3 m, which rounds down to 914 m and is consequently demoted while Mullach Coire nan Cisteachan (aka Carn na Caim S. Top) was found to be 914.6 m, rounding up to 915 m and elevation to Munro Top. The number of Tops remains 255.

Also hitting the outdoor-news headlines, Hazel Strachan (3438) Compleated a 7th Munro Round, a women's record which firmly establishes her as Queen of the Munros. She reported that her most recent Round was also her fastest, accomplished in a remarkable 9 months! Another regular correspondent, Robert H. MacDonald (375) reported a 9th Round, noting that his Compleation on Beinn Fhionnlaidh (Appin) was his 7th on that hill and probably a record. Andrew Nisbet (107) reported a 5th Round, undoubtedly a record for former SMC Presidents, one of whom to my knowledge has yet to report his first Round!

Letters notifying amendments tend to be more matter of fact and less reflective than first Munro Compleations. Kenneth J. MacIver (290) was an exception and was very reflective when reporting his 4th Round. Referring to 'coverage in some recent Munro publications' he wrote 'since May 1968 I have made 1478 Munro ascents, 130 without a beard and 1348 with. I have had canine companions to share my sandwiches on 252.' Ken has a particular fondness for what he describes as Skirosis and explained 'Since my first Munro ski ascent, Ben Macdui in April 1983 I have ascended 81 Munros on ski with a total of 302 ski ascents of Munros and Tops, including 41 tours on Macdui. Needless to say, ski descents have covered the full range from the sublime to the ridiculous! My fastest 10 Munros on ski were traversed on a wonderful day from Glas Maol to Lochnagar.' In the course of his Round of Furths, Chris Pine (4006) reported carrying ski-mountaineering gear over Helvellyn to enjoy 'an unforgettable ski off Seat Sandal.'

Graeme Morrison (1533) also reported a 4th Munro Round, accomplished in a

100day continuous outing, accompanied by his dog Penny (who achieved a 2nd Round) with the help of a campervan and 8 nights in bothies. His GPS watch recorded a total of 1317 miles (including 141 biked) and a total ascent of 145186 metres. Reporting his 4th Round J. Brian Dick (364) reminded me 'as far as I know I am only the 33 Munroist to do four or more Rounds.' That total is now of course 34 with Peter Hamilton (2861). Another remarkable amendment was reported by Simon Waddicor (2308) who wrote 'I finished the Munros while living in Nottingham and having no driving license. Since then I've done Corbetts and Grahams from Stuttgart, with the help of a car and many ferries.' He has kept diary entries for over 500 days in the Scottish hills.

Thomas Bailey (2114) has always been fussy about the weather and enjoyed views from all but 14 summits on his first Munro Round. On Round 2 he 'fixed those 14 and am pleased to be able to say that I have seen the view from the summit of all 282 Munros.' Patricia (3461) and Adrian Chapmen (3462) have now Compleated Rounds of Munros, Corbetts and Grahams together. Stephen Bateson (332) finished his 2nd Round on the Inaccessible Pinnacle explaining 'the fear factor probably caused me to leave it to the end. I actually bought a new rope just for the descent. Having got to the summit block (in somewhat ungainly fashion) I began pulling said rope from my sac whereupon the team that was already abseiling from the block offered me the use of their rope. So I still have a virgin rope.'

Six people reported a Full House having Compleated all the six Lists on our website. Over 40 people have now accomplished this. Martin Almond (1911) came up with a Gaelic term 'sarbheanntair' for these 'compleat compleatists' suggested by the Gaelic Translation Service in Inverness. Apparently 'bheanntair'

Roger Robb on the way to the summit of Beinn More Mull to celebrate completing a third round of the Munros. Photo: Peter MacDonald.

means mountaineer and 'sar' compleat. I will be interested to see if this term catches on. Something that has caught on is the new *SMC Hillwalkers Guide to the Grahams and the Donalds* which has attracted many enthusiastic comments along the lines of Norman Wares (4151) who wrote 'I would like to pay tribute to those who have been involved in the new guidebook. I couldn't wait to get my hands on it and have found it to be very helpful in planning how to tackle all the various hills.' With a double Full House Bert Barnett (3112) is another regular correspondent whose 17 List entries now equals the record set last year by Hamish Brown (62). Bert warned me 'I am working through another set of Munros at present, so you might hear from me again next year.'

At the end of each year I always end up with a small bundle of letters filed as MISC. Most of this relates to mundane stuff, correcting errors (usually mine) and apologizing for underpayment of postage but sometimes seeking your Clerk's judgment. Elizabeth McKinnon (5586) faced a dilemma regarding her dog Molly. Unlike Lynsey Fitzpatrick (5694) and Rabbie mentioned earlier, she was unable to find anyone prepared to help facilitate a four legged ascent of the Inaccessible Pinnacle and finished her letter with the plea 'can we say Molly will have climbed all the Munros if she hasn't been hoisted up that piece of rock?' Having politely but emphatically replied 'no way!' I was delighted to subsequently hear that when Elizabeth took Molly up to Sgùrr Dearg 'she scaled the rock face of the In Pinn without any problems.' In the course of her Compleation Molly helped raise more than £550 for Scottish Mountain Rescue and the Search and Rescue Dog Association.

Not all stories have such a happy ending. Writing from Somerset to request a Compleation certificate, Andrew Kilbride (741) lamented 'sadly my motivation to travel North decreases year by year in direct proportion to the rate at which wind turbines continue to multiply and desecrate the precious Scottish landscape.' On a lighter note, he also lamented his failure to climb the East Top of Lurg Mhòr on three occasions by paraphrasing Frank Sinatra (see below).

As ever I am always pleased to hear from anyone seeking immortality by having their achievements added to our six Lists. Please write to Dave Broadhead, 17 Drumdyre Road, Dingwall, IV15 9RW. For a Munro or Corbett Compleation certificate please enclose an A4 sae (with correct postage please). Check <smc.org.uk> for further details and to view the picture galleries of Munroists and Corbetteers celebrating on their final summit.

Enjoy your hills.

Dave Broadhead (Clerk of the List)

Lurg Mhòr, (My Way)

Regrets, I have a few…but then again too few to mention
Three times I climbed Lurg Mhòr…but never once its top extension.
I will return, in years to come…when knees are frail and sight be dimmer,
Disabled access will be there…I'll do it on my trusty zimmer.

Andy Kilbride

WILLIAM RUSSELL MORRISON j. 1983

My father Bill Morrison died on 11 February 2016 and I have been asked to write a few words for the Journal to cover his activities in the hills.

Born in Glasgow in 1932 and brought up in Bearsden during the war years, his introduction to the hills was with friends roaming the Kilpatrick hills and soloing climbs on local crags like the Whangie in the late 1940s and early 1950s. Leaving Glasgow High school at the age of 16, he was too young to go to university. Initially working in the bakery industry, the six-day working week with night shifts thrown in and two weeks of annual leave was not conducive to weekends away climbing. Nevertheless he managed to visit a few climbing spots with friends such as the Cobbler, Glen Coe, Arran and even climbed the Hörnli ridge on the Matterhorn in 1956 with his friend R. Kerr McPhail.

National Service came along and during this time his attention became focussed more on skiing. He started with ex-US army skis made of hickory. This was the time of cable bindings, catching the Scottish Ski Club bus to Ben Lawers and the building of the SSC hut at Glen Coe ... and its replacement when the first one blew away in a gale.

It was through skiing that his career took a change in direction. Crashing head first into a snow bank on Meall a' Bhuiridh resulted in a day off work with concussion. Feeling better by lunchtime on this day off, he paid a visit to his alma mater then called the Royal College of Science and Technology and later to become the University of Strathclyde. He was promptly offered a job in the new Department of Food Science. Apart from a couple of years in California on a Fulbright scholarship, he spent the rest of his career in this department, ending up as emeritus professor on retiral. Research was his main interest and his forte.

With the arrival of children, regular skiing trips to Glen Coe followed and I have memories of family holidays with the five of us parked up in a VW campervan next to a frozen Loch Morlich, ready to hit the Cairngorm ski slopes. As we children grew older, hillwalking restarted and many of my later teenage weekends were spent accompanying him walking, scrambling and skiing over various Munros. Memories include us skiing across a frozen Loch an Daimh between Meall Buidhe and Stuchd an Lochain on a still blue-sky day in February 1979 – hacking a hole in the ice, we found that it was 15 inches thick; then there were the clouds of midges one Skye weekend where we ended up circling the tent in an effort to create a breeze while eating a hasty breakfast.

Skiing is, of course, a winter activity in Scotland. Before my teenage hillwalking years, my father spent his summers dinghy boat racing. He worked his way up through Enterprises, Albacores, 505s and into keelboats, collecting a hoard of pewter cups, medals and glass tankards on the way. He served time on the committee of the Helensburgh Sailing Club, including as Commodore in the early 1970s. He also found time to make some of these dinghies. This maritime interest extended to service with the RNLI inshore service until barred by age.

Back to the hills. Piste-bashing morphed into ski mountaineering and the start of some SSC-organised touring trips, initially in Scotland but later including the Alps. These trips brought him into the orbit of skiing SMC members such as Malcolm Slesser, Donald Bennet, Bill Wallace, Alan McNicol and Mike Taylor. Touring trips were made to the Silvretta region in Austria, along the Haute Route, to the Vanoise in France, the Oberland in Switzerland, to Svalbard in Spitzbergen and Reindalen in Norway.

Back in Scotland, Donald Bennet asked him to make some contributions to the SMT publications The Munros and Ski Mountaineering in Scotland, giving my brother and I the dubious pleasure of decorating the scenery in some of his photos as well as justifying some research trips. It was not long before his first Munro completion materialised in 1986. A second was to follow in 1992.

Retirement brought new activities in the form of golf and Scottish country dancing as well as annual SMC-populated ski trips to Europe. He also moved from Helensburgh to the Black Isle, spending his last twenty-five years or so within sight of Ben Wyvis. He noted with regret how the ranks of climbing and skiing friends thinned during these years. Then his own ill health brought the skiing to an end as well as curtailing the hillwalking, then the dancing and eventually the golf.

His heritage includes a family-wide interest in the Scottish hills, including a further three Compleaters. My own SMC membership can trace its roots to our shared hillwalking trips and to his encouragement to join the JMCS.

John Morrison

KEN ARMSTRONG j. 1954

George Kenneth Armstrong was a farmer's son, born near Twynholm in Kirkcudbright in 1922. The death of his father when he was only 8 led him and his mother to move to Glasgow, but Galloway remained a happy haunt for the rest of his life. Cubs and Scouts developed an early enthusiasm into a lifelong passion for outdoor activities.

Ken's training as an accountant was interrupted by the Second War, where he eventually became a flying instructor in what was then Southern Rhodesia. At the

end of hostilities he came back to Glasgow to complete his CA training, but he also enrolled as one of the first students at the newly established Glenmore Lodge. His enthusiasm for climbing was fired by that introduction; despite taking up a post in London for three years, he was ardently active throughout the early 1950s with the Glasgow JMCS, climbing with the notables of the time, Len Lovat, Malcolm Slesser, George Roger. But he also explored Harrison's Rocks and the crags of North Wales in the company of Ian Roberts of the London JMCS, a fellow Scottish accountant who had also served in East Africa with the RAF.

In February 1953 Ken was in a party of four led by Tom Weir that was avalanched from steep ground south of the Upper Couloir of Stob Ghabhar (in writing it up later, Tom doesn't disguise the evident avalanche hazard). Three of the four were injured in varying degrees – Tom was hors de combat for some months afterwards, and Ken had sprained both ankles badly – but they fought their way down in vile conditions to Forest Lodge. After first aid and tea from the stalker's wife, the battered party managed to make their own way back to the haven of Inverarnan for further succour, and on to Glasgow. In several published accounts Tom never gave the full names of his companions, this in response to Ken's pressing request that his mother, then living at Broadford, should not get to hear about this misadventure. Indeed you will search in vain for a record of these events in the SMCJ accident reports of the time…

When Ken submitted his application to the SMC in 1954 he was proposed by Hamish Hamilton and seconded by Bill Mackenzie, a Dream Team pairing which probably guaranteed his election to the Club. At much the same time his work took him to Edinburgh, and to a long and successful career with the National Coal Board. In the 1960s he put his professional skills to the service of the Club as Auditor, being succeeded in that role by his old friend Ian Roberts.

In his middle years Ken's interests turned more to skiing, which he pursued avidly at home and in the Alps; he became a life member of the Scottish Ski Club. He married relatively late, and took huge pleasure in introducing his two daughters to the varied delights of the Scottish countryside, to skiing and rowing; he was proud and pleased when his younger daughter June became a ski instructor.

To the last Ken retained his affection for the hills of Galloway and the Highlands, for Mull and Speyside, and for the SMC. Over several decades he was an annual fixture at Club Dinners: a big, broad-shouldered, genial figure, bespectacled and trimly moustached, come to commune and reminisce with the comrades of his Great Days on the mountains.

Robert Aitken

JOHN BERKELEY j. 1948

It might be said of John Berkeley that he seemed all his life to be the right man in the right place at the right time – or perhaps he made himself so. Born and schooled in the south of England, he came north to Edinburgh University to study medicine just after the War. Besides winning a Blue in rowing, he took avidly to climbing with the EUMC alongside such luminaries as Derek Haworth, Gordon Parish, Iain McPhail, Malcolm Slesser, Geoff Dutton and Iain Smart. Immensely active, John became Secretary of the EUMC in 1947-48 and President in 1948. He participated in the bold explorations of that time by the University Club and the JMCS in the forbidding canyons of Five Finger and Surgeon's Gullies, and joined fellow members in providing mountaineering instruction for the then CCPR at the newly-established Glenmore Lodge.

Iain Smart gives us two vignettes of John from the famous winter of 1947. He recalls tramping through the silent snow-smoored streets of the capital with John to assail the pièce de résistance of that Arctic season, the monster cornice over the Cat Nick; and 'a traverse of An Garbhanach and the ridge beyond one bright moonlight night of crisp snow, hard frost and overwhelming silence. The view from the ridge over a silver landscape remains with me still. I also remember that

we ate dried bananas, considered a delicacy at that time.' John joined the SMC when he was just 21, proposed by Gordon Parish and seconded by the Rev. Robert Clark, who had left his charge in Fort William for the post of first Principal of Glenmore Lodge.

John started his professional career as an orthopaedic houseman at Raigmore, where he met his wife Muriel, but he was promptly summoned away to National Service with the RAF from 1950 to 1952. He was recommended to join the Air Force, reportedly, by T. Graham Brown, whom he had met through the EUMC. Graham Brown – irreverently tagged 'Lord Brown of Brenva' by the students – was at that time a Vice-President of the RAF Mountaineering Association, and had recognised the urgent need to reinforce the RAF Mountain Rescue service. Stationed in South-West Scotland at Wig Bay and West Freugh, John played a key role in the transformation of the RAF service in the wake of the grim experience of the Lancaster crash in Coire Mhic Fhearchair in 1951, which had cruelly revealed basic deficiencies in equipment and training. He led the first RAF MR winter training course in the Cairngorms in February 1952. Based at Rothiemurchus Lodge (a good deal more basic in those days than now), the course provided a stern test of men and equipment in typical Cairngorms winter conditions. John also contributed, along with Johnnie Lees, his RAF colleague and frequent rope-mate, to the preparation of the official training handbook for RAF MRTs by Michael Holton of the Air Ministry (and the Alpine Club).

Once he was demobbed, John and Muriel moved to Fort William, where John's boundless energy found expression in a wide range of mountain work beyond the 'mere' role of GP in a large family practice. Over 13 years in Lochaber, he was inevitably drawn into the development of the local mountain rescue team. In 1955 he took over training and leadership of the team from Donald Duff. He provided medical support for the Ben races, was custodian of the CIC Hut for a dozen years from 1955; and (presumably in his spare time) acted as District Commissioner of the Lochaber Scouts. Gwen Moffat records that during her arduous self-education towards mountain guiding around Lochaber in the 1950s, the Berkeleys provided her with warm hospitality and hot baths. Her *Space Below my Feet* includes a dramatic account of a typically epic winter ascent of Observatory Ridge with John.

John's intimate and extensive engagement with mountain accidents and rescue in Lochaber made him a key player in the very necessary formalisation of Scotland's civilian mountain rescue in the 1960s, partly prompted by notorious accidents on Nevis, at Loch Ossian, and in the Cairngorms. These multiple-casualty disasters impelled a review that led to the first clear articulation of the symptoms and effects of exposure, a condition which – extraordinary to us now – had hitherto been hardly recognised. They also led to the restructuring of the Mountain Rescue Committee of Scotland, partly at the initiative of WH Murray as President of the SMC at the time, with John as Chair, Hamish Macinnes as Secretary, and John Watson of the Grampian Club as Treasurer. The MRCS became the key foundation on which our modern rescue services were developed. John was also involved with Graham Tiso in developing the 'Berkeley Bag', a cushioned plastic sleeve to provide shelter for exposure cases, an interim technology later overtaken by the development of modern windproof fabrics.

From the mid 1960s John and Muriel made a fundamental change in their medical careers that stemmed from their profound Christian faith. After retraining in relevant specialisms they served with a Leprosy Mission in south India, then from 1968 in Bhutan, where their care and commitment won the warm regard of the whole nation. Thereafter their lives were a kaleidoscope of selfless medical service and education at home and abroad, in Edinburgh and Bhutan, Aberdeen and Yemen, that barely abated with John's retirement. Based in Coylumbridge, he became a member of the Highland Health Board and continued to provide advice and direction in palliative care.

From Coylumbridge John, himself an ordained lay preacher, often led Sunday Worship at Kincraig Church. It was fitting that in 2007 he should conduct the funeral service there for Malcolm Slesser, his old EUMC rope-mate, and that his own memorial service should also be held there: a service of gratitude for the life and work of a modest and amiable man to whom the SMC and the wider mountaineering fraternity owe a large and largely unacknowledged debt.

Robert Aitken

Gwen Moffat writes: it sometimes happens that you don't know a man for long: a few winter evenings of hospitality, baths when there's no hot water in your lodging, gossip, idle chat, but you did one climb: a hard route, a winter epic – and in a thousand feet and nine hours the essence of the man is revealed: skilful, balanced, eminently reliable, and at the end delighting in the achievement and the glory of the Mamores in the moonlight. This was himself on Observatory Ridge.

Obituaries for Bob Brown, Des Rubens and James Edwards will appear in 2017.

PROCEEDINGS OF THE CLUB

At the Committee Meeting of October 2015, the following mountaineers were admitted to membership of the Club. We welcome:

MICHAEL BARNARD (34) Tree Surgeon.
RUAIRIDH B. FINLAYSON (32) Equity Analyst.
ANDREW S. HEIN (41) Research Fellow.
LISA HUTCHISON (60) Retired Teacher.
OLE J. KEMI (42) University Lecturer.
PETER G. NELLIST (34) Sport Development Officer.
KENNETH ROBB (65) Retired.
LIBBY SOUTHGATE (22) Climbing Instructor.
MICHAEL P. WATSON (45) IT Consultant.
ANDREW WIELOCHOWSKI (68) Retired Teacher.
ANDREW J. WOOLSTON (29) ROV Pilot.

And at the Meeting of April 2016:

ERICK BAILLOT (37) Secondary Teacher.
ANDREW S. CLARK (42) Head Teacher.
DREW CONNELLY (57) Accountant.
PAULINE A. KELL (47) Retail Manager.
MARCUS PEABODY (24) Graphic Designer.
MASAAKI SAKANO (44) Company Director.

The-One-Hundred-and-Twenty-Seventh AGM and Dinner
5 December 2015

Over recent years it had become the norm that Club Dinners would be in Fort William, as the town was the only one in the Highlands with a hotel containing a large dining room, a separate room for our AGM and accommodation for the numbers involved. However the Carrbridge Hotel has recently expanded and as such was very pleased to take our booking.

The move east did not improve the commonly experienced weather of early December, although members who ventured to the most easterly hills did get intermittent dry spells. The poor weather did mean that the Afternoon Talk was extremely well attended. Peter Gillman gave a talk on his recent review and update to his 1966 book, *The Eiger Direct*, recording the direct winter ascent of the North Face on what became known as the Harlin Route. Much of the new information has come from the German members of the team and was unknown to Peter when he and Dougal Haston wrote the first book. The ascent was a riveting episode in Alpine climbing and the talk generated many questions and comments from the audience.

Later in the afternoon the Club had its AGM. Amongst the matters for discussion were the Journal being given a hard back and plans for another hut. The hard back for the journal was well received and members recognised this would reduce possible cost of binding their own copies in the future. The Huts

The President's Walk, 6 December 2015 – on the summit of Beinn Mhòr.
Photo: Richard Bott.

committee reported they were working on the venue for a new hut and that Skye was a likely option. The Club also plans to continue to explore how our Routes and Guides can be best made available as digital versions and in commercially appropriate operating systems.

For many years the Journal has been a source of information on accidents in the hills. In recent years this has lapsed. The Club would like to be able to publish this information but currently Police Scotland are not assisting with the release of data.

The AGM finished in a timely manner and members and guests had ample time to familiarise themselves with Carrbridge Hotel bars after so many years at the Ben Nevis Hotel. Our Guest speaker was Charles Clarke from the Alpine Club. Charles clearly knew just the tone for the Club and spoke on a range of topics from his early climbing days to more recent trips and expeditions. The Dinner closed with the President thanking the Carrbridge Hotel for doing a good job of managing our expectations and providing a fine dinner. He then announced that there would indeed be a President's Walk on Sunday.

The President's Walk proved popular with a brief stop at the Roches Moutonnées near Dulnain Bridge, before parking a little further east in Glen Beag and ascending Beinn Mhòr (471m) via a hillfort. This is neither a Munro, a Corbett or even a Graham. However all enjoyed the walk and took the chance to chat to members not seen at the Dinner.

Chris Huntley

Lakes Meet, Robertson Lamb Hut, Langdale

September 2015

It was Dick Allen's valedictory meet and I received the archivist short straw.

'You'll write something won't you Bob? I've read some of your articles in the SMCJ.' Cornered, I thought, but quite happy to be cornered in such climbing hut grandeur as the Robertson Lamb Hut. Low ceilinged with beams designed to catch the tall unawares and stone spiral staircase with climbing rope banister and old fashioned triple deck bunks. Most conducive I'd say.

The SMC Lakes Meet has a habit of assembling a diverse company intent on seeking out the pleasures of the surrounding hills and crags. Like the hut, the crags and hills seem comfortable. Langdale doesn't seem to have retained the wild grandeur that I recall from the salad days of youth, forty-five years ago. It was nevertheless my stamping ground from a teenage stint in Lancaster and home to the first ever climb I did (aged 14). So I have a soft spot for everything Wainwright through to Alan Austin whose 1973 FRCC Guide to Langdale was the first climbing guide I ever bought. It was £1.50, in the new decimalised currency of the day replete with W. Heaton Cooper crag diagrams and a graded list topped by *Aragorn* on the Neckband Crag, with *Astra* on Pavey Ark running it a close second.

Dick Allen must be a weather god – as ever since I've been attending Lakes Meets, the sun has shone. No exception this weekend.

Saturday saw the usual headlong rush up to White Ghyll as it is virtually on the doorstep of the hut. Routes ascended included White Ghyll Slabs (always a favourite) and several Knots. Those climbing perhaps wouldn't have noticed that two of the guests on the meet – Ian (Blue) Grey and Max Biden, both of the Fell & Rock – were attempting the Pico Harrisons Integrale or their variant of it. At 2.5km long (that's 8 x 125ft in old money) it is one of the longer outings available on rock south of the border. Ian and Max climbed it (in their words) 'alpine style', moving together, grading the ascent AD-/PD+. Taking in routes on Lower Scout, Upper Scout, Lower White Ghylll, Upper White Ghyll, Pavey Ark and then finally Harrison Stickle Crag – it amounts to as good an 'enchainment' as you'll come across (I repeat) south of the border.

Other rock outings included visits to Kettle Crag and on the Sunday to Long Scar and Black Crag across toward the Wrynose Pass where various routes were climbed up to VS by various of the meet.

Several of the elders present engaged in hill walking. My weekend this year was curtailed somewhat by the accident in April 2015 that had befallen Ian Crofton in the Peak, where he'd fallen from the top of a Froggatt route and decked headfirst. Ironically he'd been training for the first SMC Peak Meet the following weekend – from which I visited him in Sheffield General. He is still recovering, but I agreed to hill walk and see him safe about the place on his first return to the hills.

Circuits were made up White Ghyll, and over Blea Rigg, Rosset Pike and Silver How. Notably, John Temple, celebrating his 80th, took his partner around the Mickleden Horseshoe taking in Crinkle Crags, Bow Fell, Pike of Stickle and Harrison Stickle, where Ian Crofton and I met them on the Saturday. They were somewhat tired-out, but had bagged the biggest hill walking tick of the meet.

Ian and I walked up Harrison Stickle via Pike How. Wainwright says, 'It is not only the quickest and easiest way to the top but has two other distinct virtues;

Lake District Meet September 2015

(L. to R.) Peter Bettess (guest), Ian Crofton, Kath Fryett (guest), John Temple, Pete Sterling (guest), Max Biden (guest), Jane Murdoch, Stuart Murdoch, John Wood, Bob Reid, Laetitia Sterling (guest), Ian Grey (guest) - not in photo Hamish Brown, Dick Allen. photo Dick Allen first, it is pleasant underfoot, which is more than can be said for many Langdale paths, and, secondly, it is the "purest" route being a direct climb which does not encroach upon neighbouring fells.' (A. Wainwright, *The Central Fells*, 1958). Ian was glad of the 'pleasant underfoot'. Most remarkable was the view from the summit. We could clearly see Snowdonia in the south, the Isle of Man and the Southern Uplands in the north. A walk up Weatherlam via Greenburn Copper Mines on the Sunday completed our couple of Wainwright outings.

Dick Allen as meet organiser laid on a splendid repast on the Saturday night. It was his last meet as organiser and those who have attended over the years raised a glass in thanks. The Robertson Lamb Hut in Langdale is a comfortable base in a comfortable valley. I can only hope that those attending in future will enjoy it as much.

Members present: Dick Allen, Ian Crofton, John Temple, Jane Murdoch, Stuart Murdoch, John Wood, Hamish Brown and Bob Reid.

Guests: Pete Bettess, Max Biden, Ian Grey, Peter Stirling, Laetitia Stirling and Kath Fryett.

Bob Reid

Ski Mountaineering Meet, Ledgowan Lodge Hotel, Achnasheen

20-21 February 2016

The Ski Mountaineering Meet was held at the Ledgowan Lodge Hotel on the outskirts of Achnasheen. The hotel itself provided excellent accommodation and there is a 10 bed bunkhouse adjacent to the main building.

On the evening of Friday 19 February, many members dined in the lounge bar of the hotel after pre-booking their order by telephone, usually as they travelled across the Kessock Bridge. Neither the weather nor the forecast prompted any early retirals to bed in anticipation of the following day.

The forecast, and reality, of the weather was such that the attendees enjoyed a leisurely breakfast, even debating who had the most posh muesli. This resulted in the phrase for the weekend 'pimp my muesli!' A state seemingly achieved by adding extra seeds and nuts.

After clearing wet snow from the windscreen, Moira, Brian, Adrian and Colwyn headed south down the A890 to Loch Sgamhain where a hydroelectric dam is being constructed by the Coulin estate. They followed the construction track, then the stalkers path close to the Allt Coire Crubaidh up to the summit of the Graham Càrn Breac (678m). The wind on the ridge necessitated a 30° list to the right to avoid being blown over. The large summit shelter provided some respite from the strong wind, so a speedy lunch was eaten here. From there a direct descent down into the corrie got out of the wind and a pleasant walk back, past the workmen at the dam completed the day.

In view of the inclement weather, Ann, Bob, Anthony and Chris decided upon an exploratory expedition to Coire Lair with the hope of climbing up either a Corbett or Munro (Fuar Tholl, Sgòrr Ruadh or Beinn Liath Mhòr). Battling against the gale force winds blowing directly into their faces they reported that they pushed their way up the wide corrie. After an initial sheltered climb up the good stalkers path excellent views of Fuor Tholl appeared and even a ray of sun shone seducing the team into thinking they could get to the summit of Ben Liath Mòr.

Like the wind, reality soon hit and after enjoying good views of the target at around 450m as another, then another, squall of hail and wind gusted through the corrie preventing forward movement with any comfort, a sensible mountaineering decision was taken to retreat to the cars. On the return journey some exploratory cragging was undertaken, with the potential for a summer return by Chris and Anthony. There were excellent views of the coire of Fuar Tholl with the classic climbs on Mainreachan buttress and Fuar Tholl East Coire.

Pauline, Dave and Richard decided to head for a mighty Corbett Ruadh Stac Beag part of the Beinn Eighe massif. The wind was ferocious and the spindrift and hailstorms made progress very difficult. On occasion an enticing glimpse of cliffs and the summit appeared. After ascending to the col at 803m Dave took to the air, involuntarily. After Dave's fifth flight it was decided, despite their proximity to the summit, that it would be madness to continue and a hasty retreat was made.

The excellent facilities of the hotel (including drying room) were therefore enjoyed on the Saturday evening with convivial conversation following an excellent bar supper.

Sunday started with an early visit by the CIC hut custodian and a companion en route from The Ling Hut to attempt a climb on Fuar Tholl.

After a second prolonged breakfast, Ann, Anthony, Brian, Chris and Colwyn eventually decided to attempt the hill closest to the Ledgowan Lodge Hotel and parked on the A832 next to Loch a' Chroisg (NH124588). The short walk through the trees initially shielded them from the westerly gale blasting across the country. On reaching the end of the plantation they turned east and ascended following the ruined fence, then passed below a small ravelling crag up onto the desolate summit plateau. Skis might have been useful from this point and the route choice kept the wind to their backs, so swift progress was made to the summit of Meall a' Chaorain (706m). The wind and spindrift made progress difficult and the modest summit cairn afforded little shelter to the team.

Thereafter the party split with three returning directly to the cars while the fourth continued east and after a long traverse was collected in Achnasheen.

Pauline and David plodded round to the back of Liathach to reconnoitre the climbing routes for a less heroic day. It was damp and slushy underfoot and they were intermittently battered by hail and spindrift with the odd patch of blue sky here and there. On inspection the routes looked a bit thin.

Bob made a bee line for the Lecht ski area – which turned out to be a mistake. He'd hoped to skin up Càrn Ealasaid or Càrn Liath/Càrn Mor (Ladder Hills) – but was deluded in expecting there to be significant levels of snow. He thinks Friday did for it all. Having seen an Iain Cameron tweet the previous night of someone skiing down what looked like the Garbh Uisge Beag off Càrn Etchachan – the snow cover is indeed fickle. Indeed Christine abandoned visiting the Slochd x-country ski area and ended up going for a local walk at a low, more friendly altitude mostly in trees.

So once again the Ski Mountaineering meet was a fine success, despite skis never being used. However, I cannot be sure that the skis enjoyed their weekend away!

Members present: Richard Bott, Adrian Hart, Colwyn Jones (convenor), Ann MacDonald, Chris Ravey, Bob Reid, Brian Shackleton, Anthony Walker, Chris Watkins.

Guests: Moira Baptie, Pauline Kell, David Lilly.

Colwyn Jones

Skye Winter Meet, Glenbrittle Memorial Hut

26–28 February 2016

On what was probably the first ever meet to Skye organised for the specific purpose of winter mountaineering, eight members enjoyed a splendid weekend of calm, sunny but cold weather, with ample snow in good condition on the Cuillin. John Fowler, who organised the meet, wisely insisted on taking bookings from pairs only. Accordingly the eight resolved themselves into four teams on Saturday morning.

Des Rubens and Steve Kennedy climbed a new route on Sgùrr nan Eag taking a line up the large face left of Western Buttress in Coir' a' Ghrunnda. A hidden ramp lead to three fine pitches of ice and mixed climbing at Grade IV,4   later

Steve Kennedy in Coire a' Ghreadaidh approaching An Dorus Buttress; Gauche IV,4 is right of centre. Photo Des Rubens.

named Age Concern. This may be the first winter route on the west flank of Sgùrr nan Eag. Time was sufficiently in hand to allow an hour of idleness on the summit, enlivened by the swooping of an eagle nearby, close enough to pick out the golden neck feathers. An incident-free walk across Loch Coir' a' Ghrunnda completed a perfect day.

Geoff Cohen and Dave Broadhead tackled Abraham's Climb on Sgùrr Alasdair. The early pitches went well, but considerable difficulties were encountered higher up where the route finding was awkward. The sun was setting as they got to the top and on the descent they found that they had only one functioning head-torch. They arrived at the hut several hours after dark. While conceding that they might have been slightly off route on the climb they reckoned that IV,5 was certainly not an over grading.

Geoff Cohen, Peter Wilson, Steve Kennedy, Pete Biggar, Alan Smith, Roger Robb, Dave Broadhead and Des Rubens on the Skye Winter Meet in February 2016. Photo: Roger Robb.

Peter Wilson and Alan Smith went to Coire a' Mhadaidh and climbed the Foxes' Rake III which was reported as being most enjoyable apart from one rock-step near the top necessitating a high reach which suited Peter but apparently not Alan.

Pete Biggar and Roger Robb had a long scenic walk into Coire a' Ghreadaidh intending to climb the NW Ridge of the mountain (of which Roger was a first winter ascentionist 40 years ago in 1976), but the plan had to be abandoned as Roger was, to his great disappointment, taken unwell. Fortunately it was nothing serious and a few drams back at the hut restored equilibrium.

On Sunday Dave and Geoff climbed the Foxes' Rake which they too enjoyed. Des and Steve went to Sgùrr a' Ghreadhaidh and made the first winter ascent of Gauche on An Dorus buttress, giving a fine Grade IV,4 climb, largely on ice but with an entertaining final pitch on mixed ground. The summit of Sgùrr a' Ghreadhaidh was near cloud level, giving highly atmospheric views of the range.

While Peter and Alan went for a walk in Glen Sligachan, a now much recovered Roger and Pete climbed Garbh-bheinn on the way home, revelling in the quality of the upper ridge and noting several winter possibilities in the corrie.

The redoubtable Keeper of the Lists enjoyed the peace and tranquility of Glen Brittle so much that he determined to stay for an extra night to refresh himself for the labours to come. Only time will tell whether this meet will become firmly established in the club's calendar, but this was a most promising start. Let's hope for similar weather, conditions and good companionship next year. Our thanks go to John Fowler for making the arrangements.

Peter Biggar

Easter Meet 2016 – Kinlochewe

Standing (L to R): Bill McKerrow, Simon Fraser, Phil Gribbon, Colwyn Jones, Gordon Macnair, Bob Aitken, John Fowler, Dave Broadhead, John Hay, Hamish Brown, Andy James, Paul Brian, Lisa Hutchison, Raymond Simpson, Roger Robb, Sarah Atkinson, Campbell Forrest, Geoff Cohen, Peter Biggar.
Front row (L to R): John Mackenzie, Eve Mackenzie & Lucy (guests), Robin Campbell, Robin Chalmers, Margot Gribbon (guest), Noel Williams (President), Helen Forde, Ken McKinley (guest), Ann Macdonald, John Wood, Colin Stead, Peter Macdonald, David Stone.   Photo: D Stone.

Easter Meet, Kinlochewe Hotel, Torridon

31 March–3 April 2016

The 2016 Easter Meet was held in the Kinlochewe Hotel where we once again enjoyed the hospitality of the proprietors, Andrew and Gail Staddon. The weather was a mix of good and bad days with damp conditions ruling out the higher crags but never-the-less the Friday evening reception at John Hay's property on the shores of Loch Torridon got us off to a good start. As leaden skies sent down a constant deluge, members rubbed shoulders with each other and John's priceless antiques in great good humour, precariously balancing plates of smoked salmon and venison and searching earnestly for their glass which they had put down somewhere and someone else had taken.

The hills ascended were a mixture of high and low and it is notable how on Easter Meets Marilyns are making an increased appearance in the lists! In various groups and combinations, we ascended Sgùrr Fhuar-thuill in Glen Strathfarrar, Meall Lochan a' Chleirich above Stone Valley, Beinn a Chearcaill, Meall a' Ghiuthais, Ruadh-stac Beag, Spidean Coire nan Clach, Sgùrr nan Fhir Duibhe via the Black Carls, Mullach an Rathain, Sgùrr a'Chaorachain, Ben Shieldaig and Ben Alligin, together with a number of long lower level walks on the wetter days.

Rock climbing was confined to the low level crags between the showers with visits made to Diabaig, the Inveralligin sea-cliffs, Stone Valley, the Aztec Tower near Gairloch, A' Bhainlir Crags in Applecross and of course, Crag X, where a new route was claimed.

Dinner on Saturday evening was a splendid affair with substantial withdrawals being made from the Malcolm Slesser Memorial Whisky Fund.

Those attending the meet were the President, Noel Williams, R Aitken, Sarah Atkinson, PJ Biggar, PV Brian, RN Campbell, DJ Broadhead, HM Brown, RDM Chalmers, G Cohen, Helen GS Forde, C Forrest, JRR Fowler, S Fraser, PWF Gribbon, JYL Hay, Lisa Hutchison, AM James, C Jones, Ann Macdonald, PF Macdonald, JR Mackenzie, WS McKerrow, G Macnair, RJC Robb, GR Simpson, AC Stead, D Stone and JA Wood. Our guests were Margot Gribbon, Eve Mackenzie and K McKinlay.

At the Saturday evening consultation, members bravely decided to forsake the north-west in 2017 to travel to the Island of Arran. I do hope we made the right choice!

JRRF

Skye Spring Meet, Allt Dearg Cottage

7–14 May 2016

At last we had the superb week of weather we've been dreaming of for years. For three days the Cuillin were the hottest place in Britain. Although there was a very cold wind on the clifftop at Neist, the main problem of the week was avoiding heatstroke in the more sheltered corries. It must have been galling for Robin Campbell as he was poorly and had to call off.

The honeypots on Skye have become extremely busy in recent years and places like the Old Man of Storr and the Fairy Pools get hordes of visitors. Ken Crocket. on his first attendance at the meet, made very early starts to avoid the crowds.

The trio of Dave Broadhead, Tom Prentice and Peter Wilson started with a

Left: John Mackenzie follows the traverse pitch on The Scorcher (HVS 5b), Coire nan Laogh.

Right: Andrew Wielochowski on the FA of All the President's Men (E1 5b), South-East Face of Central Peak, Bidein Druim nan Ràmh. Photos:Noel Williams.

traverse of Glamaig and the Beinn Deargs. The following day they climbed *Grande Diedre* and bagged Sgùrr Dubh Mòr.

Andrew Wielochowski and Noel Williams joined friends Mike and Michelle to visit Lùb a' Sgiathain, east of Rubha Hunish, at low tide. They encountered several dead sheep and cows on the approach before negotiating treacherous seaweed-covered boulders. They then roped up to climb a spiky sea stack. Only Mike managed to place three fingers on the very top.

On the Monday John Mackenzie and Noel revisited Coire nan Laogh at the southern end of the Cuillin. In baking hot conditions they climbed the central Barrier feature at its highest point to produce *The Scorcher*. Noel struggled with severe cramp on the return because of dehydration.

On the Tuesday people took it a bit easier with visits to Storr Lochs, Waternish, Rubha Hunish and Suidhe Biorach, though Tom joined Mike and Michelle to bag Sgùrr nan Gillean.

On the following day a large team set off for Bidein Druim nan Ràmh. After an ascent of Tuppenny Buttress, a traverse line was taken round to the south-east face of the Central Peak where a prominent right-facing corner was climbed.

Full advantage was taken of the weather and among the many other outings Tom, Peter and Raymond Simpson climbed the two *Dooms* by the Cioch and Paul Brian visited Raasay and bagged Dun Caan.

Members present: Paul Brian, Dave Broadhead, Ken Crocket, John Mackenzie, Tom Prentice, Raymond Simpson, Andrew Wielochowski, Noel Williams and Peter Wilson. Guests: Eve Mackenzie and Linda Simpson.

NW

JMCS REPORTS

Edinburgh section: the Club acted its age this year; it went soft and bought a key for the track up to the 'guides' car park on Ben Nevis so that lucky members could avoid that steep bit through the wood at the beginning and end of their days or weekends. Some difficult allocation decisions have been necessary at peak times, but most people who wanted the key have had their turn. Unless one is made of sterner stuff than me and regrets the passing into history of the approach through 'the Everglades', so that even the track from the North Face car park seemed an unwelcome innovation, having a key can only be A Good Thing. Not that our efforts this winter were confined to the Ben – members went to all points of the compass and reported ascents of a variety of routes such as Monolith Grooves, Poacher's Fall and Sticil Face. I'm not aware of anyone having visited Lochnagar, however – the flood damage to the Braemar road early in the season tended to put people off, even after access had been restored.

As is usual these days, lots of members have had climbing holidays abroad. For a good part of last summer in the Alps the temperatures were probably higher than they often are in sun rock destinations at other times of year. Ironically, a Club trip to the Ecrins in September met rather mixed weather and an attempt on the Barre des Ecrins petered out on a bare, trackless glacier in thick mist, the penalty for following a guide who turned out not to know where he was going. You can read more about our various foreign and domestic adventures in the lavishly illustrated Annual Newsletters which can be found in the Library section of our website. A selection of the photos shown at our annual slide night can also be seen there.

Our AGM and dinner was held in Glen Clova in November 2015 during a spell of weather that made most people happy to be inside. Hardy souls with good navigation skills made it to the top of the odd Corbett or Munro while others retreated early, worried about having to dig out their cars. Those who'd seen it all before stayed in the glen. But our spirits were raised by Dan Bailey's after dinner talk, illustrated as it was by splendid sunlit photos of classic ridges in Scotland and elsewhere. A notable feature of the occasion was that three generations of one family of members were present – it is good to be able to see where the Club stalwarts of the future are coming from.

If you are interested in joining the Edinburgh JMCS, we always welcome new faces. Please come along to our Monday or Wednesday night activities and meet and climb with some of the existing members. We go to Ratho on winter Wednesdays and Alien Rock on winter Mondays. During the summer we will be inside or out, depending on the weather; you can see where we are going by looking at our website which also lists our forthcoming weekend meets. Just Google 'Edinburgh JMCS'. It is probably best to contact Nils Krichel, the Membership Secretary, beforehand to make sure there has been no last minute change of venue.

Our huts are available for booking by kindred Clubs; please contact the Custodians whose names are shown below. We have 'the Cabin' in Balgowan, between Laggan and Newtonmore, and 'the Smiddy' at Dundonnell in the North West.

The present committee includes; Honorary President: John Fowler. President: Ruth Love. Vice President and Smiddy Custodian: Helen Forde (30 Reid Terrace, Edinburgh EH3 5JH, 0131 332 0071). Secretary: David Small (5 Afton Place,

Edinburgh, EH53RB, <secretary@edinburghjmcs.org.uk>. Treasurer: Bryan Rynne. The Cabin Custodian: Ali Borthwick (01383 732 232, before 9 p.m. please). Membership Secretary; Nils Krichel <nils.krichel@gmail.com>.

David Small

Glasgow Section: the Glasgow Section of the Junior Mountaineering Club of Scotland had another very successful, busy and varied year in 2015. The Club President is Philip Smith. Secretary: Charles Craig. Treasurer: Justine Carter. Meets secretary: Neil Wilkie. Coruisk hut custodian: Iain Sneddon. New members secretaries: Mark Gorin and Simon Taylor.

Club membership currently stands at 88 members, comprising 46 ordinary members and 42 life members. The new Members Secretary role is split between committee members Mark Gorin and Simon Taylor. You should contact them if you want to go on a meet or find out more about the club. <newmembers@glasgowjmcs.org.uk>. New members are very welcome to come along to all of the club meets.

Reflecting the enthusiasm within the club, throughout 2015 there were 22 official weekend meets including the annual work meet to the club hut at Coruisk on the late May bank holiday 22/23 May. In addition to general maintenance, native tree planting was undertaken and solar panels for the electric lighting was installed. Coruisk provides simple, cheap and ferry accessible accommodation in a beautiful setting; see the website for details <www.glasgowjmcs.org.uk/coruisk.php> or to book the hut e-mail Coruisk Hut Bookings – Iain Sneddon <coruisk@glasgowjmcs.org.uk>.

The varied JMCS meets were held across Scotland, the Lake District and many were held in SMC huts: CIC, Lagangarbh, Raeburn, Ling and Naismith. The indoor wall of the Glasgow Climbing Centre hosts an indoor Thursday night meet every fortnight, with cappuccinos available in the Balcony Café (other hot drinks available!) Midweek meets are held at local outdoor rock climbing venues in the central belt over the summer; please see the club website for details <www.glasgowjmcs.org.uk/index.php>.

The annual general meeting and club dinner on 31 October 2015 celebrated the 90th anniversary at Hughenden Sports Club in Glasgow where 45 members and guests met to celebrate this milestone in the history of the club(see report below). The weekend of 20/21 November 2015 saw the annual presidential retiral meet in Auchope bothy in The Cheviots.

Winter routes climbed by members in 2015 included Boomer's Requiem, Satanic Verses, Point Five and Indicator Wall. Raven's Gully on Buachaille Etive Mor, proved to be very thin on the chockstones. Spindrift and falling snow recalled the *Cold Climbs* description:'legs threshing wildly and absolutely no technique' past the chockstones. They had the same experience of wondering what to do about protection when the snow collapsed in front and they found themselves 'deposited in a tiny ice cave'.

On the 16 July two members climbed the fine greywacke sea stack, The Soutar on the Berwickshire coast. Shortly afterwards they visited the compact blue hone granite of Ailsa Craig with a scramble to the summit and ended with an ascent of the awesome sandstone sea stack The Old Man of Hoy on the 8 August. Over three days in mid-August a member canoed down the length of the river Tweed.

Adventures abroad started early with a January winter climbing trip to Cogne in Italy where there was scant ice but members managed to climb each day. In

Colwyn Jones on one of the many frozen waterfalls in the Sellraintal, Austria, January 2016

March members were ski touring in the Bernese Oberland. Sadly poor weather at altitude meant only minor peaks were ascended.

Over the summer, ascents in the greater ranges included the Promontoire Ridge and La Meije Traverse. This apparently included getting a little bit lost and forcing a new F6a/UIAA VI variation, over steep, chossy and essentially protectionless terrain to get back on route.

One member cruised to the Lofoten Islands via The Western Isles, Shetland,

and the coast of Norway on a magnificent trip with eight other members joining for various legs of the voyage.

Using Randa as a base two members traversed the Oberer Theodulgletscher from Zermatt to the Rifugio Teodulo Hut in the Aosta Valley. They climbed the Festigrat of the Dom from the Domhütte, having previously been driven back off the Rotgrat on the Alphubel by fresh snow. The Valais Alps were visited at the end of August and this year two different members ascended the South ridge of the Lagginhorn, plus the Holaubgrat on the Allalinhorn after climbing routes on the Riffelberg and Egginer as training peaks.

One retired member fed the mosquitos when he cycled 5000km across Canada, from Vancouver to Halifax over a three month period and not without incident. The main problems were bears, the heat (it was 44 degrees at one point) and having dogs set on him when cycling through First Nation reserves! Just another typical year for the Glasgow JMCS.

Colwyn Jones

Glasgow JMCS 90th Anniversary Dinner: on Saturday 31 October 2015, following a swift and non-contentious AGM, 45 members and guests sat down to dinner at Hughenden Sports Club in Glasgow to celebrate 90 years of the JMCS and 20 years of mixed sex membership.

Phil Smith the current president introduced and welcomed the guests, principle amongst them was Iain Macleod of the senior club who gave a sincere view of the social aspects of shared days on the hills followed by a hilarious rendition of *The US Orlandez*. Claire Gilchrist, one of the pioneering lady members followed and using her finest headmistress style scythed the old chauvinist guard leaving some of them staring sheepishly into their beer glasses. From his exalted position as both senior member and principal proponent of mixed membership Iain Cumming then followed with a reply to the lassies and a history of the JMCS.

The individual dinner menus, designed by Dave Eaton and based on a Toblerone wrapping, were received with great amusement and while dinner was being served Niel Craig ran a powerpoint show comprising images scanned from several decades of club activity. The boots of the assembled company had climbed and explored every continent and season of our planet and while there were no superstars, few clubs could match the breadth and depth of experience shared that night.

A truly fitting occasion enjoyed by male members representing over half a century of JMCS activity, by some of the earliest female members of the JMCS and by current potential members, all of which bodes well for the future and reflects the stature of the Glasgow JMCS.

Charlie Craig

Lochaber Section: in the past we have held our first weekend meet in February, but have often encountered poor weather, despite periods of good weather on either side of our weekend. This year we continued the winter evening slide shows, with the first one being held early in February as a get together and had our first weekend meet in early March. By good fortune and perhaps a bit of design, we had excellent weather for the meet to Kincraig, as well as slightly longer daylight hours. Our programme of weekend meets continued with trips to Crianlarich, Glen Affric and Glen Brittle, with good turnouts and a variety of excursions tackled on each.

The club hut, Steall in Glen Nevis, has seen its second year of improved bookings which is ensuring the club's finances remain healthy. This is in part down to the works that were carried out on the hut over the previous year, but perhaps more significantly, is due to the the the new website 'www.steallhut.co.uk' created for Steall and to advertising through the MC of S huts Directory.

The club dinner was held this year at the Cairndow Inn, with more members and guests than usual choosing to attend for the two nights. This gave everyone the chance of a good catch-up. As before, we held the club AGM prior to the dinner with two new members being introduced to the club although they had been attending meets previously. Both new members are friends of a current member, making it easier for them to get to know the club and its members.

The year was brought to a close with a slide show on working and trekking in the Himalaya by Tom Gilchrist. Tom's experience goes back a couple of decades and it was interesting to see that in some ways these poorer countries are almost consigned to hardship, generation after generation. None the less the area has stunning scenes and from Tom's stories, a very friendly and welcoming people.

President: Simon Fraser; Secretary: Iain MacLeod <ia.macleod@btinternet.com>; Treasurer: Ken Scoular; Hut bookings: Ewen Kay; Hut Custodian: John Matheson.

Iain MacLeod

London Section: meets took place in Scotland (winter and summer), Mid Wales, Pembroke, the Lake District, the Peak District and in our hut in Bethesda, North Wales. Once again, the activity was mixed but with less mountain biking and more rock climbing and hill walking than in recent years.

Our winter meet in Scotland was not blessed with the best of weather but we filled the Raeburn Hut, enjoyed some good days on the hill, and were once again very well fed and watered by our Treasurer and catering maestro, David Hughes. Other forays to Scotland were successful, with ascents of Centre Post Direct on Creag Meagaidh, Savage Slit in Coire an Lochain on Cairngorm and Grooved Arête on Aonach Mor.

Spring arrived and there was a good turn-out for our return to the Solihull Mountaineering Club's excellent hut in Dinas Mawddwy from where we climbed at Tremadog and on Cadair Idris, went mountain biking at Coed y Brenin and ventured into the local hills. After a washed out meet in Cornwall in early May, it was good to be back on familiar ground in North Wales in late May enjoying some long days in the mountains and on Gogarth on Anglesey.

Summer saw us in Little Langdale, and in the Peak District at Rivelin Edge, Lawrencefield, Millstone and Bamford Edges. We returned to Scotland for a soaking at the end of August but enjoyed a sunny weekend in south Pembroke in September on some of the classics including Rock Idol and Straight Gate in Mother Carey's kitchen with celebratory liquid refreshment afterwards in the St Govern's Country Inn. Members were also active abroad in the Bernese Oberland, the Swiss Alps and later in the year in New Zealand.

Climbing in the 'winter sun' is now a feature of our programme, thanks to Jamie Ward. Half a dozen members set off for the Costa Blanca in November, making use of cheap flights and off season tourist accommodation, to go climbing on the Penon d'Ifach. Routes climbed included Via Gomez-Cano (nine pitches) by Chris Comerie and Marcus Harvey. Another visit is planned in November 2016 to an area with great ridges to walk/scramble as well as a variety of limestone climbing. The year closed on home ground, with an enjoyable Section dinner at the Ogwen Bank Country Club in Bethesda.

Sailing has become increasingly popular in our Section, as the average age rises! In 2015 members sailed in the Outer Hebrides and off the northern coast of Norway. The latter included visits to the islands of Senja, Andoya and Kvaloya and on them ascents of Luten, Storseteinnestinden and the ridge to Husfjellet.

Back home, we continue to make improvements to our hut, Glanafon, which now has a new chimney. Thanks to Simon Gladstone, the Section now has a fine newsletter and a new web site. Looking ahead, the two main issues facing the Section are attracting new members and increasing the use made of Glanafon. A marketing drive is resulting in more lettings to external parties. Membership, including life members, remains constant at 47.

Officers for 2016: President: John Howes; Secretary: John Firmin (07845 732189); Treasurer: David Hughes; Glanafon Hut Bookings: Dave L Hughes <davidlewishughes@hotmail.com>.

John Firmin

Perth Section: the Perth MC is a small club of 70 members who enjoy meeting throughout the year either in the Scottish mountains or abroad. In 2015 we had 7 new members and currently have several perspective members attending meets with a view to joining.

We started the year with an exceptionally wet and windy local walk up Craig Rossie where many of our lighter members were literally blown off their feet, and all waterproofs let in some water around the edges.

In January the Day Meet to Glen Clova was attended by only two adventurous souls, who had a very blustery wintery walk. Mid-month saw an impromptu weekend of ski touring for some, in variable weather, on the Cairnwell and Drumochter hills. The Burns Supper meet at Invergarry was a huge success with some excellent winter days completed including the Forked Gully, The Saddle in Kintail, Gleouraich and Spidean Mialach.

In February the Meet to Lagangarbh provided wonderful conditions for climbing Stob Coire Sgreamhach via Sròn na Lairig, NC Gully, Forked Gully and Broad Gully, in Coire nan Lochan, Glas Bheinn Mòr in Glen Etive, Beinn a Chrulaiste, Stob Coire Raineach and also Ledge Route and The Curtain on Ben Nevis.

In March the Raeburn meet was again wet and windy: Geal Chàrn, Monadhliath was climbed. On the Aviemore Day Meet the Runnel in Coire an t-Sneachda was climbed despite running water.

In April on the Meet to Glen Lyon Meall Dearg was climbed and nine of our members took part in the Loch Ness Etape cycling event at the end of the month.

The May meet to Kintail saw some members taking advantage of the much better than forecast weather for a sunny traverse of the South Sheil Ridge starting at the Clunie Inn end. The Sunday was grim but Beinn Fhada, Sgùrrs an Airgid and Mhic Bharraich were climbed.

In June the meet to Glenbrittle saw a damp claggy day of 'team' scrambling on Sgùrr a' Mhadaidh, Sgùrr a' Ghreadaidh, Sgùrr na Banachdaich and Sgùrr Dearg concluded by a very cold ascent of the In Pin for a large group.

In July the Invercroft meet saw Spidean Coire nan Clach, Beinn Lair, Beinn a' Chearcaill, Ben Wyvis, Meall a' Buachaille summited in dismal weather.

In August a meet to Naismith's saw members on Ghlas Bheinn, Stac Poillaidh, Foinaven, Arkle, Ben Stack, Meallan Liath Coire Mhic Dhughaill, Canisp, Breabag, Cul Mòr, the Knockan geological trail and a fine coastal walk from Blughasary out to the fort at Dun Canna. A day meet saw a wonderful if midge-full ride from Bridge of Orchy up Glen Orchy, down to Kinglass and along to Armaddy on Loch Etive, to the Fishery at Loch Awe and across to finish at Taynuilt. (Presumably on bicycles – Ed.)

In September a meet to Shepherd's Crook Bunkhouse saw a relaxed weekend avoiding as much rain as was possible with a circuit of St Sunday Crags to Fairfield and the ridge above Deepdale, up and over Place Fell. A day meet to Killin – a windy day over Ben Lawers via Beinn Ghlas and back on the wind free path below Beinn Ghlas – with wonderful lunchtime views to the North.

In October the meet to Black Rock, Meall nan Eun and Stob Coir' an Albannaich, in Glen Etive were climbed in lovely weather. Beinn Bhuidhe for others on the way to the meet. Buachaille Etive Beg and Ben Challum were climbed on Sunday.

In December the meet to Crianlarich – The Annual Dinner: Well, 2015 was wet but the worst was still to come and it started that Dinner Weekend with very wet travels for all, some having to go via Loch Lomond to make it from Killin to Crianlarich! And some being rescued by firemen! The only walking done was on the West Highland Way. A lovely chance to catch-up with the folks who braved it.

Climbing: we have continued to have healthy winter, Wednesday evening climbing turnouts at the Dundee Climbing Wall from about 5 p.m. onwards, with many also climbing on Monday evenings at the Perth Grammar School.

Further afield: trips were enjoyed by member groups motor-sailing around the Norwegian coast ski touring from the boat; two weeks in the Vanoise, getting in a few peaks; there was activity in the Pyrenees and the Alps, some warm weather sport climbing in Kalymnos; and a near completion of the Selvaggio Blu, Sardinia.

Other activities: many of our members also get together for road biking, mountain biking, skiing and paddling.

The 2015 Joint PMC and PSNS Lecture at the Perth Museum was entitled 'Yaks, Marmots and Mountains' and followed three weeks spent in the Kuillu Valley, Kyrgystan. First ascents of many 4000m peaks were accomplished.

President's Evening had a good turn-out with wonderful slide presentations.

The mountain mind quiz saw the PMC winning again.

The PMC has a website: <perthmountaineering-club.co.uk> which shows our activities and lists upcoming meets together with recent meet reports. It has an e-mail link to our secretary to allow prospective members to enquire about joining. We have a Facebook site used by some for showing photos and to provide details of impromptu meets and activities. Member communication is for the most part via a group email account to ensure that all members are aware of all of the club's activities. We have periodic newsletters featuring upcoming and past activities and events.

We always welcome new members.

The 2016 PMC Committee: Alasdair Dutton (President), Desmond Bassett (Treasurer), Sue James (Secretary), Jeff Harris (Meets Secretary), Ron Payne (Newsletter Editor), Phil Taylor (Website Secretary), Jeff Banks (Auditor), Tim Storer, Pamela Dutton and Karen Murray.

Karen Murray

SMC ABROAD

ALPS 2014

Considering that July 2014 had some pretty execrable weather, Des Rubens and I had a reasonably satisfying Alpine campaign. Here are a few brief highlights. Our best route was the south face of the Tete de Fetoules, which is approached from the beautifully situated Lavey hut near St Christophe en Oisans. This is a long traditional rock climb, first done about 1971 with quite a number of pitons, but now very out of fashion as being neither easy nor very hard. We found several really good pitches at about HVS. We tried (unsuccessfully) to escape the bad weather by driving to the Alpes Maritimes, having been given an inkling of their delights by Malcolm Slesser and Bill Wallace over thirty years ago. The CAF Refuge de la Madonna de Fenestre is a good base that can be reached by car. The rock is excellent sound gneiss; however our one attempt at a worthwhile route was rained off. In the Aosta valley the locals directed us to 'Il Paretone', which can be thoroughly recommended for long bolted slab climbs – an Italian Etive; with the attraction of an easy walk off that takes you through beautiful woods to a cafe in an old fort. Finally we squeezed in a couple of conventional mountain days on the Dent d'Herens and Castor and Pollux. We had stunning views from the latter and (embarrassing though it is to admit) were happy to add three 'ticks' to our four thousander list.

Geoff Cohen

SKI MOUNTAINEERING IN THE MIDI PYRENEES

Notes from fellow member Charlie Hornsby had sufficiently fired the imagination to check out the French side of the Central Pyrenees. Not being quite so well set up for hut to hut touring as the Alps we opted for a valley base. Ewan Clark and I chose Saint-Lary-Soulon in the upper reaches of the Vallee D'Aure – the main road up to the Tunnel de Bielsa crossing into Spain. We opted to ski up separate peaks each day averaging 800–1000m of ascent. We climbed the Pic de Bataillence (2604m), Pic d'Augas (2213m), the remarkable Lenquo de Capo (2976m), the Cap de Laubere (2179m) and the Sommet de l'Aigle (2078m). It was this latter ascent which prompted this note. Although it is the lowest of the peaks we skied, l'Aigle is the central peak of an area known as the 'Balencous'. It is an area similar to the Cairngorms in scale and shape. This was quite unexpected in the alpine Midi Pyrenees and provided a delightful home-from-home experience. Reasonable weather, good snow, alpine feel, and the almost complete absence of any alpine pretension made for an excellent trip.

Bob Reid

ALPS 2015

In late June 2015 Des Rubens and I set off for our annual Alpine campaign. The journey out never fails to offer its uncertainties, this year involving a French railway strike plus closure of the road from Grenoble over col de Lautaret. After a few days acclimatising in the Vanoise at the delightful Refuge La Femma we did a long drive via the Italian plain to Switzerland and set out at 8 p.m. on 30

Climbing the upper part of the Lauteraarhorn. All photos: Des Rubens.

The Schreckhorn from Lauteraarhorn.

Des Rubens climbing on the South Pillar of the Schreckhorn.

June to go to the Aar Bivouac. We had long wanted to sample this remote site, a good six hours walk from the Grimsel see. After a pleasant night in the heather an hour or so along the path we applied our routefinding skills, honed by years on our mist-clad Scottish hills, to missing the path up the Unteraar glacier. After an unnecessary climb of 300m up to the Lauteraar hut we had the pleasure of descending 300m on steep ladders over bald granite walls, marvelling at the depth of glacier that must have disappeared in the last few decades. It took many hours of walking to reach the hut. 'Bivouac hut' hardly suggests the level of comfort to be found in this well-appointed Swiss eyrie. There were even complimentary bottles of coke awaiting us (hideous stuff)! The ambience was definitely Himalayan with an outlook wilder than anywhere else I have been in the Alps; so it was pleasant to read in the hut book the names of fellow club worthy John Allen, and a certain Dougie Williamson of Inverness who had made the trek twice in the space of a month. We were fortunate indeed to spend four days of perfect weather in this excellent nook, undisturbed by a soul.

   Our first outing was a somewhat laboured ascent of the Lauteraarhorn by its south face, the only distinguished part of the route being the last few hundred feet of excellent rock scrambling. This thirteen hour day was enough to require me to give my aging body thirty-six hours of rest, much of which passed most pleasantly in the sunshine! The desire to knock off both Lauteraarhorn and Schreckhorn in a single traverse had been outweighed by unwillingness to contemplate carrying the necessary bivouac gear; however after our rest we were prepared to tackle the Schreckhorn in spite of the necessity to cross the Strahlegg Pass in both directions. The result was a 22 hour day. We were able to enjoy the splendid knobbly gneiss of the Schreckhorn's south pillar and were only about two hours over guidebook

On the Täschhorn–Dom traverse.

On the Täschhorn–Dom traverse.

time on the way up, but the descent is quite long and it was dark by the time we were descending from the Strahlegg. The solar powered nightlights that illuminate the exposed traverse from the hut to the toilet saved us from further wanderings among boulder fields.

After a day of recreation near the Reichenbach Falls, scene of Sherlock Holmes' mortal struggle with Professor Moriarty, we repaired to the Zermatt valley for our next target, and ascended to the Tasch Hut. This is reached in an easy two hour walk from TaschAlp, or by Landrover if you are a hut guardian. It is a modern functional Swiss Hut, clean and devoid of character. Despite the availability of vehicular access the cooking was entirely from packets of powder or tins, resulting in a meal of quite staggering dullness (at a typically exorbitant Swiss cost!). Next day we climbed the very pleasant Rotgrat on the Alphubel and descended to the Mischabeljoch bivouac hut – a large metal box on stilts, screwed into the mountain at 3855 metres. Two huge bags of chopped wood had been deposited by helicopter on the metal ledge outside the entrance – almost completely preventing entry! Fortunately two French climbers whom we'd met on the Alphubel summit were slightly ahead of us and helped greatly in squeezing in, passing all the wood inside and finally getting the stove alight. The interior is modern and well equipped (not quite at the standard of the Aar bivouac) with a fabulous picture-window view from the Matterhorn right round to the Weisshorn with Mont Blanc behind; one could gaze all day but especially at the unearthly colours of sunset and dawn.

Life in the hut was quite entertaining. To get water it was necessary to go down a ladder with a bucket on a rope and chop ice. Productions from the exterior toilet fall into a huge black plastic container that must be collected by helicopter. About an hour after our arrival two young Dutch lads whom we'd overtaken on the Rotgrat arrived. They were at least 30 years younger than us and had been going much faster on the lower part of the ridge, but they were unacclimatised, and carrying far too much gear; and on the steeper finishing tower they had chosen to pitch it whereas we had moved together. Our French friends were our sort of age and able to join us in the usual conversations about how everything has changed so much since we first started climbing.

There had been a biting wind on the Alphubel and I was very doubtful if we would be able to continue over the Täschhorn and Dom, which in any case had the appearance of unattractive tot. Des however maintained his enthusiasm, so we settled into our planned rest day which would, we hoped, improve acclimatisation. During the day various Swiss and German parties arrived, some also intent on the Täschhorn–Dom traverse. Expecting them to be faster we did not attempt to leave next day until 4 a.m., a good half an hour after them, and we only ever saw distant figures far ahead. The weather remained excellent and the snow extremely well frozen but with such well-made steps along the arêtes that crampons were unnecessary – although handholds on the filigree edge felt none too solid. We enjoyed a day of continuous outstanding views with climbing that was not particularly difficult or distinguished but absorbing enough to require concentration, especially as we did most of it unroped. We reached the Dom summit at 2 p.m., but the 3500m descent took another eight hours, and weary legs rolled into the campsite well after dark!

Geoff Cohen

REVIEWS

4000m – Climbing the Highest Mountains of the Alps: Dave Wynne-Jones (Whittles Publishing, 2016, 236pp, softback, ISBN 978-1-84995-172-2, £25).
Climbing all the 4000 metre peaks of the Alps is a major undertaking whether done fast or slow. At the end of 2013 only 18 British mountaineers were known to have completed the main mountains, never mind the subsidiary tops. Anyone who completes the 4000ers will have endured many an epic and will have a good tale to tell.

Though rather more exclusive than Munro-bagging, the 4000m peaks obsession has generated a similar sub-genre of literature. Richard Goedeke's guide, *The Alpine 4000m Peaks by the Classic Routes* started the ball rolling with its English translation in 1991. *The High Mountains of the Alps* (1994) by Dumler and Burkhardt and edited by Ken Wilson was a notable landmark in lavish photographic celebration of mountains. Will McLewin wrote a quirky and engaging account of climbing all the 4000ers, *In Monte Viso's Horizon*, which won the Boardman-Tasker prize in 1993. I entered the fray a year later with Alps 4000 – the story of an odyssey to climb them all in a non-stop journey. In 2007, again under my authorship, the Alpine Club published a more detailed guidebook specifically devoted to the 4000ers, *The 4000m Peaks of the Alps*, which has been a best-seller for the Club. Barbara Swindin's *All But One* (2012) provided a poignant perspective as a 4000m peak-collector who fell agonisingly short of her goal. An excellent new guidebook by the Italian climbers Marco Romelli and Valentino Cividini appeared in English in 2015. As well as these English-language publications there is a wealth of books devoted to 4000 metre peaks in French, German and Italian.

Dave Wynne-Jones has added a further layer to this stockpile with *4000m*. His personal accounts of ascending all the major 4000m mountains are interspersed with many good photos and informative interludes on tactics, techniques and practical advice. The author completed the peaks, largely in company of fellow Alpine Club members, over a 26-year period from 1981 to 2007. He was obsessive in his quest for many years, but had a five-year layoff before completing his last mountain, the Grandes Jorasses.

His narratives are set in chronological order and read as expanded diary accounts. Inevitably, this leads to many switches of location as he moves between the Oberland, Valais and Mont Blanc ranges in the course of individual holidays. This approach is fine if, like me, you know the peaks well, but in the absence of any maps or photo-diagrams the book's structure offers no geographical insight for an alpine aspirant.

Wynne-Jones is strident in some of his opinions. At the outset he dismisses the 'official' list of 82 mountains and subsidiary tops which was published with affirmation from the UIAA in 1993. Some tops are derided as 'insignificant excrescences', others as 'unworthy of the name'. Instead he follows Robin Collomb's list of 52 major mountains which was published back in 1971. I don't have any issues with his choice. Indeed, I recommend anyone setting out on a 4000m quest within the restriction of annual holidays to stick to the major mountains as an achievable goal. However, the author would have better cultivated this reviewer's sympathies had he explained the considerably greater difficulty and challenge of completing the tops as well as the main mountains.

The sections of practical advice are peppered with personal opinion, many entertaining but some insulting. I fully agreed with his lambast against the evils of black clothing. As a proud amateur climber he is brusquely contemptuous of mountain guides – both modern and ancient – and even less flattering about their clients. He might better have skewered the pomposity of the guiding fraternity by a little light satire rather than crushing condemnation. I agree that Ranulph Fiennes's ascent of the Eiger N Face was on one level a pointless stunt, but surely it is right to express some admiration for Cool and Parnell, his guide and cameraman? I wouldn't have fancied taking a crotchety old man with a vertigo problem up there, whatever the financial rewards!

Wynne-Jones is clearly an able and determined alpinist. To traverse the Matterhorn on-sight in 7½ hours is a fine effort. He can also write with passion and lyricism about the beauties of the Alps and the joys of moving fast with a compatible partner, most notably in his account of traversing the whole Monte Rosa range in three days. Other chapters reveal considerable personal angst. A ski tour in the Oberland is soured by his perceived abandonment by less able and less motivated companions. In fact, one could conclude that Wynne-Jones was the guilty party, insisting on pursuing his mission by going off solo in doubtful weather and abandoning them! Though these events are long in the past there is no sense of resolution in his account. Surely we can laugh off such episodes of hubris and petulance with the benefit of hindsight.

While 4000m is an enjoyable read for those in the know, both author and publisher have missed the opportunity to produce a more targeted and saleable book. Had the narrative chapters been structured in a format of 'lessons learnt' and then linked with the practical interludes, this could have become a popular book to entertain and inform novice alpinists setting out on their own careers. Whilst it is beneficial to mountain literature that small publishers like Whittles of Caithness are willing to take on such projects, positive editorial direction appears lacking in this instance, and by setting an eye-watering price of £25 the publishers have further diminished the book's potential reach.

Martin Moran

The Adventure Game – A Cameraman's Tales From Films At The Edge: Keith Partridge (Sandstone Press, 2015, 224pp, ISBN 978-1-910124-31-4, £24.99).

The Edge, Great Climb live, Touching The Void, Human Planet, Alien Versus Predator – just some of Keith Partridge's handiwork you may have enjoyed in the cinema or at home on TV. Thanks to a chance meeting between the author and Bob Davidson of Sandstone Press, we can take a fascinating look behind the scenes and discover what happens when film-makers and mountaineers meet. Cover endorsements by Joe Simpson and Stephen Venables and a Foreword by the ever enthusiastic Steve Backshall suggest that the author is more than just a competent technician, though he starts his Introduction by admitting modestly: 'More often than not I am the film equivalent of a hod carrier.' On reading a summary of his background and career development, we soon discover that as well as enjoying working in difficult and dangerous situations he has also used these opportunities to think and reflect about the motivation and rewards of adventure sports such as mountaineering. Always at the heart of the action, he is far from being self-centred, and admits disarmingly: 'It's all about the people you're with, kindred spirits if you like, and for me it's so much more than a job, being an adventure cameraman'.

After 'growing up in the flat-lands of North Norfolk' he left school to join the BBC with a secure job as cameraman and sound-recordist, becoming a week-end mountaineer at the same time. Most of us manage to find a balance between work and play, but for the young Partridge the lure of adventure proved too strong, and he packed in his job in 1990 and went on an expedition to Iceland. He describes in detail their epic struggle with horrendous weather on the Vatnajokul Icecap and his subsequent decision to work in 'Outdoor Education', only to be thwarted by a nasty ankle injury sustained at a climbing wall. Now with a wife, Andrea, to consider, a chance meeting with Richard Else led to work as sound-recordist on *The Climbers* and then the six-part series *The Edge – 100 Years of Scottish Mountaineering*. For me the story really hots up here, with a lot of familiar characters and locations. All through the book the author emphasises the importance of team-work in producing the important action shots, relying on the safety back-up of the likes of Brian Hall, Dave (Cubby) Cuthbertson, Paul Moores and Mark (Digger) Diggins, all outstanding climbers in their own right. As Partridge's career developed, so did the technology, and he makes a good job of keeping the reader up to date with the changes. For a new series of climbing adventures, *The Face*, video replaced film in an orgy of climbing in dream locations around the world, continuing with a follow-up series, *Wild Climbs*.

Joe Simpson's book *Touching the Void* gripped readers from all walks of life and unusually the film, directed by Kevin MacDonald, was as successful as the book. With Partridge behind the camera, there is plenty to be told, with understated good humour, especially the notorious cutting-of-the rope scene. The sequel, Simpson's *Beckoning Silence*, filmed on the infamous North Face of the Eiger, is equally moving and the author is clearly as sensitive to the history of the climb as to the sensational filming situations. The viewing (and paying) public's interest in mountains is limited, unlike their apparent appetite for jungles and caves which have given plenty more opportunities for Partridge's filming skills. My eyes tended to glaze over while reading these chapters (only 2 out of 11), but we are soon back in the real mountains; following rescue teams in the Cairngorms for *Inside Story*, reconstructing Whymper on the Matterhorn with Venables, and repeating the Old Man of Hoy with Bonington, 47 years after the original historic ascent. I can still remember being inspired to go rock-climbing by the sensational live broadcasts from Hoy in 1967, as a teenage schoolboy in suburban Liverpool. Perhaps the *Great Climb* featuring Dave Macleod and Tim Emmett climbing Sròn Ulladale on the Isle of Harris in 2011 had the same effect on someone else? I can still also recall the excitement of those childhood grainy black and white TV travel documentaries revealing the amazing diversity of human life which has so quickly disappeared over the course of my lifetime. The BBC's *Human Planet* series has continued this documentary tradition, and Partridge recounts filming goose-barnacle gatherers in Spain, catching and eating fruit-bats in Papua New Guinea, mining sulphur in Java and hunting with eagles in Mongolia, treating the local people involved with respect rather than as mere curiosities.

With several Himalayan filming assignments under his belt, the climax of Partridge's climbing career came in 2012 when Kenton Cool invited him to film the Everest Olympic Pledge Expedition, reaching the summit on 25 May, ninety years to the day after the record-breaking but unsuccessful attempt by Finch and Bruce. Without stringing the story out, the author convincingly describes the physical and emotional highs and lows of the whole endeavour and we can empathise with his conclusion that 'ultimately, coming home to family and friends proved to be the highest of highs'.

For the final chapter we finish in Antarctica, where the author reflects on the past, present and future capacity of adventure films to 'inspire and educate, beg questions and, importantly have the ability to tell a story'. In this book Keith Partridge does all of this in a way which can be appreciated by both seasoned climbers and armchair adventurers. Once again Sandstone Press have done an excellent job with production. The large format does full justice to the many excellent photographs, including some dramatic double-page spreads, contributed by many of his climbing subjects and their safety teams, clearly experts with cameras as well as climbing gear.

Dave Broadhead

The Fight for Everest 1924: E. F. Norton and other members of the Expedition (Vertebrate Publishing, 2015, hardback, 305pp, ISBN 978-1-910240-39-7, £24.) Everyone has heard about Mallory and Irvine, haven't they, but how many people have actually read the official record of the expedition, first published in 1925 and long out-of-print? Well, now's their chance with the release of this new edition which, as well as the original text and illustrations, includes more of Norton's pencil sketches and watercolours plus some extra material from his private archives as well as a pertinent foreword by Doug Scott. But why now, some ninety years on? In the absence of any new evidence about the duo's fate, hasn't the story been squeezed dry? Just how many golden eggs can the Everest goose lay? One might be forgiven for taking this somewhat cynical view, especially when an ice-axe reputedly owned by Mallory and gifted by his wife Ruth to the Pinnacle Club somehow ended up in a Christie's auction in 2014 and was cashed in for £132,000. However, the preface in the new version justifies its publication as it is apparently difficult to obtain a copy of the original volume (although one is available from the Club library), and adds that any royalties from book sales will be donated to the Mount Everest Foundation.

Lieutenant-Colonel Norton took over leadership of the 1924 Expedition from the ailing Brigadier-General C.G. Bruce and so it was his name that appeared as the main author although he only wrote about 25% of the book, the rest being contributed by C.G. Bruce, J.G. Bruce, Odell, Beetham, Hingston, Somervell and Shebbeare. The original edition was reviewed in the SMCJ (April, 1926) which recorded that 'this is a most admirable and interesting account' but does this still hold true today when Everest's aura of remote, mysterious invincibility has been shredded and blown away with the jet-stream wind? The answer all depends on your interest in mountaineering history, on whether you can identify with these early pioneers albeit that their backgrounds might seem very alien to us today and on your imagination but, for me, it definitely does. It is almost irrelevant that the mountain has since been climbed; that's not the point. The interest resides elsewhere: in the motivation and resolve of the mountaineers in the face of a unique challenge, what we can detect about their personalities and relationships, and in the details of the organisation of the Great Adventure to the 'Third Pole'. In short, what it was like to be wearing their boots in an era so different from ours in the 21st century.

The 1925 book was also reviewed in The Geographical Journal by A.Wollaston, who had been a member of the 1921 Reconnaissance Expedition, and he pointed out that although Norton wrote 'with evident enjoyment, a keen observation and a fund of humour ... his single failing was an occasional confusion of his right-hand with his left' which led to confusion for the knowledgeable reader who tried to visualise the country from the narrative. Although Vertebrate Publishing have adopted a policy of minimum editing of the original book they did make a handful of corrections in their 2015 publication, including Wollaston's particular criticism, which indicates commendable thoroughness. Otherwise the book is largely unchanged, and so it is no surprise to encounter some out-dated attitudes, such as Younghusband's introductory remark that the Sherpas 'have not the spirit' to reach the summit, reference to the native Mongolian porters as coolies, or the killing of wildlife in the name of science.

The book is a straightforward, comprehensive account of the Expedition with at least half of the content comprising appendices, observations, notes and a large selection of Mallory's letters home. Each of the contributors has his own style: the General's dry humour, Norton's lucid and evocative turn-of-phrase, J.G. Bruce's efficiency, Odell's compelling chapter and Beetham's more perceptual prose. Although it clearly isn't 'stream of consciousness' writing, that does not mean that there is a lack of feeling or apt comment and, if you want a more tangible form of artistic expression, then just look at Somervell and Norton's spellbinding watercolour pictures of Tibet. Even to an untutored eye like mine there is a clear difference between the two painters; perhaps they are technically as skilful as each other but I prefer Norton's freer, more atmospheric style. The pencil sketches of various people and scenes may be naive but they capture movement and character perfectly. The maps on the inside-covers are excellent and include Jacot-Guillarmod's original, masterly piece of cartography of the area immediately north of Everest.

All the 1920s expeditions involved sea journeys to India and the long march from Darjeeling, where extra personnel, predominantly Tibetan-speaking Sherpas and Bhotias, were recruited, to Shekar Dzong in Tibet. Easy to describe in one sentence but the organisation involved was staggering. Just getting to the East Rongbuk Glacier to establish Base Camp involved more than 300 miles of trekking albeit that the climbers were advised to buy their own ponies and to take a leisurely pace across the Tibetan plateau. Courtesy visits to Dzongpens (local headmen) to negotiate purchases were a necessary part of the journey. One of them was described by the perceptive Gen. Bruce as 'a grasping, avaricious but feeble, albeit well-mannered individual, who was really in the hands of his subordinates, the Gyembus, a truculent but determined crowd of cheerful rascals', and it is descriptive detail such as this that makes the narrative easy to follow, so I had little need to skip passages out of boredom. I have to admit, however, that I found some of the appendices rather tedious.

The establishment of the route and its various camps holds the attention, culminating in Norton and Somervell's oxygenless summit attempt across the slabs of the North Face on 4 June. At midday Somervell had to stop, and Norton continued alone with incipient snow-blindness, heading for the couloir which now bears his name. Remember that the effects of climbing at this altitude without supplementary oxygen were completely unknown and that clothing and equipment were rudimentary. Now on steep, loose and dangerous ground with unconsolidated powdery snow concealing the footholds, he reached a height calculated at just over 28,000ft before accepting that he had no chance of reaching the summit and retreating. One can study Somervell's photo [Plate 31] of Norton making his attempt and wonder what all the fuss is about but the picture fails to capture the true angle (40°–45°, apparently) of the terrain, and later, when Somervell dropped his ice-axe, it cart-wheeled down, never looking like stopping, and 'disappeared from our view'.

Four days later, Mallory and Irvine made their ill-fated attempt and it still makes for gripping reading, even if the story has become somewhat hackneyed. Inevitably, Odell's intriguing and oft-quoted account of his apparently final sighting of the pair still arouses one's curiosity. Odell described in his dispatch to The Times newspaper that he saw 'one tiny black spot silhouetted on a small snowcrest beneath a rock-step in the ridge and the black spot moved ... the place on the ridge mentioned is a prominent rock-step at a very short distance from the base of the final pyramid'. Odell initially identified this as the Second Step, later changing his mind to the First Step, and much analysis of his words, speculation about the crucial location and what happened have raged ever since. Some questions were answered with the discovery of Mallory's body in 1999 – for example, that the pair fell to their deaths rather than being benighted and dying from hypothermia – but whether or not they reached the summit continues to tantalise.

'We were a sad little party; from the first we accepted the loss of our comrades in that rational spirit which all of our generation had learnt in the Great War, and there was never any tendency to a morbid harping on the irrevocable', Norton wrote. The expedition was, to all intents and purposes, over.

Now even the northern approach to the summit has become a trade-route; you can approach Everest by road from the Kathmandu-Lhasa highway, there are lines of queuing climbers at bottlenecks and dead bodies littering the upper parts of the rope-fixed, beladdered way. 'Mountaineering is over', Reinhold Messner is reported to have said in 2004: 'Alpinism is dead. Maybe its spirit is still alive a little in Britain and America, but it will soon die out.' I think I know what he means, and if Everest's reputation has become tarnished and diminished to one of high-altitude tourism then read this book and recapture the unadulterated essence of the challenge.

One impression about the 1924 Expedition is of harmonious discipline and the suppression of selfish motives for the good of the team; a code of conduct imposed by the men upon themselves, a Great War culture of stiff upper lips and no back-biting, for they would all have been aware of the necessity to avoid internal strife. For any of that sort of thing we need to look at private diaries, which brings me to what can be considered a companion volume…

Mike Jacob

Everest Revealed – The Private Diaries and Sketches of Edward Norton, 1922–24: edited by Christopher Norton (The History Press, 2014 reprinted 2015, hardback, 156pp, ISBN 978-0-7509-5585-0, £20.)

Edward Felix Norton came from a privileged background: born in 1884 and raised in Argentina to a prosperous horse-loving family, sent to Charterhouse public school and thence the Royal Military Academy at Woolwich which trained potential officers exclusively for the Royal Horse Artillery. His maternal grandfather, judge Sir Alfred Wills (third President of the Alpine Club, 1863–65) owned a chalet in the French Alps and encouraged his grandson's interest in alpinism. Norton's early military years from 1903 to 1913 were spent in India and the N.W. Frontier, and much of his leisure time was spent shooting big game and indulging his passion for mounted sports. However, he remained a focused, professional soldier and went on to serve the entire period of the First World War in Belgium and France; he was awarded the DSO and MC and was thrice Mentioned in Dispatches.

Not really a man of the common people, then, but no more or less likely to possess noble qualities or human frailties because of it. 'Norton is really one of the best, and we have a splendid leader in him .... is really full of interest, easy yet dignified, or rather never losing dignity, and is a tremendous adventurer,' wrote Mallory. This opinion was reflected by his other companions, and he was especially commended for his sympathetic treatment of the non-European expedition members. It is interesting that his grandson, Christopher, hasn't titled the book 'Norton Revealed', because his grandfather's diaries, reflecting the custom of the time, reveal little about the man's innermost feelings. Norton probably kept his 1922 and 1924 expedition diaries in the knowledge that he would require notes for contributions to the Expedition books rather than as an outlet for his feelings. In this respect, it would be interesting to know if he also kept diaries during the Great War and, if so, whether or not he expressed any deep emotion on their pages.

So what did he have to say about an incident on the mountain on 23 May, 1924 when Hazard, in charge of a descending group of porters from the North Col in dangerous conditions, had unwittingly allowed several men to become marooned? Their safe rescue would become one of the outstanding achievements of the expedition. But all Norton confided to his diary was '... here was a pleasant situation!' We can only imagine, then, what he would have thought about a revelation made in 2001 by one of the Expedition Sherpas, 97-year-old Ang Tsering. One man had already died, morale was low and it was felt that all would appreciate a visit to the Rongbuk Monastery (sadly now demolished by the Chinese) for a blessing by the Head Lama.

Norton noted that the Lama was 'a most impressive man – courteous, dignified and with a curiously plastic, humorous face full of character ... he made a short address ... we all came back much impressed by what we take to be a genuine saintly man.' What Norton didn't know was that the Lama told the Sherpas, in their own tongue, to do what the Sahibs told them but not so that they reached the summit because this would be a bad omen, which explains why several of the hand-picked high-altitude porters (the so-called 'Tigers') refused to carry beyond Camp Five at an altitude of around 25,000ft. Norton wrote that 'apparently, the wind has taken the heart out of them ... two professed to be sick and totally unable to carry a load.' We now understand their true motives.

Whilst doing some background research I discovered a discrepancy with reference to Norton's solo effort on Everest, described in the previous review. In an item for the Alpine Journal[1] Michael Ward wrote that he visited Norton's widow in 1991 and that she allowed him to study her husband's then-unpublished diary and sketchbook. Ward claimed that the diary describes part of the traverse towards the Great Couloir 'as being so steep that his shoulder almost knocked against the mountain ... in some places, too, the rock was overlapping like the tiles of a roof and so loose that the holds had to be replaced after use,' but the actual diary entry (p111) says nothing so graphic. So, although this book does provide us with Norton's original written material rather than hearsay, it doesn't really add very much to what Norton wrote for the 1924 Expedition book, nor does it provide much further insight into what is already known about his character. He was too much of the restrained gentleman to even spell 'damned' or 'bloody' in full, using 'd-d' (p42) and 'bl-dy' (p107), and his only implied criticism of anyone was to query why Hazard hadn't gone to Camp V rather than

---

[1] Ward's item, which includes several of Norton's watercolours, can be downloaded from <www.alpinejournal.org.uk/Contents/Contents_1993_files/AJ%201993%2082%20Ward%2 0Norton.pdf>

'send Odell', writing 'God knows why he didn't go himself' (p112). Generally, then, the diary itself is a bit bland for general public interest.

This is a large, handsome book of the coffee-table ilk; in other words too big for a conventional bookshelf, but then, if you bought it, it would probably be for its paintings and sketches rather than for its words and so it needs bigger pages to do justice to them. Photographs of the period were always black-and-white and the landscape paintings with their vivid colours are a revelation, Norton writing that Tibet without colour was like Hamlet without the prince. The paintings of Chomolhari from Jelep La (Plate 47), the elusive Gaurisankar (Plates 88–91) and the various ones of Everest itself all stand out, but all the artwork is worthy of perusal and one wonders how Norton found the time to produce so much.

Both books are praiseworthy productions; the first a satisfying main course, the second a tasty sweet. Some might baulk at paying £44 for the combined serving so I am more than happy to pass on these review copies to the Hon. Librarian.

Mike Jacob

Highland Outcrops South – Climbers' Guide: A.D.Nisbet & others (SMC, 2016, 448pp, paperback, ISBN 978-1-907233-22-7, £28).

The new SMC guidebook *Highland Outcrops South* was finally published in May 2016. The replacement of the existing *Highland Outcrops* book from 1998 has certainly been a long time coming. The title reflects a decision to have two outcrop guides for the Highlands, with *HOS* covering everything 'Highland' south of Inverness and the Great Glen. A future *HON* is likely to contain all the outcrops covered by the three Northern Highlands guides, with mountains summer and winter in a separate guidebook.

This means *HOS* now includes outcrops in Arrochar, Mid-Argyll, Mull of Kintyre, Ardgour and Ardnamurchan. In addition, the main Highland crags of Craig a Barns, Glen Nevis, Binnein Shuas and Creag Dubh are updated and supplemented with more than 50 new crags, covering some 700 new routes in a total of 2500, illustrated by more than 170 topos, 25 maps and 95 action photographs.

The book is in the new SMC larger format, which certainly makes for a very hefty tome (830g). This is not a guide that you will be slipping down your front or into your back pocket. Some of the crags require a fair walk or cycle run, and for folk who prefer to have the book with them rather than using smart-phone technology, the size of this and other recent guidebooks (not just SMC) may result in a slightly more vigorous discussion with your partner to decide who will be carrying in the guidebook. My solution in the Lake District recently was to take photos of the relevant pages from the new FRCC guide, and carry in the old pocket-sized guidebook as a back-up. So perhaps I won't be retiring my 1998 edition quite yet.

The big change from the 1998 *Highland Outcrops* is the photo topos and detailed plans and maps. The number of these is amazing, and demonstrates the sheer amount of effort that has gone into visiting each crag by all of the contributors. As highlighted in the Introduction, Andy Nisbet has visited nearly every one of the 50 new crags with 700 new routes in the book. There are photo topos available for new crags and for crags where routes were previously only described, which is very welcome; for example, these cover the popular Ring Crags at Ardnamurchan and the topos for Creag na h-Eighe, Duntelchaig and Dirc

Mhòr. However, even for the established venues the quality, clarity and detail of the topos compared with what currently exists are exceptional. I would highlight Polldubh, Creag Dubh and Binnein Shuas in particular. At the established venues I have already spotted lots of routes to do that I didn't know about, as well as many new crags that appear to offer a welcome change from the usual suspects.

The wider coverage of the guide means that information about the history of the crag and local amenities for the less remote areas is available separately on the SMC website. Overgrown and unpopular crags are also described separately on the website. Again, this information resource is thorough and comprehensive.

The colour-coded layout for the different areas is easy to follow. Crag details and route descriptions are comprehensive and have a refreshing degree of honesty, indicating for example cases where a visit is more for the general ambience and situation than the quality of the climbing. Only for Indian Slab in Glen Gour have I managed to road-test the approach time, and this seemed pretty accurate for reasonably fit folk. A great deal of effort has clearly been put into giving accurate and updated information in the route descriptions, even for established classics. There is a notable amount of detail on the extent of bracken and bog. For example: 'The approaches are boggy so expect to get your feet wet at some point or just relax and don't try to stay dry'. Elsewhere there is said to be quite a bit of bracken but not of the 'man-eating variety'. The only small question I noticed in another review is whether there is scope for this sort of guidebook to have some sort of crag selector that shows the number of routes of a particular grade or style of climbing.

Given the long gap since the 1998 edition, *HOS* shows the changes in fashion over the years, and reflects the need for a modern guidebook to have high quality action shots. The photo on p126 of Brian Davison on the wonderfully situated *Silver Surfer* in Argyll is just one of many inspiring images; no longer is a snatched bum-shot of a lead climber sufficient. These photos have also taken time and effort to get. In many cases ropes have been set up separately to ensure that the camera gets the right angle, with model climbers asked to wear suitably bright clothing. Eagle-eyed readers may spot the same top appearing on different climbers. 'Hard on the eyes!' and 'Could you not Photoshop some of those breeks black?' were the comments from one traditionalist at the primary colour explosion on a Creag Dubh 'photo-shoot'. In this respect the photographs also show the changing fashions over the years. In the 1998 edition there seemed to be a more casual feel, with shorts and tee-shirt or Ron Hills and no helmet being *de rigour* for the crag. In *HOS* more climbers are wearing helmets and colourful combinations. There is not a Ron Hill in sight. Longer trousers may be favoured as protection against the increased tick problem. A few climbers show their longevity by featuring in photos in both editions.

In summary, for me this is a classic must-have guidebook that should stand the test of time and will, I hope, inspire folk to do some of the less established routes at the standard venues and to visit and explore new venues. Thanks must go to all those involved in its production.

Alison Coull

In Some Lost Place: Sandy Allan (Vertebrate Publishing, 2015, hardback, 224pp, ISBN 978-1-910240-37-3, £24).
This book describes the successful first ascent of the Mazeno ridge of Nanga Parbat in 2012 by Sandy Allan with Rick Allen in a small team of six in total. Sandy and Rick won the coveted Piolet d'Or in 2013, reflecting the wide acclaim

from the international climbing community for completing this 10 km long ridge which contains a number of separate summits over 7000m along its length and was considered one of the last great problems in the Himalayas. No fewer than ten expeditions had tried and failed on what is the longest route to the summit of any 8000m peak. It is likely that Sandy and Rick's achievement will stand the test of time as one of the finest by British climbers of their generation, with this book being the definitive account of the eleven days to reach the summit and the three days for the descent.

The book contains eleven chapters in three sections, with early chapters covering Sandy's own background, how his climbing life developed with Rick, and how they became involved with the Mazeno ridge project itself. Although his chosen life as a mountain guide has taken him all over the world, the mountains on his doorstep clearly remain important to Sandy and have provided a source of strength for his greater adventures elsewhere. There is also an interesting insight in the book into his experiences with other well-known figures in British climbing circles, and how the team was put together to support Sandy and Rick in their endeavour.

The final section of the book describes the last few days of the Mazeno ridge to the summit, and the difficult descent from Nanga Parbat. It comes over all too clearly just how serious and demanding it had all become, with Sandy and Rick having run out of food and lacking means of melting snow for water. Drawing on an inner strength and a determination that they could descend to safety, Sandy and Rick were perhaps fortunate to encounter two Czech climbers who provided them with food and more importantly water on the third day of their descent. The bond that existed between the pair, born from many years of climbing together, probably tipped the balance in getting them down to this point – a younger and less experienced team might not have been so successful, I fear.

The title of the book is taken from the chapter describing the final day's climbing, when they found problems locating the summit of Nanga Parbat. As described by Sandy, it certainly reminded me of quite similar experiences in locating the top of many a Scottish peak in poor weather!

As I understand it, this is Sandy's first book and a very fine one at that, of which he should be justly proud. I found I could re-read sections and pick up something new each time, whether a small point of detail or reminiscence from the past. Perhaps Sandy might find time in years to come to relate some of his other adventures in his own special engaging way!

Brian Shackleton

Lake District Climbs & Scrambles: Stephen Goodwin (Vertebrate, 2015, 176pp, paperback, ISBN 978-1-910240-02-1, £16.95.)

This guidebook is written by a former editor of the Alpine Journal, and is clearly the work of a man with wide knowledge of the Lakeland fells. It could prove very useful to the visitor who has some mountain experience but little detailed knowledge of the 'Lakes'.

In his introduction the author states that his objective is to recommend twenty itineraries, each of which could best be described as 'a mountaineering day', and from the estimated duration these are indeed full days out. It should however be pointed out that his timings assume reasonable weather and no difficulties with route-finding. When using the book the climber would accordingly be well advised to take account of the effects of poor visibility, bad weather, and limited daylight.

The suggested routes typically combine hill-walking with rock sections that range from easy scrambling to VDiff or Severe standard, and the itineraries may not always be obvious to the visitor. A 1:25000 map is provided for every excursion, and the walker should be careful to follow the suggested route and not simply take to the main footpaths, as the routes frequently cut across these. Furthermore, although a picture or plan illustrates each rock-climb or scramble, it is essential that the user has enough knowledge or experience to interpret this information and successfully follow each actual pitch on the rock.

There are many colour photographs to add interest. Those that feature climbers seem deliberately chosen to emphasise or indeed exaggerate the rock sections.

John Wood

Make or Break – Don't Let Climbing Injuries Dictate Your Success: Dave MacLeod (Rare Breed Productions, 2015, 228pp, paperback, ISBN 978-0-95642-813-4, £28.99.)

The leader never used to fall but now she never crimps. Climbing has changed over the last forty or fifty years. Dave MacLeod in his latest book *Make or Break* ventures into the quagmire of medical research, immerses himself in the world of physiotherapy, and delves into the dark worlds of sports nutrition and osteopathy. In a review of climbing-related injuries he explores the causes, preventative strategies and state-of-the-art treatments.

A signed copy of *Make or Break*, weighing in at a mighty 651 grams, provides a highly detailed review of some of the latest medical research applicable to climbing related injuries. From cutting your toenails to anterior cruciate ligament surgery, the book is an ambitious attempt to cover a lot of ground. At times reading like a PhD thesis, the book (running to 160 references) is clearly a labour of love, and it attempts to pull together worldwide data on the current knowledge of climbing injuries and treatments.

Dave rightly commands enormous respect within the climbing community, with a climbing CV of the highest quality. In the book he reveals an extensive catalogue of personal injuries incurred over his relatively short 20-year climbing career and the range of treatments he has tried. His commitment to climbing and training, shaming most of us mere mortals, is reflected in his attitude to injury and his quest for the best possible treatments available. In pursuit of cures for his injuries he describes in detail a range of exercises and treatments. At times treatment has cost him greatly as he sourced experts around the world and paid for surgery. He enlightens the reader on the levels he has gone to in search of cures, including a description of experimenting on his elbow injuries with drugs intended for the treatment of angina.

The book is in two sections. The first focuses on the perceived cause of climbing injuries and suggestions on prevention and corrective climbing techniques, along with specific exercises to protect against injury. The second section goes into detail about specific injuries and current treatments; for example elbow injuries, the downfall of many top climbers, are covered extensively. Detailed anatomical diagrams provide a background along with photographs of Dave demonstrating a range of climbing techniques and various physiotherapy exercises. Dave is clear at the start that evidence-based treatments are lacking in many areas and at times can be influenced by fashions: many will have noticed the drift of coloured physiotherapy taping from the beach volleyball teams to their local climbing wall.

The photographs, in black and white, are informative, but some are difficult to evaluate, and specific exercises perhaps should have been demonstrated in a correct anatomical position rather than on the edge of a bouldering mat.

A section on injuries in young climbers touches on the potential for serious orthopaedic hand injuries, and should send those involved in coaching juniors scrambling to check that their insurance policies provide adequate protection against litigious parents.

To readers who dip into the references it will be clear that Dave has used a range of high quality data sources such as the *British Medical Journal* to support the text, but these have to be balanced against information from other sources. For example, there are multiple references to articles appearing in the climbing magazine *Rock and Ice* written by an antipodean osteopath. Consequently readers will need to decide if the damning of the use of non-steroid anti-inflammatory drugs and steroid injections, where rich data have been extracted from peer-reviewed medical journals, is as valid as advice quoting 100% cure rates for certain conditions extracted from articles in *Rock and Ice*.

Where Dave has been able to source little or no data on treatment for specific injuries he provides personal anecdotal experience of treatments that he has found helpful. He also recommends further reading, although the reader may need to decide if they wish to spend $369 (£255) on a surgical textbook or buy a set of new cams and a few wires. He also covers the potential of new treatments on the horizon such as the use of haluronidase for elbow injuries, though these may need to be viewed with a degree of caution until full safety and efficacy data become available.

Declarations of conflict of interest become increasingly important as data are used to support new developments in medicine, and one must assume that Mountain Equipment and its parent company, whose logo appears from time to time in photographs, have no climbing coaching companies or medical treatments in their portfolio of products.

This is not an easy book to read, and it should be viewed as a reference source which, as Dave advises, can be dipped into depending on your level of interest or injury. The more senior cohort of climbers may need to read the book cover to cover, as most things probably hurt most of the time. This is most definitely not a book for those with hypochondriasis!

As Dave correctly points out in the book, there is a significant delay in the implementation of new best practice within the medical world. However, because it is new does not necessarily mean it is better, and perhaps one should proceed with caution with new treatments until it is known that they are both safe and effective, without risking one's own health and purse. Sources suggest that there is an exponential rise in medical knowledge: in 1950 it doubled in roughly 50 years, but by 2020 it is predicted that it will double every 73 days. Perhaps the third (or possibly fourth) edition of *Make or Break* is already overdue!

Dave must be commended on pulling together an enormous amount of information on what is a specialist area, with relatively few data. It is likely that this latest book will follow the influence of his previous book, *9 Out of 10 Climbers Make the Same Mistakes*, and the power screamers at your local climbing wall will now be seen working hard on their deep tissue massage and using their copies of *Make or Break* for eccentric exercise programmes. Most of us will have googled our own injuries from time to time and been overwhelmed by the range of information on the Internet. Google, as ever, remains excellent for shopping but limited in its use for medical diagnostics and treatment, and should really carry a health warning. And why those pains that have been grumbling for ages suddenly disappear one morning has yet to be explained.

Should you buy it? Probably yes, even if you are not yet injured, as this is about as good as we have at the moment.

David Crookes

The Maverick Mountaineer – The Remarkable Life of George Ingle Finch: Climber, Scientist, Inventor: Robert Wainwright (Allen & Unwin, 2016, 409pp, hardback, ISBN 978-1-76011-192-2, £17.99.)
On viewing one of J.B. Noel's photographs of an early Everest expedition, George Bernard Shaw likened the sepia scene to 'a Connemara picnic surprised by a snowstorm'. Impose on this tweedy pheasant-shoot a rack of glistening oxygen cylinders and a tall figure in quilted clothing, and you behold a disturbingly surreal juxtaposition of the old and the new. The man wearing the down coat of his own design is George Ingle Finch, and it was his advocacy of 'supplemental oxygen' that especially unsettled the old guard.

Finch was born in Australia in 1888, the elder son of a wealthy judge and his much younger wife, who was of Scottish extraction. Though in later life he attributed his self-reliance and his love of the outdoors to a boyhood in the outback, in fact George Finch had left Australia by the time he was twelve, and his teenage years were spent with private tutors in Paris, where his bohemian mother had taken up residence. After a couple of years of study at the Ecole de Médicine, he moved to the prestigious ETH in Zurich and graduated a few years later in chemistry. By 1911 he was managing a fertiliser works in Germany, before moving to London to take up an academic post. Apart from his distinguished army service in the First World War, during which he devised an aerial mine and was awarded a military MBE, Finch's professional life was spent at Imperial College, where as a pioneer of electron diffraction he became professor of physical chemistry in 1936 and FRS in 1938. The great British industrial firms of ICI and Ferranti retained him as a consultant, and towards the end of his working life he was recruited by Nehru to set up India's National Chemistry Laboratory in Poona.

Though Robert Wainwright's biography (first published last year in an Australian imprint) does deal tangentially with his scientific career, the dominant strands are Finch's mountaineering activities, his marital vicissitudes, and his personal characteristics. The main facts were already accessible from Finch's own books *The Making of a Mountaineer* (1924) and *Der Kampf um den Everest* (1925), and from the excellent biographical note that Scott Russell contributed to the 1988 edition of the former book. More recently, in his admirable *Into the Silence*, Wade Davis thoroughly explored Finch's part in the Everest expedition of 1922 and his controversial exclusion from the 1921 and 1924 expeditions. Wainwright has thus had wide shoulders to climb upon, and through Finch's descendants he has additionally enjoyed access to his extensive private papers.

Along with his younger brother Max, George Finch learnt the art of climbing early in life, taught by the old Murren guide Christian Jossi, who had made the first winter ascent of the Eiger in 1890. As Wainwright puts it, 'Thanks to Jossi, ice craft would become a hallmark of George Finch's career.' Early dare-devil exploits included Beachy Head and a nocturnal ascent of Notre Dame in Paris, but by the age of twenty he had undertaken guideless ascents of many of the major peaks in the Oberland and the Pennine Alps. In 1909 he made the first ascent of the N face of Castor, and in 1911, again with his brother Max, climbed the SSW ridge of the Aiguille du Midi. A weakness of Wainwright's book is his failure to benchmark these climbs against the standards of the period; in modern guidebooks they are graded only AD or AD sup, but would have been adventurous undertakings in the days of long axes, step-cutting and rudimentary belays. The author also (presumably through ignorance of the mountain's topography) describes Finch implausibly descending the Italian ridge of the Matterhorn to the Hörnli Hut, after his 1911 ascent of the Zmutt ridge with Valère Fynn. (In fact he shepherded a party of inexperienced climbers to the safety of the old Savoia Hut, which was now so overcrowded that Finch and Fynn had to continue to Breuil, arriving there after a 21-hour outing.)

No sooner had Finch's achievements begun to attract favourable attention from Percy Farrar and G.W. Young than he alienated the rest of the establishment by writing a piece about mountaineering for *The Field*, in which he disparaged the Alpine Club as a superannuated body that overvalued guided ascents. Wainwright quotes only briefly from this controversial 1913 article, and omits to mention a pronouncement that might raise hackles equally in our own Club: 'Ice is rarely met with in Great Britain.'

After the Great War, when the RGS and AC were laying plans for the 1921 Everest reconnaissance, Finch's inclusion in the climbing party was achieved through Farrar's persistent advocacy. Then, just days before he was due to set sail for India, this tall, erect and powerfully built young man was dropped from the expedition owing (he was told) to an unsatisfactory medical examination. The 48-year-old SMC President, Willie Ling (not 'Arthur Ling', as Wainwright calls him), was proposed as a substitute by the climbing leader, Harold Raeburn (himself 56), but he graciously declined. At the last moment George Mallory's friend, Guy Bullock, was instead enlisted. (It seems to have gone unnoticed by Wainwright – normally so quick to suspect elitism – that Ling, Mallory and Bullock were Wykehamists to a man: the old school tie, as Tom Patey sang, may be expected to go high.)

As Finch had recently performed exceptionally well in a low-pressure chamber at Prof Dreyer's Oxford laboratory, his omission was perverse, owing more to animosity and clashing personalities than any physiological deficit. Wainwright identifies Arthur Hinks, secretary of the RGS and of the organising committee, as the villain of the piece, and indeed devotes a whole chapter to 'The Bastardy of Hinks'. Is this demonisation justified? While the RGS archives (which were a major source for Wade Davis's earlier book) do include letters in which the indefatigable Hinks lobbied for the exclusion of Finch, there were not a few other men who thought him arrogant, irksome and opinionated. Indeed even his son-in-law Scott Russell, who found so much to admire in Finch, wrote 'It was no surprise that he inspired great friendships and equally great enmities, for his personality and appearance made it scarcely possible for him to be ignored in any company.' And elsewhere, 'He held strong opinions which he did not hesitate to air … but it may still be regretted that he gave little thought to the fact that his critics, who usually had little scientific understanding, had genuine difficulty in following his reasoning.'

Notwithstanding his climbing prowess, there were thus grounds for arguing (in the words of Younghusband) that '… he had characteristics which several of the committee who knew him thought would cause friction and irritation to the party and destroy the cohesion which is vitally necessary in an Everest Expedition.' Moreover it is likely that at least some details of Finch's messy domestic life would have been known to the committee. In the space of six years he had been thrice married and twice divorced. In 1916, while Lieutenant George Finch of the Royal Field Artillery had been serving king and country in Salonika, Captain

Wentworth Campbell of the Poona Horse had been serving the first Mrs Finch at an address in Portsmouth. On discovering this, Finch had tracked down his wife's lover to his army billet in France, where (in his own words) 'I found him, thrashed him into unconsciousness but unfortunately (so I thought for a long time afterwards) did not kill him. I narrowly avoided having to face a court martial.' When Wainwright says 'His crime was simply that he had the audacity to disagree with, challenge and defy the establishment who believed themselves untouchable,' is he not being a trifle partisan?

When the 1922 Everest expedition was being organised, with serious designs upon the summit, it became impossible for even his sternest critics to resist the inclusion of Finch. Having been persuaded by Dreyer of the worth of bottled oxygen, Finch now became its most active proponent and engaged the London firm of Siebe Gorman to manufacture cylinders of thin steel, which were very much lighter than those taken to Kamet a couple of years earlier by Kellas. To these he attached an early version of his 'open circuit' breathing apparatus, which was essentially the prototype of much subsequent breathing equipment for mountaineering. It is a pity that Wainwright provides so few technical details of this, and neglects to include that striking laboratory photograph of Finch, resplendent in three-piece suit, with the hookah-like apparatus plumbed to his moustachioed mouth. (It might also have interested the reader to know how hasty had been the prototyping of his design, as this was arguably the cause of subsequent difficulties on the mountain.) It is surely a miracle that Finch, with his oxygen tanks, 1000 cigarettes, benzene-fuelled Primus stoves and sacks of sodium peroxide, was able to ride across the Tibetan uplands without blowing the entire caravan to smithereens.

The story of the 1922 expedition is widely known, and gains little in being recounted once more by Wainwright. The heroic efforts of Finch, when teamed with Geoffrey Bruce (on his first ever climb) and the Gurkha Tejbir, have for example been grippingly described by Bill Murray in his Story of Everest. That Finch and Bruce, 'having had practically no rest for two nights and a day, half starved and suffering acutely from hunger,' were able to climb higher than any man before (27,300 feet) was both testament to Finch's indomitable will and a vindication of supplemental oxygen. (Had Bruce fallen to his death, as so nearly happened when his oxygen supply failed, a very different judgment would have been handed down.) Why Finch found himself partnered by the cheerful but woefully inexperienced Bruce has never been properly explained. According to Wainwright, the composition of the parties had been hastily arranged by Colonel Strutt in light of the approaching monsoon and his distrust of the oxygen sets; but Finch had been suffering from dysentery just a few days beforehand, and this may have warranted Strutt's omission of him from the select grouping of Norton, Somervell, Mallory and Morshead. By 7 June, just days after his record-breaking ascent, Finch was on his way back to Darjeeling, unaware of the avalanche that was sweeping to their deaths seven Tibetan porters and ending the whole expedition.

Having returned to Britain in the summer of 1922, Finch (and separately Mallory) undertook a gruelling campaign of lectures, totalling over eighty appearances by March, 1923. Wainwright explains how a loosely worded agreement allowed the lecturer to retain 30% of the net profits, while the bulk of the proceeds went towards defraying the debts of the Mount Everest Committee. When subsequently Finch (who spoke German and French fluently and had a large collection of his own slides) was invited to deliver a lecture series in Switzerland, he told the committee that he would feel no further obligation to share the revenues. Undeterred by the resulting outrage, he then threatened legal action. Though on Farrar's entreaty he later retracted this letter, Finch's conduct undoubtedly tarnished his reputation and made his subsequent exclusion from the 1924 expedition easier to justify. 'What an absolute swine the man is,' wrote General Bruce, who had earlier proposed him for AC membership. That Finch was now an impecunious family man, whose inherited investments in the Russian railways had evaporated at the Revolution, would have counted for little with the heavily indebted committee.

Of Finch's climbs after Everest, Wainwright has little to say, though he does mention the diagonal 1923 *Finch Route* on the N face of the Dent d'Herens. Eclipsed a few years later by Welzenbach's more direct line, this was nevertheless a bold and enterprising ice climb that presently became a speciality of some of the Zermatt guides. Beyond that, we know from Scott Russell's memoir that Finch spent a month or so in the Alps every summer, frequently climbing with his Scots-born third wife, Agnes Johnston. But in August 1931, when Finch was descending the Jungfrau, his friend Raymond Peto and two others slipped and fell to their deaths over the Rottal precipice. Wainwright says of Finch on p362 that thereafter 'He never climbed again,' though earlier in the book (p350) he stated that he gave up climbing on medical advice. A gastric condition was also Scott Russell's explanation, but elsewhere Peter Hawkes (though not quoted by Wainwright) has written that Finch celebrated his 60th birthday (in 1948) by making his 16th ascent of the Matterhorn, while John Hunt recalled meeting him at the Rothorn Hut as late as 1949, so it is misleading of Wainwright to imply a desertion of the mountains.

Presently, with the mellowing or mortality of the old guard, *l'enfant terrible* came to be venerated as *l'éminence grise*, and in 1959 Finch was elected President of the Alpine Club; meetings were now called to order by striking an empty oxygen cylinder. Our down-coated alien and his sinister tanks had blended into the landscape.

While a reader with specialist knowledge of mountaineering or of chemistry will not be wholly satisfied with this book, it does perform the service of bringing a remarkable man to the notice of the wider public. It also explores the controversy surrounding him. In analysing the hostility that Finch encountered, which went well beyond the denigration of his supplemental oxygen, the Australian Wainwright takes his cue from Russell (New Zealander) and Davis (Canadian), and depicts an 'outsider' cold-shouldered on account of his colonial roots. The existence of any such prejudice, so soon after Gallipoli and the Vimy Ridge, is hard to credit. Certainly Finch regarded himself unequivocally as British – a man who had returned to the Home Country and wished that the conquest of Everest '... should fall to the credit of one of British race.'

It is regrettable that Wainwright should touch only briefly on *The Making of a Mountaineer*, as it was an influential classic that deserves to be widely read. Captain Farrar (the *homme sans peur et sans reproche* to whom it was dedicated) judged it '...worthy to be set alongside Scrambles in the Alps and My Climbs in the Alps & Caucasus as indicating, as they did in their day, the high-water mark of mountaineering of the period.' In the dark days following the First World War, it fired the imagination of many a youngster, including John Hunt who received it as a Christmas present in 1924. Sixty years later he recalled, 'I was fourteen at the time, and it is that book which sowed the seeds of my desire to climb...... the book that has had such a profound influence on my life.' There is also barely a mention of Finch's chairmanship, from 1959–61, of the Mount Everest Foundation.

Wainwright's prose is serviceable, and from his antipodean pen flow some colourful verbs: thus Finch is 'spruiked' by Val Fynn, while Kellas's plans are 'cruelled' by the War. (Look them up yourself!) With numbers he has more difficulty, however. Thus Beachy Head is 1500ft high (p23), and the May temperature on Everest (p338) falls to minus 56 degrees Celsius. (It was actually minus 31 degrees that was recorded by Noel Odell – not 'John Odell' – in 1924. Quite cold enough, in all conscience!)

These are minor cavils. A less pardonable fault is the absence of an index, which would have added so much value to a book that ranges across many places and personalities. It is also strange that so few of Finch's own photographs (he took two thousand on Everest alone) are included. What has become of that collection? The next decade will doubtless see an avalanche of books on the early Everest expeditions, and we may dare to hope that Wainwright's biography, now copiously illustrated and properly indexed, will run to a second edition. Better still, we should pray for a reprint of Finch's own book.

Graeme Morrison

Mountaineering in the Pyrenees – 25 Classic Mountain Routes: François Laurens (Vertebrate Publishing, 2015, 96pp, paperback, ISBN 978-1-910240-56-4, £14.95).

I have not done any mountaineering in the Pyrenees, but have been there once as a hut-to-hut mountain walker, as recently as 2015. A ten-day section of the Pyrenean [sic] Haute Route (Cicerone Guide by Tom Joosten) was my aim. Like many of us I have done plenty of guidebook reading for ascents in the Alps, and plenty of ascents there too. Reading guidebooks can take over from the mountaineering, especially in huts during bad weather, but the Pyrenees do have some good weather, as seen in all the photographs in this guide – blue sky and bright sun. The photos make the whole prospect of mountaineering in the Pyrenees very attractive.

The author was born in the Luchon valley of the Pyrenees and now works there as a mountain guide. (This is in France, on the northern side of the frontier with Spain.) Published by Vertebrate and translated into English by Paul Henderson, the book's cover says much: 'Each route features technical notes, a topo and route description, and photos illustrating the character of the climbing.' In the sub-title of the book the word 'Classic' appears and, from my experience of the word in the Alps, it seems to mean middle grade (up to D+) routes of good climbing quality in the spring-to-autumn period, with scenery, variety, atmosphere, and even a sense of adventure (i.e. the route is not obvious, waymarked, fitted with fixed ropes or pegged up, but expect exposure and some loose rock).

Featured routes include a selection of climbs on the renowned peaks of Monte Perdido, the Maladeta, the Balaïtous, the Vignemale and the Grand and Petit Astazous. At least one route is 'technically straightforward' and 'within the capabilities of any experienced hiker' (the Espadas Ridge of the Pico de Posets, PD). Grades are from PD to D+. There are some snow routes (i.e. requiring ice-axe, crampons and ice gear), but mainly rock routes and traverses with relevant racks of gear, and mostly to be done in boots, not rock shoes.

The book seems aimed at climbers raised on climbing walls and bolted routes who do not have much experience outdoors or of placing gear. Classic mountaineering routes here include the greater demands of a full day on mixed ground with technical grades occasionally up to grade V that feel harder than V. The Pyrenees seem to be a good area to teach yourself about 'greater mountaineering': moving quickly and confidently on mixed ground, keeping to guidebook times, and not being so exhausted that you couldn't do the same again on the next day.

The book is bendy and slim, neither heavy nor bulky, 22.5cm x14cm. The text is rather small, i.e. rather difficult to read: a bold rather than medium typeface might have been better for my aging eyes. With only a third as many pages as a SMCJ for the same price, it might seem expensive. However, when you have no experience of a new area, and need a starter guidebook, it would be a good buy. Despite not having tried it out, I would feel confident to use it.

In fact, in 2016 I am planning to continue my trek, with companions, on the French side of the Pyrenees from the Atlantic to the Mediterranean, for another ten-day stint. We might take on a peak or two *en route*. By the time this review is published I will know more, including how to get there. The book contains no information for those travelling from outside France. There are no direct flights from Scotland to a start point, so after the flight you additionally need to get to grips with transport in France (buses and trains). For that you will need Google, the Lonely Planet or the good old-fashioned road atlas. This slight remoteness means that once there, you probably won't see another English speaking Scotsman en route, but all the other Europeans speak English anyway.

John Allen

Mountains and Rivers – Dee Valley Poems from Source to Sea: Brian Lawrie (Malfraneaux Concepts, 2015, 40pp, paperback, ISBN 978-1-87097-861-3, £9.50)

This is a book of poems by Aberdeen writer Brian Lawrie, with photos by Mick McKie. It is a little gem. Brian Lawrie is a real mountain man with many serious climbs and new routes to his credit. He has a life-long knowledge of Aberdeenshire hills, from both climbing and walking. His writing comes from a deep relationship with the mountains and evokes a sense of our own impermanence and inferiority in the face of the majestic surroundings at the source, but it grades to a more intimate relationship as the river gets closer to the sea and the land gets quieter. The sequence as we follow the Dee downstream will resonate with us all. His stones are not mere lumps of rock or pieces of geology but real and living, with a story to tell. It ends with glimpses back to the cherished mountains.

The author's images of the 'retired climber' or 'getting your sticky boots out at Clachnaben', but particularly the phrase 'their hopeful smear', will give extra pleasure to those of us who have climbed in the area. For walkers, we have 'stalking the silent overtures of the high plateau', or 'launched heroically across a granite pluton'.

The photographs by Mick McKie are arresting and stunningly different. None of your classic coffee-table pictures here. Many are of familiar aspects, but not as we've seen them before. They are an excellent accompaniment to the poems.

Let me finish with a quotation from the well-known Robert Macfarlane on this book: 'Such writing is rare and valuable.' With a celebrity endorsement like this, need I say any more? Go and get a copy.

Dave Windle

This may not be the first time a poet or composer has borne us downstream with a great river, from mountain spring to 'roar of surf', but seldom has the journey been such a revelation. Whether Lawrie is contemplating granite rocks, '… dragged here / by the ice and left' or responding to the 'exhibitionist' pine at Glen Tanar and 'Those magnificent arms / flexing with the wind,' he sees the world differently, and opens the reader's eyes in turn. His collection of poems is dedicated 'to all those who defend the wild places of the earth,' and we are heartened to hear this son of the north-east bringing his distinctive voice and imagery to that watchful community. If everyone saw the Cairngorms through his poet's eyes, that grand wilderness would be safe from disfigurement.

While mountain, river and forest are the fabric of these poems, there is also a human presence haunting most of them. Sometimes the walker is afoot early, 'wanting again / the ecstasy of scarlet dawns,' but more often there is a hint of eventide and elegy. To the reader whose voyage is now nearer sea than source, the poem called *Mountain Meditation* will especially appeal: 'On a day like this it seems / a man need never go down. / One day the trail will end, / why not here? / Let the sun and stars / officiate, the whistling wind / carry me off. It would be ceremony / enough. Better than go down / to a cold box, a few songs, / far from the earth's embrace.'

The verse-forms are not classical. In *Source (Garbh Choire Dhaidh)*, the words (one or two to a line) cascade down the page like a mountain cataract, while pieces like *The Dead Stag* comprise paragraphs of prose presented arbitrarily as verses. But at his best Lawrie has something that the most polished versifier lacks: the poet's eye.

Graeme Morrison

Rock Climbers in Action in Snowdonia, revised and extended edition: John Cleare and Tony Smythe. (Mountain Camera, 2016, 197pp, ISBN 978-1-84546-805-7, hdbk £25 pback £20; see <www.francisfrith.com/uk/pages/john-cleare> for orders).

At my secondary school there were two climbing books in the library: Joe Brown's autobiography *The Hard Years* and *Rock Climbers in Action in Snowdonia*. It wouldn't be an exaggeration to say that John Cleare and Tony Smythe's book was the reason I started climbing, though the images scared me as much as they inspired. The biggest revelation was that the venues featured were less than an hour from my home. Its influence spread far and wide, with Americans crossing the Atlantic to climb *The Corner* and *The Gates*. It became a rarity with a high price tag attached to the first edition, a cult classic whose disciples were often heard quoting the lyrical captions. Cleare was repeatedly asked if it would ever be reissued, and here it is 50 years later in a revised and extended edition.

The original had 39 full-plate images; the new edition has expanded to 132, of all sizes but all taken in the same era so continuity is ensured. If you have followed Cleare's work over the years you will have seen many of the action shots before, especially if you have *Hard Rock*, *Classic Rock*, *The Black Cliff*, *Welsh Rock* and the Welsh Climbers Club guides, but it's great to have them all in one volume. The images are positioned in synchrony with the text, and there are now landscapes and climbers' portraits too. Thus there are shots of Tryfan and its goats, the Devil's Kitchen, the CC hut Ynys Etws, a great study of Cloggy as well as Brown, Whillans, McNaught-Davis, Crew and Ingle, and the latter's cottage, Bryn Bigil, above Llanberis. This added material contextualises the text better.

Cleare's black and white is the perfect medium for his compositions and the gothic austerity of the Welsh crags. With no bolts, chalk, gear racks or manufacturers' logos, and with scant sunshine, his images are the antithesis of modern magazine-type climbing photography. They go beyond a mere 'factual' representation of a route, and still evoke a strong emotional response, perhaps now cloaked in personal nostalgia. Cleare took the trouble to hang on a rope to get the novel and intimate shots, and he is so good at giving you the bigger picture, defining the setting and atmosphere of a route. Bas Ingle in the saltire position on Hangover while Crew nonchalantly belays on a micro ledge, and the space below Duggie Baines's and Barbara Spark's feet on Mur y Niwl are two personal favourites. The authors' original captions are retained, and how memorable they are: 'Baillie bombing up The Gates' and 'I had this dream, see, and I was falling upwards in a shaft of light'.

The easier routes now get a look in, with *Milestone Direct*, *Flying Buttress* and ones on the Idwal Slabs and Tryfan's East Face. Some routes receive more than one appraisal: *Hangover*, *Tensor*, *Bovine*, *MPP* and *Troach* now have a whole sequence for each. On the latter, the lassoing and aiding of the tiny spike looks more precarious than climbing it free. The slate pictures were more anachronistic in 1966; who would have predicted back then the revolution that would take place in the disued quarries?

Fashion and gear were sparse: sweaters, breeches and jeans; no helmets or harnesses. Rope slings were carried, with pegs and hammers on the harder routes as well as pebbles to place in cracks and then thread for protection. Bottle was an important attribute for getting you up a route. Crew about to commit himself to the 5c crux of *Erosion Groove Direct* with a hawser sling barely sitting on a small shallow spike exemplifies this. Beer, fags, motorbikes and mini-vans all completed the scene.

Tony Smythe's text tends to be forgotten, and this was the first time I'd read it in full. It's rather good and takes his own personal journey from Ogwen apprentice to tackling the harder Brown and Whillans classics, the fear when a fall is imminent on Tryfan and the two he takes from the final groove of *Vector*. There's an explanation of belaying, and ethical considerations about placing pegs versus threading your own pebbles in cracks. Along the way we meet Joe and Don, established legends even back then, as well as court jester McNaught-Davis and the young Alpha Club Turks, Crew and Ingle. Creagh Dhu member John Maclean leaves his own indelible mark (not physical, I hasten to add) on Smythe. There's a hint of the wilder times with the driving antics, but for a real feel for sybaritic, sixties Snowdonia you need to read Jim Perrin or Al Harris and Lucy Rees's novel, *Take it to the Limit*.

It ends with a 'where are they now' section for the climbing models, and a portrait of each. This is fascinating but could have been developed into at least a whole chapter, particularly for more information about the likes of the inscrutable Crew, who gave up climbing for good for archaeology, and Kris Paterson, who died as a result of a drug-related killing.

If I have one criticism it is that the paper used is thinner than the original, so for instance you can see the outline of the Great Wall shot coming through on a *Troach* plate, and on the *Aries* one you can see the text from the other side. The tone of some shots looks a little lighter than those in the original edition.

I've met John Cleare a couple of times. He's a genial and articulate man who can paint a scene vividly in words. But if you want to know what life at the sharp end was like in the sixties his pictures say it all and a lot more. It may be from half century ago, but as an artistic statement the material is timeless.

Mike Dixon

Rock Queen: Catherine Destivelle (Hayloft Publishing, 2015, 228pp, paperback, ISBN 978-1-91023-707-6, £12.)
This short but intense book is a very welcome translation of *Ascensions*, first published in Paris by Flammarion in 2012, and charts the climbing initiation and development of an exceptional woman who needs no introduction. Catherine Destivelle, the author, was a girl from a large, boisterous, Fontainbleau family who dreamt of being a shepherdess. Now think role-reversal, and this book amusingly chronicles how an aspiring shepherdess becomes the boldest of sheep, with no need of rescue as she nimbly wanders onto the highest and most precarious of rocky ledges.

Her Big Three outstanding adventure solo climbs, the Grandes Jorasses, the Eiger and the Matterhorn, as described in these pages have all the ingredients of a mentally exhausting, 'edge-of-the-seat', Herman Buhl epic tale. But what this book really conveys, bravely and as never before, are the depth and range of emotions that are a vital part of climbing. The author does not try to hide her driven and competitive nature but exposes her fears and the vulnerabilities that run alongside. Tears are not uncommon.

In relating her achievements, Destivelle is grateful to those who have paved the way for her, modestly paying tribute to them and their legacy. But she is not spared from running the gauntlet of criticism for having had more than a brush with commercialism. What we read of, however, is her skilful and stoic navigation through the realms of commercial and pure mountaineering, from which we come to understand and judge that she remains a climbers' climber.

Rock Queen is accessible to non-climbers too. Technicalities and mechanisms are described in simple and interesting terms. Cams are 'sugar tongs'. Yes, the many references to food are part of a brave revelation of a sometimes difficult relationship with eating. But, as with many things, she overcomes her problems and finds a point of balance.

This is a sensitive translation of not only the French language and all its nuances but the French psyche as well. Marguerite Wright has ensured that Catherine's great sense of humour shines through, leaving one almost believing that she could be an honorary Brit!
Read when ready!

Ruth Love

In the Shadow of Ben Nevis: Ian Sykes (Baton Wicks, 2016, paperback, 242pp, ISBN 978-1-878573-98-2, £12.99; also available as an e-book, ISBN 978-1-878573-99-9).
'One man in his time plays many parts.' This is certainly true of Spike, and this autobiography takes us through them – RAF MRT member in the primitive pre-helicopter days, outdoor instructor, FIDS 'gash man', entrepreneur, Lochaber MRT member, and throughout it all a climber whose experience ranges from hitch-hiking and barn-dossing as an impoverished teenager to helicopter drops into exotic locations. Not a typical climbing autobiography – and all the better for it.

The whole book is well-written, and illustrated with apposite photographs with subjects ranging from Langdale to Antarctica to Yukon to Siberia and Chile. Refreshingly, they are largely of people. People are indeed a major feature of this book, and Ian either has a remarkable memory for names or has kept a diary throughout his career; the roll-call of people he has encountered is enormous. The few anonymous characters are so for good reason. The book has no index, and I

REVIEWS 309

can understand why: there would have had to be many extra pages.

His experiences with the Kinloss MRT in the early 'sixties are a reminder of how primitively equipped and arduous mountain rescue was in those days, both for the RAF boys and for the civilian volunteers who willingly involved themselves. His account of the Cuillin tragedy over the New Year in 1963 is both vivid and harrowing. He also brings out the lighter side of these times when the Highlands (in my memory also) were littered with hospitable and eccentric characters.

His time at Locheil Outdoor Centre was before the Health and Safety culture had set in, and he recounts tales of taking groups of semi-delinquents into the wilds of Morvern and Ardgour on trips that would be frowned upon nowadays. At this time, he met Ian Sutherland (Suds) with whom he was eventually to form Nevisport. He also found time to climb in the Alps and Dolomites, and was one of the many British climbers who gravitated to the Leysin scene and the charismatic John Harlin.

Johnny Cunningham pointed Spike in the direction of Antarctica, and he decided to join the Falkland Islands Dependency Survey. This was a career move followed by several Creagh Dhu members (and other Scots climbers such as Bugs McKeith) in the early 'sixties. You signed on for three years and got to drive dog sleds in wild country and ferocious weather, and at the end you had a pot of money to come home to. To earn that pot was no easy task in those days. The bases were primitive, radio communications were poor and there were long weeks of isolation on sledging trips. Plenty of adventure though, and the company of the dogs. Spike is not the first to wax lyrical about these sledging huskies, but they do seem to have been something special and he expresses his bitterness about the eventual decision to dispense with them and shoot most. (The sad fate of the few survivors is a story told elsewhere.)

On his return from Antarctica he went back to instructing but soon he and Suds made the decision to open a climbing shop in Fort William when some premises became available. Personally, I think it is fair to say that Nevisport and the subsequent development of Nevis Range played a major part in the economic survival of Fort William in its post-industrial phase. The failure of the pulp mill and the decline of the aluminium works had left the 'Armpit of the Highlands' in an economic depression. Its transition into the 'Outdoor Centre of the Highlands' owes a lot to Spike and Suds, who acted as a nucleus for several other far-seeing Lochaber businessmen.

The story of the development of Nevisport is more interesting than you might think, involving *inter alia* brushes with the Wee Frees, internal piracy and a Chinese Triad murder. Throughout this period the two Ians remained heavily involved with the Lochaber MRT, and there are descriptions of hairy rescues on the Ben and elsewhere. Climbing was not neglected, and trips to Mount Kenya and the Eiger are described.

The birth of Nevis Range was a prolonged and complex process, and Ian's description of the political, financial and technical problems encountered in establishing the ski centre and gondola demonstrates the remarkable persistence of all the parties involved. Potential developers of outdoor facilities be warned!

The book concludes with accounts of climbing trips to the Yukon, Wadi Rum and southern Chile, where Spike demonstrates that the aging process has not dimmed his enthusiasm for climbing and the mountain environment. There is also an account of a rather surreal trip to Siberia to act as consultant to a ski resort in the middle of nowhere but with a neighbouring Gulag as a source of labour (cheaper than the Lochaber Mafia). As I said earlier, not your typical climbing autobiography.

Bob Richardson

The Hughs – Scotland's Best Wee Hills under 2000ft: Andrew Dempster (Luath Press, 2015, paperback, ISBN 978-1-91074-503-8, £14.99).
On opening this pocket-sized book I immediately looked for Cruach nam Miseag, the first hill I ever climbed in Scotland, and for Ben Hutig, my favourite unsuspected gem from years ago. Both were included. Andrew Dempster has been roaming the hills for decades (two Munro rounds, the Corbetts, and the Grahams – to which he wrote a guide) so was well placed to produce this attractive wee book, and to illustrate it profusely. Perhaps we need to be reminded that small can be beautiful, fascinating and full of character: hills like Ben A'an, Dumgoyne, the Eildons, Criffel, Clachnaben, Bennachie, Beinn Lora, the Stack of Glencoul, Maiden Pap – dozens of them, loved before any list appeared.

This is a very personal selection of one hundred mostly worthy mainland entries (with an islands' hundred to follow), rather than a list of everything as with Munros, Corbetts, et al. Entries are brief but give all the practical information needed, together with a sketch map showing the route, and many photographs. All guidebooks are out of date on publication as nature and, more often, man keeps on altering the landscape, and one may have other ideas of routes than those given, but these are general niggles rather than particular faults. Apart from the name to make one squirm, this is a companionable book of 'hills with character …. big in character, charisma and clout'. Like all lists, this selection will impel walkers into fresh explorations, the best justification for having them.

Hamish M Brown

Up and About – The Hard Road to Everest: Doug Scott (Vertebrate Publishing, 2015, hardback, 404pp, ISBN 978-1-910240-41-0, £24).
Doug Scott is a household name in the British mountaineering world and needs no introduction. Now in his seventies, this is a first volume of autobiography from his birth in 1941 to the successful ascent of Everest's SW face in 1975.

Usually I find the early chapters of an autobiography among the most fascinating, but in this case I felt that the book had too slow a start. For readers with a strong interest in the social history of post-war Britain there is plenty of good material, but we have to wait for about 60 pages before there is much about climbing. For my taste there are too many somewhat irrelevant family photographs, although those showing his father's excellent physique, which Doug inherited, were well worth inclusion.

At age 12 Doug had the classic introduction to climbing with his mum's washing line and his friend's dad's tow rope. After some instruction at the White Hall outdoor pursuits centre in Derbyshire his extraordinary climbing career began to take off, although he continued playing rugby into his twenties. The following chapters recount his early Alpine experiences, with typical narrow escapes from disaster, and then his innovative expeditions to Morocco, Tibesti, Cilo Dag and Afghanistan, with a first ascent of the south face of Koh-i-Bandaka (6850m) in 1967. By the end of the sixties we have his ascent of *The Scoop* on Strone Ulladale, marred in his own account by the use of a single bolt which he greatly regrets. Interleaved are the stories of his early married life, his teacher training course and first teaching jobs, and his climbs in UK and Dolomites with the wide-ranging Nottingham Climbing Club.

The next section of the book starts with an excellent chapter on 'a changing world', a brief conspectus of the early seventies counterculture, and specifically the changes in the climbing world with the influence of Ken Wilson's *Mountain Magazine* and the popularity of outdoor climbing television spectaculars. Somehow Doug manages to bring within the ambit of the same chapter a detailed summary of the 1971 Cairngorms disaster and its effects on the world of training for mountain leadership. There follow splendid stories of Yosemite, where Doug's affinity with the top American climbers makes for lively reading, then an ascent of the Troll Wall and fabulous big wall climbs on Baffin Island.

Doug took part in two unsuccessful attempts on Everest's SW face in 1972. The spring international expedition also included Don Whillans, and this allows him to recapitulate some of the choicest Whillans stories that have entered climbing legend; the autumn expedition, led by Bonington and excluding Whillans, had a strong Scottish contingent but failed again through trying the wrong side of the rock barrier at 27,000 feet. Chapters on the highly successful first ascent of Changabang and the tragic international Pamirs camp, both in 1974, lead on to an interesting chapter on Doug's ideas at that juncture about how to tackle Everest. Had his proposals been taken up, the first ascent of the SW face would have been a more democratic and much less commercial affair, though he does suggest that his ideas might have been as disastrous as the earlier international expeditions. Although his inclinations were rather different from Bonington's he paints a largely sympathetic picture of CB's leadership. The penultimate chapter on the 1975 success is a tale well told with several intense personal vignettes.

Although consumed by his passion for climbing and mountaineering, Doug is anything but narrow-minded. He was well aware of, and is happy to sketch, the social and political events that formed the background to his adventurous life. He has a capacious grasp of mountaineering history which he uses to set his own experiences in context. He is not afraid to quote poetry and of course he is known for his interest in eastern philosophy, which is referenced occasionally but not overdone. He has a fantastic memory for detail and an ability to paint vivid pen portraits of many famous characters. Not least one admires his honesty about his own personal failings whether in relation to his marriage or excessive ambitions. His great open-heartedness has become well known through his work for Community Action Nepal, though that is not dealt with in this volume. Instead here we are able to enjoy, in addition to his seemingly endless climbing, some hilarious anecdotes from younger and more rambunctious days.

In all then, this is a good book that I am sure will be enjoyed by his very many fans. It could however have been even better had the publisher and editor made more demands on Doug. His style is sometimes too rambling, and the huge number of names can make it hard to follow who was who on different trips. More seriously the accounts of many of the expeditions are not easy to follow without maps. Even though I have been to the Spanish Sierra Nevada and the Atlas, I found the accounts of his visits there to have far too many named cols, peaks and valleys that are impossible to appreciate without a map. That goes even more for the path-breaking Tibesti and Hindu Kush expeditions. Given that maps must exist in his expedition reports, I think the publishers would have been well advised to push Doug to resuscitate and improve them. Equally, while the glossy photos are mostly excellent the black and white reproductions scattered throughout the text are very varied in quality; some, such as portraits of Warren Harding and Don Whillans, are superb but many others lack definition. I am a bit surprised that in this age of Photoshop even poor quality originals could not have been sharpened up. Maybe we will be treated to an improved second edition of this invaluable history of a climbing era and one of its most famous activists.

Geoff Cohen

McIntyre's Parcel of Fine Red Herrings: Ann I. McIntyre (FastPrint Publishing, 2014, paperback, 405pp, ISBN 978-178456-039-03, £12.50).
This book is all about the life of one of our own members, Donald B McIntyre (1923–2009), and is subtitled 'A Life of Learning, Love and Laughter'. There will not be many of us that can justify a book about our lives, but a few moments with this book will reveal what a truly extraordinary character Donald was and what an outstanding career he had as a geologist and computer scientist.

This is not a standard biography, but rather a collection of writings and speeches by Donald and interviews, eulogies and notes by various colleagues and students, as well as family notes and letters. This material has been gathered, selected and added to by his wife with much help from various people, including Gilbert Summers and Meg Cowie. We are indeed fortunate that Donald lived at a time when letter writing was the main means of communication and that his parents saved his letters from his childhood onwards. Few keep long term copies of e-mails nowadays and future generations will struggle to match the kind of record his family has preserved.

To give you a flavour of Donald's mountaineering career; as an 18-year-old he climbed the seven highest Cairngorm summits in a day (*SMCJ* 1941, 22/132, 388); he became President of the Edinburgh University Mountaineering Club; and after the war he climbed with Bill Murray when he was working on the new guidebook to Glen Coe. Weekend after weekend Donald took the train through to Glasgow to meet up with Bill and travel north in his car. Many of their outings are described in *Undiscovered Scotland*.

The book includes a letter from Bill to Donald about his accident on the Barre des Écrins in the Alps in which Bill fractured his skull and one of his companions died. Bill in his book *The Evidence of Things Not Seen* describes how Donald 'came alive when he spoke of rock'. He also said 'he used to pause on a steep pitch to lick the rock to bring out its texture and colour.'

Donald later confessed that when out on the hills he became too distracted by his interest in geology and gave up climbing. And what a career he had as a geologist… One of his lecturers as a geology student, in a class of three(!), was Arthur Holmes, famous among many other things for his classic textbook *Principles of Physical Geology*. After he graduated Donald joined the Geology Department in Edinburgh. Holmes sent him to Switzerland to gain experience with the very difficult Professor Wegmann. There he was taught stereographic projection and much else about structural geology, but he also learned about wine-tasting.

Donald had all sorts of gifts and interests. He was, for example a keen bagpipe player, but one of the most impressive tales in the book is how Donald displayed his new-found skill as a wine connoisseur. Shortly after his spell in Switzerland he went on a visit to Berkeley and during a convivial evening of wine-tasting he was put on the spot. In a room full of distinguished worthies, including Nobel Prize winners, he was asked to tell the company about a particular wine. He was able to identify not only that it was from the village of Auvernier in the Neuchâtel region but also the year it was bottled. This inspired deduction may have contributed to him later landing a job as Professor at Pomona College in Claremont, California where he spent all his subsequent career.

At Pomona Donald became involved in the pioneering use of X-ray fluorescence to analyse rocks. He developed an interest in computers 'to have efficient quality control in our work in X-ray Fluorescence'. As a result he became an expert in the computer languages APL and J.

Donald, on reflecting on the histories of these two languages, was 'struck with the number of chance occurrences that have played so great a role in determining my professional life.' That may be so, but it is only special individuals that can capitalise on such occurrences.

After retirement Donald moved back to Scotland and settled in Perth. In 1992 Donald became the Club's very first Archivist, a post which he held for five years. Robin Campbell eventually took over the reins, and, in his obituary of Donald, he remarked on the 'immaculate paper trail' that Donald passed on to him of the items he had placed in the National Deposit Library.

Donald was a great authority on James Hutton, widely acknowledged as the founder of modern geology. In 1997 he co-authored a very informative and readable booklet about Hutton which is still published by the National Museums of Scotland. Hutton made a crucial discovery at Siccar Point east of Edinburgh, which led to the concept of 'deep time'. It would be no exaggeration to say that it is one of the most important geological exposures in the world. Donald used to visit this location on a regular basis, which is why there is a photo of Siccar Point on the cover.

As a fellow geologist I would love to have met Donald, but regrettably our paths never crossed. If I'd known then what I know now after reading this book, I would certainly have tried to rub shoulders with him. By its nature the material in this book is a little disjointed at times, and there is inevitable repetition, but overall it is a fascinating read about a very remarkable man.

Noel Williams

******

ERRATA

'God helpe the man so wrapt in Errour's endlesse traine.'
(Edmund Spenser, *The Fairie Queene*, Canto I, xviii).

In the 2015 edition the frontispiece photo of Des Rubens climbing *The Wand* on Creag Meagaidh was wrongly credited to Geoff Cohen; it should have been Andrew Rubens.

The caption of the photo on p349 conflates two places: Patey is playing the accordion in Aviemore (pub unknown) and not in the Fife Arms, Braemar.

ORDERING THE SMC JOURNAL

Members should automatically receive a copy of the Journal when it is published. Members wishing to order extra copies or non-members wishing to place a regular order should contact the Distribution Manager, Roger Robb, by **e-mail** <journal.distribution@smc.org.uk>.

SMC JOURNAL BACK NUMBERS

Back numbers of the Journal may be obtained from Clifford Smith:
16 House o' Hill Gardens, Edinburgh, EH4 2AR.
e-mail: <journal.archive@smc.org.uk>
tel: 0131-332 3414   mob: 07748 703515

The following years are available: post and packaging are extra.

	Year			Year
£5.00	1972		**£12.95**	2000
	1977			2001
	1978			2002
	1979			2003
	1980			2004
	1983			
			£13.95	2005
£5.50	1985			2006
				2007
£5.70	1986			2008
	1987			
	1989		**£14.95**	2009
	1990			2010
	1991			2011
	1992			2012
				2013
£6.95	1993			2014
	1994			
	1995			
£8.95	1996			
	1997			
	1998			
£11.95	1999			

SCOTTISH MOUNTAINEERING CLUB HUTS

Bookings can be made to stay at any of the five Club Huts by contacting the relevant Custodian.

CHARLES INGLIS CLARK MEMORIAL HUT, BEN NEVIS
Location: (NN 167 722) On the north side of Ben Nevis by the Allt a' Mhuilinn. This hut was erected by Dr and Mrs Inglis Clark in memory of their son Charles who was killed in action in the 1914–18 War.
Custodian: Robin Clothier, 35 Broompark Drive, Newton Mearns, Glasgow, G77 5DZ.
e-mail <cic@smc.org.uk>

LAGANGARBH HUT, GLEN COE
Location: (NN 221 559) North of Buachaille Etive Mor near the River Coupall.
Custodian: Bernard Swan, 16 Knowes View, Faifley, Clydebank, G81 5AT.
e-mail <lagangarbh@smc.org.uk>.

LING HUT, GLEN TORRIDON
Location: (NG 958 562) On the south side of Glen Torridon.
Custodian: John T Orr, 8 Fleurs Place, Elgin, Morayshire, IV30 1ST.
e-mail <ling@smc.org.uk>.

NAISMITH HUT, ELPHIN
Location: (NC 216 118) In the community of Elphin on the east side of the A835.
Custodian: Andrew Tibbs, Crown Cottage, 4 Crown Circus, Inverness, IV2 3NQ.
e-mail <naismith@smc.org.uk>.

RAEBURN HUT, LAGGAN
Location: (NN 636 909) On the north side of the A889 between Dalwhinnie and Laggan.
Custodian: Clive Rowland, Inverene, Links Place, Nairn, IV12 4NH.
e-mail <raeburn@smc.org.uk>.

SCOTTISH MOUNTAINEERING CLUB GUIDEBOOKS
Published by THE SCOTTISH MOUNTAINEERING TRUST

HILLWALKERS' GUIDES
The Munros
Munros GPS data sets – from
The Corbetts and other Scottish hills
The Grahams & The Donalds
The Cairngorms
Central Highlands
Islands of Scotland including Skye
North-West Highlands
Southern Highlands

SCRAMBLERS' GUIDES
Highland Scrambles North
Skye Scrambles

CLIMBERS' GUIDES
Scottish Rock Climbs
Scottish Winter Climbs
Scottish Sports Climbs
Inner Hebrides & Arran
Ben Nevis
The Cairngorms
Glen Coe
Highland Outcrops South
Lowland Outcrops
North-East Outcrops
Northern Highlands North
Northern Highlands Central
Northern Highlands South
Skye The Cuillin
Skye Sea-Cliffs & Outcrops

OTHER PUBLICATIONS
Ben Nevis – Britain's Highest Mountain
The Cairngorms – 100 Years of Mountaineering
A Chance in a Million? – Scottish Avalanches
Hostile Habitats
The Munroist's Companion
Scottish Hill Names – Their origin and meaning

e-BOOKS
Cairngorms Scene and Unseen
A Century of Scottish Mountaineering
A History of Glenmore Lodge

APPLYING FOR MEMBERSHIP OF
THE SCOTTISH MOUNTAINEERING CLUB

The following notes are provided outlining the principles by which climbers may be admitted to membership of the Club.

The Committee does not lay down any hard and fast rules when considering applications but considers each case on its own merits. Candidates must be over 18 and have experience of mountaineering in Scotland in both summer and winter. This experience should have extended over a period of at least four years immediately prior to application and should not be confined to just a single climbing district.

The normally expected climbing standards include:

- Experience of winter climbing including several routes of around Grade IV standard and the ability to lead climbs of this level of difficulty.

- Rock climbing experience including climbs of Very Severe (4c) standard and the ability to lead routes of this level of difficulty. In considering applications, emphasis will be placed on multi-pitch climbs in mountain locations.

- The ascent of at least 50 Munros of which at least one third should have been climbed in snow conditions.

In short, the candidate should be able to show – by producing a detailed list of climbs – that they are competent to lead a variety of outings in the mountains of Scotland in both summer and winter. The technical standards specified refer to applicants currently active and may be varied at the discretion of the Committee for older candidates provided that the applicant's routes reflect a reasonable standard for their time. Climbing in the Alps and elsewhere is taken into consideration. Candidates who do not fulfil the normal qualifications listed above but who have made special contributions to Scottish mountaineering in the fields of art, literature or science may receive special consideration.

It is essential that each candidate, before applying, should have climbed with the member proposing the application. It is also desirable that a candidate should be introduced to a member of the Committee before the application is considered. Application forms must be obtained on behalf of candidates by members of the Club who may not propose or support candidates for election during their own first two years of membership. The annual membership fee is £40.00 (£30.00 for those aged 65 and over) which includes the Club Journal.

A fuller version of these notes for members wishing to propose candidates is available from the Club Secretary who is happy to advise candidates and members on any aspect of the application process. Please contact John R R Fowler, Honorary Secretary at:

e-mail: <jrrfowler@tiscali.co.uk>
tel: 0131 226 4055.

OFFICE BEARERS 2015–16

Honorary President: Neil Quinn
Honorary Vice-President: Robert T. Richardson
President: D. Noel Williams
Vice-Presidents: Derek A. Bearhop and Helen G.S. Forde.

Honorary Secretary: John R.R. Fowler, 4 Doune Terrace, Edinburgh, EH3 6DY. **Honorary Treasurer**: J. Morton Shaw, 7 Kirkbrae Terrace, New Deer, Turriff, AB53 6TF. **Honorary Membership Secretary**: Geoff Cohen, 198/1 Grange Loan, Edinburgh, EH9 2DZ. **Honorary Meets Secretary**: John R.R. Fowler. **Honorary Editor of Journal**: Peter J. Biggar, Hillhead, Craigton, North Kessock, Inverness, IV1 3YG. **Honorary Librarian & Honorary Archivist**: Robin N. Campbell, Glynside, Kippen Road, Fintry, Glasgow, G63 0LW. **Honorary Custodian of Images**: David Stone, 30 Summerside Street, Edinburgh, EH6 4NU. **Honorary Reporter on Accounts**: David Small, 5 Afton Place, Edinburgh, EH5 3RB. **SMC Website Manager**: Tony Stone, 36 Huntingtower Road, Sheffield, S11 7GR. **Convener of Publications Sub-Committee**: Rab Anderson, 24 Paties Road, Edinburgh, EH14 1EE. **Convener of Huts Sub-Committee**: Andrew M. James, 41 Urquhart Road, Dingwall, IV15 9PE. **Representative to the MCofS**: Brian R. Shackleton, 4A Campbell Road, Edinburgh, EH12 6DT. **Committee**: Richard K. Bott, Simon Fraser, Graeme N. Hunter, Ruth Love, Alison J. Coull and Colin A. Simpson.

Journal Information

Editor: Peter Biggar, Hillhead, Craigton, North Kessock, Inverness, IV1 3YG. **e-mail** <journal@smc.org.uk>
New Routes Editor: Andy Nisbet, 20 Craigie Avenue, Boat of Garten, PH24 3BL. **e-mail** <newroutes@smc.org.uk>
Photos Editor: Ian Taylor, 15, Pulteney Street, Ullapool, Ross-shire, IV26 2UP. **e-mail** <itandtf@hotmail.com>
Reviews Editor: Graeme Morrison, 42 Orchard Drive, Edinburgh, EH4 2DZ. **e-mail** <g.d.morrison@btopenworld.com>
Distribution: Roger Robb, Blaven, Upper Knockbain Road, Dingwall, IV15 9NR. **e-mail** <journal.distribution@smc.org.uk>
Back Numbers: Cliff Smith. **e-mail** <journal.archive@smc.org.uk>

INSTRUCTIONS TO CONTRIBUTORS

The Editor welcomes contributions from members and non-members alike. Priority will be given to articles relating to Scottish mountaineering. Articles should be submitted **by the end of April** if they are to be considered for inclusion in the Journal of the same year. Material is preferred in electronic form (.txt, .pdf, .odt, .rtf or .doc/docx) and should be sent by e-mail direct to the Editor.

Those without access to e-mail can send hard copy (typewritten and double-spaced) by post to the Editor's home address. Illustrations not relating to an article should be sent to the Photos Editor. All photographs should be of high resolution and must include explanatory captions including the photographer's name.

Books for review should be sent to the Reviews Editor by the end of April, though they can sometimes be sent later by prior arrangement.

The Editorial team reserves the right to edit any material submitted.

INDEX OF ILLUSTRATIONS

INDEX OF AUTHORS

INDEX OF PEOPLE AND SUBJECTS

Notes: Indexing of people is limited to those who figure fairly prominently in the article or note indexed. Indexing of matter following the Miscellaneous Notes section is reduced to the minimum necessary.

INDEX OF BOOKS REVIEWED

(Reviewers in brackets)